THINKING ABOUT THE FAMILY:

Views of Parents and Children

THINKING ABOUT THE FAMILY:

Views of Parents and Children

Edited by

Richard D. Ashmore
David M. Brodzinsky
*Rutgers — The State University
of New Jersey*

 LAWRENCE ERLBAUM ASSOCIATES, PUBLISHERS
1986   Hillsdale, New Jersey   London

Lawrence Erlbaum Associates, Inc., Publishers
365 Broadway
Hillsdale, New Jersey 07642

Library of Congress Cataloging-in-Publication Data
Main entry under title:

Thinking about the family.

Includes bibliographies and index.
1. Family—United States.   2. Parent and child—United
States.   3. Socialization.   4. Cognition in children.
I. Ashmore, Richard D.   II. Brodzinsky, David.
[DNLM: 1. Family.   2. Parent-child Relations.
WS 105.5.F2 T443]
HQ536.T445   1986   306.8′5   85-16229
ISBN 0-89859-693-9

Printed in the United States of America
10   9   8   7   6   5   4   3   2   1

Contents

List of Contributors

Richard D. Ashmore, *Rutgers — The State University of New Jersey*
Margaret K. Bacon, *Rutgers — The State University of New Jersey*
Jay Belsky, *The Pennsylvania State University*
Anne Braff Brodzinsky, *Rutgers — The State University of New Jersey*
David M. Brodzinsky, *Rutgers — The State University of New Jersey*
Maurice J. Elias, *Rutgers — The State University of New Jersey*
Rhonda L. Gilby, *University of Western Ontario*
Sharon D. Herzberger, *Trinity College*
Robert D. Hess, *Stanford University*
Lawrence A. Kurdek, *Wright State University*
Richard Lehrer, *University of Wisconsin*
James C. Mancuso, *State University of New York at Albany*
Teresa M. McDevitt, *Stanford University*
David R. Pederson, *University of Western Ontario*
Michael Rovine, *The Pennsylvania State University*
Dianne Schechter, *Rutgers — The State University of New Jersey*
Irving E. Sigel, *Educational Testing Service*
Howard Tennen, *University of Connecticut School of Medicine*
Michael Ubriaco, *Rutgers — The State University of New Jersey*
Mary J. Ward, *The Pennsylvania State University*

Introduction: Thinking About the Family

Richard D. Ashmore
David M. Brodzinsky
Rutgers-The State University of New Jersey

Over the past decade and a half the rising divorce rate, coupled with other changes in family life, has led some observers to conclude that the traditional nuclear family today is analogous to a species of dinosaur facing an inevitable Ice Age and, with it, extinction. However, though perhaps beaten, battered and—most importantly—transformed, the family seems unlikely to die (cf. Scanzoni, 1982).

During this recent period of social upheaval, in which the American family has undergone considerable change, there has been an exciting upswing in research on the family and the introduction of novel perspectives for seeking to understand this most important societal institution. This volume brings together the writings of a set of researchers who represent one of these emerging approaches. Although they are not adherents of a single theory, all of the authors of this collection of chapters believe that to understand the family, and the socialization of children more generally, requires recognition that the family is a social-interactional entity and that the participants (parents and children) are active cognitive creatures.

Historically, the family has been viewed as the primary socialization agent of the child. Because of its central importance in the development of the child, the family has been the focus of considerable research. In the past, this work was dominated by psychoanalytic and behavioral theories and focused primarily on the impact of parental (especially maternal) practices on the behavior and adjustment of the child (cf. Goslin, 1968). A basic assumption of most of the early research was that socialization influences were largely unidirectional—that is, from parent to child.

Recently, however, psychological research on the family has undergone considerable change, both in terms of the theoretical orientations guiding the research and the assumptions regarding the direction of socialization influences and the mechanisms underlying these influences. Although psychoanalytic and behavioral theories still play an important role in the conceptualization of the family, they are being challenged by a number of perspectives, including social-cognitive theories (e.g., attribution theory), cognitive-developmental theory, ethological theory, and systems theory (Bell & Harper, 1977; Belsky, 1981; Bowlby, 1969, 1973; Dix & Grusec, 1985; Goodnow, 1984; Sigel, 1985a). These newer approaches to the family tend to emphasize the multi-directional and transactional nature of family influences. In other words, there is a clear recognition that children influence the behavior and adjustment of parents (both as individuals and as a couple) as much as parents influence children. Moreover, these influences are not assumed to be time-bound, but rather are viewed as having a continuing impact on subsequent parent–child interactions (Sameroff & Chandler, 1975).

In addition to adopting a more comprehensive and complex view of the family, current researchers, particularly those operating out of a social-cognitive and cognitive-developmental framework, are also placing more emphasis on mental processes as mediators of family practices and ultimately developmental outcomes. Thus, it is becoming increasingly clear that the beliefs, attitudes, and value judgments that family members adopt about their own and other's behavior have a significant impact on the way in which these members interact and influence one another (McGillicuddy-De Lisi, 1982; Sigel, 1985b). In light of this realization, more and more researchers are focusing on parents' and children's perceptions and conceptualizations of family practices as a way of explaining the development of individual family members, as well as the development of the family as a unit.

It is precisely this topic that is the focus of this volume. A talented group of authors has been asked to present their theoretical and empirical work on parents' and children's thinking about the family. A variety of theoretical perspectives are included—cognitive-developmental theory, cognitive social psychological theory (including attribution theory), and personal construct theory. In addition, the authors invoke a wide range of affective and cognitive variables—beliefs, values, emotions, goals, strategies, expectancies, and structures—in an attempt to account for family processes and child and parent outcomes. Finally, a diversity of methods (e.g., indepth idiographic analyses of single families, quasi-clinical interviews, open-ended interview formats, panel studies, and causal models) are ingeniously used to explore the interconnections of adult and child thinking and feeling with numerous other variables. Given this overall introduction, it is now time to introduce each contribution in a bit more depth.

The volume is divided into two parts—Views of Parents and Views of Children. The first part consists of six chapters, all of which focus on the thoughts and feelings of parents in the socialization process. The first two chapters—by Bacon and Ashmore and Sigel are primarily conceptual analyses. In the first of these chapters, Bacon and Ashmore present a general heuristic model for conceptualizing the role of parents' cognitive activities in the parent–child socialization interaction. Their framework, which is in the information processing tradition, is similar to recently proposed general social cognition models (e.g., Hastie & Carlston, 1980) and more specialized social-cognitive frameworks (e.g., Ashmore, Del Boca, & Wohlers', 1985, analysis of gender stereotypes). Basically, Bacon and Ashmore argue that through their own socialization as well as through on-the-job learning, parents develop a complex set of cognitive and affective structures (e.g., implicit theories about how children learn, beliefs and feelings about specific children, etc.) and that these structures influence parents' cognitive processes (including, for example, attention and categorization) in parent-child encounters.

Bacon and Ashmore illustrate the heuristic value of their framework by a brief discussion of research generated within the framework. A particularly striking finding is that multidimensional scaling analyses of parents' responses to both the social behaviors and personalities of their own and others' children reveal a strong evaluative (or good–bad) dimension underlying their judgments. This suggests that such cognitive contrasts as "mature versus immature behavior" and "parent should change versus encourage the behavior" are an important part of parents' (or white middle-class American parents') thinking about children.

In the next chapter, Sigel provides an insider's view of the genesis, development, and results of a major research project on parental beliefs about development and their relationship to both parental teaching strategies and child outcomes. Sigel begins his narrative by tracing the origin of his ideas on the parental belief-parental strategy-child outcome relationship to early educationally based research on representational competence. He notes how the variability in children's capacity to deal with representational material was linked to differential teaching and socialization practices manifested by parents. In turn, these teaching strategies were traced to a set of fundamental beliefs about how children learn and develop. Out of this early research emerged a general causal model of the relationship between parental beliefs about development, parental teaching strategies, and specific developmental outcomes within children.

In this chapter, Sigel goes on to show how his basic assumptions and ideas about the connection between parents' beliefs and actions were evaluated in two separate research projects. In summarizing the results of the research, he reports that parental beliefs about children and development did influence their teaching strategies, but in more restricted ways than originally thought.

In the final section of his chapter, Sigel reflects on the apparent frailty of the belief–behavior relationship. He observes that the notion of a one-to-one correspondence between parental beliefs about development and specific teaching strategies was not supported by the data. Instead, parental teaching strategies were associated with *patterns* of beliefs. In completing his narrative, Sigel re-analyzes the basic assumptions underlying the nature of beliefs and the methodology researchers have used to study them. He concludes by suggesting the need for a multi-contextual methodology for further assessing the relation between parental beliefs and actions.

The remaining four chapters in Part I are more data oriented than the first two. The Mancuso and Lehrer contribution is a nice bridge—in the first part of the chapter they outline a theory of reprimand based on Kelly's (1955) personal construct psychology together with Carver and Scheier's (1981) control theory of self-regulation. Following this, they present data on the development of children's conceptions of reprimand—the results of several investigations support the conclusion that beliefs about reprimand follow the cognitive developmental progressions suggested by Piaget. Mancuso and Lehrer then turn to adult constructions of reprimand. They find that adults consistently judge reprimands along a bad–nice dimension (which is parallel to the evaluative continuum obtained by Bacon and Ashmore). Further, and perhaps more importantly, adults do not see a single reprimanded transgression as having much efficacy in reducing future transgressions. Mancuso and Lehrer suggest that perceivers expect such a change only if they have evidence that the transgressor's belief system has changed and they do not see single reprimands as likely to bring about such change.

Whereas Mancuso and Lehrer are concerned with parents' thinking about an important aspect of children's "social-emotional development" (i.e., how to reprimand in order to reduce or eliminate "negative" behaviors), Hess and McDevitt, in the next chapter, focus on a topic generally subsumed under the rubric "cognitive development" (i.e., academic performance). More specifically, they seek to understand how mothers account for their children's performance in mathematics. Their study is, from one perspective, an application of attribution theory (cf. Jones, Kanouse, Kelley, Nisbett, Valins, & Weiner, 1972), the dominant orientation in social psychology in the 1970s, to an important issue in developmental psychology. Hess and McDevitt summarize their major findings with a preliminary causal model in which the child's level of performance, the mother's own perceived mathematics ability, and the affective relationship between mother and child are antecedent to maternal attributions regarding their children's mathematics performance.

The final two contributions to this part of the volume move us even closer to the child. Belsky, Ward, and Rovine are concerned with the transition to parenthood—how mothers, fathers, and the marital relationship itself change with the birth of the first child. They first pinpoint the "pluses" (e.g., a sense of self-enrichment) and "minuses" (e.g., fatigue and role overload) that accompany becoming a parent. They then raise the issue of individual differences in this transition and suggest that violations of parents' expectancies may be a key to understanding adjustment to parenthood. They tested this hypothesis by gathering prenatal expectations, postnatal perceptions, and self-report assessments of the quality of the marital relationship on such dimensions as marital conflict, cooperation, and the like. For mothers, but not for fathers, violated expectancies did have a deleterious impact on the marriage.

In the final chapter of Part I, Elias and Ubriaco place parental beliefs at the core of their attempt to account for the development of children's social competence. They first articulate a cognitive-behavioral assessment model that identifies parental beliefs and teaching strategies as crucial inputs, together with a set of mediator variables (e.g., degree of interparental accord, quality of family environment), for the developing child's social competence. They illustrate the utility of the model and, in the process, refine it through an idiographic analysis of four families. Their conceptual framework and the data derived from it demonstrate not only the importance of parents' thoughts and feelings in the socialization process but also the complexity of this set of phenomena. One factor contributing to this complexity is that the child, like the socializing adult, is an active cognitive creature and not simply an organism that builds up thoughts and behaviors through rewards and punishments or exposure to various stimuli. Thus, to understand the family and socialization from a cognitive and social-interactional perspective requires attention not only to the views of parents, but to the views of children as well. With this in mind, we turn to the chapters in the second part of the volume.

Part II—Views of Children—includes four chapters. The first of these, by Pederson and Gilby, consists of a review of the research on children's conception of the family. The bulk of this research was carried out within the context of Piaget's theory of cognitive development. In summarizing the results of this literature, the authors suggest that young children have a qualitatively different view of the family than older children and adults. Preschool and early school age children generally understand kinship relations, family roles, and the structure and function of the family in very concrete terms. As they mature, however, their comprehension of the family becomes more abstract. Older children, in comparison with younger children, appreciate the recursive and reciprocal nature of kinship relations (e.g., if one has a brother, then one's brother also has a sibling), and see family roles as the interaction of spousal and parental roles. They also are more likely to define a family in terms of legal and genetic criteria than residential criteria.

One of the more interesting conclusions reached by Pederson and Gilby is that children's understanding of the family does not appear to be strongly influenced by their personal experiences within the family, including the type of family structure in which they live. The authors argue that children's level of cognitive development is more important for their comprehension of the family than the specific experiences derived from living within their own unique family.

The second chapter in this section, by Brodzinsky, Schechter, and Brodzinsky, provides additional insight into children's understanding of the family. In this case, however, the focus in on a very specific form of family life—adoptive kinship relations. Working within a cognitive-developmental perspective, the authors delineate the specific way in which adopted and nonadopted children's thinking about adoptive family life changes from the preschool period to adolescence. Brodzinsky and his associates conceptually link these developmental changes to the more general changes in cognitive and social-cognitive domains that emerge during this period.

Like Pederson and Gilby, Brodzinsky and his co-workers report that children's family structure and background experiences, including their adoptive status, play a minor role in their understanding of family life—or in this case, adoptive family life. The authors suggest that this finding is more supportive of a constructivist, as opposed to a mechanist, view of knowledge development.

Finally, Brodzinsky and colleagues note that children's knowledge of adoptive family life is associated with their psychological and school-related adjustment. Specifically, as children move into the middle childhood years, positive ratings of adjustment by parents and teachers are linked to a more sophisticated view of adoption—one that takes into account the many complications that are part of this form of family life. The authors conclude their chapter with a discussion of the implications of their data for fostering positive psychological growth and adjustment in adopted children and their parents.

The last two chapters in Part II, by Kurdek and Herzberger and Tennen, focus on children's perspectives on family disruption. The chapter by Kurdek examines the area of parental divorce and its impact on children. After briefly reviewing the research literature on children's divorce adjustment, the author presents a cognitive-developmental framework for undestanding the way in which children cope with this life stressor. Kurdek suggests that one must examine the way in which divorce is perceived by children in order to understand the variability in adjustment found both within and across age periods. Kurdek notes that compared to younger children, older school age children and adolescents are more aware of incompatibility and emotional distance between parents. Furthermore, their reasoning about divorce is more inferential and abstract, and they are better able to see both the positive and negative consequences of divorce. The author also observes, however, that most children in the elementary and high school years do not believe their parents will reconcile, and they are more likely to blame the noncustodial father for the divorce than either the custodial mother or both parents. In explaining children's reasoning about divorce, Kurdek draws heavily on the more general changes in logical thinking and social knowledge that emerge in the school age years—a strategy Brodzinsky and colleagues also rely on in their explanation of children's comprehension of adoption.

The final chapter of the book, by Herzberger and Tennen, examines the issue of child abuse. In analyzing this serious familial and societal problem the authors adopt a perspective that is compatible with the other contributors in this section of the book—namely, that the way in which children cope with and adjust to life stress, including abuse, is determined to a great extent by the specific meaning that they attribute to their life experiences. Herzberger and Tennen begin their chapter with a brief review of characteristics of abusive parents and the consequences of abuse for children. They then examine abusive parental practices from the perspective of the child. The authors suggest that abused children seek to gain some sense of control over their abusive environment. Most often they begin by attempting to utilize direct or primary control strategies such as changing their behavior, fighting back, running away, or telling someone about the abuse. If these strategies prove inadequate, however, secondary controls are adopted. These control strategies may include, among other things, such diverse behaviors as ascribing new meaning to the abusive acts (e.g., believing that the severe punishment was deserved), selectively attending to the positive aspects of the abusive situation (e.g., comparing oneself to less fortunate individuals) and believing that one's own behavior caused the parent to engage in abusive actions. Herzberger and Tennen suggest that these secondary control strategies, which involve denial-like processes, perceptual distortions, and clear attributional errors, allow the child to cope, at least to some extent, while remaining within the abusive context. What remains unanswered, however, is the extent to which or the manner in which such coping strategies affect the abused child's psychological development.

In summary, this volume brings together a group of researchers whose work is shedding light on a new and exciting area of family development and socialization. What unites these researchers is their commitment to a cognitive approach to family interaction. Underlying this commitment is the assumption that parents' and children's knowledge of the world, including their perceptions of family life and the socialization process, results from an active process of construction rather than a gradual build-up of facts or bits of information. To be sure, the contributors to the volume do not hold to a single model of cognition or social cognition. Numerous differences are apparent as one compares the content of the chapters. Nevertheless, the basic commitment of these researches to understanding family life from the perspectives of family members (i.e., parents and children) is a strong bond uniting them together.

Although social cognitive and cognitive-developmental approaches to the family have opened up exciting and potentially fruitful avenues of research on the socialization process, the area certainly is not without its problems. Possibly the most fundamental issue that remains unresolved is the very definition and/or meaning of such core concepts as beliefs, expectancies, structures, and the like (cf. Sigel, 1985b). Furthermore, controversy exists concerning the best way to measure these concepts. As the field develops, however, these issues are likely to be clarified further and some resolution obtained. As editors of this volume, it is our hope that the set of chapters we have gathered together will serve as a springboard for further theoretical and empirical explorations into this promising research domain.

REFERENCES

Ashmore, R. D., Del Boca, F. K., & Wohlers, A. J. (1985). Gender stereotypes. In R. D. Ashmore & F. K. Del Boca (Eds.), *The social psychology of female-male relations: A critical analysis of central concepts.* New York: Academic.

Bell, R. Q., & Harper, L. V. (1977). (Eds.). *Child effects on adults.* Hillsdale, NJ: Lawrence Erlbaum Associates.

Belsky, J. (1981). Early human experience: A family perspective. *Developmental Psychology, 17,* 3–23.

Bowlby, J. (1969). *Attachment and loss. Vol 1: Attachment.* New York: Basic Books.

Bowlby, J. (1973). *Attachment and loss. Vol II: Separation, anxiety, and anger.* New York: Basic Books.

Carver, C. S., & Scheier, M. F. (1981). *Attention and self-regulation: A control-theory approach to human behavior.* New York: Springer.

Dix, T. H., & Grusec, J. E. (1985). Parent attribution processes in the socialization of children. In I. Sigel (Ed.), *Parental belief systems: Psychological consequences for children* (pp. 201–234). Hillsdale, NJ: Lawrence Erlbaum Associates.

Goodnow, J. J. (1984). Parents' ideas about parenting and development: A review of approaches. In M. Lamb & A. Brown (Eds.), *Advances in developmental psychology* (Vol 13, pp. 193–242). Hillsdale, NJ: Lawrence Erlbaum Associates.

Goslin, D. A. (Ed.). (1968). *Handbook of socialization theory and research.* Chicago: Rand McNally.

Hastie, R., & Carlston, D. (1980). Theoretical issues in person memory. In R. Hastie, T. M. Ostrom. E. R. Ebbeson, R. S. Wyer, Jr., D. L. Hamilton, & D. E. Carlston (Eds.), *Person memory: The cognitive basis of social perception* (pp. 1–53). Hillsdale, NJ: Lawrence Erlbaum Associates.

Jones, E. E., Kanouse, D. E., Kelley, H. H., Nisbett, R. E., Valins, S., & Weiner, B. (Eds.). (1972). *Attribution: Perceiving the causes of behavior.* New York: General Learning.

Kelly, G. A. (1955). *The psychology of personal constructs.* New York: Norton.

McGillicuddy-De Lisi, A. V. (1982). The relationship between parents' beliefs about development and family constellation, socioeconomic status, and parents' teaching strategies. In L. M. Laosa & I. E. Sigel (Eds.), *Families as learning environments for children* (pp. 261–300). New York: Plenum.

Sameroff, A. J., & Chandler, M. J. (1975). Reproductive risk and the continuum of caretaking casuality. In F. D. Horowitz (Ed.), *Review of child development research* (Vol. 4, pp. 181–241). Chicago: University of Chicago Press.

Scanzoni, J. (1982). *Sexual bargaining: Power politics in the American marriage.* (Second edition). Chicago: The University of Chicago Press.

Sigel, I. E. (Ed.). (1985a). *Parental belief systems: The psychological consequences for children.* Hillsdale, NJ: Lawrence Erlbaum Associates.

Sigel, I. E. (1985b). A conceptual analysis of beliefs. In I. Sigel (Ed.), *Parental belief systems: The psychological consequences for children* (pp. 345–371). Hillsdale, NJ: Lawrence Erlbaum Associates.

VIEWS OF PARENTS

1 A Consideration of the Cognitive Activities of Parents and their Role in the Socialization Process

Margaret K. Bacon
Richard D. Ashmore
Rutgers—The State University of New Jersey

Although there is a large and diverse literature concerned with socialization, little work has been done on how parents think about children or how the cognitive activities of parents influence the parent–child interaction sequence. A conceptual framework that explicitly recognizes the central role of parental cognition in the socialization process is presented. This framework posits a set of cognitive variables that intervene between the child behavior presented as a stimulus to the parent and the parental response. These intervening variables consist of affective and cognitive structures that influence cognitive processes and which, in turn, may be modified by background factors.

This chapter, then, focuses on the cognitive activities of parents in interpreting and responding to the behavior of children. We begin by presenting a preliminary case for the importance of parental cognition in the socialization process and by briefly reviewing some recent work that has been guided by a cognitive perspective. Next, our own cognitive-affective framework for the socialization process is presented. This heuristic model, which derives from a more general information processing approach to human behavior, focuses on the affective and cognitive structures and processes of the perceiving adult in adult–child socialization interactions. The chapter concludes with a brief review of our empirical work generated by the framework and suggestions for future research.

PARENTAL COGNITION AND SOCIALIZATION: QUESTIONS, METHODS AND SIGNIFICANCE

In view of the extent and diversity of socialization research, it is surprising that so little attention has been paid to the cognitive activities of parents in the

3

interaction of parent and child (cf. Goodnow, 1984; Hess, in press; Parke, 1978). The importance of these parental cognitive activities can hardly be questioned. Parents are bombarded with child-induced stimuli and events for which they are not only a captive audience but are also made to feel responsible in varying degrees. Certainly in the light of what Mischel (1979) calls "cognitive economics" parents must (in self-defense) cognitively organize these events in order to experience them as meaningful units and thus determine their own response or lack of it. Furthermore, the child behavior that is responded to by the parent is not necessarily that which is perceived by the investigator but that which is filtered through the cognitive apparatus of the parent.

Questions raised by a consideration of these cognitive activities are numerous and important. Four prominent examples are:

1. How do parents break up the behavior stream of the child?
2. Do parents apply labels to the units they perceive? (If so, what are they?)
3. Do parents respond primarily in an affective, unverbalized fashion? (And, if so, is there any recognizable resemblance among the units that evoke such responses?)
4. How do parents organize these units (whatever they may be) along dimensions or in categories that are consistent with the implicit theories that they carry in their heads?

Cognitive activities such as these must be crucial in determining parental response to child behavior. For example, if a given fragment of child behavior is labeled *fighting,* the response to it will be quite different than if it is labeled *horse play.*

What do parents really think when they view their children's behavior? We don't know, of course, but differences in interpretation of behavior may result from differences in vocabulary used to describe such behavior. The following examples of psychological and colloquial word usage may clarify this issue. When Mrs. Walker looks out of her kitchen window and sees her older son, Charlie, chasing her younger son, Peter, she might say to herself, "Charlie is being very aggressive today," or "They are engaged in rough and tumble play." It seems unlikely. It seems more possible that Mrs. Walker might say something like, "I'll bet Peter's been teasing Charlie about flunking his arithmetic test," or "Charlie's getting like that bully next door," or "Maybe Charlie has inherited a mean streak from his Grandfather Walker. I must speak to his father." Or maybe she would merely say, "They are playing."

Situations involving greater extremes of evaluative response are frequent. For example, suppose the Smiths are entertaining friends for cocktails when their oldest son appears and delivers a long and detailed account of the varieties and habits of the spiders that inhabit the Smiths' garage. How will the Smiths view this behavior on the part of their son? Will it be seen as a rude interruption of adult conversation, an embarrassing display of "show off" behavior, an awkward but charming attempt to be a good host, or an impressive example of precocity in a gifted child? Here, the parental response may range from strongly negative to strongly positive.

In our conceptualization of the socialization process, then, we include the cognitive activities of parents as a crucial set of variables intervening between the behavior stream of the child and the parent's socializing response or non-response. Very little is known about the nature of these cognitive activities that mediate parental response to the child. In fact, much socialization research has employed methods that may obscure parental affective and cognitive responses. For example, in many knowledge domains, people tend to organize objects into categories of things that go together (cf. Schneider, Hastorf, & Ellsworth, 1979; Warr & Knapper, 1968). This permits the individual to respond to objects as members of classes and by this means greatly reduces the complexity of the world around them (Bruner, Goodnow, & Austin, 1956). It seems, therefore, that it is extremely important to know how parents categorize the behavior of their children. In traditional studies, however, this has not been investigated. Such studies have, instead, asked parents to respond within a categorical framework imposed by the investigator. This may account for some of the unreliability of interviews as a method of data collection, a point that has been noted elsewhere (cf. Maccoby & Maccoby, 1954; McCord & McCord, 1961; Sears, Maccoby, & Levin, 1957).

The early studies of child rearing made extensive use of interview techniques. For a consideration of parental cognition in the socialization process these techniques present a special problem. This may be illustrated by an example. Parents have often been asked the following question: "How about when X is playing with one of the other children and there is a quarrel or a fight, how do you handle this?" (Sears, Maccoby, & Levin, 1957; also used by Minturn & Lambert, 1964; Peterson & Migliorino, 1967). The question is one of many designed to investigate individual and cultural differences in the parental handling of aggressive interaction between children. An important issue not considered concerns the point at which the observing parent perceives the interaction as "fighting" (or something else) and as sufficiently intense to warrant intervention. The parental response to such a question is undoubtedly influenced by the perceptual structure evoked by the question that may be influenced more by parental concepts of appropriate behavior in the interview situation than anything else. Thus, the parent may construe this interview as a means of determining how good a parent she or he is rather than an effort to learn her or his real beliefs. Also, the parent may not use the same dimensions in interpreting the behavior as that intended by the interviewer. The answer, therefore, may have little relationship to the parent's actual behavior when faced with what is called fighting by the interviewer but something else by the parent.

In addition to interviews, parent–child relations have been extensively studied by means of observational methods. Most studies of parent–child interaction, whether in the laboratory or in more naturalistic surroundings, involve coding of the behavior of the parent and/or the child either directly at the time of observation or later, using a running account of the behavior as raw data. By such coding, the investigator has imposed his or her own cognitive structuring on the data. The selection of categories and dimensions of attitude, perceived personality or behavior has been investigator-determined. As an important means of quantifying data, coding is very widespread. For example, Lytton (1971) reviewed 50 studies of parent–child interaction emphasizing observational methods (structured and unstructured observations in the laboratory and naturalistic observations in the home). Inspection of his summary tables clearly demonstrates the limitation: 46 of the 50 studies involved coding the observed behavior into investigator-determined categories.

This is not to suggest the elimination of coding as a method of considerable importance in psychology. Indeed, the analysis of data can hardly proceed without some kind of coding. We wish rather to emphasize that parents are information-processing organisms, that they select from the behavior stream what they consider to be units of behavior and that they organize these units into categories or along dimensions of their own. And these categories, together with the attitudes, beliefs, theories, which parents carry in their heads, are extremely important in the socialization interaction and should be investigated.

In recent years there has been increasing recognition of parental cognition in parent–child interaction. Emmerich (1969) presented a conceptual framework that emphasized the importance of cognitive factors as mediators of parental role performance. His methodological approach, however, involved the administration of a Parental Role Questionnaire, a device based on "certain principles of behavioral modification studied by behavioral scientists" (p. 7) rather than on beliefs about parenting obtained from parents themselves. Bacon and Ashmore (1975) offered the initial version of the cognitive-affective heuristic model to be discussed below and reported preliminary findings from a study of parental categorization of child behavior using a vocabulary for such behavior derived from parents. Parke (1978) explicitly urged a cognitive perspective by offering "a cognitive mediational approach to parent-infant interaction." As we do, Parke recommended abandoning the notion (implicit in much socialization research) of "the parent as a black box reactor" and suggested instead that researchers "treat parents as information-processing organisms." Parke noted four types of cognitive variables relevant to parent–infant socialization interaction: parental knowledge of infant behavior (e.g., there are wide differences between adults in their knowledge of the capabilities of children of various ages); parental perceptions of infant behavior; parental stereotypes (including discussion of the considerable evidence that, from birth, male and female infants are perceived and treated differently); and parents' implicit theories of children's personalities.

Goodnow (1984), in her wide-ranging review entitled "Parents' Ideas About Parenting and Development" organizes her material in five categories relevant to socialization.

1. *The effects of social class*. Major reliance is placed upon Kohn's (1969) work attempting to link the conditions of father's employment (especially whether the job requires or does not require autonomy) to the father's and mother's values for their children (e.g., curiosity, obedience).

2. *Becoming "modern" or "mainstream"*. The focus of research in this category is on culture change, exploring how parents' ideas about children and child rearing change as a particular society becomes "modern."

3. *Values across generations (within-family)*. Workers in this category are concerned with how beliefs (particularly political and religious values) are transmitted from parent to child.

4. *Home, school, and achievement*. How do parents' beliefs about how children learn (their implicit theories of learning) influence their behavior toward children and ultimately impact on children's achievement? A major project on this topic is a large E.T.S. study (e.g., McGillicuddy-De Lisi, 1982; Sigel, 1982).

5. *Life with children: Ongoing interactions*. Socialization researchers have long been concerned with "ongoing interactions." However, those taking a cognitive approach do not rely solely on observational methods but, in addition (or sometimes instead of), use self-report techniques to explore how parents make sense out of specific child actions. For example, Dix and Grusec (1985) have studied parental attributions for children's pro- and anti-social behavior, and Holloway and Hess (1982) have assessed parents' explanations for their children's school achievement.

The five categories of cognitive approaches identified by Goodnow concern cognitive structures (e.g., values, implicit theories) and processes (e.g., attribution) and the background factors shaping these (e.g., social class, culture). The next section presents a general framework that incorporates these and other issues.

COGNITIVE ACTIVITIES OF PARENTS IN THE SOCIALIZATION PROCESS

We turn now to a more detailed analysis of the cognitive structures and processes as we conceive of them and to the variables involved in their interrelationships. Possible effects on the cognition of the developing child are also considered. All of this is presented in a framework which we have developed over the past several years and which we have labeled "Heuristic Framework for Parental Cognition" (see Fig. 1.1).[1] The framework has three primary components: (a)

---

[1]It is important to note that this is the present form of the schematic framework. It has changed over the years, and there still remain some points of disagreement between the authors about the framework and how best to represent it graphically.

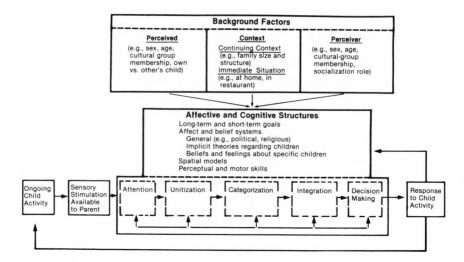

FIG. 1.1.   Heuristic framework for parental cognition.

the socialization interaction; (b) affective and cognitive structures in the perceiving parent; and (c) background factors influencing parental perceptions of child behavior. The parent–child socialization interaction begins at the lower left of the figure with "Ongoing Child Activity" and "Sensory Stimulation Available to Parent" and terminates with "Response to Child Activity." These end points are the familiar S and R of behavioristic approaches. The significant part of the socializer-child interaction, as it is here conceived, is the set of cognitive processes that are placed in between the S and the R. These cognitive processes, which are posited to be crucial in determining the adult's response to the observed child behavior, are discussed in detail later. It should be noted that parental cognitive activities do not occur in a vacuum. Rather, parental cognitive structures and processes are influenced by a variety of factors that are discussed later under "Background Factors." Affective and cognitive structures are discussed first.

Affective and Cognitive Structures

How parents perceive and interpret child behavior is directly influenced by the cognitive and affective structures that the adult brings to the socialization interaction. These structures are conceived to be quite similar to what some cognitive psychologists term *long-term memory*. That is, it is assumed that the affective and cognitive structures are "the 'repository' of our more permanent knowledge and skills" (Bower, 1975, p. 57). We use the term, *affective and cognitive structures*, rather than long-term memory, in order to highlight the importance of affective and conative factors, as well as cognitive factors, in shaping parents' cognitive activities.

Long-Term Goals

Protection.   As can be seen in Fig. 1.1, we distinguish several general classes of affective and cognitive structures, which parallel the types of "knowledge" most often assumed to be stored in long-term memory (Bower, 1975, pp. 56–57). Long-term goals are among the most important of the cognitive and affective structures the perceiver brings to the socialization interaction. Two long-term goals are distinguished: (a) to protect the child from harm, and (b) to socialize the child. Of these, the goal to protect the child represents the most powerful motive. Because it seems to be evident in all known societies, it appears to be universal (cf. LeVine, 1974). Certainly parents the world over guard their children from what they conceive to be danger. They protect them from germs, from the evil eye, from the crocodiles in the river, from the spirits of the dead, from falling or drowning or being burned or bewitched and from being bussed to school in an "alien" culture. And parents in many nonhuman species protect their young. These protective responses may represent some biologically based mechanism related to the survival of the species.

It seems likely that parents also carry in their heads acquired mechanisms related to scanning the environment or picking up information related to the immediate welfare of the child. This group of related mechanisms might be called into play by alerting signals (perhaps accompanied by or precipitated by affective arousal in response to distress signals from the child). Such structures are conceived to be largely affective and to have a pre-emptive function overriding all other cues, alerting the organism for immediate response with a minimum of cognitive elaboration. The mother, working in her kitchen and simultaneously monitoring the many sounds emanating from the backyard where her children are playing, responds instantly and with an urgency overwhelming all other signals to a cry of distress from one of her children. The strength of this motivation and the predominance of its effect on the behavior of the parent would be expected to vary systematically with certain attributes of the child, for example, the health, intelligence and especially the apparent age of the child. Thus, although "danger-to-child" signals would pre-empt all other signals at the point of sensory input or behavioral response, the need for parental intervention would presumably decrease as the child's capacity to deal with its environment increased.

Socialization.   The second major long-term goal identified is what might be called the "motivation to socialize"—to guide the child so that his or her behavior is such that the child becomes an accepted member of his or her group. It is likely that this motive to socialize would lead to an increased tendency to "notice" or attend to behavior prescribed or proscribed by the society. Societies, however, appear to differ in the degree to which children of various ages are expected to conform to social expectations. They also differ in the manner in which children are expected to learn acceptable behavior, e.g., by direct tuition or by imitation. Such variations should influence the degree to which different kinds of child behavior may be noted or remain unnoticed.

The strength of the motivation to socialize should also vary with belief systems regarding the malleability of the child. Thus, parents who believe that they profoundly influence the behavior of children would be more concerned with the task of socialization than those who believe that child behavior is largely determined by genetic, or supernatural or other preordained influences. The strength of the motivation to socialize should also vary with the degree to which parents feel responsible for the behavior of their children. Bacon and Ashmore (1985) found a strong tendency for parents, in responding to descriptions of the social behavior of early school-age children, to cognitively organize these along an evaluative continuum. This continuum was empirically indexed by three bipolar rating scales: Good–Bad Social Behavior; Mature–Immature; Parent Should Encourage versus Change the child behavior. This evaluative emphasis might be viewed as reflecting a strong socialization motive (at least for the white, middle-class parents who served as subjects for the study). If a perceiver feels she or he is responsible for a child's development, then it is likely she or he will think of the child's behavior in terms of such distinctions. This, of course, might be less pronounced in parents of other class, ethnic, or cultural groups.

There are probably many other long-term goals related perhaps to the personal ambitions and values of the perceiver. Parents who value achievement may be expected to perceive child behavior in different ways than those without such an orientation. Similarly, sports-minded parents may monitor the athletic tendencies of their children with special interest and rewarding attention.

Short-Term Goals

By short-term goals we mean any intention or purpose that is of relatively short duration. Such goals are also generally more situation or context specific than long-term goals. One example: It is early Monday morning and Mrs. Smith has three short-term goals. By 8:30 she must get herself showered, dressed, and ready to leave for her job, prepare breakfast for her 4-year-old daughter and 34-year-old husband, and make sure that her daughter is dressed and has her lunch and other materials for nursery school.

Affect and Belief Systems

Affect and belief systems, the second major category of affective and cognitive structures, are structured sets of "knowledge," more or less affectively charged. By knowledge, we do not mean "facts" or even simply verbal or verbalizable information. Rather, we see affect and belief systems as composed of any cognitive or affective distinctions or discriminations made by the parent (see Kelly, 1955). Although we do not take a stand on how these distinctions are represented in memory, we believe that several types of contents must be included: (a) verbal knowledge (e.g., "Mary gets A's in math"); (b) images (e.g., the "picture" of Mary in the class play last year); (c) feelings (e.g., the warm happy feeling when she comes in the door from school); and (d) expected action sequences (e.g., waking Mary up, preparing breakfast, checking to make sure she has lunch money, driving her to school).

General.   As can be seen in Fig. 1.1, three types of affect-and-belief systems are posited to influence cognitive processing. Under "general systems" we include the various structured sets of knowledge held by the perceiver concerning politics, economics, religion and so on. These general systems influence parental cognitive activities in various ways. For example, the Protestant work ethic subscribed to by many middle-class Americans probably leads to child-rearing methods emphasizing approval and other rewards for persistent, goal-directed and productive activity on the part of the child. And, children who grow up in societies where it is believed that the souls of dead relatives may reappear in children are often subjected to influences suggesting that they have inherited personality traits from a particular dead relative (cf. the Dogon [Griaule, 1965] or, in general, Frazer [1890/1981]).

Implicit Theories Regarding Children.   "Implicit theories regarding child behavior and child rearing" is another general component of affect-and-belief systems. The term *implicit theories* derives from early work in person perception concerned with the concept of "implicit personality theory" (cf. Bruner & Tagiuri, 1954; Cronbach, 1955; Hays, 1958). Applied here it carries the assumption that socializers have a relatively stable set of beliefs and expectations concerning child behavior and the role of adults in relation to children. Because these beliefs and expectations are seldom verbalized except in a fragmentary and piecemeal fashion, most socializers remain unaware of their "theories," hence the term *implicit*. The implicit theories that concern us here are of two general types, one pertaining to children and child behavior, the other to adults and their role-relationship to children. The beliefs that adults have about their role in child socialization include ideas about what is appropriate behavior for them in their role-relationship (e.g., teacher, parent, older sibling). Adults' belief systems about children contain ideas about types of children and kinds of child behavior. They also may include theories concerning the causes of different varieties of children and child behavior, as well as the remedies for child behavior viewed as in need of change. Another very important set of implicit theories or beliefs about children concerns the manner in which they learn and what they should be taught. A pertinent study here is that by McGillicudy-De Lisi (1982) that studied the teaching strategies used by mothers and fathers as related to parental beliefs about child development, family constellation, and socio-economic status. The study involved two-parent families including equal numbers of those with one and three children divided equally between "working-class" and "middle-class" categories. Parents' beliefs about children and children's learning were investigated by individual interview, presenting vignettes of child behavior and probing parents' beliefs about children's knowledge and learning; teaching strategies for specified tasks were observed by videotape. Coding and analyses of this mass of data led to the conclusion that parental behavior was more influenced by parental beliefs related to teaching, support and feedback behaviors than by demographic characteristics, supporting the author's "contention that beliefs are mediating variables between family constellation, SES and parental practices."

Beliefs and Feelings About Specific Children.   Beliefs and feelings about specific children have an important influence on the cognitive activities of socializers. In addition to theories about children as a group, adults, especially parents, have special theories with regard to specific children. Parents, for example, who have been the principal caretakers of their own child have in their memory a large body of facts and feelings concerned with the individual history of the child—the illnesses, accidents, traumas, joys, sorrows, and fears of the child as well as the parental feelings that accompanied these and other events and that persist and grow as a part of the parental attachment to the child. All of this stored affect and information influences how the parent experiences the behavior of his or her own child in contrast with, say, the neighbor's child.

Spatial Models

The affective-cognitive structures labeled *spatial models* refer to the cognitive maps parents develop in response to the task of child care. We presume that adults who occupy living quarters over some time have a more or less detailed picture in their minds of the various rooms in the dwelling, their relationship to each other, and the furniture and other objects in them. As her infant matures to the first stages of mobility, the mother's cognitive map of her house probably changes to include areas of possible danger (or destruction of valued objects) available to her creeping child. Thus, she notes the location of open stairways, the presence of electrical wall plugs, hot radiators, stoves, tables that are easily upset—every space and object of possible danger to her child. As the child begins to walk and moves outside the house into play areas, the mother's cognitive map of the child's area of movement with its safe and potentially dangerous areas (streets, sunken driveways, swimming pools, dogs) increases in size to include the play area.

We assume that this process continues with the growth and increasing competence of the child so that parents have, as a part of their cognitive equipment, a cognitive map of the area of usual movement of the child, marking areas of possible danger or difficulty. It seems probable that mothers, as a consequence of more prolonged contact with and greater responsibility for their children, would possess more elaborate and accurate cognitive maps of this type than fathers. We have no data on this point, but if it should be true it would suggest that males are not consistently superior in visual–spatial ability (see Maccoby & Jacklin, 1974) and that such abilities develop, in part, according to the demands of adult sex roles.

Perceptual and Motor Skills

The final type of affective-cognitive structure discussed is skill, both perceptual and motor. *Skill* is described as procedural (Anderson, 1980) or "how-to" knowledge. A wide variety of perceptual skills are involved in socialization. For example, a mother learns to perceive that her child is ill through slight changes in behavior not noticed by others. Also, the mother learns to interpret correctly the sounds made by children playing in an adjoining room. Caretakers of children also probably develop some motor skills. Bathing a wiggling slippery baby represents an acquired motor skill. Putting a snowsuit on an active exuberant toddler provides another example.

Background Factors Related to Affective and Cognitive Structures

An important part of our conceptualization concerns the development of the parental affective and cognitive structures that influence the parents' manner of perceiving the behavior of children. Much of this is probably learned through the socialization experiences of the parent. The future socializer as a child was born into an ongoing household that might contain several other children. The child observed the parents' interaction with the other children—the "chunks" of behavior they noted, the names they applied to those units, how they evaluated them, and otherwise responded. The child also heard the naming of his or her own sequences of behavior and experienced related responses. These experiences in the family may be added to those occurring in other contexts, e.g., the school, mass media. Thus, through years of childhood and adolescent experiences and observations, the affective-cognitive structures of the future socializer are built.

These structures also develop from on-the-job learning, which in some cases may begin quite early. Among the tribal societies of the world, most girls (and occasionally boys) have babies tied to their backs when they are barely able to carry them and take care of them for hours daily. They quickly learn how to pacify a crying baby (for a review, see Weisner & Gallimore, 1977). As adults, parents learn a great deal about children, especially from their first child (cf. McGillicuddy-De Lisi, 1982).

At the top of Fig. 1.1 are three general classes of background factors that are assumed to influence the cognitive processes of the adult in the adult–child interaction sequence. The first two types of factors include the attributes of the perceived child and the immediate and long-term context of the socialization interaction. The third class of background influences refers to the attributes of the perceiver.

Attributes of Perceived Child.   Of the many attributes or characteristics of the perceived child that might influence socializer cognitive activities, those mentioned here are: sex, perceived age, perceived social status, attractiveness, and competence. The effect of each of these factors is mediated by the affective and cognitive structures of the perceiver. The behavior of children of different social status is undoubtedly perceived in terms of the adult roles they are expected to occupy (Whiting & Whiting, 1971). For example, aggressive behavior shown by the son of a chief might be viewed quite differently from that of a boy of lower social rank. Similarly, children of different sex are generally assigned different characteristics. Parents of newborn infants during the first 24 hours of life, both when informed and also when misinformed about the sex of their child, demonstrated stereotyped ideas about the characteristics of the infant according to their belief as to its sex; for example, infants believed to be male were seen as firmer, larger, and more active; whereas those believed to be female were perceived as prettier, smaller, and looking like their mother (Rubin, Provenzano & Luria, 1974). Physical attractiveness and perceived competence (physical or mental) may also affect parental perception. A great deal of work also has been done on differential response of parents to other attributes of children, e.g., children with impairments and those with different temperaments (cf. Maccoby & Martin, 1983).

Context.   The second general class of background influences, Context, includes all aspects of the situational context in which the parent–child interaction sequence occurs. The immediate situation is clearly important. Behavior that is accepted without comment in the backyard will be viewed quite differently if it occurs in a crowded restaurant. Parents also cognitively "take into account" contexts that transcend the immediate situation. For example, a mother's perception of a particular fragment of a child's behavior is likely to be influenced by the fact that she feels the child "is sick." As with attributes of the perceived, the influence of contextual factors is mediated by affective and cognitive structures, e.g., beliefs about the appropriateness of various behaviors in different settings.

Long-term contextual factors also influence the manner in which child behavior is perceived. The economy of a society often determines the degree to which children are expected to work and the nature of the tasks assigned (Whiting, 1980). In addition to factors influencing perception arising from the economy of the society, there are those associated with the family structure—nuclear, extended or mother-child, etc. For example, in his analysis of some of the data from the Six Cultures study, Lambert (1971) found that aggression among children is perceived much more negatively when it occurs in an extended family than in a nuclear family.

Attributes of Adult Perceiver. The final type of background factor concerns the attributes or characteristics of the perceiver. We expect, for example, that the parent's perception of the behavior of his or her child will vary according to the cultural background, the social class, race, sex, or other characteristics of the parent who experiences the event. Variations in cultural background, for example, could result in variations in affective and cognitive structures, including implicit theories concerning children. Thus, parents who believe that it is in the nature of babies to spend a certain amount of time crying would tend to respond differently to crying behavior from parents who consider crying a kind of communication between infant and caretaker. Also, parents who believe that exposing babies to the cold (cf. Le Vine & Le Vine, 1966) will "harden" them and thereby promote health will differ in their cognitive structuring of child behavior and parental role from those who believe that various respiratory diseases result from "drafts." Variations associated with social class differences may be mediated by differing parental values (cf. Kohn, 1969). Those associated with parental sex roles may arise from differences in the amount of time spent with the child and in the degree of responsibility assumed for children, as dictated by social custom.

The relationship between the perceiver and the perceived is assumed to be an important determinant of the cognitive processing of the perceiver. Teachers, grandmothers and neighbors may differ in their perceptions of the same behavior of the same child. Certainly the distinction between "my child" and "not my child" strongly affects parental perception (Ashmore, Bacon, & Del Boca, 1981). Parents generally have much more information about their own children and this information is derived from a wide variety of situations. Also, parents generally have positive affective attachment to their children.

Cognitive Processes

Before discussing the cognitive processes distinguished in our framework, we would like to emphasize that the affective and cognitive structures we have described are assumed to form a cognitive frame of reference against which any given fragment of child behavior is perceived at the time of occurrence. These structures help to give meaning to observed child behavior. For example, if an American parent saw a 7-year-old child who could not print his or her name, the parent might conclude that the child was "backward." In societies where children seldom attend school, however, the child would be regarded as unremarkable. In fact, the adult who asked the child to print his or her name might be considered "foolish."

Parents' cognitive processing, as we conceive it, is indicated in Fig. 1.1 by the five boxes at the bottom middle of the diagram. These five boxes are intended to represent what we conceive to be important processes that may intervene between the S and the R. We do not, however, view these as slow and conscious processes or as separate and sequential stages. More likely they generally occur very rapidly, often in parallel, and without conscious recognition.

Attention

Various writers in the field of cognition have discussed the importance of attentive processes in the analysis of information. No individual in any situation attends to all of the stimuli in his or her environment. Why do some events catch the attention whereas others do not? Or, in the context of child behavior, out of the mass of child activity available for observation, why do parents notice some things and fail to notice others? Anderson (1980) points out that a great deal of information enters sensory memory but must be attended to and recoded in order to be retained and enter into further processing. Attention, therefore, is seen as important in the operation of selection for processing. The question of what determines the process of selection, however, seems not to be addressed.

Shiffrin's (1975, 1976) theoretical approach to attention seems most compatible with our view of parental cognition. Shiffrin proposes a memory system consisting of two structures: a temporary structure, short-term-store (STS), and a permanent repository called long-term store (LTS). Sensory information enters STS where it is encoded in a series of stages. This sensory information may activate existing knowledge structures with which it is compatible. This knowledge structure may, in turn, activate higher knowledge structures. If the appropriate knowledge structures do not exist for a given individual, then they cannot be activated. Thus, a person perceives an event in terms of the knowledge she or he possesses. Even if the knowledge structure has been activated, without further processing, it will quickly decay. Attention (selective) determines which cognitive structures receive further processing.

The framework in Fig. 1.1 suggests that there are many variables that may influence what is noticed and what is not. The goals of the perceiver seem likely to be an important factor. Cohen (1981) has recently demonstrated the influence on perception of the observational goals of the perceiver. Certainly, it would seem reasonable that the motive to socialize her children would lead a mother to notice certain kinds of behavior more than others. For example, a mother who plans to entertain her husband's family for Thanksgiving dinner will be oriented to ''notice'' the table manners of her children. Similarly, the figure would suggest that the parent who feels responsible for the behavior of his or her child would notice more items of behavior produced by this child than by the neighbor's child.

The emphasis by Anderson (1980) and others (e.g., Neisser, 1976) on the development of perceptual skills seems pertinent to the learning in naturalistic situations that may occur with child caretakers. It is possible that mothers or their surrogates may become skilled in their perceptions of auditory stimuli associated with the activities of their children. Full-time mothers may become especially proficient in this skill because of their feelings of responsibility and their goals of protection and socialization. Thus, as they proceed with their household tasks, mothers seem to monitor the activities of their children in the backyard or the playroom through the sounds that accompany the child activity. By such means, they may be able to identify the children present, the activities engaged in, and the situations requiring their intervention.

Attention is often conceived of as being "single minded" in the sense that a person can "attend" to only one task or item at a time. Experiments on selective looking (Neisser & Becklen, 1975) and selective listening (Cherry, 1953; Cherry & Taylor, 1954) clearly demonstrate that subjects can easily attend to one set of stimuli and ignore another, simultaneously presented, according to the directions of the experimenter. As already indicated, it seems evident that perceptual selection of sensory stimuli may be an important aspect of parent–child interaction in naturalistic settings. For example, as mothers monitor the activities of their children through the sounds that accompany their activities, selective listening may occur. Also, the behavior of mothers in their supervision of children seems closely related to what has been called dual or divided attention. While "keeping an ear on the children," they not only perform the more routine household chores but also plan menus and perform complicated tasks. Whether such simultaneous activities can really be said to represent attending to two things at the same time can certainly be questioned. However, experimental evidence suggests that people can "attend" to two things at once and that they get very much better at it with practice. An experiment by Spelke, Hirst, and Neisser (1976) provides evidence on this point. Two subjects were asked to read short stories while writing lists of words at dictation. After several weeks of practice, they were able not only to write words but to discover relations among the dictated words and to categorize them for meaning while reading for comprehension at normal speeds. Thus, with practice, these subjects were able to extract meaning simultaneously both from what they heard and what they read. The authors note that these findings are inconsistent with the idea that there are fixed limits to attentional capacity. They suggest that attention is based on the development of situation-specific skills.[2]

This idea that individuals through practice can become proficient in dividing attention seems possibly applicable to women's performance of the routine tasks of mothering and housework. Thus, as suggested earlier, through many hours of child care mothers may become very adept at extracting meaning from the various sounds that accompany child activity. This extraction of meaning from

---

[2]All this raises a number of interesting questions. What are the units of attentional capacity? Can such be devised? Writers frequently imply that there are greater or lesser "amounts" of attention. Thus, when Anderson (1980) describes the overlearning of certain skills with the resulting lesser amounts of attention required, *complete* automaticity is not claimed. Some remnants of attention are apparently assumed to be retained. Is there a dimension of agility of attention or capacity to shift attention rapidly along which people may vary and which can be improved with practice?

child sounds could also involve the use of cognitive maps of the area the sounds come from and the objects it contains. Sounds from the kitchen where a cake is cooling on the counter suggest quite different information than the same sounds from the family room. It also should be noted that mothers extract information not only from sounds but from silences. Even young sibling caretakers know that hearing no sound from a room occupied by a small child who is not asleep is a signal for immediate investigation.

Unitization

Another cognitive activity that enters into parental action in the parent–child relationship involves the breaking up of the observed behavior stream into units. Writers in the field of person perception have noted that we perceive the behavior of others as discrete actions rather than continuous behavior (cf. Heider, 1958; Schneider, Hastorf, & Ellsworth, 1979). In other words, in the process of perceiving the ongoing activity of another, the observer segments the behavior into units meaningful to him.

Newtson and his associates (Newtson, 1973, 1976, 1980; Newtson, Enquist, & Bois, 1977) have investigated the ''units'' of behavior that perceivers abstract from an observed sequence of action. His method consists in presenting to subjects a film or videotape of an actor involved in a series of behaviors, and instructing them to press a button (attached to a continuous event recorder) whenever one meaningful action ended and another began. Perceptual units were then equated with distances between presses of the button. These units were defined as *actions*. Newtson (1973) showed that some people divided the behavior stream into a small number of relatively large units, whereas other subjects partitioned the same behavior stream into a relatively large number of small units. At the same time there seemed to be a good deal of consensus as to ''break points'' in action (i.e., points at which one kind of behavior ends and another begins [Newtson & Enquist, 1976]). It should be noted that the videotaped sequences that Newtson presented to his subjects consisted of simple motor behavior (such as getting up and closing a door) without any affective implications for actor or observer.

Cohen (1981) has pointed out the limitations of this type of analysis and has suggested that the ''observational goal'' of the perceiver is important in determining the features of behavior relevant to the goal and the basis for unitization. Cohen supports her view with empirical evidence. Two groups of subjects with different observational goals showed highly significant differences in their unitization of the same observed behavior stream. Cohen's point of view and supportive data are consistent with the implications derived from our framework where it is suggested that the unitization of behavior will be influenced by a number of factors related to the perceiver, including specifically the perceiver's goals. A recent study by Russell (1979) is also consistent with this view. Russell investigated the perception of action units as a function of the subjective importance of the units. He found that greater subjective importance resulted in the discrimination of a larger number of action units in the behavior sequence. Because the operational definition of subjective importance in this experiment consisted of promised payment for students' performance, it seems possible to subsume this under Cohen's observational goal of the perceiver and consider it support for her hypothesis as well.

In considering these various findings in relation to our general concern with parental perception of child behavior, it should be noted that Cohen presents a tentative taxonomy of observational goals. Cohen (1981), in defining observational goals as "the purpose for which an individual plans to use the information gathered from the observation of another's behavior" (p. 47), distinguishes (a) Information Seeking or Learning Goals; (b) Personality Analysis Goals; and (c) Judgment Goals. According to Cohen, goals in the latter category are generally concerned with judgments regarding the position of the observed behavior along some dimension (probably evaluative). It seems possible that parents at various times make use of all three of these types of goals. For example, our first experiment (Bacon and Ashmore, 1985) indicated the existence of a strong evaluative dimension (reflecting a judgment goal) governing parents' categorizations of verbal descriptions of the social behavior of children.

Categorization

Another important step in the cognitive activity of the parent in response to child behavior is categorization. The necessity of categorization in the human response to the world of objects, people, and events has been emphasized by many writers in anthropology and psychology (e.g., Frake, 1961, Goodenough, 1956, Rosch, 1977, Schneider et al., 1979, Spradley, 1972). Bruner, Goodnow, and Austin (1956) defined categorization as follows: "To categorize is to render discriminably different things equivalent, to group the objects and events and people around us into classes, and to respond to them in terms of their class membership rather than their uniqueness" (p. 3). Categorization appears to be an integral part of all aspects of human cognition, from the simplest perceptions to the most complex type of thinking. As a result, a great deal of research attention has been directed to investigating the nature of categories and the processes of categorization. This is especially true in the recently developing field of social cognition where our present interest lies (cf. Lingle, Altom, & Medin, 1984).

Earlier work on categorization was concerned with concrete objects and "things" in the environment. The concept of "attributes" was important in this work. Attributes are aspects or characteristics of objects. Two legs, feathers, wings, beaks, and hatching of young from eggs are attributes of birds. Attributes form the basic elements of categories. Thus, the perception of the above attributes would be associated with the categorization "bird." Originally, the category concept included the notion of "defining attributes," i.e., groups of attributes or single attributes which were necessary for the determination of the category and without any one of which the entity in question was not a member of the category. This has been called the "classical view" (cf. Lingle, Altom, & Medin, 1984).

Rosch (1977) has contributed extensively to our understanding of the nature of categories through her explorations of the nature of category membership. She found that people readily make judgments as to the typicality of a category member and show substantial agreement. Thus, although robins and chickens are both categorized as birds, people agree that a robin is a more typical bird than a chicken. Cognitive psychologists now agree that categories are not defined by necessary and sufficient features but are seen rather to be organized around prototypes. According to Anderson (1980) a prototype "is a construct of a hypothetical most typical instance of a category" (p. 133). Lingle, Altom, and Medin (1984) include the prototype concept under the "probabilistic view" of category representation. Here, prototype is seen as a summary representation, consisting of an abstraction from specific exemplars, which is used to determine category membership.[3] This does not assume that the abstracted attributes must necessarily be defining. They instead may be merely salient. A new instance will be considered a category member if its similarity to the abstracted summary or prototype of that category is greater than to the prototypes of other categories.

In the domain of child socialization, the categorization of observed child behavior by the parent would seem to be of the utmost importance. At present, little if anything is known about this question. A good deal is available concerning how psychologists categorize child behavior (many parents are also familiar with such categorizations by psychologists) but little knowledge exists concerning the categories parents use to mentally organize child behavior if left to their own devices. In approaching the problem of parental categorization of child behavior it is necessary first to delineate the attributes of child behavior as they are perceived by parents. How do parents label or describe various fragments of behavior that they observe? From these attributes and their interrelationships, categories are presumably built.

Figure 1.1 indicates that the categorization process may be influenced by a large number of factors including variations in cultural background of the perceiver. It is assumed that such influence would enter at the level of the determination of the attributes of child behavior as well as how these are organized to determine prototypes and category boundaries. For example, it is assumed that lower class parents would conceive the basic attributes of child behavior differently from middle-class parents and that the differences between Ifaluk, Mexican, and New England parents would be even greater.

---

[3]Others regard categories as being represented in memory in terms of concrete exemplars and "mixed representation" models (involving both abstracted summary representations and knowledge of specific instances; Anderson, 1980; cf. Lingle et al., 1984).

Questions regarding the underlying bases for the development of categories must also be considered. Zajonc (1980) has pointed out the importance of affective systems that seem especially pertinent for parent–child interaction. Indeed, it is likely that most interactions involving parents and their children have strong affective elements that may, at times, dominate the interaction. It is entirely possible, of course, that parents form categories of child behavior primarily on the basis of affect, such as: "behavior that makes me angry" or "behavior that makes me glad," (although the parent need not—and probably does not—have explicit verbal labels for these feelings).

Certain constraints on the categorization process may also be operative. For example, parents have limited energy, time, and emotional resources. These limitations might lead to larger and less finely discriminated categories than would be the case with no limitations. It seems intuitively reasonable that (as an adaptation to the limitations) parents might come to categorize the behavior perceived in terms of what they should do about it. Thus, all observed child behavior might be divided initially into two categories: (a) "Behavior I should do something about," and (b) "Behavior I can safely ignore." As a consequence, on a good–bad or acceptable–unacceptable continuum there might be at the positive end a large, relatively undifferentiated group of behavior items that parents would not respond to at all. In contrast, at the other end of the dimension might be found behavior, such as "picks fights," "hassles neighbors," or "spits at other kids," that would ordinarily demand some kind of action from the parent. We would hypothesize here that behavior at the negative end of the distribution would be more differentiated than that at the positive end because negative behavior usually requires a decision about parental response.

Such an initial categorization into these two major groups (if it does occur) should be useful to parents in reducing their load of responsibility. We have no real data related to such a basic categorization. However, commonly overheard parental conversations using such phrases as "it's just a stage," "all boys do that," "she just wants to get attention" suggest a parental need to place behavior in a "safe to ignore" category. Such phrases seem to relieve parents of responsibility for action by removing the observed child behavior from the category of disapproved and, hence, to-be-changed category.

How adult perceivers categorize observed child behavior is also influenced by the relationship between the socializer and the child. In our earlier discussion, this relationship tended to be defined as a role-relationship (e.g., "own-child" vs. "other child," "parent-child" vs. "teacher-child"). Here, we wish to point out that affective relationships between parent and child may also be an important factor. A mother may well view the behavior of her favorite child in a more favorable light than she does the same behavior in a less favored child. A parent may also tend to identify more with the child of the same sex than with the child of the opposite sex.

Integration

During "Integration" the incoming information regarding child activity is related to all the stored knowledge about the child held by the perceiver. It is assumed that this integration goes on throughout the earlier steps in the cognitive process but reaches some sort of completion at the time of categorization. In fact, integration is so closely allied with the categorization process that the two might be combined as one, resulting in a single box in the framework (as depicted in Fig. 1.1) labeled *Categorization-Integration*. We have here given Integration a separate heading in the text and a separate box in the figure, not because we consider it a separate step in the structuring process, but because of its on-going nature and its extreme importance in final parental decision.

In Integration, a parent viewing a given fragment of child behavior will, in interpreting it, take into account factors in the immediate and past history of the child and the events surrounding him or her as well as his or her general competence in dealing with his or her environment and his or her state of health at the moment. The cultural expectations for socialization will be important here as well as the parents' implicit norms for children of a given age.

Another factor to be considered in the integration of child behavior is the attribution process (cf. Schneider, Hastorf, & Ellsworth, 1979). People not only seek to categorize behavior, they also seek to understand it, and, in the course of understanding, they generally assume that behavior is caused, either by factors within the individual or in the external environment. Parents are certainly motivated to understand the behavior of their children, because their attribution of the causality of the behavior may determine parental response or nonresponse. Because white middle-class mothers generally take more responsibility for the behavior of their children than do fathers (cf. Gecas, 1976), it seems likely that they are more motivated to infer the cause of child behavior than fathers. Thus, we would suggest that white middle-class mothers might have more elaborate theories about the causes of child behavior than would fathers.

Many situations arise in parent–child interaction in which the parent makes attributions of various sorts to the child. We shall consider here only a few of them with their possible consequences. In an achievement-oriented society, for example, attributions as to the causality of success or failure of their children are a frequent concern of many parents. Occasional lapses in an otherwise adequate school performance are usually attributed to temporary (i.e., "unstable"; cf. Weiner, Frieze, Kukla, Reed, Rest, & Rosenbaum, 1972) and external conditions, e.g., "she had a cold when she took the test," "she was distracted by the noise outside the classroom," "she was thinking of her birthday next week." If, however, the poor performance persists, then the parent, who feels he or she must "do something," is usually forced to attribute the failure to either limited competence or inadequate effort, i.e., to internal factors. These alternative categorizations create a difficult situation for both the parents and the child. Most parents are reluctant to accept the categorization that their child is possibly below average in intelligence. It thus seems preferable to explain the situation by such phrases as, "he is just not trying," because lack of effort is an "unstable" attribution that implies that the child's performance can be changed.

If parents are in conflict over the causes to which the poor performance may be attributed, they may take special steps—seek tutors, special testing programs, psychiatric consultations—all for the purpose of discovering the "cause" and means of alleviation of the condition. Meanwhile, the child may suffer various kinds of labeling by the school system, parents, and peers: "under-achiever," "learning disabled child," "lazy," "daydreamer," "stupid," "dummy," "in the lowest reading group." Such labels categorize the child in terms of the presumed cause of his or her poor school work. These categorizations may follow the child throughout his or her school career and certainly influence the child's peer interaction and self-image.

Parents of school-age children are often involved in situations in which attribution of intent to the child is of considerable importance in determining parental response. When Susie places a crown of burrs on her playmate Ellen's curls, is she pretending that Ellen is a lovely princess or is she jealous of those curls and fully aware of the prolonged and painful procedure required to remove the burrs? Children learn early the value of categorizing various events as "accidents." Johnny will assert that the lump on Susie's head is not the result of a deliberate blow from the stick he holds in his hand. "I didn't *mean* to. We were just playing and the stick jumped out and hit her on the head." There is a need for research on the many questions of attributions in parent–child interaction. At what age do parents begin to "hold children responsible" for their actions? How much variation is there in this judgment and to what factors are such variations related? It certainly seems unlikely that age is the only factor considered. What other signs of maturity are taken into consideration by parents? Few studies seem to have dealt with parents' attributions for child behavior (see, however, Dix & Grusec, 1985; Hess & McDevitt, this volume).

Most of the research on attribution has been concerned with the attributions of cause of the behavior of adults made by other adults. Are the generalizations derived from such research applicable to the attributions made by adult socializers for the behavior of children? For example, the fundamental attribution error (Nisbett & Ross, 1980) states, in essence, that people show a general tendency to see their own behavior as caused by situational factors and the behavior of other people as internally caused. Does this hold for parents observing the behavior of children? And what about the "defensive attribution model" (Schneider et al., 1979) that indicates that people are less likely to hold themselves responsible for their failings than are others. Perhaps people are also motivated to avoid blaming the perpetrator of a bad act to the extent that the perpetrator is related in some way to the observer. If so, it is possible that parents might be more reluctant to attribute blame to their own child than to the neighbor's child and the difference would be even greater for an unknown child.

Decision Making

Our framework provides also for some sort of decision process. In response to child activity, filtered through the parental cognitive process, what does the parent decide to do? There are obviously many factors involved in this process about which we know very little. At present we can only point out factors that must be operative and speculate on others. Our use of the terms *decision* and *decision making* does not refer to the conscious choice among clear alternatives but to a consideration of possible factors affecting parental reaction to perceived behavior. The decision-making process in parental response to child behavior seems to vary greatly in the time elapsing between perception and response. As noted earlier, any signal communicating "danger to child" is presumed to pre-empt all others and lead immediately to parental behavior designed to protect, defend, or otherwise care for the child. In most instances, however, decision making is not so immediate.

Parental response to observed child behavior need not always be active. The parent may decide to do nothing, filing the observation in the appropriate storage area for future consideration or combination with subsequent behavior. Or, the parent may deliberately ignore the activity for various reasons, implicitly classifying it as "unimportant," "just play," "part of growing up," or "wants attention."

If, as we have suggested, parents initially categorize child behavior in terms of their own response or non-response (i.e., "behavior I can safely ignore" vs. "behavior I must do something about"), then the action decided upon in many cases is determined by the categorization (e.g., if the categorization is "behavior to be ignored" then there is no separate decision-making process). If the do-nothing, do-something categorization coincides with a good–bad dimension, then the decision process may be concerned almost entirely with what to do about disapproved behavior. It is assumed that every parent develops a repertoire of parental response to such disapproved behavior that ranges on a dimension of severity from mild to severe in punitiveness. Parental goals as well as implicit theories about how children learn may influence the choice of response. (See Mancuso and Lehrer's discussion of implicit theories of reprimand, this volume.) Great variability in these repertoires both across cultures and within cultures must exist, both with regard to the nature of punishment and the type of behavior punished. "Disobedience," for example, is a child act that is treated quite differently by different parents and varies by the child's developmental level. Cross-culturally even greater variations may appear.

Effects of Cognitive Structuring

The last part of the diagram to be considered is the feedback loop, the arrow connecting parental "Response to Child Activities" with "Ongoing Child Activity."[4] Because this involves the effect of parental behavior on child behavior, a great deal of the literature on socialization might be expected to fit here.

It is essential to note that the child, too, is a cognitive being who through experience actively constructs his or her world. Information or stimuli provided by parents and others are understood or given meaning within the constraints of the child's existing cognitive and affective structures.

Throughout this chapter we have repeatedly pointed out examples of the manner in which parental perception of child behavior might affect parental response. An additional important implication of the present cognitive framework with feedback is that parents may influence the child by other means in addition to the immediate reinforcing or shaping parental response. Three such means are noted. First, what is the effect on the child of a lack of overt response by the parent? As noted previously, parents may elect not to respond as a result of some categorizations of child behavior or fail to respond for other reasons. How does the child experience or interpret nonresponse from a parent—as disapproving, permissive, rejecting, indifferent, lacking in appreciation? Obviously the answer to this question depends on a variety of factors (e.g., age and sex of the child, role relationship of adult to child, circumstances surrounding the behavior, the child activity itself, and the child's affective and cognitive structures). Second, however the parent categorizes the child behavior, it seems inevitable that this categorization will be, either wittingly or unwittingly, transmitted to the child who may come in time to adopt it as his or her own. Thus, the child may come to organize the world as his or her parent does—to perceive objects, events, people, and behavior (of others or self) as "good," "bad," "normal," "dangerous," "unimportant," "helpful," whatever. Third, parents also sometimes categorize children according to perceived personality characteristics and these, too, may be transmitted to the child. The child who overhears his or her mother refer to him or her as a "sensitive" child may come to view him or herself as "sensitive," whatever that may mean to the child. Thus, the child's self-concept is influenced.

We would question whether there might not be a number of variables influencing the child's acceptance of parental views. Can the age of the child be an important factor, with younger ages more susceptible to such influence? Also, is the affective relationship between parent and child influential in the child's incorporation of the parent's categorizations? It seems likely that a boy who has a

---

[4]The arrow from "Response to Child Activity" back to "Affective and Cognitive Structures" is also worthy of note, suggesting that parental perception and response may also influence the parent's cognitive structures.

warm affectionate relationship with his father, and who strongly identifies with him, might accept his father's categorizations of the world and himself and hold these into adulthood. On the other hand, a child who experiences negative or conflictful affect toward a parent may partially or wholly reject the parental view of himself and the world.

RESEARCH GENERATED BY THIS COGNITIVE-AFFECTIVE FRAMEWORK

Our own research, following the outlines of this framework, has been diverse in area and method of approach. It has been united, however, by the common goal of uncovering the cognitive and affective structures that exist in the minds of socializers and that may influence the manner in which they perceive and respond to the behavior of children. To this end we have made use of the least directive data-gathering approaches possible. Every effort has been made to avoid asking subjects to respond in terms of an investigator imposed categorical framework. We have made extensive use of open-ended questions and when a closed-ended format has been employed, the items have been phrased in terms of a vocabulary supplied by parents.

Our initial investigation (Bacon & Ashmore, 1985) addressed what seems to be the central question of our conceptualization: Do observers of child behavior "see" the same bit of behavior differently as a function of differences in their background? We began with the collection of a body of verbal descriptions of the behavior of children in the 6 to 11 year age period, spontaneously produced by parents. These descriptions were obtained from the tape recordings of parents who were asked to talk about the behavior of boys and girls of this age. This represents a first step in the development of a parental vocabulary of child behavior that must be helpful to parents in their thinking about their children. Our schematic framework suggests that the perception of child behavior (of which the parental vocabulary may be considered as an indirect outcome) will vary with the age, sex, social class, and cultural background of the perceiving parent and perceived child. The sample we collected was obtained from a group of white, middle-class mothers and fathers in New Jersey describing the behavior of their early-school-age girls and boys. Each descriptive phrase was placed in two sentence frames, one of which attributed the behavior to a girl, the other to a boy. Thus, the sex of the perceived child was varied as well as that of the perceiving parent.

In an effort to explore how mothers and fathers might categorize these verbal descriptions (e.g., "hassles neighbors," "is definitely a part of the conversation at dinner"), another sample of parents (of both a boy and a girl in this age range) were given the task of sorting these descriptions into piles in terms of how they would think, feel, or respond if the behavior occurred in a boy (or a girl) of their own. In line with our basic goal of uncovering mothers' and fathers' cognitive structures, we chose the least directive instructions we could think of. The sorting task was used to devise a measure of similarity between all possible pairs of the behavior descriptions. The basic assumption here is that items that often co-occur in the same sorting pile are psychologically similar, whereas those that are seldom sorted together are psychologically distant. These measures of similarity were subjected to multidimensional scaling and hierarchical clustering which are statistical analyses designed to uncover underlying structure in this type of data.

The most outstanding finding of this study was the existence of a strong evaluative dimension which appeared for both sexes of parent and both sexes of child and was strongly supported by all statistical measures employed. This seems consistent with the "socialization goal" that we postulated for parents (also Cohen, 1981, Judgment Goal).

We also found a clearly delineated group of behavior descriptions that seemed to represent hostile-aggressive behavior. Further, mothers viewed the hostile-aggressive not hostile-aggressive dimension as more closely aligned to the good–bad dimension than did fathers. That is, mothers were more likely than fathers to consider hostile-aggressive behavior as "bad." We have tentatively suggested that this may be because such behavior is difficult to deal with and mothers usually have more constant contact with children than do fathers.

Evidence for a normal-problem dimension used in parents' thinking was also found. Of particular interest is the finding that the parents we studied saw the normal-problem distinction as more closely related to the good–bad dimension for daughters than for sons. This suggests that parents may think that good behavior is normal for girls but not necessarily sons, whereas bad behavior is a problem in a girl but not necessarily something to worry about in a son.

Thus, although this is a greatly abridged account of our first study, it does serve to indicate that our first question was answered in the affirmative: Yes, categorization of verbal descriptions of the social behavior of children does vary with the sex of the perceiving parent and the sex of the perceived child.

Figure 1.1 also suggests that variation in role relationship between the perceiving socializer and perceived child may have an important influence on the perception of child behavior. As a partial test of this proposition, we asked a group of college students (male and female), who had younger brothers and/or sisters in the appropriate age range, to perform the same sorting task using the same sample of behavior descriptions. Again, we found evidence of a strong evaluative dimension underlying the organization of the descriptions by siblings. We also found differences in the categorizations between parents and siblings, suggesting that role relationship might be an important factor (Bacon & Ashmore, 1982). A major difference appeared to consist of less emphasis on an evaluative dimension by older siblings. That is, the cognitive distinction "good–bad" was a less indispensible part of the cognitive structuring for older siblings than for parents. This seems intuitively reasonable if we assume that siblings are generally less concerned with the goal of socialization than parents.

In another series of studies we attempted to discover how parents described the personalities of their own and other children. In experimenting with different methods, we first asked mothers and fathers to list at least 30 words or phrases describing the personalities of their sons and daughters. This method, however, tended to produce lists that were very positive and internally consistent. We found that if we simply asked parents to describe their children and tape recorded their responses, the data obtained were much richer, various, and distinctive. These taped responses of parents were transcribed verbatim and an elaborate system of coding was developed and applied to each transcription. These data are still in the process of analysis. They do indicate clearly that mothers produce more extensive descriptions of their children than fathers do.

In another study, some of the clusters of behavior descriptions derived from the hierarchical clustering analysis of the first study (e.g., "shows off," "acts up in class," "clowns around") were presented to another sample of parents who were asked what they would call the behavior, how they would react, and the type of child who showed such behavior. By far the most frequent response given to the first question was "normal." This is interesting from a number of points of view. It suggests that a major and quite conscious concern of white middle-class parents is that their children be "normal." It also appears to be consistent with our speculation in the section on categorization that parents initially dichotomize observed behavior in terms of whether or not they should take any action. "Normal" behavior presumably requires no intervention.

Parents' open-ended responses to the clusters also provided a vocabulary of child personality descriptors. Those that occurred most frequently were given to a new sample of parents who were asked to sort them into piles on the basis of their likelihood of going together in the same 6- to 12-year-old child. As in our initial study, the sorting data were subjected to multidimensional scaling, and again there was evidence of an evaluative continuum. More positive attributes were assigned to "own" child and girls than to "other" child and boys.

FUTURE RESEARCH SUGGESTED BY THE FRAMEWORK

Our first studies addressed questions arising from the top section of the figure where "Background Factors" were considered. Much remains to be done in this area. A study, similar to our first (Bacon & Ashmore, 1985), including development of the vocabulary in use by the parents, should be carried out comparing middle- and lower class parents. If Kohn (1969) is correct in his analysis of the link between father's occupation and parental values, lower socio-economic status parents should, in comparison with the middle-class sample, emphasize obedience and de-emphasize independence.

Teachers should also provide interesting material with respect to vocabularies and categorizing. We would expect, for example, their vocabularies to contain references to academic skills (e.g., "strong in math," "behind grade level in reading") and to classroom comportment (e.g., "can't sit still," "works well alone").

The nature of the evaluative dimension should be investigated further. The "good" and "bad" social behavior categories could be divided and multidimensional scaling done on each half. This might increase our understanding of parents' interpretation of "good" and "bad" behavior. The whole subject of vocabularies of parents for child behavior should be of considerable interest cross-culturally. If anthropologists who know the language well could collect such information, it should further our knowledge considerably.

Much more can be done concerning context and attributes of perceived child. For example, what is the effect of divorce on parental categorization of child behavior? Also, what effect does the introduction of stepchildren and half brothers or half sisters have on the mother's and father's categorizations? It should also be noted that all of this previous research and that suggested previously are directed to the cognitive process of categorization. Within the categorization area, the influence of affect on the development and nature of categories should be investigated.

The framework also suggests that a variety of factors might be expected to influence other aspects of cognitive processing such as attention, unitization, attribution and decision making. Methodological techniques must be developed. Newtson's (1973) method of studying unitization might be adapted to the study of parents' segmentation of child behavior. Phenomena of attention suggested in the text might be approached through studying parental responses to videotaped sequences of child play. Questions of attribution can be approached in many cases by traditional methods.

Further study of the central section of the framework—the "Affective and Cognitive Structures"—should include investigation of parents' theories about the development of behavior and personality of children. One obvious and important next step would be to extend our work on early school-age children to the perception of both older and younger boys and girls.

CONCLUDING REMARKS

In this chapter we have presented an heuristic framework that outlines our current conceptualization of parental cognition in the parent–child interaction sequence. The basic logic of our analysis is that what the observing parent "sees" depends not only on sensory receptors but on a complex set of cognitive and affective structures and processes. These affective-cognitive factors are, in turn, a function of variables associated with the child, the observer, and the context, generalized and specific, within which the observation occurs.

In this discussion we have applied this logic to parents. It can, of course, be applied to all others who observe the behavior of children: those who "help" children, such as teachers, pediatricians, social workers, as well as those who "study" children, namely developmental psychologists.

We hope this tentative framework serves to stimulate new questions and hypotheses concerning socialization as well as assists in developing new strategies in data gathering for this complex and difficult field.

ACKNOWLEDGMENTS

The research by the authors reported in this chapter was supported by National Institute of Mental Health grant 27737 and Office of Education grant 222-BO97. We also wish to thank the Rutgers Research Council.

We thank the following individuals for their comments on an earlier draft of this paper: Selden Bacon, David M. Brodzinsky, Sara Harkness, Jeannette M. Haviland, Charles M. Super, John Lingle, Mark Altom, Irvin Child, and John and Beatrice Whiting.

REFERENCES

Anderson, J. R. (1980). *Cognitive psychology and its implications*. San Francisco: Freeman.

Ashmore, R. D., Bacon, M. K., & Del Boca, F. K. (1981, November). *American parents' implicit theories of children's personalities*. American Anthropological Association Convention, Los Angeles.

Bacon, M. K., & Ashmore, R. D. (1975, November). *Cognitive structuring of parental perceptions of children's behavior*. American Anthropological Association Convention, Mexico City.

Bacon, M. K., & Ashmore, R. D. (1982). The role of categorization in the socialization process: How parents and older siblings cognitively organize child behavior. In L. M. Laosa & I. E. Sigel (Eds.), *Families as learning environments for children* (pp. 301–341). New York: Plenum.

Bacon, M. K., & Ashmore, R. D. (1985). How mothers and fathers categorize descriptions of social behavior attributed to daughters and sons. *Social Cognition. 3*(2), 193–217.

Bower, G. H. (1975). Cognitive psychology: An introduction. In W. K. Estes (Ed.), *Handbook of learning and cognitive processes, Vol. 1: Introduction to concepts and issues* (pp. 25–80). Hillsdale, NJ: Lawrence Erlbaum Associates.

Bruner, J. S., Goodnow, J., & Austin, G. (1956). *A study of thinking*. New York: Wiley.

Bruner, J. S., & Tagiuri, R. (1954). Person perception. In G. Lindzey (Ed.), *Handbook of social psychology* (Vol. 2, pp. 634–654). Reading, MA: Addison-Wesley.

Cherry, E. C. (1953). Some experiments on the recognition of speech with one and with two ears. *Journal of Acoustical Society of America, 25*, 975–979.

Cherry, E. C., & Taylor, W. K. (1954). Some further experiments on recognition of speech with one and two ears. *Journal of Acoustical Society of America, 26*, 554–559.

Cohen, C. E. (1981). Goals and schemata in person perception: Making sense from the stream of behavior. In N. Cantor & J. F. Kihlstrom (Eds.), *Personality, cognition, and social interaction* (pp. 45–68). Hillsdale, NJ: Lawrence Erlbaum Associates.

Cronbach, L. J. (1955). Processes affecting scores on "understanding of others" and "assumed similarity." *Psychological Bulletin, 52*, 177–193.

Dix, T. H., & Grusec, J. E. (1985). Parent attribution processes in child socialization. In I. E. Sigel (Ed.), *Parent belief systems* (pp. 201–234). Hillsdale, NJ: Lawrence Erlbaum Associates.

Emmerich, W. (1969). The parental role: A functional-cognitive approach. *Monographs of the Society for Research in Child Development, 34,* 1–71.

Frake, C. O. (1961). The diagnosis of disease among the Subanum of Mindanao. *American Anthropology, 63*(1), 113–132.

Frazer, J. G. (1981). *The golden bough: The roots of religion and folklore.* New York: Avenel. (Original work published 1890)

Gecas, V. (1976). The socialization and child care roles. In F. E. Nye (Ed.), *Role structure and analysis of the family.* Beverly Hills, CA: Sage.

Goodenough, W. H. (1956). Componential analysis and the study of meaning. *Language, 32*(1), 195–216.

Goodnow, J. J. (1984). Parents' ideas about parenting and development. In M. Lamb, A. L. Brown, & B. Rogoff (Eds.), *Advances in developmental psychology, Vol. 3* (pp. 193–242). Hillsdale, NJ: Lawrence Erlbaum Associates.

Griaule, M. (1965). *Conversations with Ogotemmeli: An introduction to Dogon religious ideas.* New York: Oxford.

Hays, W. L. (1958). An approach to the study of trait implication and trait similarity. In R. Tagiuri & L. Petrullo (Eds.), *Person perception and interpersonal behavior.* Stanford: Stanford University Press.

Heider, F. (1958). *The psychology of interpersonal relations.* New York: Wiley.

Hess, R. D. (in press). Approaches to the measurement and interpretation of parent-child interaction. In R. W. Henderson (Ed.), *Parent-child interaction: Learning and adjustment in children.* New York: Academic.

Holloway, S. D., & Hess, R. D. (1982). Causal explanations for school performance: Contrasts between mothers and children. *Journal of Applied Developmental Psychology, 3,* 319–327.

Kelly, G. A. (1955). *The psychology of personal constructs.* New York: Norton.

Kohn, M. L. (1969). *Class and conformity.* Homewood, IL: Dorsey.

Lambert, W. W. (1971). Cross-cultural backgrounds to personality development and the socialization of aggression: Findings from the Six Cultures study. In W. W. Lambert & R. Weisbrod (Eds.), *Comparative perspectives on social psychology* (pp. 49–61). Boston: Little, Brown.

LeVine, R. A. (1974). Parental goals: A cross-cultural view. *Teachers' College Record, 76,* 226–239.

LeVine, R. A., & LeVine, B. B. (1966). Nyansongo: A Gusii community in Kenya. In B. B. Whiting (Ed.), *Six cultures: Studies of child rearing* (pp. 15–202). New York: Wiley.

Lingle, J. H., Altom, M. W., & Medin, D. L. (1984). Of cabbages and kings: Assessing the extendibility of natural object concept models to social things. In R. S. Wyer, Jr., T. K. Srull, & J. Hartwick (Eds.), *Handbook of social cognition* (pp. 71–120). Hillsdale, NJ: Lawrence Erlbaum Associates.

Lytton, H. (1971). Observation studies of parent–child interaction: A methodological review. *Child Development, 42,* 651–683.

McCord, J., & McCord, W. (1961). Cultural stereotypes and the validity of interviews for research in child development. *Child Development, 32,* 171–185.

McGillicudy-De Lisi, A. V. (1982). Relationship between parents' beliefs about development and family constellation, socio-economic status and parents' teaching strategies. In L. M. Laosa & I. E. Sigel (Eds.), *Families as learning environments for children* (pp. 261–300). New York: Plenum.

Maccoby, E. E., & Jacklin, C. N. (1974). *The psychology of sex differences.* Stanford, CA: Stanford University Press.

Maccoby, E. E., & Maccoby, N. (1954). The interview: a tool of social science. In G. Lindzey (Ed.), *Handbook of social psychology* (pp. 449–487). Reading, MA: Addison-Wesley.

Maccoby, E. E., & Martin, J. A. (1983). Socialization in the context of the family: Parent–child interaction. In P. H. Mussen (Ed.), *Handbook of child psychology 4th edition* (Vol. 1, pp. 1–101). New York: Wiley.

Minturn, L., & Lambert, W. W. (1964). *Mothers of six cultures: Antecedents of child rearing.* New York: Wiley.

Mischel, W. (1979). On the interface of cognition and personality (Beyond the person-situation debate). *American Psychologist, 34,* 740–754.

Neisser, U. (1976). *Cognition and reality.* San Francisco: Freeman.

Neisser, U., & Becklen, R. (1975). Selective looking: Attending to visually-specified events. *Cognitive Psychology, 7,* 480–494.

Newtson, D. (1973). Attribution and the unit of perception of ongoing behavior. *Journal of Personality and Social Psychology, 28,* 28–38.

Newtson, D. (1976). Foundations of attribution: The perception of ongoing behavior. In J. H. Harvey, W. J. Ickes, & R. F. Kidd (Eds.), *New directions in attribution research* (Vol. 1, pp. 223–247). Hillsdale, NJ: Lawrence Erlbaum Associates.

Newtson, D. (1980). An interactionist perspective on social knowing. *Personality and Social Psychology Bulletin, 6,* 520–531.

Newtson, D., & Enquist, G. (1976). The perceptual organization of ongoing behavior. *Journal of Personality and Social Psychology, 12,* 436–450.

Newtson, D., Enquist, G., & Bois, J. (1977). The objective basis of behavior units. *Journal of Personality and Social Psychology, 35,* 847–862.

Nisbett, R., & Ross, L. (1980). *Human inference: Strategies and shortcomings of social judgment.* Englewood Cliffs, NJ: Prentice-Hall.

Parke, R. (1978). Parent-child interaction: Progress, paradigms, and problems. In G. Sackett (Ed.), *Observing behavior, Vol. 1: Theory and applications in mental retardation* (pp. 69–94). Baltimore, MD: University Park Press.

Peterson, D. R., & Migliorino, G. (1967). Pan-cultural factors of parental behavior in Sicily and the United States. *Child Development, 38,* 967–991.

Rosch, E. (1977). Human categorization. In N. Warren (Ed.), *Advances in cross-cultural psychology* (Vol. 1, pp. 1–49). London: Academic.

Rubin, J. Z., Provenzano, F. J., & Luria, Z. (1974). The eye of the beholder: Parents' views on sex of newborns, *American Journal of Orthopsychiatry, 44,* 512–519.

Russell, J. C. (1979). Perceived action units as a function of subjective importance. *Personality and Social Psychology Bulletin, 5,* 206–209.

Schneider, D. J., Hastorf, A. H., & Ellsworth, P. C. (1979). *Person perception (Second Edition).* Menlo Park, CA: Addison-Wesley.

Sears, R. R., Maccoby, E. E., & Levin, H. (1957). *Patterns of child rearing.* Evanston, IL: Row, Peterson.

Shiffrin, R. M. (1975). Short-term store: The basis for a memory system. In F. Restle, R. M. Shiffrin, N. J. Castellon, H. R. Limchuan, & D. B. Pison (Eds.), *Cognitive Theory* (pp. 193–218). Hillsdale, NJ: Lawrence Erlbaum Associates.

Shiffrin, R. M. (1976). Capacity limitations in information processing, attention, and memory. In W. K. Estes (Ed.), *Handbook of Learning and Cognitive Processes, Vol. 4: Attention and Memory* (pp. 177–236). Hillsdale, NJ: Lawrence Erlbaum Associates.

Sigel, I. E. (1982). The relationship between parental distancing strategies and the child's cognitive behavior. In L. M. Laosa & I. E. Sigel (Eds.), *Families as learning environments for children.* New York: Plenum.

Spelke, E., Hirst, W., & Neisser, U. (1976). Skills of divided attention. *Cognition, 4,* 215–230.

Spradley, J. P. (1972). Foundations of cultural knowledge. In J. Spradley (Ed.), *Culture and cognition (rules, maps, and plans)* (pp. 3–38). San Francisco: Chandler.

Warr, P. B., & Knapper, C. (1968). *The perception of people and events.* New York: Wiley.

Weiner, B., Frieze, I., Kukla, A., Reed, L., Rest, S., & Rosenbaum, R. M. (1972). Perceiving the causes of success and failure. In E. E. Jones et al. (Eds.), *Attribution: Perceiving the causes of behavior* (pp. 95–120). Morristown, NJ: General Learning Press.

Weisner, T. S., & Gallimore, R. (1977). My brother's keeper: Child and sibling caretaking. *Current Anthropology, 18,* 169–190.

Whiting, B. (1980). Culture and social behavior: a model for the development of social behavior. *Ethos, 8,* 95–116.

Whiting, B., & Whiting, J. W. M. (1971). Task assignment and personality: A consideration of the effect of herding on boys. In W. W. Lambert & R. Weisbrod (Eds.), *Comparative perspectives on social psychology* (pp. 33–45). Boston, MA: Little, Brown.

Zajonc, R. B. (1980). Feeling and thinking: Preferences need no inferences. *American Psychologist, 35,* 151–175.

2 Reflections on the Belief– Behavior Connection: Lessons Learned from a Research Program on Parental Belief Systems and Teaching Strategies

Irving E. Sigel
Educational Testing Service

This chapter tells the story of a research effort that began with two basic assumptions: (a) that developmental psychologists should attend to the family as a unit—that after all, children usually grow up in families where they are influenced by fathers, mothers, siblings—in fact, a broad social network; and (b) that parents' beliefs are an important input into their socialization actions. Yet, at the time this set of studies began, relatively little interest was evident among developmental psychologists in the family as a set of mutual influences (Sigel, Dreyer, & McGillicuddy-DeLisi, 1984). Further, relatively little consideration was given to parents' cognitions regarding children's development (Sigel 1985).

With these convictions, my colleagues and I began an exciting, yet frustrating, journey. Exciting because we believed we set for ourselves new challenges. Frustrating because we soon began to realize how complex and difficult the task we elected to undertake was. In this chapter I describe our efforts—an insider's view, so to speak—of an 8-year research effort. The narrative proceeds developmentally, first dealing with the conceptualization of parental teaching strategies, and then focusing on a description of parental beliefs about children's cognitive development that were conceptualized as undergirding parents' teaching strategies. Following this I detail our thinking about the linkage between parental beliefs and parental teaching strategies and how each of these major components and connections was addressed empirically. The results of our empirical research are presented, and the chapter concludes with reflections on my experience and a recommendation for new research directions.

OVERALL CONCEPTION OF THE FAMILY AS A
SYSTEM OF MUTUAL INFLUENCES

The basic hypothesis guiding the research program was that the development of representational thought in children is, in part, an outcome of a particular class of teaching strategies parents use with their children, both formally and informally. This teaching goes on in the context of the family. The types and frequencies of strategies parents use are influenced by a number of contextual factors such as family size, spacing, ordinal position of the child, sex of the child and the parent, and socioeconomic status. In addition to these social and family context status factors, I was interested not only in what strategies parents use, but *why* they use the particular kind of strategies they do. Thinking along these lines led me to conceptualize the research effort as addressing two questions:

1. How do parents' teaching strategies impact on children's cognitive functioning?
2. How do parents' constructions of children's cognitive understanding and development influence their teaching strategies?

Answers to these questions were sought in the context of the family. I begin with a description of the family unit and its components as a backdrop for subsequent discussion.

The First Model

A model of family interactions was developed as a prelude to collecting our data and to establishing analytic procedures. The model that is depicted in Fig. 2.1 represents the connections among family behaviors initially believed to cover the major relevant components.

There are three primary interactive components in the model: parental beliefs regarding the child's development (i.e., mothers' and fathers' beliefs about children's development), parental teaching behaviors (i.e., how mothers and fathers teach their children), and child outcomes (i.e., child's level of cognitive development). Each component can be affected directly or indirectly by each of the other components. Parents' teaching strategies, for example, influence the child's behavior—a direct influence—but the child's behavior can influence the parents' teaching strategies—another instance of a direct influence. Parents' beliefs influence their teaching strategies, *but* the way children respond to parents' teaching strategies may influence not only the these teaching strategies, but also parents' beliefs about their children. This is an indirect effect (McGillicuddy-DeLisi, 1985). The schematic of the model depicts these direct and indirect influences of parent–child interactions.

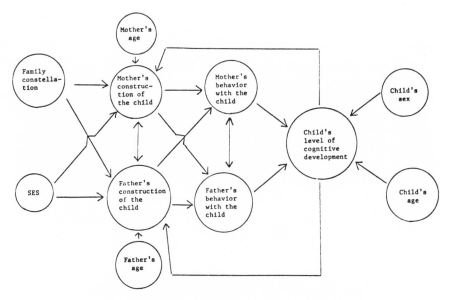

FIG. 2.1.   First model of the mutual influences within the family.

However, additional sets of factors influence each of these components. In addition to family size, specific characteristics of each family member are sources of influence, e.g., for parents, age, education, and occupation, and for children, age, sex, ordinal position and educational level. In sum, the model of the family can be described as a system of mutual influences wherein each component is not independent of any other component.

Within this overall framework and for the purposes of this chapter, I abstract and focus on the relationships between parents' beliefs and their teaching behaviors, realizing that I am decontextualizing a part of the model from the total.[1] I begin with a discussion of the conceptualization of the parents' teaching behaviors, because the linkage between parents' beliefs about children and their teaching and managerial strategies can only be understood in the context of a clear conceptualization of parental behavior. In this way, theoretical linkages can be articulated between behaviors and their underlying determinants.

CONCEPTUALIZATION OF PARENTAL TEACHING STRATEGIES

The original model was developed in a study of children's cognitive development in the context of a preschool environment. The conceptualization and methods of

---

[1]The relationship between parents' teaching strategies and children's cognitive functioning is described in detail in Sigel (1982, 1985).

study were virtually in place when the present study began. I incorporated that component into the research described below (Copple, Sigel, & Saunders 1979–1984).

The focus in this section is on teaching strategies, which from the model are considered as major influences on children's representational competence. This argument is based on the proposition that what parents do with their children makes a difference in children's cognitive development. In my previous work in the preschool, I found that these strategies, when used by teachers, did impact on children's representational competence (Copple, et al., 1979/1984; Sigel, 1982). The teaching strategies are conceptualized as *distancing strategies,* which I (Sigel, 1982) define as follows:

> [Distancing is] a construct that is used as a metaphor to denote the psychological separation of the person from the immediate, ongoing present. The distancing metaphor suggests that individuals can project themselves into the past or into the future or can transcend the immediate present. This process of distancing is conceptualized as critical in the development of representational thinking. (p. 50)

Distancing is instigated by strategies that are operationally defined to include those behaviors that place cognitive demands on the child to reconstruct the past (reconstructive memory), to employ his or her imagination in dealing with objects, events, and people (transcend the immediate), to plan and to anticipate future actions (with particular attention paid to the articulation of such intentions), and finally, to attend to the transformation of phenomena from one symbol system to another. Distancing strategies have a demand quality wherein the parent engages the child to be an active participant in an interaction.

A cognitive demand is intrinsic to the message of the distancing strategy. Strategies range from a concrete to a conceptual level, from a demand to label (e.g., ''What is the name of _____ ?'') to a demand to express such relationships as cause–effect, (e.g., ''How come there is no water left in the pot after it boils for some time?'').

Distancing strategies vary in the degree to which they activate the separation of the person from the ongoing present. Simple declarative statements, for example, require passive listening and associative responses; *open-ended inquiry* demands active engagement (Sigel & Cocking, 1977). Open-ended inquiry serves to instigate, to activate, and to facilitate reorganization of mental operations because it demands active engagement.

A further function of distancing strategies is to generate discrepancies that create disequilibrium that the child strives to resolve via some mental actions assumed to be representational in nature. Hence, *distancing strategies are hypothesized as fostering the development of representational thinking* (Sigel & Cocking, 1977). The discrepancy resolution perhaps is short-lived, because another inquiry can reinstitute the cycle. The impact of inquiry has been found to be most effective when a dialogue of followup questions or cognitive demands is used (Rosner, 1978).

The foregoing discussion emphasizes the functional aspect of distancing strategies. Obviously, distancing strategies take some form. Two basic forms were identified: *telling* and *posing a question*. The conceptualization of effects of distancing strategies was derived from a constructivist perspective that holds that each participant in the interaction has the opportunity to construct new information and thereby alter his or her perspectives (Kelly, 1955). Strategies that are types of telling or closed, and/or highly structural questions have less chance for generating a discrepancy that *demands* resolution compared with an open-ended inquiry wherein the respondent has an implicit or explicit choice as to how to organize a response. Asking the child questions demanding a *yes* or *no* answer or single-word utterance allows for a limited range of responses, compared with inquiry-type questions.

Over 40 types of distancing strategies have been identified, and they have been organized into three hierarchical levels defined in terms of the complexity of cognitive demands inherent in the message (see Table 2.1 for examples). Strategies that demand association or a passive attitude are at the lowest level, whereas more *demanding* inferences or hypothetical deductive reasons are high-level. Details of these characteristics can be found in Sigel, McGillicuddy-DeLisi, and Johnson (1980), and Sigel, McGillicuddy-DeLisi, Flaugher, and Rock, (1983).

TABLE 2.1
Mental Operational Demands on the Child
through Parent Distancing Strategies

High-Level Distancing	Medium-Level Distancing	Low-Level Distancing
evaluate consequence	sequence	label
evaluate competence	reproduce	produce information
evaluate affect	describe similarities	describe, define
evaluate effort and/or performance	describe differences	describe—interpretation
evaluate necessary and/or sufficient	infer similarities	demonstrate
infer cause-effect	infer differences	observe
infer affect	symmetrical classifying	
infer effect	estimating	
generalize	asymmetrical classifying	
transform	enumerating	
plan	synthesizing within classifying	
confirmation of a plan		
conclude		
propose alternatives		
resolve conflict		

Historical Development of the Distancing Model

The conceptualization of distancing, as I indicated, emerged from an educational context (Sigel, Secrist, & Forman, 1973). Let me turn now to the story of why and how the model was applied to the family environment.

A number of studies have been reported dealing with parents' teaching strategies demonstrating the influence of such techniques on children's socio-emotional and/or intellectual development (Baumrind, 1971; Hess & Shipman, 1965; Laosa, 1982, 1983; Martin, 1975; Sigel, 1982; Sigel et al., 1984). Although none of the other authors alluded to the term *distancing strategies,* I believe many of the strategies they describe can be categorized according to my system. Hence, I consider those studies as indirect evidence supporting my argument that parents' teaching strategies are significant influences in the child's cognitive development. In reviewing such research it became evident that relatively little attention had been paid to *detailing* the parents' contribution to the children's intellectual development.

My interest in detailing parents' actions in the context of teaching their children (teaching conceived in the broadest sense of guiding, instructing or modelling) did not emerge from arm-chair speculation. Rather, the history of the distancing model evolved from early studies in which my colleagues and I discovered that young children from underprivileged backgrounds had considerable difficulty in classifying pictures (Sigel & McBane, 1967) or in engaging in dramatic play. Classification of pictures or engagement in dramatic play require the individual to emancipate him or herself from the immediate physical characteristics of stimuli to relate to these stimuli as symbolic material (Sigel, 1970). In an earlier publication (Sigel, 1970) I addressed this problem and concluded:

> On the basis of these data one is left with the conclusion that differences between lower- and middle-class children in intellectual functioning found at later ages may well have their roots in the transitionary period, the last stage of the sensorimotor intelligence and the beginning of preoperational thought, approximately that period between 2 and 4 years. It may well be that it is during this period of life that the adult assumes a more significant psycho-social role in increasing distance between self and object and hence contributes to the development of representational competence.
>
> During this transitional period, language and extended social contacts occur. My contention is that during this period significant experiences begin to occur, experiences necessary for acquisition of representational thought. It is at this time in the life of the child that lower-class parents behave differently from middle-class parents in how they interpose in terms of time, space, and language to create distance between the child and his environment.
>
> The experiences necessary for the acquisition of representational thought are presumed to occur through the parents' provision of: (1) a relatively orderly, structured, and sequential environment; (2) a linguistic environment that contains a high frequency of words denotative of distance between reference (object) and level

of language (concrete-descriptive versus abstract-inferential); (3) models indicating the relevance and pragmatic value of distancing. (pp. 114–115)

Further research with middle-class children demonstrated that teachers' use of distancing strategies did in fact influence children's ability to deal with representational material (Sigel, 1982). In addition, findings from the educational programs demonstrated that children's cognitive competence is enhanced by an educational program where teachers employ distancing strategies to a greater extent than in the more traditional preschool program (Rosner, 1978; Sigel et al., 1973).

Although such findings are of sufficient moment to support the *distancing theory* model, the question still arises as to the impact of distancing strategies in more general terms: Are effects of distancing strategies restricted to educational settings, or are they significant in other settings? It has already been suggested that the home environment is one such setting, because it is the crucible in which significant experiences occur influencing the child's cognitive competence. After all, children come to preschool with some years of experiencing parental influence. To get closer to the ontogenetic factors contributing to children's cognitive growth, it was necessary to study family environments. Further, it was necessary to study families where *no* educational intervention had been involved. Thus, our initial family studies were with children who never went to school.

In 1978 Ann McGillicuddy-DeLisi and I undertook the first of three major research endeavors to study the relationship of parental distancing strategies to children's cognitive functioning. To study the relationship of distancing strategies in the context of the family raised a number of relevant issues such as: Should fathers and mothers be included? What about parents' justification of their particular choice of distancing behaviors? Do distancing behaviors that vary in level of cognitive demand differ in their impact as far as children's representational competence is concerned? Do parents differ in the types of distancing behaviors they use as a function of their children's language comprehension? Answers to these questions, I believed, could be found by studying how each parent interacts with his or her child, and also by learning how parents interpret the kinds of interactions they have with their children. Further, because it was assumed that parental behaviors may well be primarily reflections of their cognitions and/or constructions of children's development, the idea of focusing on beliefs of fathers and mothers, as well as their behaviors, was incorporated into the research design.

CONCEPTUALIZATION OF PARENT BELIEF SYSTEMS

The conceptualization of the belief construct that would predict to distancing behaviors evolved in the early days of our work. The problem at this initial point was how to study beliefs (McGillicuddy-DeLisi, 1982a). Early on we interviewed parents to get at their preferred ways of teaching and/or disciplining their children. Each parent was presented with a hypothetical vignette depicting typical parent–child encounters and the parent was asked what he or she would do and why. This technique allowed for maximum parent input, and consequently we were able to get a good sample of the parents' constructions. In the course of this pilot interviewing ". . . we found that parents' rationales for their behaviors with children ranged from well-articulated theoretical statements to intuitive comments regarding their ideas about children's intellectual and social development" (McGillicuddy-DeLisi, 1982a, p. 193).

Reflecting on these data it became clear that in spite of considerable variability among the parents in their stated reasons for their particular behavior, their rationales appeared to be presented as well-developed beliefs or constructions. For example, asked to respond to the question "How do children develop emotional control?," some parents would say, "They develop emotional control through experiences;" whereas other parents would say, "They develop control by parents using praise and punishment when they act out." For each parent in this example, his or her rationale was stated as a belief. Studying these pilot data, two theoretical points become clear: first, parents had a complex set of constructs about child development; second, and very important, many of the child development constructs were based on the parent's personal experiences as a child and as a parent (McGillicuddy-DeLisi & Sigel, 1982). It was this latter discovery that renewed my interest in Kelly's *Personal Construct Theory* (Kelly, 1955) and further influenced the development of our methodology, which I describe in a later section. Personal constructs are indeed products of an individual's construing of experience, but more relevant for this research effort, individuals use personal constructs as hypotheses to predict events and evaluate the accuracy of these predictions. In the normal course of experience, when one's constructs are confirmed they are likely to be maintained. When, however, they are disconfirmed the construct could change. Kelly referred to this process as *constructive alternativism.*

Parents' teaching or disciplinary behaviors operate in interactional contexts with children where their ideas can be confirmed or disconfirmed. Such a context is clearly one that is consistent with Kelly's notion of constructive alternativism. Children, however, do not necessarily conform to the parents' wishes and so the parents' particular strategy may fail, or at least yield unexpected results. It is under such circumstances that, as Kelly contends, the parents' constructs and behavior may change. The parent may elect another strategy that might work and in this way alter the underlying construct.

Kelly's notion of personal construct and my notion of belief are in some ways similar, but derived from different conceptual frameworks. Kelly's personal construct theory initially provided a point of departure for conceptualization of beliefs because it appeared to be compatible with the Piagetian orientation my colleagues and I shared. With further study of Kelly, I became aware of its incompatibility with my own neo-Piagetian perspective. Consequently, I moved away from personal construct theory as an overarching perspective and reconceptualized beliefs influenced, admittedly, by Kelly, but also Piaget (1977), Polanyi (1958), Pepper (1942/1967), and Scheibe (1970), among others. Consequently, the term *belief* is used in describing my work instead of personal construct. The reasons for such reconceptualization become clear as the narrative unfolds and culminates in a discussion of the propositions guiding my view (cf. for those readers unfamiliar with Kelly's theory and the measurement of personal constructs, I refer you to the seminal volume by Bannister and Nair, 1968).

Although beliefs held by parents are hypothesized as influencing parental behavior, it is necessary not only to define beliefs in general, but identify the content of parental beliefs. Further, to understand the role of beliefs as influences of parent distancing strategies, it is necessary to determine what factors influence belief content—factors that traditionally have been considered significant include education, sex of parent, occupation of fathers, and so on.

These were the questions about beliefs that guided our initial efforts in designing studies. Our interviews were set up to elicit the parents' beliefs, control strategies, and teaching strategy preferences and goals for their children. (In this chapter I only focus on the belief portions of the interview.)

Belief-Distancing Strategy Linkage: An Epistemological Framework

In the preceding section I described the initial conceptualization of beliefs and of distancing strategies. Further, the relationship between the two constructs was described as beliefs underlying distancing strategies. These two were not specified in greater detail a priori, because we had not initially defined categories of beliefs. Distancing strategies, as was mentioned, were defined in great detail from observation of teachers. The assumption was that parents would exhibit as full a range of distancing strategies as teachers. For that reason, the distancing categories were not expanded, but organized into levels such as those described in Table 2.1. Having a list of distancing categories in advance influenced our thinking theoretically and empirically about the relationship of distancing strategies to beliefs.

The theoretical issue refers to the nature of beliefs and their conceptualization. Because distancing strategies are behaviors that occur in a dyadic context and hence are subject to the influence of the respondent (the child), the issue became one of whether beliefs were constructed in the overall dyadic interaction or whether beliefs become fixed to specific behaviors. That is, the question is whether beliefs function as generalized schemata incorporating relevant behaviors that express the belief, or whether they are particularized and situation specific.

The methodology of choice, which is described in detail in a subsequent section, was an interview that elicited specific behaviors as well as parents' constructions regarding child behavior. The parents' responses to the probes, e.g., "How do you think a child comes to know about _____ ?" were studied and categories of beliefs were derived from them. These probes, my colleagues and I believed, got directly at the parents' beliefs or their constructions. A list of the belief-like categories was generated (see Table 2.2) categorizing parents' statements. The labels accrued were the closest that our group could come to, to reflect the meaning or the intent of the parents. The belief–behavior linkage on empirical grounds could now be established, but not with a priori hypotheses because I was not in a position to be specific about the relationships between belief constructs and distancing behaviors. In hindsight, I can discuss

TABLE 2.2
List of Parental Beliefs

Innate Factors	child's natural growth
Readiness	child's mental or physical preparedness
Empathy/Contagion/Projection	child's fusion of own inner state with that of another person
Negative feedback	unpleasant state produced in child serving to change child's behavior
Dependency	child's reliance on others for support, guidance, etc.
Rigidity	child's thinking/behavior unyielding
Impulsivity	child's tendency toward spontaneous action
Conflict	child's internal struggle between external and internal demands
Logic/Reasoning	child's ability to think logically
Structure of Environment	external influences acting upon child
Accumulation	child's growth in knowledge/behavior by passive accumulation
Creativity/Imagination	child's ability to form original ideas
Cognitive Restructuring	child's ability to reintegrate ideas, reflect, and restructure them into a logical whole
Self-Regulation	child's ability to exercise control over own actions
Absorption	child's incorporation of material/ideas without transformation
Modelling/Identification	child's tendency to incorporate traits of another person
Direct Instruction	external information presented directly to child
Proximity/Exposure	external information occurs in presence of child
Observation/Perception	child's awareness of an event and making a judgment about it
Stage	progressive step in child's life
Generalization	child's ability to apply knowledge to another situation
Infusion	injection of material from environment into child
Positive Feedback	pleasant state produced in child serving to change child's behavior
Positive Affect	child's possession of a positive internal state
Negative Affect	child's internal state marked by anxiety
Balance	child's tendency toward harmonious resolution of personal and nonpersonal material
Experimentation	child's application of a new idea/behavior to a situation, receipt of feedback, and modification of his behavior

the linkages, but these ideas would not be accurate depictions of the historical perspective I wish to maintain in this chapter.

DATA GATHERING PROCEDURES

Guided by the model presented in Fig. 2.1, three sets of instruments had to be developed: one for beliefs, one for parental distancing strategies, and one for children's cognitive functioning, as well as for the demographic variables.[2]

Procedure for Assessing Parent Beliefs.   In making a decision regarding the method to study beliefs the literature was reviewed. I was not satisfied with many of the methods reported in the literature due to their incompatibility with the constructivist conceptualization of beliefs that guided this research. It was necessary to provide a research strategy that would elicit parents' constructions rather than having parents respond to already defined constructs. The use of questionnaires was rejected because it employs items that the investigator defines and is basically a closed system. The method of choice in this research program was to use open-ended interview items in a critical-incident format. These critical incidents provided opportunities for parents to express their beliefs underlying their reported actions. The decision to proceed in this fashion was to ensure that the parents' belief responses were directy tied to the behavior addressed in the vignette given. In this way, the linkage between beliefs and reported parental distancing strategies becomes manifest. With such a strategy, beliefs and behaviors were disambiguated. Following the aforementioned rationale led to the construction of the interview I now describe.

Parent Construction Interview Schedule.   The final interview schedule consisted of 12 hypothetical situations involving preschool children. These hypothetical situations were purposely varied with respect to content (e.g., teaching physical facts and principles, social interactional and child management themes). The 12 situations were selected from an array of 20 having been judged as relevant to parental childrearing practices by a group of 28 adults enrolled in an adult education course in child development. A group of 24 pairs of parents of children enrolled in our Educational Testing Service preschool program also agreed that the situations we constructed represented typical kinds of interactions they had with their children.

The parent interview, which was audiotaped, took about 2 hours. The name of the child in the vignettes was the real name of the parent's child. This procedure

---

[2]Because the focus of this chapter is on the belief-distancing behavior connection, the results of the distancing behavior-cognitive functioning relationship is not presented. (See Sigel, 1982, for a major set of findings).

was intended to personalize the situation and presumably to give it a sense of reality. From parents' comments I believe we succeeded in accomplishing this goal.

To get at parents' beliefs underlying their reported behavior to deal with the situation represented in the vignette, a set of probes was constructed to establish the parents' views of the preschool child's developmental level or capabilities; e.g., "Does a 4-year-old understand time?" In addition, probes were aimed at eliciting the parent's views of developmental and learning processes; e.g., "How does a child come to understand the concept of time?" For every vignette the same pattern of probes was used.

Reliability and validity studies were done with the interview.[3] On the basis of these analyses we had considerable confidence in the interview as a reliable measure of parents' beliefs. The coding system also proved to be reliable. Although the system is complex and time-consuming, it provided rich material. If one were to inspect Table 2.2, it is evident that the coding of parent responses to the vignettes with the categories requires careful disembedding of the content from a complex response containing much extraneous material. These coding procedures were done from audiotapes and hence provided considerable information such as expressions of affect, structure of language, etc. The coding system, however, focused on the content of the utterance. In spite of the embedded nature of the belief constructs in the overall response, coders were able to achieve high coding reliability for each of the belief constructs identified (see McGillicuddy-DeLisi, 1982a, for details).

Observations of Parent–Child Interactions.   In the interview the parents were asked to report how they would handle a number of different situations. The question still remained—what would they actually do in a real-life situation? Of course, the only way to find out was to observe parents teaching their children. Again, a number of decisions had to be made: what kind of observations, where to observe, and what kind of interactions? These were crucial decisions because to test the distancing model it was necessary to get a good sample of parents' distancing behavior.

The decision was made to observe the parents in a laboratory setting because in so doing the conditions in which parents interacted with their children would be consistent for everyone. Once this decision was made, the next question was what should be going on in the interaction? It was believed that the interaction should be one in which a parent could teach a child a task that would be equally novel for all parents. Further, the task should be one that could vary in difficulty because we also wanted to use the same task for older children. A Japanese paper-folding-type task seemed to fit the bill in all particulars. The idea came

---

[3]The data are available from the author.

from Croft (Croft, Siegelbaum, & Goodman, 1976) who used this type of task in her studies with preschool children.

Although this task equates parents for novelty, my colleagues and I decided to add another task that in all likelihood all parents use. Asking the parent to teach the child a story would fit that requirement.

Thus, the two tasks decided on were the paper-folding task, which provided opportunities for parents to teach the child a task that was structured and had a specific definable outcome, and the story-telling task, which is relatively unstructured and does not have a definable product outcome. By using these two a broad range of distancing strategies should be elicited.

Each mother and father was videotaped teaching the child the paper-folding and the story task. Each parent–child pair received a different paper-folding item so that the child was exposed to two different paper-folding tasks and two different stories. (Details of this procedure are available from the author.)

PROGRAM POPULATION SAMPLE

The program of research that I report deals with two studies, each involving preschool children (ages $3\frac{1}{2}$ to 5)[4]. The first study involves 120 middle- and working-class families varying in family size; the second study involves 120 families, 60 with a communication-handicapped child and 60 with a non-communication-handicapped child. These two studies served two distinct purposes. The first study was directed at assessing the role of beliefs and distancing behaviors as influenced by spacing and birth order between two social class groups. The model depicted in Fig. 2.1 identifies all of the pertinent variables and the role each played in influencing other variables. The second study applied the same model and used the same variables as in Fig. 2.1 to determine whether belief structures and distancing strategies varied as a function of the child's difficulty in language expression. Because the distancing behaviors under scrutiny are essentially verbal and often require a verbal response from the child, I wondered whether families with children who were communication-handicapped would demonstrate similar or different relationships among the belief-distancing behavior and child outcome connections than families with non-communication-handicapped children. In effect, the second study represented a test of the basic model under more adverse conditions. Because the communication-handicapped children's IQ scores were within the normal range, findings should be indepen-

---

[4]Although I use the first person, it is for editorial purposes, I wish to make it clear that throughout this research program Ann McGillicuddy-DeLisi was equally involved as a codirector and many of the ideas were hers or derived jointly. In this essay, however, I am solely responsible for the interpretation. I wish to acknowledge the helpful editorial comments of the editors of this volume.

dent of the child's intellectual level. The same interview and parent–child observational procedure was used in each study.[5]

RESULTS AND DISCUSSION

Variations in Belief Constructs Among Parent Groups. The results from
both of the research projects did reveal a relationship between parental beliefs
and parental distancing strategies. However, as is shown in the following discussion, the relationships are not simple or consistent across subgroups of parents.

Analysis of parent interviews initially yielded 47 belief categories. These
were statements parents used in response to the probe questions asking how
children come to understand a particular concept or behavior, e.g., how children
come to understand time, or to control their emotions, etc. Belief frequencies
were established across the 12 vignettes in the interviews. Subsequent to a
correlational analysis, the number of belief constructs that were included in the
final list was 16. A series of analyses was performed to identify differences in
beliefs among the groups using SES, sex of parent, size of family, and handicap-
ping condition.

The data were analyzed to answer a number of interrelated questions focusing
on the relationship between parental beliefs and a number of demographic and
family status variables including parental education, sex of parent, age of child,
family configuration, and the child's communication status. Following these
analyses the relationship between parental beliefs and distancing strategies was
investigated. The results indicated that beliefs stated by the parents in the first
study were related to each of the demographic factors listed earlier, but were not
distinctive between parents of communication- and non-communication-handicapped children. Because the purpose of this chapter is to address the belief-
distancing issue, I will not present the findings relating demographic and family
status characteristics and parental belief constructs. Those details are not relevant
here. For those interested in the specific findings, see McGillicuddy-DeLisi
(1982b). Suffice to point out that parents' educational level, experience with
children, sex of parent, and sex of child are relevant variables associated with
differences in stated parental beliefs. Findings of this type do inform us that the
notion of beliefs has some validity.

The findings to be reported in the following section focus on the relationship
between parental beliefs and parental use of distancing behaviors as expressed in
the parent–child teaching interactions.

---

[5]The complete interview schedule is available from the author. Some additional interview questions were used in the research involving the communication handicapped children, but these are not
relevant in this chapter.

Relationship of Beliefs to Parental Distancing Strategies.   The general problem of predicting activity, in this case distancing behaviors, from mental state, e.g., beliefs or attitude, has plagued investigators for many years. Compelling as the argument is that behaviors are determined by exogenous and endogenous factors, the power of endogenous variables to predict behaviors has generally been limited. In spite of the general skepticism regarding the predictive power of mental states, my colleagues and I reasoned that within a relatively narrow domain of childrearing, what parents believe should be proximal to what they do.

Types of Observational Data Found.   The observation of parent–child interactions also yielded a large number of categories because the parent behavior coded included distancing strategies and non-distancing behaviors. The reason for coding both classes of actions was that distancing strategies occur in a social context. How, then, would all this observation data be used? First, a stringent definition of distancing strategies was used, applying the label only to those strategies that clearly generated mental operational demands (see Table 2.1). Other control strategies such as imperatives, structuring, and positive and negative reinforcement were considered non-distancing strategies. In this way we established two broad categories that would distinguish distancing behaviors from non-distancing, with the sum of the two categories covering the major types of parental teaching strategies.

Some Guiding Hypotheses and Outcomes.   From our constructivist perspective, my colleages and I reasoned that parental use of distancing strategies would be related to expressed beliefs about how children learn. Specifically, it was expected that parents who believed that children are self-regulating, developing organisms who acquire knowledge through experimentation would engage their children in teaching/learning tasks by using high mental operational demands and would use inquiry as a primary teaching strategy. By contrast, parents who construe children as relatively passive recipients of parental directives, and as having a knowledge base that is a product of assimilation and accommodation, would use directives as low-level distancing strategies, thereby creating few opportunities for the children to problem-solve. Essentially, the latter type of parental teaching strategy would minimize children's autonomy as problem solvers, whereas the former approach would have the opposite effect. Although the cognitive consequences for the children of these teaching strategies are not the topic of this chapter, it is important to point out that these expectations were generally born-out, particularly for the effects of low-level distancing strategies and other authoritative type control strategies (Sigel, 1982, Sigel & McGillicuddy-DeLisi, 1984).

On reflecting on the complexity of factors influencing the belief–behavior relationship, not only were demographic and family status factors relevant, but also the type of task the parent was teaching. I should mention that the tasks elicited different kinds of teaching strategies. It was expected that the teaching behaviors exhibited in the paper-folding task would be consistent with those on the story-telling task. However, striking differences occurred between the two tasks, so it seemed unwise to combine the two.

A series of zero-order correlations was performed revealing *many* mixed patterns of findings with few consistent one-to-one correspondences beween beliefs and behaviors across groups (McGillicuddy-DeLisi, 1982b). The decision in the first study was then made to relate beliefs to teaching strategies by undertaking four stepwise regression analyses. The control variables in this analysis, SES and family constellation, were first entered followed by the explanatory variables, i.e., parental belief variables. This procedure was followed for each parental teaching behavior variable in each of the two observation tasks.

What we found by using this procedure was that several beliefs, when considered together, did relate to parents' distancing strategies as revealed by the significant increments found in the regression analyses. The results are complex because they vary by task (paper-folding or story), and by sex of parent. The results, however, can be summarized from McGillicuddy-DeLisi (1982b) as follows:

1. Mothers' beliefs about how children develop cognitively did predict to their teaching behaviors with the story and paper-folding tasks. For example, mothers' belief that that children develop cognitively through the children's own accumulation of knowledge was related positively to the mothers' use of high-level distancing strategies and related negatively to the use of low-level distancing strategies. This is consistent with distancing theory, which holds that children construct their own reality through interaction with other people. High-level cognitive demands then should emanate from an environment replete with such people.

2. Fathers' belief scores also produced significant increments in multiple regression coefficients after SES and family constellation were stepped into the regression analysis. As with the mothers, fathers' beliefs did predict to their distancing strategies, but differently from mothers, especially as a function of task. Where mothers' belief–behavior relationship was more frequent on the story task, for the fathers the predominant relationship occurred on the paper-folding task. For example, mothers' beliefs in modelling and empathy were related to their distancing behaviors on the paper-folding task; for fathers on this same task, beliefs in the child as an active processor were related to high-level distancing. In general, fathers who believed children develop through exploration, experimentation and active learning tended to use high-level distancing strategies. The converse also held. Fathers who viewed the child as passive and as a recipient of knowledge tended to use low-level distancing and structuring. (pp. 294–296)

In sum, the results indicate that parents' beliefs, when viewed as a *pattern*, do predict to parents' distancing strategies.

For example, mothers' beliefs in processes of experimentation and self-regulation were negatively related to mothers' scores for not placing mental operational demands on the child during the story task. If mothers do not think that children develop through self-regulatory processes and their own experimentations, an assumption within distancing theory, it would be inconsistent to place demands on their own child to perform mental transfomations. Fathers' use of high-level mental operational demands on the paper-folding task were positively related to belief in stages of development and the process of experimentation and negatively related to belief in absorption. Their pattern is also consistent with distancing theory, which posits that children construct knowledge in a stage-like sequence based on their own internal action and do not simply absorb knowledge presented to them in a directive fashion.

On the basis of this study, it seems clear that in broad outlines parents' beliefs concerning child development states and processes are related to parents' distancing behaviors in association with family constellation and SES. Further, these results indicate that there are mediating factors internal to the parent from which parental childrearing styles emerge, and which may help to account for variation in parental distancing strategies.

Because the study focused on the family unit, and because the child is obviously subject to the behaviors of both parents, the next step in our analysis was to undertake a series of multiple regressions involving both parents' beliefs as predictors to each other's behavior. Results indicated that one parent's beliefs may be related to the other parent's behaviors. The findings revealed that indeed fathers' scores on beliefs about development produced significant multiple correlations with mothers' behaviors on each of the two tasks, and mothers' beliefs were related to fathers' behaviors. Such relationships are best exemplified by the path analysis described below.

A path analysis was undertaken that included all of the major variables described in Fig. 2.1. For the purposes of the topic under discussion here (i.e., the belief–behavior connection), it should be noted that the beliefs of mothers and fathers were related to each other ($r = .43 < .05$) and mothers' beliefs had a slight impact on fathers' behavior (path coefficient .11, not significant). Of considerable interest, however, was the fact that fathers' and mothers' *behaviors* were not significantly correlated ($r = .03$). This suggests that parents may construct their own beliefs together, but behavior may be either complementary or differentiated rather than consistent across pairs of parents. Mothers' and fathers' behaviors both influenced the child's cognitive development in spite of the fact that their beliefs do not mutually impact their behavior (Sigel et al., 1980).

Turning now to the results from the study with communication-handicapped children, it should be kept in mind that two groups of families were involved:

those with children without a communication handicap and those with communication-handicapped preschool children between the ages of $3\frac{1}{2}$ and $5\frac{1}{2}$ years of age. The design of this study was similar to the previous one, with the exception that questions dealing with parents' responses to handicaps were included (see Sigel et al., 1983 for details).

Procedures for analyzing these interviews were similar to the previous study. For each of the subsamples of parents, correlational analyses between beliefs and distancing strategies in each of the two tasks were computed.

One of the most striking findings was that with two exceptions, no significant differences were found between parents of communication-handicapped and non-communication-handicapped children. More parents of communication-handicapped children stated that negative feedback, i.e., unpleasant consequences, is a relevant basis for cognitive development, and second, these same parents believed that children were passive recipients of knowledge.

In view of the aforementioned findings, it might be expected that the relationship between beliefs and behaviors would be similar for these groups of parents. This was not consistently the case. Results of our analyses revealed relationships between parent beliefs and distancing strategies that again varied as a function of the sex of parent, and task, and additionally as a function of the handicapped status of the child. Thus my conclusions are general and do not apply equally and completely to each subsample. (See Sigel et al., 1983 for all details.) Evidence was found that high-level distancing strategies tend to relate to parents' belief in the self-regulating nature of the child. Findings of this type are consistent with distancing theory and with the previous study. In general, the results show that the types of distancing behaviors parents use are associated with their expressed beliefs, particularly those that focus on the nature of the child as a learner; high-level distancing strategies are linked to a view of the child as an active learner, low-level distancing strategies seem to express parents' view of the child as a passive learner. Furthermore, it is of interest that strategies like structuring and imperatives, i.e., those that are highly didactic, relate to parents' views that the child is a passive recipient of knowledge.

I have provided an array of findings from two studies that in sum allow for some meaningful generalization. There is sufficient evidence to support the basic proposition that parents' beliefs about child development processes do influence the level of distancing behaviors they use. For those who hold that children's intellectual development is, in part, a function of such endogenous factors as self-regulation and efforts at exploration and experimentation, distancing strategies that respect the child's active efforts at coming to know his or her world are used. In effect, the parents make high-level cognitive demands on the child. Conversely, parents who view the child as the passive recipient of parental direction use low-level strategies or directives, i.e., make minimal cognitive demands. This latter view can be referred to as the exogenous perspective of child development.

These generalizations, however, need to be qualified because of the constraints of demographic, contextual, and personal variables (see Fig. 2.1). In spite of the qualifications, I am of the mind that the belief construct is of sufficient import to warrant further intensive study. In the context of the studies reported here, the justification for more conceptual and methodological work becomes readily apparent when considered in terms of the significant effects the distancing strategies had for children's cognitive functioning (Sigel & McGillicuddy-DeLisi, 1984). In other words, the linkages between parental behaviors and child outcomes are sufficiently strong to warrant study of their antecedents, thereby providing some explanation for the types of distancing strategies parents use.

Lest it be thought that my colleagues and I believed linkages in the long term are unidirectional, let me correct that impression by presenting a set of results from the study with communication-handicapped children. The findings from this study reveal a reciprocal relationship between parent and child characteristics, where the less intellectually able the child the more likely the parent would use low-level distancing strategies, and where the child was intellectually able, the parent would more likely use high-level distancing strategies (Sigel et al., 1983). In other words, the intellectual level of the child influenced the parents' distancing strategies. Whether this relationship would affect parents' beliefs, I do not know. I would venture an educated guess that the reciprocal relationship between the intellectual level of the child and parental use of distancing strategies probably illustrates the idea of child characteristics influencing the parent's beliefs and behaviors. This is another example of mutual influence of parents and children.

REFLECTIONS

As I look back on this program of research I ask myself the question: If I were to do these studies again on the basis of what I now know, what would be different? Two answers to this question seem appropriate: (a) I would reconceptualize the belief construct; and (b) I would not have changed our basic method, but would have sought ways to make it more efficient, yet more complex.

Beliefs Reconceptualized.   As I reflected about the research while working on this chapter, I began to realize how simplistic my original thinking was. I became increasingly aware and sensitive to the idea that the study of beliefs was more complex, because of the way they appeared to function in the context of other beliefs and in the interview.

In preparation for the path analyses discussed earlier, the number of independent beliefs had to be reduced. This was done by employing a principal component analysis. These results revealed a cluster of beliefs that represented mothers' beliefs that children's knowledge develops through abstraction from experience. A similar analysis for fathers resulted in an identifiable component reflecting the belief that children's knowledge develops as a function of interactions between internal processes and feedback from the environment.

Such a componential analysis informs us that organization of beliefs varies for mothers and for fathers. On rethinking why mothers and fathers produced different clusters, I ask, could it be due to our definition of beliefs? The definitions that were developed were inductive, and perhaps the context in which the parents stated them was not taken into account in developing the codes. Because this may well be the case, it becomes necessary to rethink how to generate data on beliefs. For example, if an interview is used, how to structure it, or perhaps ask if an interview should be the method of choice.

Because parents produced belief statements in response to a probe in the interview, it is reasonable to assume that for the most part they were conscious of and deliberate in their statements. Accepting this assumption leads me to view beliefs as cognitions, rather than as personal constructs as described earlier, because cognitions refer to a knowing, thinking function, the transformation of experience. As Neisser (1967) writes, "Cognitions refer to all processes by which sensory input (my concept of experience) is transformed, reduced, elaborated, stored, recovered and used" (p. 4). Cognitions are organized into schemas, and I propose that the schema contains a number of connected cognitions. The distinction between a cognition in general and a belief is that the belief is a cognition that is based on knowledge and is *accepted as truth*. I have defined beliefs elsewhere (Sigel, 1985) as "knowledge in the sense that the individual knows that what he (or she) espouses is true or probably true, and evidence may or may not be deemed necessary; or if evidence is used, it forms a basis for the belief but is not the belief itself" (p. 348). Using this definition of belief, in conjunction with the concepts and findings in this study, as well as my reading during the course of writing this chapter, I came up with seven propositions and integrated my ideas as the basis of a conceptual framework for organizing further study about beliefs.

1. Beliefs arise from an array of social experiences and come to define an individual's psychological reality. Because knowledge is a social construction, and is integral to beliefs, the assertion here may appear self-evident. However obvious it appears, it still leaves open the question of how and under what conditions particular knowledge is acquired. This leads to my second assumption.

2. Beliefs may be organized in domains, e.g., political, social, religious. Relationships among domains may vary; for some they can be interrelated, whereas for others they may be fractionated. Beliefs in these areas have been studied by other behavioral and social scientists who fractionated beliefs in terms of particular domains of knowledge (Rokeach, 1980).

3. Belief domains as organized schemata are held to have boundaries varying in permeability. The degree of permeability will be related to the probability that new information can be assimilated producing reorganization of existing knowledge and beliefs. The readiness to assimilate new information and to change one's beliefs depends on the basis by which beliefs are organized and bonded.

4. Belief structures are not only organized on rational bases, but are also bonded by affect. Knowledge acquired in a social context is inexorably linked to affect; i.e., cognition and affect are indissociably linked. It is the affect bonding that contributes to the maintenance of the schema. Affect and knowledge are interdependent. The intensity of affect bound to knowledge probably influences the readiness of beliefs to change (Sigel, 1985).

5. Beliefs can vary in type, "existential and relational, abstract and concrete, expectational and historical, self-oriented, and other oriented" (Scheibe, 1970, p. 34). The beliefs parents reported might have been categorized in this fashion, because in hindsight it is clear that some beliefs are concrete; e.g., "children learn through direct instruction." This example incorporates *action* and belief; the belief that "children learn through self-regulation" is more abstract and does not have an explicit action component. Using such schemes to create hierarchical levels of beliefs may well help solve some of the problems of prediction, because direct linkages can be drawn between some beliefs and actions more than others, as in the concrete example above. For the abstract belief statements additional probes will be needed to get at the action implications.

6. Beliefs are guides to action. Actions can be initiated or reactive to particular classes of events. Beliefs guide not only the action, but also the "choice" of events to which to react. Beliefs "appear in the context of behavior" (Scheibe, 1970, p. 35). However, the range of action is limited because actions are "never free of situational constraints" (Scheibe, 1970, p. 35). Thus, observations of actions may provide but a limited understanding of an individual's belief.

7. "Apparent inconsistencies in manifestations of belief are reconciled when we acknowledge the extent to which situation and belief are tied to each other" (Scheibe, 1970, p. 35). This proposition is consistent with the idea that beliefs are expressed in action in contexts. To predict to the situation, it is necessary to know the individual's beliefs in conjunction with contextual factors.

These seven propositions represent my thinking as of now. As with so many issues in psychology, the more one reflects on one's own sources of knowledge and questions, the more one comes to recognize how complex psychological phenomena are and how linked they are to other concepts. The glaring awareness I discovered is that one of the limitations in our research was that as a developmental psychologist I was relatively naive regarding the relevant social psychological literature on beliefs. In addition, I realized that distancing strategies are verbal communications. So, I ask: What does psycholinguists' discourse analysis have to tell me about the *how* and the *what* of the significance of distancing strategies? I can continue this type of referencing to other fields. The question is: How far does one go? The over-specialization in our field does have its negative aspects. How much better our research might have been had we become more intimately acquainted with the other relevant literatures (Sigel, 1979)? Of course, in hindsight, we are all wise.

Some Methodological Issues.   What factors might account for the limited number of relationships found between beliefs and behaviors? Having come up with the foregoing propositions and their implications for theory and inter-disciplinary connectedness, I began to think about the limited results a second time. I came up with three methodological reasons that might help to account for the relatively few belief-to-behavior predictions.

First, the belief constructs were based on a limited number of situations that were tested with criterion teaching situations. It could be argued that if the reason for limited predictor power is due to the distal relationships between the inter-view and the observation, then beliefs are situation specific. If that were the case, then the approach taken in these studies may be of little value in studying beliefs, because few generalizations will emerge unless it can be shown that the sample of interview situations does represent the universe of situations parents and children engage in.

A second issue has to do with the measurement of beliefs. Is the interview method as conceived here the most effective? Listening to the audio recordings of parents' presentations of their constructions of their children's development reveals that beliefs are embedded in a rich fabric of parent cognitions and feelings, the richness of which may get lost as the specifics are decontextualized from the whole in the process of coding responses. It is possible that more global categories may yield more powerful relationships.

The omission of consistent behavioral information concomitant with belief statements may be another source of difficulty. The parents were not asked how they would express a particular belief in action. It may well be that asking parents what actions they would use to reflect their beliefs may have given us greater predictive power.

The final methodological issue deals with the behaviors that were targeted for study. In this research the behaviors being studied were distancing strategies, which are a limited class of parental actions. Could it be that the distancing strategies were too specific? It may be inherently difficult to predict to a single act without taking the context into account. For example, what beliefs might guide the parents' use of questions as teaching strategies? It may be that the decision is a function of parental beliefs, not only in terms of particular teaching strategies, but also how the parent construes the total context. The parent may eschew a direct strategy on the belief that children have something worth saying. In our paper-folding task, the parent's behavior may have been a function of beliefs about achievement, about cooperative efforts, or about experimental procedures. Each or all of such factors may play a role in guiding the parent's actions. In effect, the choice of a single teaching strategy may have multiple beliefs as guides not merely pertaining to the child's developmental status. Another example: The parent believes that children learn through exploration and experimentation, and thereby accumulate knowledge as they are ready by virtue of their developmental stage. This belief cluster may predict to the parent's single act of structuring the environment with appropriately arranged materials and telling the child, "You are free to do as you wish with these things." At the same time, the parent may believe that children should be free to explore in their own way. These latter beliefs may stem from the parent's political or social views in general.

My general point here is a continuation of the argument that there is not a necessary one-to-one correspondence between a belief and a behavior, but it may be the case that a number of beliefs coalesce to determine how the parent will act. The metaphor of a funnel may express what I have in mind. A number of beliefs are poured into the funnel and the outcome is a narrow range of actions. A particular behavior may in effect have multiple determinants, beliefs being but one. What may be necessary is the conceptualizing of the various possible determinants of a single act. For example, the parent's choice of a high-level distancing strategy may be due not only to a particular construction of the way children learn, but also the child's level of development, experience, and interest in the task.

Some Suggestions for Methods in Studying Beliefs. There are a limited number of approaches that can be used to study beliefs. Various types of questionnaires, observations and interviews have been used, and each of these has its particular virtues and defects (Fishbein, 1980; Rokeach, 1980). Common to interviews and questionnaires is their reliance on verbal reports.

The perennial question regarding these approaches is the validity of the data. Do people say what they really mean, or are the responses reflections of such factors as social desirability, resistence, lack of understanding of the item or lack of information? (Nisbett & Wilson, 1977). In the interview used in our studies, we nitially administered, in addition to the interview, the Parent Research Instrument (PARI) and the Edwards Social Desirability Scale. A factor analysis was performed with these three instruments and it was found that the PARI and the Social Desirability Scale loaded on a common factor interpreted as social desirability and our construction interview was orthogonal. Such a finding buoyed our confidence that the interview would yield information that would not be confounded by the *social desirability factor.* Although the parents' responses may not have been influenced by social desirability responding, another confound arose; namely, many of the situations that we presented to parents were new to them, situations that they claimed they never thought about before the interview. For example, many parents said they never gave a moment's thought to how children learn about *time*. In view of such reports, it is clear that the interview was getting at parent's *newly constructed* beliefs about how children learn about time, rather than already formed beliefs. These new constructions were in effect adaptations to a new problem. Thus, what is learned is that the parents can generate reasonable constructions in the here and now. These views, however, could not have been conscious guides to distancing behavior. Further, we never challenged parents to report sources of knowledge about specific events or challenged the veridicality of their knowledge.

The problems inherent in interviews are also present in questionnaires. In addition, however, questionnaires generally tend to restrict the amount and the kind of information produced. Enough has been written about problems with questionnaires, so I do not have to go into the technical details. For our purposes, the limits of questionnaires, as with interviews, are that such verbal reports about beliefs tend to be decontextualized. Even with the critical incident-type approach that we use, the respondent fills in the gaps, which of course precludes a common situation for all respondents. If a complete verbal picture is drawn, including relevant historical information, and if it were possible, would that solve the problem? I doubt it. Is it possible to create a social scene that would be *standard*, as a math problem is on a test? I doubt that also because irrespective of the number of details, respondents will still have room for constructing their own meaning. Word pictures may reduce ambiguity, but once again I doubt if they could eliminate it. Essentially, there is no historical *context* for the particular actions depicted in any vignette, i.e., it is not clear what the parent construes about the situation. In a sense, virtually every procedure has some ambiguity, irrespective of the amount of detail presented, because each respondent will generate his or her own interpretations.

Finally, interviews and questionnaires are verbal reports of states and perhaps intentions for action. However, it is well known that there is a possible gap between what one says and what one does. I believe this discrepancy, when it appears, may well be a function of the ingredients in the real situation, not because of resistance or withholding information.

If all this is the case, is there any way to get at parents' beliefs? I have discussed limitations of interviews and questionnaires—what about observations? Observations demand the most inference from behavior. If observations include discourse material as well as actions, they may be providing evidential bases for making reliable and valid inferences regarding beliefs. Nevertheless, observation procedures are fraught with their own unique problems of reliability, validity, contextual factors, and of course, the observer's interpretation of the causes of the behavior.

I have briefly described each method, acknowledging that each method provides some valuable information. Can these methods be melded in such a way as to pool each of their contributions, thereby enhancing the identification, understanding and predictive power of beliefs?

If it is acknowledged that beliefs refer to evidential knowledge about events, people, and objects, and further, the belief is held to be true, then there is need to corroborate these assertions. The question is how to do it. The final section will propose a conceptualization and a research strategy to enhance our understanding of parents' beliefs as predictions to practice. What I propose may appear at first blush to be inefficient and cumbersome. However, I am convinced that at this point in time this may be a necessary and perhaps a sufficient strategy that incorporates many of the comments presented above.

A Specific Methodological Suggestion.   The approach I propose will be referred to as a *multi-site* methodology. This strategy is based on some of the propositions I listed earlier:

1. Beliefs, irrespective of level, are guides for action.
2. Beliefs are expressed at an abstract and a concrete level.
3. Beliefs are expressed contingent on context.
4. Beliefs vary in intensity of commitment.
5. Beliefs are not necessarily consistent across domains.

Three methods are proposed: an interview using a predefined set of vignettes to get at parents' predictions of their own actions as well as parental constructions underlying these actions. *However,* whenever the *constructions* are abstract, the parent *must* be asked to state what parental *action* will best express those *beliefs.* If, for example, a parent states that, "Children develop cognitively through exploration," then the parent *must* be asked what types of parental actions would follow from such a belief. If on the other hand the parent reports concrete beliefs, such as a child learns through direct instruction, then the underlying abstract beliefs should be probed. Such a strategy yields two levels of beliefs—abstract and concrete (action). These procedures are based on points one and two above.

The interview should also contain items that get at the source of parents' beliefs and some idea of the conviction with which beliefs are held. Such data would provide a socio-historical context in which beliefs are embedded and possibly guide current contextual actions. In other words, the interview might be the place to get parents to describe the meaning a particular context has for them. This would allow for identifying contextual factors that constrain actions.

The interview can in part be validated by observation if the observation is structured to provide opportunities for parents to perform actions similar to those involved in the interview. For example, if it is of interest to get at parents' beliefs and consequent actions involving children's learning, then a learning task is an appropriate one to observe. The choice of task should be guided by the belief domain(s) under study. Because action expressed in a social context is in part influenced by the context, more than one context is needed. When studying the role of the family, the family should become the unit for an observational study and decisions will have to be made regarding which family members to include.

To minimize making inferences about what are the bases for the observed behavior, I suggest that dyadic and family interactions be videotaped to provide *frozen samples* of interactions; these can be used as the basis for an interview in which parents and the investigator would review the tapes together and the parent would be asked to explain the basis for his or her actions. In this way a second set of beliefs can be identified in the context of action.

A final set of observations should be done in the home, thereby yielding a second observational context. Under these conditions additional contextual factors come into play, such as presence of other family members, routines of the family, etc., which will provide still another sample of familial interactions, such as interactions with siblings.

The above schematic discussion is an example of a multi-site strategy that provides opportunities to obtain a range of behaviors and their underlying beliefs.

The system by which beliefs or behaviors can be categorized will have to be two-fold—hierarchical in nature and tied to social context. From the perspective of this chapter, the interviews and observations would be coded and subsequently quantified within the beliefs framework in Proposition No. 5 described earlier, and the behaviors could be coded within the distancing behaviors framework (see Table 2.1).

The methodology proposed here is by necessity schematic. To be taken seriously and tied closely to the propositions described earlier requires a different and more elaborate model than represented in Fig. 2.1. The more I thought about our findings and the relationships among the variables in the context of the family, the more convinced I became that the model depicted in Fig. 2.1 was too simplistic. Parents' beliefs and consequent behaviors are embedded in at least two types of social contexts—both the particular social context in which parents and children find themselves, e.g., a teaching situation in the laboratory or in the home, as well as in the broader socio-historical context. Even within these environments demographic and extra-familial factors impact what core beliefs parents have and what they believe are the appropriate ways to express their beliefs. Consequently, beliefs must be examined at two levels—core beliefs and beliefs regarding activity. Once I began to think in such socially relevant and interactional terms, I developed the model depicted in Fig. 2.2.

Inspection of Fig. 2.2 will reveal that the Fig. 2.1 model is elaborated on and embedded in Fig. 2.2, with the latter figure depicting detailed interactions among the identified variables. For example, note that the parental beliefs regarding the child are conceptualized as influencing beliefs about actions. These beliefs in turn influence the core beliefs parents hold regarding the developing child.

Figure 2.2, I contend, articulates a schematic that identifies a set of reciprocal factors whose relationship must be conceptualized if we are to obtain an in-depth

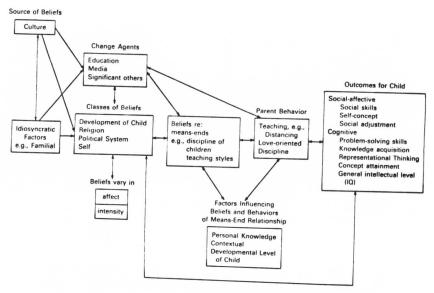

FIG. 2.2.   Schematic of revised model of belief-behavior paradigm regarding parent–child relationships. (Siegel, 1985).

understanding of parents' beliefs in the context of family interaction. Essentially, I am opting for a contextual interactional analysis of parental beliefs by embedding our initial model in the more elaborate one.

The reader may ask whether I argue that this grand scheme is a way to proceed in our research on the family. Ideally, I would say yes. However, the feasibility of employing such an extensive model is moot. One may ask, if it is not feasible, why worry about it? My argument is that rational compromises are possible as the reality demands e.g., as financial resources dictate.

Extracting components from the model and generating studies accordingly may still provide useful and important data enhancing our understanding of the origins or impact of beliefs. The studies reported in this chapter are but one example of such a compromise. Another example is setting up studies to examine the organization of classes of beliefs to determine the relationship between the beliefs regarding children's cognitive development and one's religious orientation. Other components can be selected for study to clarify relationships among variables depending on the interest of the investigators. Nevertheless, I argue that the entire model should be kept in mind as the superordinate organizing scheme. In this way not only can relevant variables be identified, but elaboration for empirical studies can be entertained.

In sum, my point is merely to argue for a multi-site strategy using the model described in Fig. 2.2, because beliefs are expressed behaviorally in a context (see

Proposition No. 6). This methodology suggests how each of the propositions can be articulated in a research design. Time will tell whether suggestions of this type will enhance our understanding of beliefs as guides to action.

FINAL WORD

The results of our research described in this chapter provide some support for the bidirectional model of reciprocal family interactons depicted in Fig. 2.1. What was also found was that although parental beliefs do serve as a guide to distancing behaviors in general, there are a number of qualifications that must be kept in mind. Specifically, beliefs of fathers and mothers differ and relate to different types of distancing strategies. However, parents' beliefs do not reveal a necessary one-to-one correspondence to their distancing behaviors; rather, *patterns* of beliefs relate to their teaching styles. Factor analysis of parental beliefs shows that identifiable clusters exist that differ between mothers and fathers. In addition to gender differences affecting belief clusters, such demographic variables as SES and age of the parents and of the children are also important.

Although our results tended to be positive and in the anticipated directions, I felt that our conceptualization constrained the predictive power of the belief construct itself, and thereby limited our findings of the role beliefs play in the family context. On reflecting on the limitations, I realized that the concept of beliefs itself should be reconceptualized, in cognitive terms, while accentuating the contextual factors that influence the way beliefs are held and expressed. The result of such thinking led to the development of a complex model that takes into account an array of conceptually linked variables.

These studies, I believe, provide a launchpad for continued investigation into the critical field of parents' thinking as they fulfill their historical role of childrearing.

Important as theoretical research is for enhancing our understanding of the human condition, its ultimate value resides in its service to the general public. The type of research reported in this chapter makes such a contribution. What has been shown is that parental behaviors have a cognitive base, i.e., beliefs.

For those clinicians and educators working with parents, my work demonstrates that the targets for diagnostic and intervention efforts should not be just what the parents do, or what the parents feel, but also what the parents *think*. The parent's belief system guides his or her practice. Targeting beliefs, for example, in an intervention program, may well lead to behavioral changes as targeting behaviors may influence beliefs. In effect, the results of these studies speak to an interactionist or bidirectional perspective that provides practitioners with a research–based model they can adopt. Admittedly, this recommendation needs to be field tested, since there are no data suggesting which point of entry in the intervention effort—targeting parents' beliefs or behaviors—will be the most effective. Until such studies are carried out, the data reported here can serve to sensitize the practitioners to the significance of parents' cognitions in the childrearing effort. By transforming the initial model of the research (Fig. 2.1) to the complex, yet comprehensive, perspective (Fig. 2.2), I believe we expand our horizons to effect more productive research and practice.

ACKNOWLEDGMENTS

Part of the research reported in this chapter was supported by the National Institute of Child Health and Human Development Grant No. R01-HD10686 to Educational Testing Service, National Institute of Mental Health Grant No. R01-MH32301 to Educational Testing Service, and Bureau of Education of the Handicapped Grant No. G007902000 to Educational Testing Service. These grants were awarded to Irving Sigel and Ann McGillicuddy-DeLisi. Significant contributions to this research program were made by J. E. Johnson, J. Flaugher, and D. Rock. We would like to thank Linda Kozelski for her help in preparing this chapter.

REFERENCES

Bannister, D., & Nair, J. M. M. (1968). *The evaluation of personal constructs.* New York: Academic Press.

Baumrind, D. (1971). Current patterns of parental authority. *Developmental Psychology Monographs, 4*(1, Part 2).

Copple, C., Sigel, I. E., & Saunders, R. (1979/1984). *Educating the young thinker: Classroom strategies for cognitive growth.* Hillsdale, NJ: Lawrence Erlbaum Associates.

Croft, R., Siegelbaum, H., & Goodman, D. (1976). *Manual for description and functional analysis of continuous didactic interactions.* Rochester, NY: University of Rochester.

Fishbein, M. (1980). A theory of reasoned action: Some applications and implications. In H. E. Howe, Jr. & M. M. Page (Eds.), *Nebraska Symposium on Motivation, 1979* (pp. 65–116). Lincoln: University of Nebraska Press.

Hess, R. D., & Shipman, V. C. (1965). Early experience and the socialization of cognitive modes in children. *Child Development, 36,* 869–886.

Kelly, G. A. (1955). *The psychology of personal constructs* (Vols. 1 & 2). New York: Norton.

Laosa, L. M. (1982). Families as facilitators of children's intellectual development at 3 years of age: A causal analysis. In L. M. Laosa & I. E. Sigel (Eds.), *Families as learning environments for children* (pp. 1–45). New York: Plenum.

Laosa, L. M. (1983). School, occupation, culture, and family: The impact of parental schooling on the parent-child relationship. In I. E. Sigel & L. M. Laosa (Eds.), *Changing families* (pp. 79–135). New York: Plenum.

Martin, B. (1975). Parent-child relations. In F. D. Horowitz (Ed.), *Review of child development research* (Vol. 4, pp. 463–540). Chicago: The University of Chicago Press.

McGillicuddy-DeLisi, A. V. (1982a). Parental beliefs about developmental processes. *Human Development, 25,* 192–200.

McGillicuddy-DeLisi, A. V. (1982b). The relationship between parents' beliefs about development and family constellation, socioeconomic status, and parents' teaching strategies. In L. M. Laosa

& I. E. Sigel (Eds.), *Families as learning environments for children* (pp. 261–299). New York: Plenum, 1982.

McGillicuddy-DeLisi, A. V. (1985). The relationship between parental beliefs and children's cognitive level. In I. E. Sigel (Ed.), *Parental belief systems: The psychological consequences for children* (pp. 7–24). Hillsdale, NJ: Lawrence Erlbaum Associates.

McGillicuddy-DeLisi, A. V., & Sigel, I. E. (1982). Family constellation and parental beliefs. In G. L. Fox (Ed.), *The childbearing decision: Fertility attitudes and behavior* (pp. 161–177). Beverly Hills, CA: Sage Publications.

Neisser, U. (1967). *Cognitive psychology.* New York: Appleton-Century-Crofts.

Nisbett, R. E., & Wilson, T. D. (1977). Telling more than we can know: Verbal resports on mental processes. *Psychological Review, 84,* 231–259

Pepper, S. C. (1967). *World hypotheses: A study in evidence.* Berkeley, CA: University of California Press. (Originally published 1942)

Piaget, J. (1977). *The development of thought: Equilibration of cognitive structures.* New York: Viking Press.

Polanyi, M. (1958). *Personal knowledge.* Chicago: University of Chicago Press.

Rokeach, M. (1980). Some unresolved issues in theories of beliefs, attitudes, and values. In H. E. Howe, Jr. & M. M. Page (Eds.), *Nebraska Symposium on Motivation, 1979* (pp. 261–304). Lincoln: University of Nebraska Press.

Rosner, F. C. (1978). An ecological study of teacher distancing behaviors as a function of program, context and time (Doctoral dissertation, Temple University, 1978). *Dissertation Abstracts International, 39,* 760A.

Scheibe, K. E. (1970). *Beliefs and values.* New York: Holt, Rinehart & Winston.

Sigel, I. E. (1970). The distancing hypothesis: A causal hypothesis for the acquisition of representational thought. In M. R. Jones (Ed.), *Miami Symposium on the Prediction of Behavior, 1968: Effect of early experiences* (pp. 99–118). Coral Gables, FL: University of Miami Press.

Sigel, I. E. (1979). On becoming a thinker: A psychoeducational model. *Educational Psychologist, 14,* 70–78.

Sigel, I. E. (1982). The relationship between parents' distancing strategies and the child's cognitive behavior. In L. M. Laoca & I. E. Sigel (Eds.), *Families as learning environments for children* (pp. 47–86). New York: Plenum.

Sigel, I. E. (1985). A conceptual analysis of beliefs. In I. E. Sigel (Ed.), *Parental belief systems: The psychological consequences for children* (pp. 347–371). Hillsdale, NJ: Lawrence Erlbaum Associates.

Sigel, I. E., & Cocking, R. R. (1977). Cognition and communication: A dialectic paradigm for development. In M. Lewis & L. A. Rosenblum (Eds.), *Interaction, conversation and the development of language* (pp. 207–226). New York: Wiley.

Sigel, I. E., Dreyer, A., & McGillicuddy-DeLisi, A. V. (1984). Psychological perspectives of the family. In R. D. Parke (Ed.), *Review of child development research* (Vol. 7, pp. 42–79). Chicago: University of Chicago Press.

Sigel, I. E., & McBane, B. (1967). Cognitive competence and level of symbolization among five-year-old children. In J. Hellmuth (Ed.), *The disadvantaged child* (Vol. 1, pp. 433–453). Seattle, WA: Special Child Publications of the Seattle Sequin School, Inc..

Sigel, I. E., & McGillicuddy-DeLisi, A. V. (1984). Parents as teachers of their children: A distancing behavior model. In A. D. Pellegrini & T. D. Yawkey (Eds.), *The development of oral and written language in social contexts* (pp. 71–92). Norwood, NJ: ABLEX.

Sigel, I. E., McGillicuddy-DeLisi, A. V., Flaugher, J., & Rock, D. A. (1983). *Parents as teachers of their own learning disabled children* (ETS RR 83-21). Princeton, NJ: Education Testing Service.

Sigel, I. E., McGillicuddy-DeLisi, A. V., & Johnson, J. E. (1980). *Parental distancing, beliefs and children's representational competence within the family context* (ETS RR 80-21). Princeton, NJ: Educational Testing Service.

Sigel, I. E., Secrist, A., & Forman, G. (1973). Psychoeducational intervention beginning at age two: Reflections and outcomes. In J. C. Stanley (Ed.), *Compensatory education for children, ages two to eight: Recent studies of educational intervention* (pp. 25–62). Baltimore, MD: Johns Hopkins University Press.

3 Cognitive Processes During Reactions To Rule Violation

James C. Mancuso
State University of New York at Albany

Richard Lehrer
University of Wisconsin

INTRODUCTION

Prologue

The following discourse attempts to frame parent–child reprimand interactions within the metaphors of modern psychological studies that emphasize *cognitive processes*. The discussion rests on a general contextualist–constructivist epistemological base (Pepper, 1942; Sarbin, 1977), which, we believe, provides the most appropriate foundation for a bridge between social processes and an individual psychology.

From our perspective, each reprimand interaction involves schematization processes—efforts after meaning. Thus, to proceed adequately we present five propositions, developed around the concept of *schema* or *construction,* which form the foundation of our analysis of reprimand. Additionally, we consider the ways in which a theory of personal constructs (Kelly, 1955) in conjunction with current explications of *cognitive control* theory can integrate our thinking about reprimand. As we proceed, we indicate the ways in which useful studies of reprimand would trace out, among other things, the strands that represent the cognitive constructions that the participants have placed on the event (Kohlberg, 1969; Newberger, 1980), the implicit behavior–change theories of the reprimander (see Applegate, 1983; Mancuso, 1979; Mancuso & Handin, 1984), and the participants' constructions or schematizations of the social roles available to them in the situation (Mancuso, Heerdt, & Hamill, 1984).

Definition of Reprimand

By use of the term *reprimand* we risk the possibility of readers carrying unwanted, ancillary meanings into this discussion. Commentators have used terms such as *socialization, discipline, induction of rule following, reprimand processes,* or *moral training* to label the kinds of parent–child interactions discussed in this chapter. At this beginning point, we hope that the term *reprimanding* refers to nothing more than that social process in which an actor intends to eliminate or reduce the unwanted behavior that has been enacted by a transgressor.

Beyond specifying this beginning caution, we must preview our basic assumption that the target of the reprimand has enacted a behavior that has invalidated the potential reprimander's construction of the context in which that behavior has occurred. In many instances a parenting person observes his or her charge enacting behaviors that reflect the child's use of constructions that the parent would not use. Every one of these instances would *not* necessarily lead to reprimand, because they are not invalidations of the parenting person's constructions in that context. In some instances, for example, the parent's construction would not be invalidated because he or she construes the child as being *incapable* of developing the agreed-on construction. The necessity of this distinction becomes clearer as we spell out our conception of the *reprimand process.*

A COGNITIVE–CONTROL THEORY OF REPRIMAND

Schemata and Reprimand: Five Basic Propositions

Five basic propositions, developed around the concept of *schema,* or *construction,* form the foundation of our analysis of reprimand. These assumptions are summarized as follows:

1. Schemata are the basic units of psychological description. " 'Schema' refers to an active organization of past reactions, or of past experiences, which must always be supposed to be operating in any well-adapted organic response" (Bartlett, 1932, p. 20). The quality and finite quantity of schemata, or *constructs,* available in a person's system establishes the ways in which a person can understand input-related events.

2. Anticipatory schematizations guide the direction of psychological processes. Schematically derived constructions act as the "feedforward" *reference signal* (Powers, 1973) against which the flow of feedback input is assessed. When the input fails to match the standard, as when the thermometer reading (input) does not match the thermostat setting (reference standard), the system is activated to negate the discrepancy.

3. Input is processed against hierarchically arranged systems of anticipatory schemata.

4. Any effort to resolve a discrepancy by a resetting of a lower level anticipatory schema would require a concomitant alteration of any superordinating or subsuming construction.

5. Schemata allow elaborations of input. "The role of the scheme is to expand the representation of an experience or message to include components not specifically contained in the experience but that are needed to make representation coherent and complete in some sense" (Greeno, 1980, pp. 718–719).

Reprimand as Self-Regulation

Recall that inputs are processed by means of a hierarchical array of schemata, or reference standards (Proposition 3). We adopt a cognitive–control theory approach (Carver & Scheier, 1981; Powers, 1973) to consider the ways in which reprimand processes function to stabilize a system of self-regulation.

To proceed, imagine a scenario rather characteristic of some family households. A 7-year-old child, Robin, interacts with her 9-year-old sister: "Brenda, you're a jerk!" The mother, Mrs. Alonzo, interrupts her reading, orients toward Robin, and admonishes: "Robin, we don't use that kind of language in this house! Mind your manners!" Robin returns a puzzled gaze to her mother, whereupon Mrs. Alonzo elaborates: "Robin, just think of how you would feel if Brenda said that to you!" To set the stage further, assume that Mrs. Alonzo internally processes the event sequence within a system of hierarchically integrated constructions of the input from herself and her children: "My children should be polite in their interaction with their siblings," and a corollary, "Don't call siblings derisory names."

Discrepancy as the Fundamental Unit of Self-Regulation. In our analysis of this reprimand scenario, we focus on the discrepancy between the mother's anticipatory schema for conduct, "be polite," and the mother's perceptions of Robin's behavior. Essentially, Mrs. Alonzo applies the socially shared construction—the *rule:* "children should be polite." Robin's use of a construction that does not earn social approval, reflected in her transgression, producing input that is discrepant from Mrs. Alonzo's constructed, prototypical representations of the ongoing social exchange among her children—that is, input that is discrepant from Mrs. Alonzo's reference standards.

The strength of the error signal, or "gain" (Powers, 1973), introduced into Mrs. Alonzo's system of self-regulation is proportional to the amplitude of the discrepancy between input and reference conditions. Mrs. Alonzo is motivated to negate the discrepancy (Proposition 2). It is important to note that in our formulation, discrepancy assumes a relativistic character in that the appropriate unit of analysis consists of a relation between quantities (inputs and reference standards), and never represents the activity of any unique input or standard. The gain of the discrepancy is associated with the particular standards that occupy attention at the time of the transgression. As we proceed, we clarify the relativistic qualities of discrepancy, especially when we consider attentive processes.

The reprimand delivered by Mrs. Alonzo represents an effort to bring about distal conditions that minimize the amplitude of her error signal. In sum, Mrs. Alonzo acts to match her *perceptions* (Powers, 1973) of Robin's behavior to her representation of the convention, "be polite." Additionally, input from her own behavior must match the standards for her own self-enactments. If effective, the reprimand reduces discrepancy by forestalling Robin's immediate repetitions of similarly invalidating input (discrepancy), and will prevent future invalidations of her mother's standard for "politeness."

Rule-Related Events Are Encoded by Multiple Standards

Figure 3.1 displays a hueristic precis of Mrs. Alonzo's hierarchically integrated system of self-regulation, as it operates to organize her cognitive processes in the reprimand situation (Proposition 3). To consider adequately the interlocking hierachy charted in Fig. 3.1, one must keep Proposition 2 firmly in mind. Schematically derived reference signals also act as feedforward templates against which one assesses all feedback input—including input from body positions. The lower level reference signals represented in Fig. 3.1, then, are regarded as the *directions* for actions that change the environment to produce input that matches higher order reference signals.

Inspection of Fig. 3.1 indicates that Mrs. Alonzo's "good parent" reference standard superordinates her construction of "maintain an appropriate home atmosphere," located at a principle level. (The terminology *systems, principle,* etc. is consistent with that established by Powers, 1973, and with Carver & Scheier, 1981). "Programs" that validate the "atmosphere" principle-level standard would require the establishment of rules regulating intrafamily social conduct. Note that higher level standards, such as those specifying systems and principles, are marked by their generality or variability across a wide range of contents, so that the subordinate standards may serve as "variable slots" (Bobrow & Brown, 1975; Mancuso & Ceely, 1980; Woods, 1975) relative to the superordinate schemata.

The specification of the rule itself, "polite exchange between siblings" (particularly Mrs. Alonzo's children), concerns a more specific context—the rela-

FIG. 3.1. A representation of a hierarchically organized system of standards that organize a reprimander's response to a transgression of a sibling–sibling interchange rule.

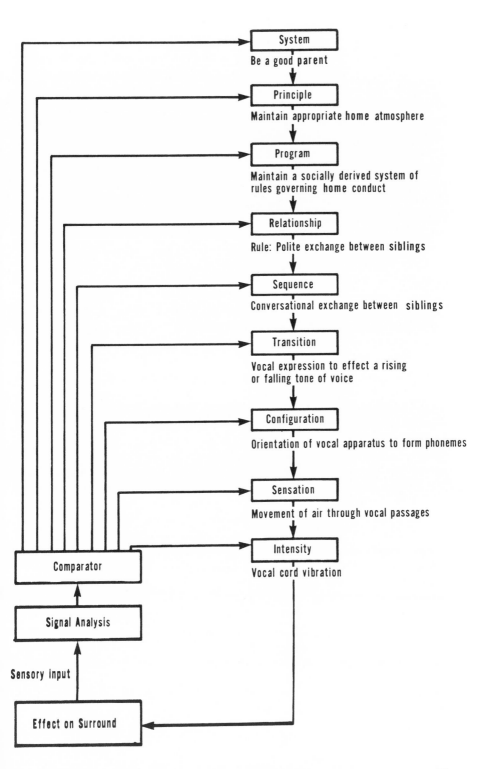

System

Be a good parent

Principle

Maintain appropriate home atmosphere

Program

Maintain a socially derived system of
rules governing home conduct

Relationship

Rule: Polite exchange between siblings

Sequence

Conversational exchange between siblings

Transition

Vocal expression to effect a rising
or falling tone of voice

Configuration

Orientation of vocal apparatus to form phonemes

Sensation

Movement of air through vocal passages

Intensity

Vocal cord vibration

Comparator

Signal Analysis

Sensory Input

Effect on Surround

tionships between siblings. By inspection of Fig. 3.1, it is apparent that this rule "sets"—within Mrs. Alonzo's system—lower order standards that define increasingly specific expectations about feedback derived from the behavior of siblings, and about Mrs. Alonzo's actions in situations where she reprimands in order to remove discrepant input relative to higher order standards concerning the conditions of "appropriate home atmosphere," "polite sibling exchanges," and so forth. Thus, at the sequence level a particular pattern of conversational exchange between siblings is expected, whereas the transitional level specifies a range of "vocal intonation" in the reprimand situation. The lowest level standards are most behaviorally specific, and ultimately provide the anticipatory patterns against which are matched intensities of stimulation, such as muscle tension, and vocal cord vibration. Inspection of Fig. 3.1 also suggests some of the ways in which schemata allow elaboration of input (Proposition 5). The encoding for the "politeness" rule, for example, is embedded within superordinate and subordinate systems of construction, and validation of the rule by the siblings' enactments also informs the mother's system of the validity of her role as "good parent."

Reprimand Serves to Minimize Discrepancy Across the System.   Referring again to Fig. 3.1, Robin's comment to Brenda violated Mrs. Alonzo's reference standard specifying polite relations between siblings, which produces a registration of discrepancy relating to the relationship level. Recall that Proposition 4, which describes the *economic* constraints on changes of standards, would stipulate that the superordinating constructions for the politeness standard—at the system, principle, and program levels in our example—will maintain their organization so long as feedback signals are congruent. In our example, Robin's transgression invalidates the relationship standard. By the negative feedback principles set out above, the transgression invalidates the mother's superordinate levels as well. By implication, Mrs. Alonzo is a "bad parent" and "maintains an inappropriate home atmosphere." In addition, through the action of anticipatory feedforward processes, wherein the reference conditions for lower order levels are specified by the relationship standard, lower level processes are also disrupted. Consequently, reprimand actions (guided by the lower level standards in the reprimand situation charted in Fig. 3.1) are initiated to restore equilibrium throughout the system, although the relationship standard serves as the focal standard (the standard specifically being matched by the particular reprimand strategy dictated by lower level standards).

Selectivity of attention also derives from the registration of discrepancy within the regulating system. Inputs for serial processing are selected by reference to the gain of the error signal describing the relation between anticipation and realization (input). The system attaches priority to resolving the most incongruous input, thereby providing an executive ordering to attentive processing (Mancuso, 1977; Moray, 1970).

Toward the Resolution of Discrepancy: Resetting Standards or Retrieving New Standards. Drawing from cognitive perspectives on *attention* (Mancuso, 1977; Moray, 1970; Norman & Bobrow, 1975) one may conclude that input stays on attention until discrepancy reaches a low level, relative to other sources of discrepancy. The disequilibration engendered by a transgression can be eliminated by recognizing that the initially applied rule does not apply to the assumed transgression. In short, the potential reprimander might "reset his or her standard." To illustrate: After orienting toward Robin, Mrs. Alonzo, noting Robin's facial expression, may enlarge her cue sampling of the transaction between the siblings, and recognize that Robin had used a "kidding tone." Thereupon, Mrs. Alonzo's system may act to refine the "politeness" standard to include those transactions wherein the tone of voice is "kidding." Thus, at the sequence and transitional levels, Robin's use of the term *jerk* may now match those standards, if the higher level "politeness" standard has been reset. After resetting the standard, Mrs. Alonzo's memory for the event is tested against the revised standard, and if a satisfactory match is obtained, the situation would not develop into the reprimand scenario charted in Fig. 3.1.

Alternatively, if Mrs. Alonzo's system did instigate a reprimand, the setting of subordinate standards would direct the ecology–changing motor actions, which *should* lead to input that reduces the amplitude of the error resulting from the mismatch between the "politeness" standard and the transgression. In short, her reprimand-construing system would be activated in order to achieve reduction of discrepancy between the input from her children's actions and her higher order standards. Following our general assumptions, we would believe that reprimand-specifying standards link into other hierarchically integrated cognitive networks, particularly those that would specify the reprimander's "implicit personality theory." A reprimand strategy, such as "speak softly and carry a big stick," is encoded with links to several schematic networks.

For illustrative purposes, we may represent reprimands in the form of production rules. Productions are bifurcated if—>then statements wherein the *if* side specifies conditions for applying a production, and the *then* side specifies procedures that are applied when conditions of applicability (if side) are instantiated (Anderson, 1983).

Mrs. Alonzo's first admonition to Robin, "Robin, we don't talk . . . ," could be represented as a production rule, as follows: *If* a child violates the rule about teasing, And the child understands the basis of the rule, And the transgression does not involve fighting, *then* remind the child of the rule by stating, "(child's name), we don't. . . ."

By application of her self-behavior specifying standards (Fig. 3.1: transitions, configurations, etc.) related to this strategy, Mrs. Alonzo acts to forestall further discrepancy within her overall psychological system by creating conditions that place the "politeness" standard—the rule—into Robin's working memory. However, Robin's subsequent puzzled expression provides input that invalidates Mrs. Alonzo's anticipatory schemata.

Perhaps one of Robin's previous transgressions was not brought into Mrs. Alonzo's working memory. Consequently, the second condition for applying the strategy (understands basis for rule) was inappropriately inferred. After noting Robin's puzzled reaction to the first reprimand, Mrs. Alonzo's system might be sufficiently complex to allow the resetting of the second condition to a null, resulting in the "firing" of a second production rule: *If* a child violates the rule about teasing, *And* he or she does not appear to understand the rationale for the rule, *then* remind transgressor how he or she would feel in victim's place. As her reprimanding expertise increases, one would expect Mrs. Alonzo's specification of conditions (*if* side) and procedures (*then* side) would become more elaborate.

Understanding the Constructions of the Transgressor.   The use of the foregoing example introduces the assumption that the ability to specify elements of the construction system of the transgressor represents an important component of a person's reprimanding expertise. Misspecification of elements of the transgressor's system may increase the likelihood of an unsuccessful reprimand. Additionally, one would expect that inexpert reprimanders would focus on surface characteristics of the event sequence, and would be unable to consider the construction system of the transgressor. Hence, the fulcrum for inexpert reprimanders may be observed behavior. For these novice reprimanders the production rules governing reprimand would contain a simple set of conditions governing the application (the *if* side of the production rule). An observation of the transgression could be a sufficient condition for setting off the *then* side of a production rule. For example, a less expert parent-reprimander might encode a reprimand for the transgression of our example as follows: *If* a child violates the rule about teasing, *then* remind transgressor of the rule by stating, "(name), we don't. . . ."

Then, when Robin returned a puzzled gaze, this inexpert reprimander might simply reiterate the rule. In contrast, the more expert reprimander in our earlier example evidenced greater strategic flexibility by acting in accordance with a second, more elaborated production.

Tangential and Relevant Reprimands.   Consideration of the transgressor's psychological system leads to the development of our only reprimand-categorizing taxonomy—the location of reprimand strategies along a *relevant–tangential* dimension. By this taxonomy we invoke the conceptions with which to discuss "shared intersubjectivity" and "sociality" (Tschudi & Rommetveit, 1982). *Relevant* reprimands reference the transgressor's constructions of the event and enhance elaboration of his or her schemata. By elaboration, we mean an increase in differentiation of conceptions about the event in a normative direction, and simultaneously, the integration of these conceptions with other self-regulatory standards. In contrast, tangential reprimands provide comparatively little elaboration with respect to conceptions about the rule-related event (i.e., the basis for the rule, its history, and its function).

To illustrate the proposed dichotomy, consider Mrs. Alonzo's first strategy: "We don't . . .". By consideration of the mismatch between Robin's and her mother's conceptions, we may say that this reprimand was not particularly elaborative for Robin. However, the mother's second, more relevant strategy— "How would you feel if. . . ."—encourages Robin to take the perspective of another and thereby induces one of the foundations for the rule. However, Robin need not share her mother's entire implicative structure about the rule, which referred to higher level standards such as "good mother" and "home atmosphere." Such an elaborate understanding would be more typical of friendly peer relationships rather than of parent-child or student-teacher relations. In addition, we note that the mother's reprimand was relationally appropriate, specifying concrete referents, rather than abstractions such as "atmosphere." Generally, the notion of relevancy is meaningful only in reference to the dynamics of a particular reprimand context. However, as Sigel (1970) notes, particular types of parenting activities are more *likely* to promote elaboration of the child's understanding than are others.

On Reprimand and Emotion

One may often detect irrelevance in those reprimand situations that involve *emotion*. Recall that the introduction of discrepancy is taken to be the motivation for the reprimander's action. Discrepancy, we assume, is accompanied by physiological arousal (Mancuso, 1977; Mancuso & Handin, 1983; Mancuso & Hunter, 1983) and the reprimander may take cues from the context to label the arousal as a particular emotional experience (Schachter, 1971). *Emotion,* however, must be seen as more than a "label" for arousal. Averill (1982), taking a constructivist perspective on emotion, says:

> The person who says I am angry with you or I love you is not simply labeling a state of physiological arousal; he is entering into a complex relationship with another person. The meaning of the relationship, not only for the individuals involved but also for the larger society, is embodied in the feeling rules (social norms) for that emotion. (p. 25)

By reference to "feeling rules" Averill allows the inference that *emotions,* as schemata, can be described within the control-system principles enunciated in this essay.

Again recall Mrs. Alonzo's reprimand of Robin. Mrs. Alonzo might apply her "anger" construction to the event. She might then admonish in a sharp tone, "Robin!!" The enactment of this anger role is enabled by context and the larger social meaning of that context. The larger social meaning refers to the notion that Robin and her mother share conceptions about the meaning of the enactment of the anger role. In a different context, involving Mrs. Alonzo and Mr. Alonzo, it might be inappropriate for Mrs. Alonzo to "get angry." In the context of the child–parent relationship, anger may not only be allowable; it might be expected. For instance, when Mrs. Alonzo admonishes Robin, Robin might expect her mother to enact components of the "anger" role. If Robin's expectations are violated, she may, by the attentional processes previously outlined, reset her standards to one wherein her mother "really doesn't mean it." Although we have not examined legitimating effects of anger displays in reprimand scenarios, it is easy to envision contexts wherein targets interpret anger display cues as defining features of the reprimand. Moreover, we think that the typical effect of a reprimander's anger enactment is to increase the tangential qualities of the reprimand, with respect to the construction system that the transgressor would apply to the rule-related event.

The enactment of the anger role, as a completely tangential reprimand strategy, could maintain a system's equilibrium at several levels. Anger displays often extract immediate compliance from other persons involved in a reprimand scenario. For example, when a mother's strategic production fails to bring validation of her constructions of "sibling relationships" she could retrieve a standard for a socially understood, "tough" anger performance. Her enactment of the anger role could be congruent with her standard for the role of "good mother," in that she "expresses her true feelings to her children."

Anger enactments may be especially cued when the rule violation is considered unjustified or avoidable (Averill, 1982). For instance, if Mrs. Alonzo has repeatedly reprimanded Robin for teasing, another instance of the misbehavior may be construed as unwarranted. Robin "should know better." One might predict, then, that chronicity of transgression may cue the selection of reprimands that contain elements of "anger."

Later in the sequence, the mother might experience difficulty ("guilt," Kelly, 1955, p. 502) with integrating her anger performance with her superordinate construction of "nice person." Or, after a particularly vehement enactment of the anger role, a mother might be hard-pressed to differentiate her conception of "appropriate reprimand" from another person's construction of "child abuse." In short, we would expect that different persons, in that they would bring notably different hierarchically ordered systems to reprimand situations, would show greater or less expertise in their ability to integrate behavior-regulating standards like "child abuser," "nice person," and "good parent." We now turn to programs of research within which such expectations might be explored.

Reprimand as Problem Solving

On the basis of the foregoing one could declare that reprimand shares many of the processes observed in problem solving, in that the problem solver (invalidated reprimander) has a goal, and attempts to apply strategies to realize that goal. The validation of a standard (the reprimander's construction of the rule) represents a goal, and the reprimand (set as a self-regulating standard) serves as a strategy. The likelihood of attaining the goal, however, depends on the system of knowledge representation the solver utilizes to represent the problem and the solution (Larkin, McDermott, Simon, & Simon, 1980). Problem solving is facilitated for experts, in contrast to novices, because their "deep structure," or principled problem representation, "automatically" (Chi, Glaser, & Rees, 1982; Schneider & Schiffrin, 1977) can cue hierarchies of specific procedures that may be applied for problem resolution. That is, principles and problems are hierarchically well integrated. In this way, expert problem solving also shares many of the features of everyday language production wherein a deep structure representation serves to generate automatically a surface structure representation (Frederiksen, 1979).

In contrast to experts, novice problem solvers typically attempt to "bootstrap" a solution by immediately applying a series of highly specific, surface-structure–compatible procedures that may be only tangentially related to the "deep structure" of the problem. The novices in the Chi et al. (1982) studies typically failed to specify linkages among surface features of problems and principles. Similarly, we would expect that novice reprimanders would be unable to describe verbally the linkages among the complex construing activities by which they process reprimand situations, just as novices cannot adequately make verbal articulations of the complex processes that are involved as they decode and encode discourse. Consequently, inexpert reprimanders may fall back on the advice of behavior change experts, just as we may have occasion to enlist the aid of formal grammar during sentence construction. The scholar looking at reprimand, then, undertakes to untangle the strands that twist through a reprimand context, just as psycholinguists have labored to describe the phonemic, syntactic, and semantic processing systems involved in discourse processing. Some labors of this sort are described in the following sections.

EXPLICATING THE CONTENT OF PEOPLE'S IMPLICIT THEORIES OF REPRIMAND

Development of Conceptions of Reprimand

As a beginning point, an investigator may explore the possibility that the development of integrated systems of constructs about reprimand parallel general cognitive development progressions. Piaget (1932) made the point that a pre-operational child, from his or her egocentric perspective, looks at reprimand as an authority's affirmation of transcendental, immanent morality. Young children do not perform the cognitive operations that allow them to know that there exist alternative ways of construing transgressive events. Thus, "In the choice of punishments, expiation takes precedence over punishment by reciprocity, the very principle of the latter type of punishment not being exactly understood by the [preoperational] child" (p. 316).

Piaget concluded that to the average child reaching the age of 7 or 8, "the idea of expiatory punishment is no longer accepted with the same docility as before, and the only punishments he accepts as really legitimate are those based upon reciprocity" (Piaget, 1932, p. 316). Once children can see that rules are invented in social concert, they can justify reprimand as an effort to prompt the transgressor toward a socially approved construction of the event.

Cognitive Developmental Levels and Constructions of Reprimand

The results of a number of investigations illustrate the kinds of developmental progressions that are linked to changes in people's constructions of reprimands. The typical format used in this body of work involves presenting varied, reprimand-related stimulus material to children of different age levels. The participating children then register their reactions to the reprimander and to the transgressor.

These studies are represented by the work of Eimer (1981, and Eimer, Mancuso, & Lehrer, 1983a, 1983b), who executed a study designed explicitly to look at developing constructions of reprimand. Samples of boys at four different levels of development (ages 5–7, 8–9, 11–12, and 14–16) observed videotaped scenarios of a transgressing boy (Roger) being reprimanded in different ways (explanatory/relevant or coercive/tangential) by his father.

As one part of this series of studies the boys registered their responses on (a) a device whereon they predicted the likelihood of Roger's continued use of aggression; (b) a device on which they made a global predictive evaluation of Roger's overall behavior following the reprimand; and (c) a global evaluation of the father. The first and second measures would indicate the participants' attributions of reprimand effectiveness, whereas the third measure would give information about their evaluations of the reprimander.

Eimer (1981) also interviewed 63 of the children (twenty 5- to 6-year-olds, twenty-three 8- to 9-year-olds, and twenty 11- to 12-year-olds) who had participated in the study. These boys had been asked a series of open-ended questions about: (a) the kinds of processes that would relate the father's reprimand enactment and the transgressor's behavior change; (b) the relation between the reprimand severity, the transgression, and the likely consequences of the administration of the reprimand; and (c) the relations between the father's reprimand and the thinking of the father and the son about that action.

Eimer et al. used information from the interviews to explore the developmental implications of the previously outlined constructivist analysis of reprimand. Developmentally linked constructions of reprimand were suggested by: (a) the findings of previous studies of children's evaluations of reprimand sequences; (b) information about children's cognitive development in related areas of person cognition (Livesley & Bromley, 1973), social-psychological causality (Karniol & Ross, 1976), social perspective-taking (Selman, 1980), and moral judgment (Kohlberg, 1969; Piaget, 1932); and (c) a review of the constructs that had been used by some of the 63 interviewees. From the interview material Eimer et al. developed a five-stage model that could be fit to the progressions reflected in the children's responses. Some of the results of using this interview-based model are reported in the following sections.

Reprimand Constructions of Preoperational Children.   Eimer et al.'s analysis of the patterns of responses to the rating scale measures showed that the 5- to 6-year-old boys rated Roger (on the global measure), the reprimanded transgressor, to be quite negative. They also appear to have attributed little behavior change effect to the reprimand and predicted (on the behavior prediction device) that Roger would frequently repeat his aggressive behavior. Mancuso and Allen (1976) reported parallel results after having gathered responses from kindergarten children who had observed a boy being reprimanded for having broken a vase. These young children judged the reprimanded transgressor (explanatory and tangential reprimands had been shown) to be more negative than was the transgressor who had not been reprimanded. These young children also predicted that the reprimanded transgressors, particularly the tangentially reprimanded trnsgressor, would more frequently engage in unwanted behaviors than would the nonreprimanded children. By contrast, older participants had made more positive evaluations of reprimanded transgressors than of the nonreprimanded transgressor.

The interviews conducted by Eimer provide some base for explaining the preoperational children's judgments of the reprimand process. The preoperational boys saw reprimand as a signal of badness (Stage 0–A). The boy's focus was on the misbehavior. The reprimand, as a kind of automatic justice, signalled the parental displeasure and reset the balance of *good–bad* that had been upset by the transgression. Some of the younger boys, located at Stage 0–B, continued to see the reprimand as a signal of badness, but they also could describe an undefined relationship between the reprimand and the transgressor's future actions.

If preoperational children see reprimand as a sign of the reprimander's badness and cannot construe the reprimand in terms of its behavior change effects, by what system do they construe a transgressor's immediate responses to reprimand? Aldrich and Mancuso (1976) explored this question by showing reprimand–transgression sequences to first and sixth-grade boys. They saw a boy doing accidental damage and then saw the child's mother reprimanding the boy for his "clumsiness." Note that the reprimand could be seen as "unjustified," and an observer, depending on his view of reprimand, could expect any one of a wide variety of transgressor responses. Separate samples of boys saw the portrayed transgressor responding to the reprimand in one of five different ways— (a) open and honest disagreement; (b) open belittlement of the reprimander; (c) acceptance of the reprimand, followed by an expression of annoyance after the mother left the room; (d) simple indication that he would follow the mother's prescriptions; and (e) no response. Data was collected by means of having the children respond to two devices, the Global Rating Scale and the Moral Behaviors Prediction Test, which had been developed for use in previous work (Mancuso, Morrison, & Aldrich, 1978; Morrison, 1975).

First-graders, like the youngest children in the studies previously discussed, gave negative evaluations to each of the five reprimanded transgressors, as well as to the nonreprimanded transgressor. The transgressor who had openly accepted the reprimand (like the nonreprimanded transgressor) though judged to be bad, was rated as being significantly better than was the transgressor in all other response-to-reprimand situations. Similarly, the young children predicted that the transgressor would go on doing "bad" things, in every case.

On the whole, then, the preoperational 5- to 6-year-old children appear to be at a stage of general cognitive development within which they can only center on the concrete events depicted in a reprimand/transgression situation. Interview responses given by preoperational children reflect no use of conceptions from which they could ascribe behavior-altering consequences to reprimands. At this level of development a reprimand serves only to *signal* adult disapproval and, correlatively, a reprimanded child's "badness." This conceptual foundation, it appears, provided the base from which the children who had viewed coercion generated more negative expectations for the reprimanded transgressor than did the children who had viewed explanatory reprimand. One can conclude that preoperational youngsters view the use of explanation as a sign that a reprimander has placed a less negative judgment on the transgressor.

Judgments of a reprimanding father also reflect the young children's physicalistic orientations. The findings of the Eimer et al. study support the Piaget (1932) conclusion that the 5- to 6-year-old children do not employ concepts of responsibility, duty, and intention as they evaluate a reprimander. Instead, they form their evaluations on the basis of the perceived noxiousness, or severity, of the father's conduct. In interviews the 5- to 6-year-old participants justified their paternal ratings with concepts such as "mean," "bad," or "nice." In this way Eimer's participants parallel Appel's (1977) 5- to 6-year-old children, who appear to have used a concrete, present-centered orientation that led them to cognize the nonreprimanding mother as "nice."

Additionally, preoperational children show that the *bad* construct, and little else, is immediately evoked when they are asked to take into account varied transgressor responses to a parental reprimand. The judgment of *bad* persists regardless of the transgressor's response to a reprimand that might have been unjustified. Only the transgressor's open acceptance of the reprimand influenced the young children to judge him to be less bad, but nonetheless bad.

Reprimand Constructions of Concrete Operational Children.   It may be said that being able to perform operations on internal representations of sensory–

motoric events is the quintessential cognitive achievement that marks a child's passage into Piaget's concrete operational stage. The concrete operational child also can recognize that other persons may perform similar operations, and they know that others can hold a perspective of an event that differs from their own. On reaching the level of concrete operations, we may expect the child to construe reprimand functioning in terms of psychological processes related to perspectives regarding the transgressive event. Children at this level of development should expect behavior–change consequences from administrations of reprimands.

These expectations were reflected in the findings of a study reported by Mancuso and Allen (1976). Third- and sixth-grade children, apparently believing that reprimand had a behavior–change aspect, judged a reprimanded transgressor more positively than they judged a nonreprimanded transgressor. Early first-graders, like the kindergartners in the Eimer et al. study, construed the transgressor more negatively if they had seen him being reprimanded by his mother. Similarly, both the 8- to 9-year-old boys and the 11- to 12-year-old boys who had participated in the Eimer et al. study made positive judgments of the transgressor whom they had seen reprimanded. The younger of these two samples produced more positive ratings of the boys who had been the target of explanation, whereas the older, 11- to 12-year-old sample made more positive attributions to the coercively reprimanded transgressor.

The analysis of the interview responses gathered by Eimer also reflects the use of concrete operations. Eimer et al. gave the following summary descriptions to Level I functioning—the functioning best reflected in the responses of the majority of children in the 8- to 12-year range:

1. *Stage I-A: Rudimentary econometric conceptions, direct counterforce and simple cost-avoidance.* Reprimand is seen to suppress undesirable behavior. Cost, evaluated in terms of physical discomfort, severity of reprimand, etc., prevents recurrence of transgression.

2. *Stage I-B: Implicative econometric conceptions: Psychological mediation of counter-force and cost.* The context of the ongoing relationships between reprimander and transgressor provides a backdrop for cost–benefits analysis. Reprimander might moderate severity in interest of maintaining a working relationship with transgressor. Transgressor's view of reprimand is considered, particularly in terms of his or her view of reprimander. Transgressor's "character" also considered. Transgressor's construction of the transgressive event is also taken into account. Means of inducing "a change of mind" are viewed as crucial.

The response patterns of sixth-grade participants in the Aldrich & Mancuso (1976), by their evaluations of the transgressors who had responded to reprimand, also gave evidence that concrete operational children incorporate input about the *internal workings* of participants into their constructions of reprimand interactions. Those sixth-graders made varied judgments, depending on the ways in which the transgressor had responded to reprimand. They rated the "no reprimand" transgressor quite positively, as they similarly rated the transgressor who openly accepted the reprimand. Concurrently, the sixth-graders predicted that these latter transgressors would engage in few unacceptable behaviors. These older participants tended to assign negative ratings to the other depicted transgressors. Their most negative ratings were assigned to the transgressor who had openly belittled his mother's reprimand efforts. Sixth-graders also predicted that there would be many unacceptable behaviors in the belittler's future actions. Some of the sixth-grade boys' responses are not clearly explainable. They predicted few unwanted behaviors from the transgressor who openly accepted and then covertly rejected the reprimand. They responded very differently to the reprimanded transgressor who failed to show any reaction to the reprimand. They predicted that he would engage in many unwanted behaviors.

The findings of this series of studies, then, indicate that children who can perform the cognitive processes one expects to see in concrete operational children do take into account the cognitive processing of the persons involved in reprimand situations. Participating children in the 6- to 12-year age range consistently show that they construe reprimands in terms of *correction*. The responses of the 11- to 12-year-old children in the Eimer et al. study indicate that they, in marked contrast to pre-7-year-old children in this and in other studies, make positive ratings of children who are coercively (tangentially) reprimanded. In the interview they show that their judgments are based on a belief in force–counterforce causality, in which the transgressor had been impelled (force) to his bad behavior, whereupon the role of an effective father is maintained by appropriate use of counterforce (coercion) to suppress his impetus to the transgression and to force the transgressor to "learn a lesson."

These general concrete operational views of reprimand's functions are also reflected in evaluations of reprimanders. Eimer et als.' 8- to 9- and 11- to 12-year level samples appear to have brought to bear a concept of *legitimate authority* (Damon, 1977) as they processed the information about the disciplining father. This is, they saw the father doing what fathers should do—exercising authority, power, and control (Lynn, 1974).

Children well into the concrete operational stage show that considerations of *internal psychological functioning* also enter into evaluations of varied transgressors' responses to reprimand. Unlike kindergartners, they take open acceptance of the reprimand to be indicative of the transgressor's "goodness," and they find open and honest disagreement to be tolerable. Conversely, the sixth-graders take an open rejection of the reprimander's constructions to be a sign of his "badness."

Reprimand Constructions of Formal Operational Persons. Adolescent males aged 16 years made equally negative attributions to the reprimanded transgressors, regardless of the kind of reprimand that they had seen administered, (Eimer et al., 1983b). In doing this they perform as did the college-aged participants in the Page (1981) study. Our consideration of this repeated finding has led us to a conclusion that will require further exploration, namely that persons operating with a complex system for processing reprimand activity will not attribute behavior–change efficacy to a single reprimand. A review of the adolescent's reponses to the Eimer interview shows some of the basis for this conclusion.

A small portion of the 11- and 12-year old children in the Eimer et al. study gave responses that show they construe reprimand using a Level II system. Reprimand construing at this level was summarily described as follows:

Level II. Reprimander Must Treat Transgressor as Coconstruer. Transgressor's thinking and alteration thereof are taken to be the central aspect of reprimand. Reprimand is considered in terms of its efficacy in leading to an understanding of the principles of prescribed behavior. Applications of tangential cost or benefits are seen as being irrelevant. Reprimand is seen to be effective when it successfully disconfirms the transgressor's way of construing the event. Thus, to disconfirm the transgressor's status as a coconstruer by use of coercion is seen as having serious consequences relative to the relationship between the transgressor and the reprimander.

Kanner and Mancuso (1984) completed a study that supplements the Eimer et al. study. Twenty persons between the ages of 14 and 16 responded to the Eimer interview. Ten of these adolescents responded so that their conceptions of reprimand processes would easily be categorized as Level II functioning. The responses of six of these persons reflected Level I–B functioning, whereas the responses of four of the participants in this sample showed the use of Level I–A functioning. The Level II adolescents regularly stressed the belief that the reprimander simply could not justify a stance that pits the view of the reprimander against that of the transgressor. Ultimately, a change in the transgressor's behavior would depend on correlative changes in his or her construction of the transgression situation. That being the case, an explanatory reprimand would be most recommended, in that explanatory reprimand would create the least possibility of disrupting the relationship between the reprimander and the transgressor, and a positive relationship would be the best guarantee of the transgressor's eventual acceptance of the reprimander's construction of the situation. Nevertheless, a single explanatory reprimand would not be expected to have a great effect on the transgressor's views of the transgression situation. If the transgressor's construction system were firmly fixed, even an explanatory reprimand would not change his or her behavior. After endorsing an explanatory reprimand, one youngster made the foregoing points by saying, ''The father had to do something, so what he did was the best thing to do, because there just isn't much he can do until Roger finds out for himself that using rough stuff can't work.''

Summary Comment on Developing Conceptions.   When one is guided by a framework like Piaget's general theory of cognitive development the results of the studies reviewed previously offer no surprising findings relative to the details that describe developing children's constructions of reprimand. A central point must not be lost among these details. The work previously described, along with the constructivist perspective guiding this essay, forces the conclusion that a child does not naively survey the world to see the ways in which reprimands work on him or her. Each developing alteration in the person's systems of cognition will affect what developing persons see in the outer world.

Adult Constructions of Reprimand

Kelly's (1955, Adams-Webber & Mancuso, 1983; Mancuso & Adams-Webber, 1982) theory of personal constructs explicates the ways in which a person's processing systems interact with input. Delia and his colleagues (Applegate, 1980a, 1980b, 1983; Delia, Kline, & Burleson, 1979; O'Keefe & Delia, 1979), who adhere to personal construct theory, have explored the relationships of qualities of an individual's person-construing system and his or her ability to adapt communications to varied listeners. In his discussion of teachers' communicative strategies, Applegate (1980b) states that, ''it is posited that teachers who have developed a more abstract interpersonal construct system for construing others will evidence more personal, adaptive communication with students in regulative and interpersonal contexts. They will refrain from formulating communicative strategies simply as a response to the student's overt behaviors and/or features of his/her status as 'student' '' (p. 163). From this, we infer Applegate's agreement with our assumption that a skilled reprimander's communications are shaped by systems that contain and use higher level standards, like those at the principle and program levels, rather than those at transitional or sequence levels.

To validate his formulations, Applegate (1980b) first assessed the level of abstractness reflected in the participating teachers' person-perceiving construct systems. Then the teachers gave verbal descriptions of their actions toward a hypothetical, transgressing child. These responses were coded by the use of Applegate's hierarchical system, which ranged from a level labelled *position-centered appeals* through to a level labelled *person-centered appeals*. Person-centered messages (the highest level) would show the respondent's ''sensitivity to the unique features of the context and of the perspectives of interactants'' (p. 73), and this sensitivity would be apparent in the elaborations of the teacher's communication. As predicted, the level of abstractness in a teacher's person-perceiving system correlated highly with the level of appeals described by that teacher.

Applegate achieved another kind of validation by first going into classrooms to observe 10 teachers in order to classify them as being either person-centered or position–centered. The portion of the sample that had been classed as person-centered, on the basis of their classroom behavior, used many more abstract person-describing terms when completing a variant of Kelly's (1955) role construct repertory test.

In concluding descriptions of his less abstract reprimanders Applegate (1980b, 1983) used terms like *issues commands and simple assertions, reliance on authority, lacking rationale,* and *uses nonverbal methods.* Person-centered teachers more often provided reasons for modifying behavior, and considered the arousal levels, the intentions, and the perspectives of those involved in the unique context of the reprimand. Additionally, the more skilled reprimanders could generate alternative strategies that were oriented to the psychological–motivational qualities of the transgressor.

The work reported by Grusec and Kuczynski (1980) suggests that certain kinds of transgression might lead mothers to generate person-centered reprimands. Seventy percent of the mothers, after considering one or another of various transgressions, recommended a tangential strategy (hitting, spanking, slapping, or yelling). Most mothers prescribed relevant reprimands for the child who had stolen from her purse or for the child who had ridiculed a debilitated old person. Grusec and Kuczynski believe that mothers recognize these transgressions to be constructions that are discrepant from universal rules (our terms), and they conclude that mothers turn to explanation when they anticipate a need for compliance to a rule that appears to be universal. To interpret these results in terms of the complexity of the reprimander's constructions system, one would want to have, among other things, information about the reprimander's knowledge of the discrepancies between the rules and the hypothetical child's construction of the rule-relevant situations. Perhaps the participating mothers could detect an immense discrepancy between the child's perspective and the perspective needed to integrate the rule, and in such cases they are able to invoke self-defining reprimand standards other than those that would be validated by immediate compliance.

Mancuso and Handin (1980a; Handin & Mancuso, 1980) undertook an exploration of the reprimand constructions of workers who functioned in an agency providing residential child care. The workers viewed and then evaluated three different kinds of reprimand (explanatory, restitutive, and tangential) addressed to a boy who had transgressed. Workers judged restitutive reprimand most positively. Whereas the participating workers made negative judgments of the strictly position–centered coercive reprimands, as a group they tended to prefer somewhat position–centered restitutive reprimands. Thirty percent of workers saw explanatory reprimand as most proper, whereas another 30% saw it as the least proper of the three types of reprimand. One cannot conclude, however, that positiveness and propriety relate to a *behavior–change effectiveness* dimension. Within these workers' construct systems, the *severity–leniency* construct was most salient. A multivariate analysis of variance located *social disapproval,* rather than *effectiveness,* to be in positive relationship with *severity,* so that there is no reason to conclude that the workers think of effectiveness in altering behavior when they think of the positive value of the reprimand. One can conclude that one of the high-level, self-regulating standards in the reprimand processing systems of many of these workers will be validated by input signifying social approval.

More recent work (Mancuso, Page, Hunter, & Kanner, 1983; Page, 1981) affirms the extent to which "social niceness" becomes a standard against which people test the input from reprimand activity. Page studied teasing as a method of reprimand, that is, as a method of disconfirming a transgressor's rule-discrepant construction of an event. Skillful teasing, one can argue, puts a person's constructions into a tolerably arousing distortion, and thereby informs a transgressor that worlds do not collapse when a favorite construction is disconfirmed. Thus, the transgressor is "teased" toward—in the sense of "edged toward"—flexible reconstruction of his self-standard relative to the transgressive event.

Some of Page's (1981) college-aged participants observed the reprimander enact, for example, word plays on the nature of the transgression. In a comparable scenario the reprimander made derogatory jokes about the character of a boy whose tardiness would detain the family from starting on an afternoon picnic (coercive teasing). Other participants saw either a straightforward coercive or an explanatory reprimand.

Participants evaluated the reprimand scene by responding to 24 five-point scales that had evolved from the Mancuso/Handin work. Factor analysis (varimax solution) of responses allow the conclusion that five meaningful dimensions define the particiants' assessments of the reprimand interactions that they had observed. By contrasting the separate samples' scores on the factors Page could conclude the following: (a) Participants' judgments relative to three dimensions—the transgressor's immediate compliance, the reconstruing done by the transgressor, and his or her overall socialization—were not systematically affected by the variations in the strategies used by the reprimander. Clearly, however, the explaining father and the father who had used benevolent teasing were judged (a) to have given more attention to the perspective of the reprimander and (b) to be "nicer" persons than were the fathers portrayed in the other reprimand conditions.

Mancuso and his associates (Mancuso, Page, Hunter, & Kanner, 1983) introduced another variable—the perceived character of the father's relationship with the transgressor—into Page's research model. Before watching the reprimand scenarios, half of the participating college students who observed each reprimand condition heard an audiotaped statement that described the father's aloofness from his children. The remaining half of the participants heard that the father worked hard to maintain a positive relationship.

Additionally, Mancuso et al. (1983) revised the Reprimander/Transgressor Rating Scales (RTRS) in an attempt to bring the items into line with an extension of the theoretical framework. Following Averill (1982) the items relating to the reprimander's "badness–niceness," as well as added items, were shaped to have respondents focus on the possibility that the reprimander was enacting an "anger strategy" in an effort to coerce the transgressor into compliance. Following these revisions, a competed factor analysis (varimax solution) again indicated that the participants used five dimensions as they responded to the 29-item RTRS.

Though the variations in the experimental conditions significantly affected the responses on several dimensions, the findings again show that participants had judged that all of the portrayed reprimands would be equally ineffective, generally, in bringing about change in the transgressor's conduct. Hence, these results corroborate those of the Eimer et al. studies. Formal operational persons seem to give the same level of "change power" to singly displayed, quite varied reprimands. By contrast, judgments relative to the dimension reflecting the father's understanding of the transgressor's perspective were dependent on the variations in the reprimand scenarios that participants had witnessed. The father's involvement with his children, as described by the experimenter, clearly affected rating on this latter dimension. Participants attributed more understanding to the "positively relating" reprimanding father than to his "aloof" counterpart, regardless of the type of reprimand he had used. As in the original Page (1981) study, the fathers who had delivered the explanatory reprimand and the benevolent reason, were judged to be more understanding than were the fathers who had used coercive reprimand and coercive teasing. When they responded to the items subsumed by the relevant factor, the participants judged that the transgressors who had been subjected to explanation and benevolent teasing would consider themselves most adequately understood.

As had been anticipated by the investigators, there did emerge a factor that coalesced the participants' judgments of whether or not the reprimand was directed toward achieving proper behavior, as opposed to representing an expression of the reprimander's effort to bring about, in a *mean* way, a resolution of his own discrepancy and arousal. Here, again, the participants judged that the explaining and the benevolently teasing reprimander had most satisfactorily addressed the behavior–change issue.

Essentially, the findings from the Mancuso et al. (1983) study replicate the original Page work. Two findings, discussed later in a broader context, require special note. First, participants regularly use a "bad–nice" dimension as they process input about reprimands, and reprimanders who tease benevolently or who use explanation are judged to be more "nice." Second, and most significantly, the participants again differentiated the reprimand in terms of the understanding shown by the reprimander, but they did not report expectations that one or another of the reprimands would be associated with more acceptable behavior on the part of the transgressor.

Parents' Views of Reprimand

Newberger (1980) has reported an investigation which, like Applegate's work, follows from the assumption that reprimand-construing systems are hierarchically related to broader person-perceiving systems. She asked 51 parents to respond to open-ended questions about issues, including reprimand issues, encountered by parents. Having evolved a classification scheme that has many parallels with that which Eimer et al. (1983b) devised to categorize developing conceptions of reprimand, Newberger concluded that "parental conceptions could be ordered hierarchically into four increasingly comprehensive and psychologically oriented levels. Within interviews, thinking was relatively consistent within and across issues" (p. 49–50).

Consider Newberger's descriptions of the kinds of construing shown by parents at her Levels 3 and 4, the highest levels of parental awareness:

> Level 3. The parental role is organized around identifying and meeting the needs of this child rather than as the fulfillment of predetermined role obligations.
> Level 4. The parent understands the child as a complex and changing psychological self-system. (p. 50).

One can readily note the relationship between the orientations seen in these two levels and the Stage I–B and Level II thinking about reprimand that has been independently identified by Eimer et al. (1983a). Additionally, Newberger's upper level parents seem to reveal the use of the same kinds of implicit personality theories that are used by Applegate's (1980b) person-centered teachers, whose reprimands included messages that focused on the intentions of the transgressor, rather than on their overt behaviors.

Parent Training Programs and Parental Constructions of Reprimand. Newberger (1980) suggested that her Level 1 or Level 2 parents would be more likely to function as inadequate parents. She suggests then that "Interventions on parental reasoning would be an important supplement to current intervention modalities" (p. 65). She also recognizes that assessments of parents' belief systems would provide useful means of gauging the kinds of changes that occur during intervention.

Similar assumptions guided Mancuso and Handin (1980b, 1983) as they implemented a constructivist parent training program. These investigators developed a Parent Repertory Role Grid (ParRep) to aid in assessing the changes in the construing systems of participants. This instrument (which may be computer administered) is modeled after the Role Repertory Grid Technique (Kelly, 1955), and yields a 16 × 14 raw data matrix. Each cell of the completed matrix contains an index of judgment, on a 3-point scale, which was derived in the following manner: A parent considers one of 14 parent role descriptors, such as, "best parent," "parent of child who can't stand new things." After careful study of the described role the respondent considers a parent belief statement, such as, "A child should settle down when he's told to settle down," "Always try to tell a kid what is going to happen before it happens." The respondent then indicates whether or not the described parent would reject, maybe accept, or accept the belief statement. To derive the 0, 1, and 2 ratings that will be entered into each of the 224 cells of the matrix, participants judge the extent to which each of the parent roles would endorse each of the 16 belief statements. Using the techniques designed by Rosenberg and his associates (Gara & Rosenberg, 1979; Rosenberg, 1977) one can subject each respondent's matrix to multidimensional scaling, cluster analysis, and subset and superset implications analysis.

Hamill (1983) has completed an extensive analysis of samples of mothers, some of whom have completed the Mancuso/Handin program. The parent trainers had judged that 9 of the 14 mothers had made significant progress during their involvement with the program. These nine mothers and the five program-involved mothers who had made less progress were compared with varied samples of nonprogram mothers. The quality of the parent role perceiving systems (as it is reflected in the organizational properites of the ParReps) found in high-progress mothers consistently exceeded that of the low-progress mothers. For example, the low-progress mothers, compared with high-progress mothers, show low differentiation of beliefs about child rearing. Socioeconomic status alone would not be expected to account for the obtained differences. In other analyses Hamill found that a comparison sample of low-socioeconomic mothers produced more well-organized ParRep grids than did the preprogram mothers. These initial explorations indicate that an instrument like the ParRep can be used as a means of assessing the extent to which parents can integrate reprimand beliefs into systems of constructions regarding the practices of parenting.

Some Conclusions about Adult Constructions of Reprimand

It is easy to say that the average person undergoes a long series of experiences before achieving the complex, hierarchically ordered person-perceiving system within which she or he construes reprimand. The complexity of the system and the problems of conducting formal studies of that system are highlighted by a major finding derived from at least four of the studies completed by Mancuso and his colleagues. Participants can process information about different types of reprimands in ways that lead them to differentiate the qualities of those reprimands. At the same time, the participants give no evidence that they believe that these perceptibly different reprimands are systematically related to varied outcomes in the transgressor's conduct. Unlike the middle-childhood participants' evaluations, separate samples of adults who had viewed the videotaped scenarios did not vary their evaluations of the transgressor—despite each sample having seen the adminstration of different types of reprimand, whereupon they demonstrated that they had detected differences on other construable dimensions.

Consider also that in studies in which participants are informed of a trangression and then are asked to recommend effective behavior–changing reprimands, they will do so with alacrity. Furthermore, after judges have seen consecutive showings of two qualitatively different reprimand enactments, they will readily judge that one or the other will produce more or less compliance. We are led to a perplexing question: Why do the adult participants, when they are asked to do so, unhesitatingly recommend a reprimand of one or another type, whereas when they are shown a single reprimand and then asked to evaluate its effectiveness they will judge that it will have little effect on behavior change?

At this point we are led to hypothesize that adults are very cautious about attributing "change power" to any single reprimand, regardless of its type. Having observed a single transgression/reprimand scenario, they can locate its definition within their construction system, but they will not deduce that the isolated reprimand will "cause" a change in the transgressor. We would conclude that adults implicitly know that a person does not change his or her construction of an event simply because one or another reprimand has been delivered. When he or she applies a complex person-perceiving system, an adult knows that a person's construction of an event is hierarchically related to a construction of self, to a construction of relationships with other persons of inferior and superior status, and to constructions of relationships with the reprimander. Adults know that unless this whole hierarchy changes, the lower level, behavior-guiding reference standards will not change.

In brief, adults and adolescents can understand reprimand as a historical process wherein reprimand scenarios must be integrated over time to be meaningful to transgressors and to reprimanders. In terms of the hierarchical processing model outlined previously, reprimand *effectiveness* relates to the superordinate levels in adults' systems. This superordinacy implies a longer feedback loop than might be charactertistic of lower order standards, such as those standards at the sequence level standard that might be affected by denying the transgressor a promised privilege. Hence, observers seeing a single reprimand have little information about effects on the transgressor's system. In short, one would need to write a novel about the transgressor and the reprimander in order to convince an adult participant/judge to evaluate confidently the outcomes of a particular reprimand.

Why then do participants pliantly offer endorsements of one or another reprimand when they are asked to do so? To explain this, we again refer to our analogy between the constructive activity in discourse processing and the constructive activity in construing reprimand. Adults continuously apply their complex discourse processing systems to create elaborate sentences. If they are asked, they can recall some of the grammar rules learned in junior high school, but they could not begin to describe the complex cognitive system by which they form sentences. Additionally, they know a good sentence when they hear or read one. At the same time, they would not believe that they can use their linguistic system to anticipate confidently that any one or another sentence would have a meaningful impact on a listener, unless they knew a great deal about all the strands of the communication context. Analogously, people apply their reprimand system in precisely these same ways.

RECOMMENDATIONS TO REPRIMANDERS

This chapter closes with a summary position relative to recommendations to reprimanders. We are led to the conclusion that behavior scientists cannot satisfactorily recommend a universally effective, all-purpose reprimand that will lead to a transgressor's happy compliance. We do believe, however, that it will be shown eventually that an effective reprimander is highly skillful in assessing, taking into account, and addressing the construction system of the transgressor. In doing this, the reprimander must recognize that children have developed their own conceptions of what does happen in a reprimand situation. Correlatively, the effective reprimander would be highly skillful in assessing, taking into account, and addressing his or her own construction system. With these skills, the effective reprimander will constantly regard his or her developing child as a construer, and will not use his or her position of power to remove the child from that role.

REFERENCES

Adams-Webber, J. R., & Mancuso, J. C. (Eds.) (1983). *Applications of personal construct theory.* Toronto: Academic Press.

Aldrich, C. C., & Mancuso, J. C. (1976). Judgments of a child involved in accidental damage and responding diferentially to adult reprimand. *Perceptual and Motor Skills, 43,* 1071–1082.

Anderson, J. R. (1983). *The architecture of cognition.* Cambridge, MA: Harvard University Press.

Appel, Y. H. (1977). Developmental differences in children's perceptions of maternal socialization behavior. *Child Development, 48,* 1689–1693.

Applegate, J. L. (1980a). Adaptive communication in educational contexts: A study of teachers' communicative strategies. *Communication Education, 129,* 157–170.

Applegate, J. L. (1980b). Person– and position–centered teacher communication in a day care center. In N. K. Denzin (Ed.), *Studies in symbolic interation* (Vol. 3, pp. 59–96). Greenwich, CT: JAI Press.

Applegate, J. L. (1983). Construct system development, strategic complexity, and impression formation in persuasive communication. In J. R. Adams-Webber & J. C. Mancuso (Eds.), *Applications of personal construct theory* (pp. 187–205). Toronto: Academic Press.

Averill, J. (1982). *Anger and aggression: An essay on emotion.* New York: Springer-Verlag.

Bartlett, F. C. (1932). *Remembering.* Cambridge: Cambridge University Press.

Bobrow, R. J., & Brown, J. S. (1975). Systematic understanding. In R. J. Bobrow & A. Collins (Eds.), *Representation and understanding.* New York: Academic Press.

Carver, C. S., & Scheier, M. F. (1981). *Attention and self–regulation: A control–theory approach to human behavior.* New York: Springer-Verlag.

Chi, M. T. H., Glaser, R., & Rees, E. (1982). Expertise in problem solving. In R. J. Sternberg (Ed.), *Advances in the psychology of human intelligence.* Hillside, NJ: Lawrence Erlbaum Associates.

Damon, W. (1977). *The social world of the child.* San Francisco: Jossey-Bass.

Delia, J. G., Kline, S. L., & Burleson, B. R. (1979). The development of persuasive communication strategies in kindergartners through twelfth-graders. *Communications Monographs, 41,* 413–429.

Eimer, B. N. (1981). *Children's conceptions of the purposes, outcomes, and styles of parental reprimand.* Unpublished doctoral dissertation. State University of New York at Albany, Albany.

Eimer, B. N., Mancuso, J. C., & Lehrer, R. (1983a). *A theoretical and empirical analysis of developmental stages in boys' conceptions of paternal discipline.* Unpublished manuscript, State University of New York at Albany, Albany.

Eimer, B. N., Mancuso, J. C., & Lehrer, R. (1983b). *Developmental differences in boys' judgments about paternal disciplinary behavior.* Unpublished manuscript, State University of New York at Albany, Albany.

Frederiksen, C. H. (1979). Discourse comprehension in early reading. In L. N. Resnick & P. A. Weaver (Eds.), *Theory and practice of early reading* (Vol. 1, pp. 155–186) Hillsdale, NJ: Lawrence Erlbaum Associates.

Gara, M. A., & Rosenberg, S. (1979). The identification of persons as supersets and subsets in free response personality descriptions. *Journal of Personality and Social Psychology, 37,* 2161–2170.

Greeno, J. G. (1980). Psychology of learning, 1960–1980: One participant's observations. *American Psychologist, 35,* 713–728.

Grusec, J. & Kuczynski, L. (1980). Direction of effect in socialization: a comparison of the parent's versus the child's behavior as determinants of disciplinary techniques *Developmental Psychology, 16,* 1–9.

Hamill, R. (1983). *The parent role reportories of parents of difficult to manage children.* Unpublished doctoral dissertation, State University of New York at Albany, Albany.

Handin, K. H., & Mancuso, J. C. (1980). Perceptions of the function of reprimand. *Journal of Social Psychology. 110,* 43–52.

Kanner, B., & Mancuso, J. C. (1984). *Parent role repertories and reprimand constructions used by adolescents.* Unpublished manuscript, State University of New York at Albany, Albany.

Karniol, R., & Ross, M. (1976). The development of causal attributions in social perception. *Journal of Personality and Social Psychology. 34,* 455–464.

Kelly, G. A. (1955). *The psychology of personal constructs.* New York: Norton.

Kohlberg, L. (1969). Stage and sequence: The cognitive developmental approach to socialization. In D. A. Goslin (Ed.), *Handbook of socialization theory and research* (pp. 347–480). New York: Rand McNally.

Larkin, J., McDermott, J., Simon, D., & Simon, H. (1980). Expert and novice performance in solving physics problems. *Science, 208,* 1335–1342.

Livesley, W. J., & Bromley, D. B. (1973). *Person perception in childhood and adolescence.* London: Wiley.

Lynn, D. B. (1974). *The father: His role in child development.* Monterey, CA: Brooks/Cole.

Mancuso, J. C. (1977). Current motivational models in the elaboration of personal construct theory. In A. W. Landfield (Ed.), *Nebraska Symposium on Motivation: Personal construct psychology* (pp. 43–97). Lincoln: University of Nebraska Press.

Mancuso, J. C. (1979). Reprimand: The construing of the rule violator's construct system. In P. Stringer & D. Bannister (Eds.), *Constructs of sociality and individuality.* New York: Academic Press.

Mancuso, J. C., & Adams-Webber, J. R. (1982). Anticipation as a constructive process: the fundamental postulate. In J. C. Mancuso & J. R. Adams-Webber (Eds.), *The construing person* (pp. 8–32). New York: Praeger.

Mancuso, J. C., & Allen, D. A. (1976). Children's perceptions of a transgressor as a function of intentionality and type of reprimand. *Human Development, 19,* 177–290.

Mancuso, J. C., & Ceeley, S. G. (1980). The self as memory processing. *Cognitive Therapy and Research, 4,* 1–25.

Mancuso, J. C., & Handin, K. H. (1980a). Comparing high- and low-rated child care worker's attributions of reprimand effectiveness. *Child Care Quarterly, 9,* 275–288.

Mancuso, J. C., & Handin, K. H. (1980b). Training parents to construe the child's construing. In A. W. Landfield & L. M. Leitner (Eds.), *Personal construct psychology* (pp. 271–288). New York: Wiley.

Mancuso, J. C., & Handin, K. H. (1983). Prompting parents toward constructivist caregiving practices. In I. E. Sigel & L. M. Laosa (Eds.), *Changing families* (pp. 167–202). New York: Plenum.

Mancuso, J. C., & Handin, K. H. (1984). Reprimanding: Acting on one's implicit theory of behavior change. In I. E. Sigel (Ed.), *Parent belief systems* (pp. 143–176). New York: Plenum.

Mancuso, J. C., Heerdt, W. A., & Hamill, R. (1984). Construing the transition to parent roles as a constructive process. In V. L. Allen & E. van der Vliert (Eds.), *Proceedings of NATO Symposium on Role Transitions* (pp. 289–300). New York: Plenum.

Mancuso, J. C., & Hunter, K. V. (1983). Anticipation, motivation, or emotion: The fundamental postulate after twenty-five years. In J. R. Adams-Webber & J. C. Mancuso (Eds.), *Applications of personal construct theory* (pp. 73–92). Toronto: Academic Press.

Mancuso, J. C., Morrison, J. K., & Aldrich, C. C. (1978). Developmental changes in social–moral perceptions: Some factors affecting children's evaluations and predictions of the behavior of a "transgressor." *Journal of Genetic Psychology. 132,* 121–136.

Mancuso, J. C., Page, R., Hunter, K. V., & Kanner, B. (1983). *Young adults' perceptions of varied features in a reprimand situation.* Unpublished manuscript, State University of New York at Albany, Albany.

Moray, N. (1970). *Attention: Selection processes in vision and learning.* New York: Academic Press.

Morrison, J. K. (1975). Developmental study of person perception of young children. In H. C. Lindgren (Ed.), *Children's behavior: An introduction to research studies* (pp. 17–22). Palo Alto: Mayfield.

Newberger, C. M. (1980). The cognitive structure of parenthood: Designing a descriptive measure. In R. L. Selman & R. Yando (Eds.), *New Directions for Child Development* (Vol. 7, pp. 45–67), San Francisco: Jossey-Bass.

Norman, D. A., & Bobrow, D. G. (1975). On data limited and resource limited processes. *Cognitive Psychology, 7,* 44–64.

O'Keefe, D. J., & Delia, J. G. (1979). Construct comprehensiveness and cogntive complexity as predictors of number and strategic adaptation of arguments and appeals in persuasive messages. *Communication Monographs, 46,* 231–240.

Page, R. (1981). *Perceptions of teasing as reprimand.* Unpublished doctoral dissertation, State University of New York at Albany, Albany.

Pepper, S. C. (1942). *World hypotheses: A study of evidence.* Berkeley: University of California Press.

Piaget, J. (1932). *The moral judgment of the child.* (M. Gabain Trans.). London: Kegan Paul.

Powers, W. T. (1973). *Behavior: The control of perception.* Chicago: Aldine.

Rosenberg, S. (1977). New approaches to analysis of personal constructs in person perception. In A. W. Landfield (Ed.), *Nebraska Symposium on Motivation: Personal construct psychology* (pp. 179–242). Lincoln: University of Nebraska Press.

Sarbin, T. R. (1977). Contextualism: The worldview for modern psychology. In A. W. Landfield (Ed.), *Nebraska Symposium on Motivation: Personal construct psychology* (pp. 1–41). Lincoln: University of Nebraska Press.

Schachter, S. (1971). *Emotion, obesity, and crime.* New York: Academic Press.

Schneider, W., & Schiffrin, R. M. (1977). Controlled and automatic human information processing: I. Detection, search, and attention. *Psychological Review, 84,* 1–66.

Selman, R. L. (1980). *The growth of interpersonal understanding.* New York: Academic Press.

Sigel, I. E. (1970). The distancing hypothesis: A causal hypothesis for the acquisition of representational thought. In M. R. Jones (Ed.), *Miami Symposium on the Prediction of Behavior: The effect of early experience* (pp. 99–118). Coral Gables, FL: University of Miami Press.

Tschudi, F., & Rommetveit, R. (1982). Sociality, intersubjectivity, and social processes: The sociality corollary. In J. C. Mancuso & J. R. Adams-Webber (Eds.), *The construing person* (pp. 33–44). New York: Praeger.

Woods, W. A. (1975). Foundations for semantic networks. In D. G. Bobrow & A. Collins (Eds.), *Representation and understanding* (pp. 35–82). New York: Academic Press.

4

Some Antecedents of Maternal Attributions About Children's Performance in Mathematics

Robert D. Hess
Teresa M. McDevitt
Stanford University

The recent activity in research on parental beliefs reflects a growing appreciation for the importance of cognitions in the daily lives of family members. The focus of much of the writing and research on parental beliefs has been on the character and function of parents' beliefs—the kinds of beliefs that parents hold, the correlates of their views, and the relation between parents' beliefs and children's behavior and skills. This chapter addresses an aspect of this topic that so far has received relatively little attention—the origins of beliefs that parents hold about their children's achievement in school.

This chapter first identifies three general sources of beliefs that may apply to parents' views about their children—personal experience, cultural values, and psychological biases. Second, it describes the particular parental beliefs on which we concentrate—causal explanations about why children did as well as they did in mathematics and why they did not do better. Third, it describes several variables that are associated with specific experiences, cultural explanations, and psychological biases, all of which may impinge on parents' beliefs. Finally, this chapter reports the results of a study that tested the influence of these antecedent variables on mothers' causal attributions.

GENERAL SOURCES OF PARENTS' BELIEFS

At least three perspectives address the origins of parental beliefs. One view suggests that beliefs and naive theories are constructed from experience (Kelly, 1955, 1963). In this view, specific life experiences with particular children are treated as sources of parents' conceptions (Goodnow, 1984; McGillicuddy-De-

95

Lisi, 1980; McGillicuddy-DeLisi, Sigel, & Johnson, 1979; Stolz, 1967). For example, parents with more than one child may observe differences in temperament or activity level among their children and conclude that personality is innate and not subject to parental intervention. Repeated reports from different teachers about performance in school or observations that a particular child always keeps at a task until it is completed help develop parents' impressions about ability and work styles. The child's repeated successes or failures may be taken as evidence about what he or she "can" or "cannot" do (Weiner, 1980).

Second, parents adopt the values and attitudes of their cultures, communities, historical cohorts, and the media (Goodnow, in press). This process of belief formation is relatively static compared with the constructivist position, for it suggests that beliefs are transmitted through "collective folk wisdom" (Whiting, 1974), handed down by cultural agents. Support for this perspective comes from a growing body of evidence on cultural differences in parents' beliefs about children and developmental processes; the reader is referred to other sources for a review of this literature (Goodnow, 1984; Holloway, Hess, Azuma, & Kashiwagi, in press; Marjoribanks, 1980). One modern variant of cultural influence in the United States is the advice to parents popularized in child-rearing books (Clarke-Stewart, 1978). Although presumably based on sound theory and research, the type of advice given to parents changes over time, reflecting changes in the society (Bronfenbrenner, 1958).

Third, psychological conditions bias the way parents perceive and interpret information from external events. One prominent bias is the tendency to hold beliefs that protect one's self-esteem. Ego-protection, or self-enhancement, refers to the inclination to protect oneself against changes, particularly negative changes, in self-regard (Greenwald, 1980). For example, we may offer explanations that shift blame for our failures to external sources or to uncontrollable events, and may place credit for successes on internal sources. These self-serving biases may also extend to include others with whom one feels a close attachment. Thus, parents may protect not only themselves but also their children. Accordingly, parents have been shown to attribute positive behavior of their children to stable, internal traits and negative behavior to external, unstable features (Dix & Grusec, 1985). Another fundamental source of bias has to do with one's perspective on the target action; events are explained in somewhat different terms by participants than by onlookers. The actor tends to emphasize situational factors, especially in attempting to explain lack of success, whereas observers tend to see behavior as more firmly rooted in dispositional causes (Jones & Nisbett, 1971). In a sense, parents play the role of observers when making attributions about their children's behavior and might be expected to offer dispositional rather than situational explanations. Another possible bias has to do with projection: parents may project onto their children their own feelings for a particular subject or task. Parents may also tend to project more strongly onto their same-sex children, on the principle that people tend to believe that individuals who are like them in observable ways are also similar in other ways.

PARENTS' CAUSAL EXPLANATIONS FOR CHILDREN'S PERFORMANCE IN MATHEMATICS

A range of different forces may thus combine to form parents' beliefs. The particular forces that operate may differ from one belief to another. In this study, we focus on causal explanations about children's performance in mathematics—accounts of why children performed as well as they did and why they did not do better. The research instrument we used included five options—ability, effort, training at home, training at school, and luck—but in this analysis we examine two explanations—ability and effort.

As explanations, ability and effort are similar in that both refer to factors internal to the actor. The other explanations, training at school, training at home and luck, refer to external and uncontrollable factors. Although ability and effort are both internal explanations, they differ along several dimensions. Effort, unlike ability, is under volitional control. In addition, ability is considered to be stable over time, whereas effort can fluctuate greatly. Because of these differences in stability and controllability, ability and effort attributions lead to dissimilar expectations about future performance. According to Weiner (1980), failure that is ascribed to low ability (or to some other stable factor such as task difficulty) decreases the expectation of future success more than failure that is ascribed to lack of effort or bad luck. Yet expectancies are highest when success is attributed to stable causes.

There is an additional reason to distinguish between ability and effort attributions. Although ability and effort are both valued, ability is preferred to effort as a means to success, at least within some cultures. Covington and Omelich (1979) argue that although successes due to sustained effort produce positive affect, one's pride depends on the extent to which the success experience reflects one's ability. Success due to diligence does not necessarily create a sense of competency in the student or arouse expectations for future success. Similarly, Nicholls (1976) found that high ability was valued more than high effort. Nicholls suggests that high ability may be preferred to high effort in an important task because of ability's association with expectations of success and concludes that although high effort is rewarded by socializing agents, the greatest rewards are usually given for "outstanding performance, not outstanding effort" (p. 313). " 'A' for effort" is a consolation prize.

SELECTION OF ANTECEDENT VARIABLES

In our analysis, we sought to identify variables that represented the effects of different experiences, exposure to cultural explanations about performance, and psychological biases. We had data on four variables that fit one or more of these criteria: the mothers' perception of their children's performance, the affective relationship between mother and child, sex of child, and mothers' attributions about their own performance in mathematics.

Mothers' Perception of the Child's Performance

This variable is particularly relevant to the argument of the constructivists, namely, that beliefs are formulated in response to experiences. Parents have many opportunities to gather information about their children's performance in school through report cards, conferences with teachers, and direct conversation (Entwisle & Hayduk, 1978). The mother is made aware of the child's performance compared with his or her peers, and although the interpretation of this information draws on cultural values and norms, the information itself is often a matter of direct experience.

Attribution theorists predict that expected outcomes are ascribed to stable factors such as ability or task difficulty, whereas unexpected outcomes are ascribed to unstable factors such as effort or luck (Weiner, Frieze, Kukla, Reed, Rest, & Rosenblaum, 1971). Thus for children who consistently perform well, success is an expected outcome and may be attributed to ability; failure is unexpected and may be attributed to effort. Similarly, for those who repeatedly perform poorly, failure is an expected outcome and may be seen as the result of lack of ability; success is unexpected and may be seen as the product of effort.

The Affective Relationship Between Mother and Child

The affective relationship between parent and child probably calls up a host of cognitive biases that influence the way parents conceive of their children's achievement. Attributional literature typically treats affect as an outcome of beliefs (Weiner, 1980), but it may also function as an antecedent. Observers who have positive affect for an actor tend to attribute actions they approve of to the actor and actions they disapprove of to external factors (Regan, Straus, & Fazio, 1974). Hence, mothers who have a good affective relationship with their children may credit them for success and blame external or unstable sources for failure. When the relationship is less positive, mothers may view their children's successes as being the result of external or unstable forces such as training at school or effort and their failures as lack of ability.

Sex of Child

The meaning that mothers attach to performance in mathematics of girls and boys comes from both cultural attitudes and observations of sex-related distinctions in performance. Because child gender has been shown to influence parents' values (Russell & Russell, 1982) as well as their normative standards (Barry, Bacon, &

Child, 1957; Rheingold & Cook, 1975), it is reasonable to expect sex-related distinctions in parents' explanations of their children's scholastic performance. Several researchers have reported differences by sex of child in adults' attributions about children's performance in school, although the results are not always consistent (Bar-tal & Guttman, 1981; Holloway & Hess, 1982, Parsons, Adler, & Kaczala, 1982). In one study that reports sex differences (Parsons et al., 1982), boys and girls performed similarly in mathematics, yet their mothers and fathers believed that mathematics was more difficult for girls than boys and that girls had to work harder to do well in this subject. More generally, evidence suggests that females' achievement failures are often explained in terms of lack of ablility (Feather & Simon, 1975) and males' failures are explained in terms of lack of effort or motivation (Dweck, Nelson, & Enna, 1978). Parents may share this bias and explain their sons' successes in mathematics in terms of ability and their daughters' successes in terms of effort. Conversely, they may see lack of effort as a reason for their sons' failures and lack of ability as a source of their daughters' failures.

Self-Attributions About Performance in Mathematics

The attributions that mothers make about their own performance in mathematics may influence the way they perceive their children's performance. Mothers may draw on their own feelings and experiences with a particular subject in forming their explanations about their children's level of performance in that subject. This may be more likely to happen for daughters than for sons.

Each of the variables we have selected for analysis reflects both the constraints of our available data and a theoretical claim to significance. We also have information on socioeconomic status (SES) of families and children's performance on a test of mathematics at grade six. We report data on the relationship between mothers' attributions and SES and children's test scores because of their possible interest to readers, but our attention centers on the four variables discussed.

PLAN OF THE STUDY

Subjects

Sixty-seven white, native-born American mothers, from a range of socioeconomic backgrounds, and their 4-year-old children were recruited through preschools and day-care centers in the San Francisco Bay area.[1] The median

---

[1]This paper was based on a longitudinal study supported by grants from the Spencer Foundation, through the Social Sciences Research Council, and the National Science Foundation, Grant #NSF BNS 91-07542. The project was a collaborative effort between a Japanese team directed by Hiroshi

education of parents was about 2 years of college; roughly a third had not attended college, and about one third had earned a college degree. There were 33 boys and 34 girls in the group of children; all were first-born. About one third of the children came from single-parent homes. A follow-up study was made of 47 of the original 67 families. Forty-nine of the original group were located; 48 agreed to participate. Arrangements could be made to interview all but one family, leaving a sample of 47. Twenty-three of the children were girls; 24 were boys.

The 20 families who dropped out of the study were compared with the 47 families who participated in the follow-up phase of the project on the following variables: SES, mothers' IQ, marital status, mothers' education, children's performance on two age-4 measures of ability, the child's IQ at age 6, and the child's performance on measures of school readiness. There was only one significant difference between the two samples: families that remained in the study were more likely to have both parents residing in the home than those who dropped out. This indicates greater difficulty in locating mothers who had been single parents during the preschool phase of the study.

Procedures

Data were gathered from mothers and children in the initial study when the children were 3 years and 8 months of age and at ages 4, 5, and 6. All data-gathering sessions except maternal interviews were conducted at a research center at Stanford University. A variety of standardized tests and interviews was administered. The follow-up phase was conducted when the children were in sixth grade. Mothers and children were separately interviewed at that time, and children were administered tests of scholastic aptitude.

Instruments

Preschool Phase

Socioeconomic Status.   Estimates of SES were made using a modified Hollingshead scale, with occupation and education of father and education of mother equally weighted.

Azuma at the University of Tokyo and an American group led by Robert Hess at Stanford University. This paper reports data from the American sample. W. Patrick Dickson served as Associate Director of the preschool phase of the study. Other staff members during the initial phase were Gary G. Price, Mary Conroy, Deborah J. Leong, and Eleanor B. Worden. Susan Holloway and Teresa McDevitt helped direct the follow-up phase of the project. Other participants included Anne Wenegrat, Satomi Sato, and Kathryn Dunton. We gratefully acknowledge suggestions made by Kathryn Dunton and statistical advice given by Dr. David Rogosa.

Mothers' Estimate of Children's Kindergarten Performance.   As part of an interview conducted when the children were age 6, mothers were asked to evaluate how well their children were doing in kindergarten. A 5-point scale was used, ranging from "much below average" to "much above average."

Age 5–6 School Readiness.   At ages 5 and 6, several tests of school-relevant skills were administered. At age 5, separate composites were formed for verbal and number-oriented items. The verbal composite included two items: (a) letter recognition, using 22 letters of the alphabet, scored from 0–22; and (b) the child's ability to write his or her own name, scored 0–4. The number composite included (a) the ability to count, in order, groups of 4, 7, 5, 13, and 11 buttons, scored from 0–5; (b) number recognition, using flashcards with numbers 2, 6, 3, 14, 21, scored from 0–6; and (c) questions that required the child to show knowledge of the concepts *half, more, as many,* and *fewer* and perform a simple addition task (adding one cookie to a group of five), each scored one pont for a range of 0–5. At age 6, the school readiness measure was a composite of two subtests of the Metropolitan Readiness Test (Hildreth, Griffiths, & McGauvran, 1964): a number scale that used 26 items and a letter recognition scale that used 16 letters. Scores for ages 5 and 6 were combined within age, using standard scores for the original sample. A total readiness score was an equally weighted composite of scores at the two age levels. The verbal composites and number composites within and between the two age levels were significantly intercorrelated (the range was $r = .41$ to $r = .65$, with a median coefficient of .52).

Affective Relationship.   This measure was a rating, from transcripts and videotapes, of the interaction between mother and child based on (a) their exchange in two interaction tasks, a block-sorting session and an unstructured 10-minute interaction that preceded it; (b) mothers' responses to questions about hypothetical disciplinary situations (e.g., "What would you say if your child hit another child with a block?"), and (c) more general features of an interview that asked about mothers' aspirations for the child, things she was doing to prepare the child for school, goals for the child's development, etc. (Cronbach's alpha = .83) (see Estrada, Arsenio, Hess, & Holloway, 1985). A high score on this composite indicates positive affect.

Follow-up Phase

Mothers' Estimates of Children's Grade-Six Mathematics Performance.   As a part of the maternal interview at the follow-up phase, mothers were asked to estimate how well their children performed in mathematics at grades 3, 4, and 6. Mothers were asked to indicate the child's level of performance on a 6-point scale ranging from "not doing as well as most" to "doing the very best in the class." Estimates at the three grade levels were intercorrelated (for grade 3 with grade 4, $r = .82$ ($p < .001$); for grade 3 with grade 6, $r = .42$ ($p < .01$); for grade 4 with 6, $r = .59$ ($p < .001$). A composite was formed of children's estimated performance at the three grade levels to provide a more stable measure of mothers' perceptions.

Mothers' Attributions About their Children's Mathematics Performance. Each mother was asked to explain her child's performance from two perspectives: why the child was doing as well as he or she was and why he or she was not doing even better. These questions were asked in reference to the mother's report of the child's performance in the sixth grade, using the aforementioned 6-point scale. Regarding why the child did as well as he or she did, the interviewer, noting the performance rating the mother had given, said, "You have indicated that your child is doing (better than some/better than many/better than most, of the other children in the class. Why do you think he/she is doing that well?" The mother was then shown five cards, each labeled with an attributional phrase. The attributions were selected on the basis of previous research (Holloway & Hess, 1982) and of appropriateness for use in Japan as well as the United States. The following attributional phrases were used:

My child has a natural ability for math.
My child tries hard in math.
My child has had good training in school.
My child has had good training at home.
My child has been lucky in math.

The mother was then asked to distribute 10 plastic chips across the five cards to indicate the importance of each reason in explaining her child's relatively successful performance. This procedure resulted in five attribution variables with possible ranges of 0 to 10.

An analogous procedure was used for questions about why the child was not doing better. The interviewer said, "You have indicated that your child wasn't at the (very) top of the class. Why do you think he/she isn't doing (even) better in math?" The attributional phrases were worded to reflect low performance (e.g., "My child does not try hard in math.").

The request to limit the number of chips to a total of 10 puts constraints on the range of scores for individual attributional options. Under this procedure, allocating chips to one source necessarily affects the number of chips available for allocation to other sources and thus an artifact from this constraint may be built into the data. Because our focus in this chapter is on ability and effort attributions, we were concerned that this procedure might also produce severe constraints on the combined value of ability and effort attributions. If this combined value were the same for all mothers, no additional information would be obtained by examining both of the attributions, because when the value of one attribution was set, the other would also be known. (The consequence of this for correlations would be that $r_{y,\ ability}$ = negative $r_{y,\ effort}$ for any measure y.)

In order to examine this possibility, we created additive composites of ability and effort attributions (separately for the two conditions, why children did as well as they did and why they did not do better) and examined the resulting distributions of scores for the 47 mother–child pairs. We found a considerable range and distribution among the scores. The range for why children did as well as they did was 1 to 8; for why they did not do better, it was 1 to 10. Both also showed nearly uniform distributions. This indicates that the constraint on ability and effort was negligible and correlations with other variables should not be influenced by the structure of data collection.

Mothers' Self-Attributions.   Mothers were also asked to make attributions about their own performance in mathematics when they were students in elementary school. Categories and procedures were identical to those used for making attributions about their children's performance, except for appropriate changes in phrasing.

Children's Mathematics Performance.   Children's sixth-grade mathematics performance was assessed by the Mathematics Concepts subtest of the Iowa Tests of Basic Skills (ITBS) (Hieronymus, Lindquist, & Hoover, 1978).

RESULTS

The results are organized into three sections. First, descriptive information is provided about the explanations that mothers offered for their children's performance in mathematics and for their own past school performance in mathematics. Second, the relationships between mothers' beliefs and antecedent variables, taken individually, are examined. Finally, antecedent variables as groups are examined to document the amount of variance accounted for by multiple predictors and to describe processes through which these sources exert their influence.

Mothers' Explanations for Their Children's and Their Own Mathematics Performance

Before attempting to trace the antecedents of mothers' beliefs about children's performance in mathematics, we describe the causes that mothers of our research group believed determined the level of their children's performance. Recall that mothers were asked to explain why the child did as well as he or she did and why the child did not do better. Mothers' responses differed somewhat to these two questions (Table 4.1). They gave most credit for their children's successes in

TABLE 4.1
Means and Standard Deviations for Mothers' Causal Explanations
About Their Children's and Their Own Mathematics Performance

Explanations	Attributions About Children		Attributions About Selves	
	Why They Did as Well as They Did	Why They Did Not Do Better	Why They Did as Well as They Did	Why They Did Not Do Better
Ability				
M	2.30	2.62	2.02	3.28
SD	1.97	2.66	2.31	2.93
Effort				
M	2.70	3.08	2.81	2.81
SD	1.40	2.56	1.86	3.11
School Training				
M	2.96	2.26	2.98	1.98
SD	1.18	2.24	1.80	1.86
Home Training				
M	1.85	1.66	1.47	1.66
SD	1.28	1.52	1.38	1.48
Luck				
M	0.13	0.38	0.72	0.28
SD	0.40	1.05	1.44	0.58

mathematics to an external source—the teacher. This belief in the role of the teacher may reflect a view of mathematics as a technical subject that requires formal instruction for mastery. Mothers gave slightly less emphasis to the children's effort, an internal source over which they and the children presumably exercise some control. Less emphasis was given to ability and to training at home. Virtually no importance was assigned to luck.

In response to the question, "Why is (Name) not doing better?" mothers put more responsibility on their children. Lack of effort was given most weight, with lack of ability second. The school was third in importance, with training at home receiving relatively little weight. It is of interest, perhaps, that the school was given credit for children's achievements more than it was blamed as a reason why they did not do better.

As a group, mothers provided somewhat similar explanations about their own performance in mathematics when they were students. They explained their own relative successes in much the same way as they did for their children's successes: training at school, effort, and ability were the most prevalent explanations. However, the primary reason given for "not doing better" was lack of ability, not lack of effort as for their children. Lack of effort and lack of training at school received moderate weightings. The emphasis on lack of ability for their own relatively low performance may represent a general tendency to underrate females' mathematics aptitude, a bias shared by men and women alike (Parsons et al., 1982). As is discussed later, these mothers also provided different explanations for their sons' and daughters' performance.

In examining the antecedents of mothers' beliefs, we have chosen to focus on attributions to ability and effort. Our major concern is with the ways that mothers view their children and draw on internal sources to explain relative success and failure.

Associations of Mothers' Beliefs with Individual Antecedents

Children's Achievement as a Source of Maternal Attributions. Our findings suggest that measures of children's early and later achievement and mothers' reports of this achievement are related to mothers' explanations (Table 4.2). Mothers of children with high performance believed that their children did relatively well because they had ability and did not do better because they lacked effort. Mothers of children with low performance in school believed that their children did as well as they did because of effort and failed because of lack of ability.

TABLE 4.2
Pearson Product-Moment Correlations Between Mothers' Causal
Explanations and Children's Achievement Indicators

	Children's Achievement Indicators	
	Mothers' *Estimates* *of Performance*	*Children's* *Achievement* *Scores*
Preschool	Kindergarten Estimate	School-Readiness Score
Ability: Why They Did As Well As They Did	.31*	.50***
Effort: Why They Did As Well As They Did	−.14	−.34*
Ability: Why They Did Not Do Better	−.30*	−.37**
Effort: Why They Did Not Do Better	.28*	.32*
Follow-up	Grades 3, 4, & 6 Estimate	Mathematics Score
Ability: Why They Did As Well As They Did	.49***	.52***
Effort: Why They Did As Well As They Did	−.50***	−.43**
Ability: Why They Did Not Do Better	−.46**	−.40**
Effort: Why They Did Not Do Better	.26*	.23

$*p < .05$
$**p < .01$
$***p < .001$

A question arises as to whether performance measures and estimates gathered at the preschool phase of the study predict mothers' attributions as well as those collected at the follow-up phase. The magnitude of the correlations for the performance measures and estimates were compared for the two time periods. One difference was significant: compared with the mothers' estimates of children's performance at kindergarten, the mothers' reports of children's performance at follow-up yielded a significantly higher correlation with effort attributions for doing well [$t(44) = 2.40, p < .05$]. In general, then, both preschool and follow-up measures of performance are important predictors of mothers' explanations.

In order to examine whether the measures of achievement from the two age periods both exerted effects on mothers' explanations, we examined the conjoint effects of these measures on mothers' attributions to ability for why children did as well as they did. In the first analysis, median splits were computed on mothers' estimate of children's performance at kindergarten and the composite of perceptions for grades 3, 4, and 6, yielding four groups (high/high, low/low, high/low, and low/high). Means were computed for each group on attributions to ability for why children did as well as they did (Table 4.3). A 2 × 2 analysis of variance was conducted using the "experimental design method" for unequal cell frequencies (Overall & Spiegel, 1969). The analysis indicated that mothers gave more credit to ability for children who were perceived as achieving at a high level at the follow-up phase than those perceived as achieving at a low level [$F(1,43) = 10.08, p = < .01$]. Mothers did not give more credit to those who

TABLE 4.3
Mothers' Attributions to Ability
for Why Children Did as Well as They Did:
Comparisons of Groups Formed
by Median Splits on Mothers' Perceptions
of Kindergarten Performance
and Grades 3, 4, and 6 Performance
(Means and Standard Deviations)

	Kindergarten Estimate	
	Low	High
Grades 3, 4, & 6 Estimate		
Low		
M	1.35	1.75
SD	1.50	1.71
High		
M	3.25	3.18
SD	1.96	2.14

TABLE 4.4
Mothers' Attributions to Ability
for Why Children Did as Well as They Did:
Comparison of Groups Formed
by Median Splits on Age 5/6 and Age 12
Achievement Measures
(Means and Standard Deviations)

	Age 5/6 *School Readiness*	
	Low	*High*
Age 12 Achievement		
Low		
M	1.18	2.00
SD	1.67	1.90
High		
M	2.00	3.56
SD	1.26	1.82

were perceived as performing well at the kindergarten phase, and there was no interaction effect. This suggests that as mothers formulate their beliefs, they are more attentive to their perception of children's recent performance than to memories of past performance.

However, a second analysis indicated that performance from both time periods influenced their beliefs. This analysis was conducted using the two achievement scores as independent variables. Median splits were computed on children's age 5–6 school readiness scores and their age 12 mathematics scores, yielding four groups (high/high, low/low, high/low, and low/high). For each group, means were computed on mothers' attributions to ability for why children did as well as they did (Table 4.4). Mothers gave more weight to ability for children who scored highly at age 12 than those who scored relatively poorly at this age [$F(1,43) = 4.30, p < .05$]. Mothers also gave more weight to ability for children who scored highly at age 5–6 than those who scored relatively poorly at this age [$F(1,43) = 4.30, p < .05$]. The interaction effect was not significant.

This is thus partial support for the contention that mothers used information from both ages when forming their beliefs about the origins of children's performance. Thus, even if children performed at a given level at age 12, mothers appeared to be affected by their knowledge that their children had performed at a different level at an earlier age. Although the correlations between children's early performance and mothers' explanations can be interpreted as stemming from the variance shared between these early performance measures and the follow-up performance measures, the finding of independent effects of the two achievement measures in the present analysis suggests that children's performances over time may have cumulative effects on mothers' beliefs.

Affect Between Mother and Child as a Source of Explanations.   The warmth of the relationship between mothers and children during the preschool phase of the study was associated with the explanations that mothers offered for their children's mathematical performance. Mothers who had positive affective relationships with their children credited them with ability as a reason for doing well and put less blame on lack of ability for not doing better. For the relative success condition, mothers' affective relationship was positively related to ability attributions ($r = .30, p < .05$) and negatively related to effort attributions ($r = -.29, p < .05$). For relatively low performance, affect was negatively related to attributions to lack of ability ($r = -.41, p < .01$) but not related to attributions to lack of effort ($r = .17, p > .05$).

Effect of Sex of Child on Mothers' Explanations for Children's Performance.   In general, mothers offered different explanations for why boys and girls did as well as they did and why they did not do better (Table 4.5). Mothers of boys used ability as a reason for why children did as well as they did more than mothers of girls [$t(45) = 2.85, p < .01$]; mothers of girls felt effort was a stronger determinant than mothers of boys [$t(45) = -2.14, p < .05$]. There was a marginally significant tendency for mothers of girls to use ability more as a reason for why children did not do better than mothers of boys [$t(45) = -1.90, p < .07$]. Mothers of boys used effort as an explanation for relatively low performance more than mothers of girls [$t(45) = 2.52, p < .05$].

TABLE 4.5
Attributions Given by Mothers of Boys and Mothers of Girls
for Children's Performance in Mathematics
(Means and Standard Deviations)

	Sex of Child				
	Boys		Girls		
Explanations	Mean	S.D.	Mean	S.D.	t value
Why They Did as Well as They Did					
Ability	3.04	2.01	1.52	1.62	2.85**
Effort	2.29	1.55	3.13	1.10	−2.14*
Why They Did Not Do Better					
Ability	1.92	2.62	3.35	2.55	−1.90
Effort	3.96	3.04	2.17	1.53	2.52*

*p < .05
**p < .01

This pattern fits the view that boys have ability but do not always live up to their potential. In the interviews, mothers often suggested that girls were more conscientious than boys. If girls are viewed as trying hard, it makes sense that lack of ability is an important variable in their failure to do better. For boys, there seems to be less assurance that they are really giving effort to the task; effort thus becomes salient for failure to do better. An alternative possibility is that mothers tend to perceive their daughters as being less able than do mothers of sons; consequently, they deemphasize ability as a reason for relative success and focus on effort. Also consonant with this view is lack of ability as a reason girls do not do better. Boys have all the skills they need, according to this perspective; their failure must be due to lack of effort.

Because mothers' attributions for boys are similar to those for children of relatively high performance and attributions for girls to those for children of relatively low performance, it may be that mothers are simply responding to different levels of achievement by boys and girls. This explanation is plausible only if boys in our research group actually achieved, and were perceived to have achieved, at a higher level than girls. In order to examine this possibility, we computed a series of one-tailed t-tests between boys and girls on relevant measures. There were no significant differences between the two groups on a composite of mothers' perceptions of children's mathematics performance in school for grades 3, 4, and 6 [$t(45) = 1.35, p > .05$] or on mothers' perceptions of children's mathematics performance during sixth grade alone [$t(45) = 1.13, p > .05$], but boys did do better than girls on the Mathematics Concepts subtest of the Iowa Tests of Basic Skills [$t(45) = 1.84, p < .05$].

These results suggest that at grade 6 the boys are developing superior competence in mathematics. Yet mothers of boys and mothers of girls did not rate their children's level of mathematics performance in school in different ways. Hence, we cannot conclude that the discrepant explanations offered for boys' and girls' performance are the result of mothers' different perceptions of their sons' and daughters' performance in school.

Mothers' Self-Attributions as Sources of Explanations for Their Children's Performance. The causal explanations that our group of mothers gave for their children's performance in mathematics probably came in part from their views about their own past experiences in mathematics.[2] To examine this possibility, we correlated mothers' self-attributions with the attributions made about children. Since mothers may project their own experience more onto daughters

---

[2]Direction of effects is an issue here because mothers were asked about their children before they were asked about their own performance in mathematics. The order in which the questions were asked may have influenced the association between mothers' views of their own experience and their beliefs about their children's performance.

TABLE 4.6
Pearson Product-Moment Correlations
Between Mothers' Self- and Child-Attributions
Separately by Sex of Child

	Sex of Child	
Explanation	Boys	Girls
Why They Did as Well as They Did		
Ability	.00	.02
Effort	−.36*	−.42*
Why They Did Not Do Better		
Ability	.14	.65***
Effort	.31	−.11

*p < .05
**p < .01
***p < .001

rather than sons, we computed correlations separately by sex of child (Table 4.6).

There are some similarities by sex in the patterns of correlations, yet there are also several apparent differences. In general, the correlations did not appear to be substantially higher for girls than boys. We were especially struck, though, by the difference between the correlations for relative-failure ability attributions for boys and girls ($r = .14$ and $r = .65$, respectively). Mothers of girls who felt that their own relatively low performance in mathematics was due to lack of ability projected this outlook onto their children, whereas mothers of boys did not. These findings provide valuable clues about the nature of mothers who see lack of ability as putting a ceiling on their own mathematics performance; of those who do, many tend to hold the same view about their daughters but not their sons.

Socioeconomic Status as a Predictor of Mothers' Explanations. We found little research or theory that would help predict what the association between socioeconomic status and maternal attributions would be. For descriptive purposes, we included SES in order to see if this global measure of family living conditions was associated with mothers' beliefs.

SES was correlated with the explanations mothers offered for why children did as well as they did, but not with explanations for why children did not do better. Mothers from high SES backgrounds placed more weight on ability as a reason for relative success ($r = .34$, $p < .01$); mothers from lower SES backgrounds put more emphasis on effort ($r = -.37$, $p < .01$). This relationship is difficult to interpret and may have arisen because of some correlate of SES, such as child achievement. Because SES may function as a surrogate variable for more specific processes and influences, we wanted to see if it added any predictive value over and above the effects of the variables already discussed. To examine this possibility, we tested full multiple regression models that included SES against reduced models that did not (Chatterjee & Price, 1977). The reduced models included the composite of mothers' perception of children's grade 3, 4, and 6 performance, the affective composite, mothers' self-attributions (in each case we selected the mother attribution comparable with the child attribution taken as the dependent variable), and child gender (as an indicator or "dummy" variable). SES was then included to compute the full models.

In only one of the four regressions did SES add any predictive power once the effects of the other variables were taken into account. When ability explanations for why children did as well as they did were examined, the five-predictor model that included SES provided a better acount of the data than the four-predictor model [$F(1,41) = 5.69$, $p < .05$]. For the other three explanations, the five-predictor models did not provide better accounts of the data (for relative-success effort, $F(1,41) = 2.82$, $p > .05$; for relative-failure ability, $F(1,41) = 0.39$, $p > .05$; for relative-failure effort, $F(1,41) = 0.38$, $p > .05$). These regression results suggest that SES does not provide much additional predictive value beyond that offered by more specific, concrete variables.

Multiple Antecedents of Mothers' Beliefs

So far we have identified several variables that were associated with the explanations mothers gave for their children's performance in mathematics. It is not obvious how these sources were related to one another and whether their contributions were overlapping or cumulative. We examined these additional questions through regression analysis. Two related approaches were taken. First, we examined how much of the variance in mothers' explanations could be accounted for by the variables taken together. Second, we performed a path analysis to examine relationships among predictor variables.

Predictive Power of Antecedent Variables. Our findings indicate that mothers' beliefs can be predicted with a fair degree of accuracy when multiple predictors are taken into account. Four predictive variables were examined in multiple regression analyses: the affective relationship, mothers' estimates of children's kindergarten and later mathematics performance, and mothers' self-attributions selected in each analysis to match the child attribution serving as the dependent variable. These four sources represent potentially independent and important influences on mothers' beliefs.

Both ability and effort attributions for why children did as well as they did were well predicted by the data. For ability attributions, 27% of the variance was accounted for by the four predictors [$R^2 = .27$, $F(4,42) = 3.98$, $p < .01$;

Adjusted $R = .20$]. An even higher prediction was obtained for effort attributions: 39% of the variance was explained [$R^2 = .39$, $F(4,42) = 6.62$, $p < .001$; adjusted $R^2 = .33$].

Ability but not effort attributions for why children did not do better were predicted by the data. For lack of ability attributions, 34% of the variance was accounted for by the data [$R^2 = .34$, $F(4,42) = 5.51$, $p < .01$; adjusted $R^2 = .28$]. Mothers' attributions to lack of effort were not explained by the data [$R^2 = .12$, $F(4,42) = 1.43$, $p > .05$; adjusted $R^2 = .04$]. With some assurance, then, we can predict three out of four of the attributions.

Two additional questions can be addressed with regression analyses. First, does information from the preschool phase help us to develop a better prediction than is given by the follow-up variables alone? Analyses comparing full and reduced models indicated that the two preschool variables (the affective relationship and mothers' kindergarten estimate) when examined together did not offer additional predictive value after the two follow-up variables (mothers' perceptions of children's school performance and self-attributions) were included. For all four of the attributions, the follow-up variables explained the variation as adequately as the full set of predictor variables (for relative-success ability, $F(2,42) = 0.77$, $p > .05$; for relative-success effort, $F(2,42) = 0.90$, $p > .05$; for relative-failure ability, $F(2,42) = 1.23$, $p > .05$; for relative-failure effort, $F(2,42) = 0.94$, $p > .05$).

Second, do the affective relationship and mothers' self-attributions—sources not directly representing child performance—add predictive value over and above mothers' perceptions of performance? For two of the attributions, the affective relationship and mothers' self-attributions did increase the prediction beyond the contributions of mothers' two performance estimates. For attributions to effort for why children did as well as they did and attributions to ability for why they did not do better, the four predictors provided a better model than the two-predictor model consisting only of mothers performance estimates [for relative-success effort, $F(2,42) = 4.75$ $p < .05$; for relative-failure ability, $F(2,42) = 3.58$, $p < .05$]. For the other two attributions, relative-success ability and relative-failure effort, the two-predictor set provided a better model [for relative-success ability, $F(2,42) = 0.46$, $p > .05$; for relative-failure effort, $F(2,42) = 0.32$, $p > .05$].

The regression results suggest that we can predict mothers' beliefs with a fair degree of accuracy from a limited set of preschool and concurrent variables. Generally, the preschool variables did not add much once the follow-up variables were taken into account. However, the affective relationship and mothers' self-attributions did add predictive value to the ability estimates. Mothers' perceptions of their children's ability played a foundational role in the formation of these mothers' beliefs, but other less objective sources also entered into the process.

Relationship Among Predictive Variables and Mothers Beliefs.   In developing a path model, we began with the idea that the beliefs and feelings mothers have for their children are closely tied to children's performance. Throughout the child's development, mothers react to observations of performance with both cognitive and affective responses. These beliefs and feelings, in turn, shape their attributions about their children's performance. Mothers' beliefs and feelings about themselves also enter into construction of beliefs about their children. In sum, we formulated our path model with the conception that children's performance and mothers' belief systems are interrelated; together, they determine mothers' causal explanations about children's performance.

Path analysis requires the development of an explicit model of causal connections among variables. We formulated a model (Fig. 4.1) by incorporating five variables that might have direct or indirect effects on mothers' attributions: (a) children's school-readiness scores taken at age 5–6; (b) children's mathematics achievement at age 12; (c) the affective relationship between mothers and children assessed from ratings of preschool data; (d) mothers' perceptions of their children's grade 3, 4, and 6 mathematics performance; and (e) mothers' self-attributions to lack of ability for their own relatively low performance in mathematics. Mothers' attributions to lack of ability for why children did not do better

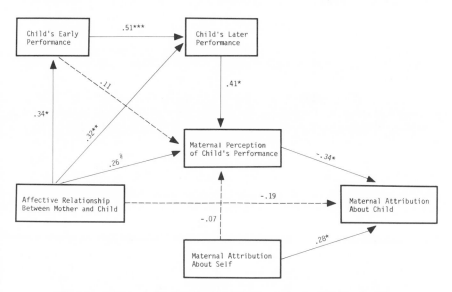

FIG. 4.1.   Path Analysis of Mothers' Attributions to Lack of Ability for Why Children Did Not Do Better in Mathematics. Standardized partial regression coefficients are shown on paths. Significant paths are indicated by solid lines; nonsignificant paths are indicated by broken lines. For significance levels, #p < .08, *p < .05, **p < .01, ***p < .001.

was selected as the dependent variable. This particular attributional option was selected for its theoretical interest and the potential impact it may have on mother's thought and behavior. If they perceive lack of ability as the reason why their children do not do better, mothers may be pessimistic about their children's capacity to improve their performance. They may make this perception known to their children and withhold encouragement.

We utilized procedures described by Heise (1969a, 1969b) that assume linearity among variables and the absence of interactions among predictors. The potential paths between children's early performance and later performance and mothers' attributions for their children's achievement were not included because we assumed that the effects of children's performance are mediated by mothers' perceptions.

Overall, the path analysis indicates two significant paths to mothers' attributions to lack of ability for children's relatively low performance: a path between mothers' perceptions of children's performance and a path from mothers' self-attributions. Maternal self-attribution is a solitary contributor to attributions about the child but mothers' perceptions of performance may be affected by two indirect sources: one is the child's performance at the preschool and follow-up phases; the other is the affective relationship between mother and child during the preschool years (though the path coefficient for the affective relationship was only marginally significant).

It is noteworthy that the affective relationship did not have a statistically significant direct path. The affective relationship is correlated with mothers' explanations, but here it seems to exert its primary influence through children's performance and mothers' perceptions of performance. Had a measure of the affective relationship been taken at the follow-up phase, we might have found a stronger and more direct association between affect and mothers' attributions.

The goodness-of-fit test we employed to test our model is based on a comparison of the adequacy of a reduced model (with some paths deleted) against a fully recursive model (with all paths included; Specht, 1975). This procedure utilizes a composite of the squared multiple correlation coefficient in a statistical test and has been shown to be commensurate with other goodness-of-fit tests.

Based on the results of this test, we found that we needed to include several non-significant paths and paths that we had initially hoped to exclude on theoretical grounds, namely, the paths between the child's early performance and mothers' perception of children's school performance, the affective relationship and mothers' attributions about children's performance, and mothers' attributions about their own performance and their perceptions of the children's performance. All of these paths produced non-significant standardized regression coefficients. However, their inclusion did enhance the model's capacity to represent the structure of the data.

Generally, the path analysis helps to indicate the relative roles of different sources of influence on maternal attributions and supports the idea that contemporary attributions are rooted in the history of the mother and child. We should point out, however, that had the paths been computed separately for mothers of sons and mothers of daughters, the results might have been different.

SUMMARY AND DISCUSSION

All of the four major sources we examined appeared to contribute to the causal explanations that mothers gave for their children's performance in mathematics. As they formulate their causal explanations, mothers attend to the children's level of performance, their affective relationship with the children, perceptions of their own past mathematics performance, and sex of child.

The child's level of achievement was a major contributor to the explanations that mothers offered for why their children did as well as they did and why they did not do better. Whether we used the mothers' perceptions or test scores, preschool data or follow-up data, achievement measures were associated with maternal attributions. In response to the question about why children did as well as they did, higher performance by children led the mothers to give more credit to ability and less to effort. This may mean that their experience with children led mothers to establish a base line of expectations for level of achievement. When this was high, mothers believed that ability was more involved than when it was low; the converse was true for effort. It is as if mothers doubted that continued high performance came from effort, whereas lack of effort could be understood more easily as the cause of consistently low performance. In response to the question about why children did not do better, mothers of children who were at the upper level of achievement tended to see lack of effort, not lack of ability, as a reasonable explanation. Mothers of children at the lower ranges of performance believed that lack of ability was responsible.

These responses given by the mothers are not merely reports of observations; there is no compelling reason why ability or lack of ability, rather than effort, is a more plausible explanation for a high-achieving child than for one who does less well. Attributional research suggests that repeated successes are attributed to the stable cause of ability, yet the reasons for this inference need to be examined further. This pattern may arise at least in part out of cultural interpretations, making cultural comparisons on the antecedents of mothers' beliefs worthwhile. Preliminary analyses of the Japanese data in our study indicated that children's achievement levels did not predict mothers' causal explanations.

Psychological states appeared to play a role. Mothers who had a poor affective relationship with their children during the preschool years tended to believe that their children's relatively poor performance arose from lack of ability. Lack of ability is an internal, stable source over which the mothers and children have little control; mothers who called on this explanation may have been disassociating themselves from their children's failures. By doing so, they protected themselves and in a sense blamed their children. In the path analysis, the impact of affect appeared to be indirect, through an influence on the children's actual performance and mothers' perceptions of performance. This measure of the affective relationship between mothers and children was taken from preschool data. A stronger or more direct effect might have emerged if information about the current relationship had been available. In any case, the indication that affect has some effect on mothers' explanations suggests that the role of internal psychological states deserves more careful analysis in the study of parental beliefs.

Mothers' recollection of their own experience in mathematics was associated with their beliefs about their children, possibly through some sort of projection of their own experience. They did not project consistetly more often onto daughters than onto their sons, but self-attributions seemed to have considerable impact for girls where relatively low performance was involved. Mothers also used somewhat different sources to explain performance levels of boys and girls. Not only were boys given credit for ability when they did well, but boys' relatively low performance was blamed on lack of effort. Girls' relatively low performance was ascribed to lack of ability.

These results indicate that mothers drew from several different sources in forming attributions about their children. The constructivism and cultural transmission arguments are supported by the connection between mothers' causal explanations and perceptions of their children's performance and gender. The relationship between affect and explanations seems to support the ego-protective hypothesis and presence of cognitive biases; the connection between mothers' self-attributions and those offered for their children bolsters the notion that we project onto others our explanations for our own successes and failure. These findings, when taken together, indicate that mothers are eclectic in the sources they attend to as they construct beliefs. They also give us additional confidence in the predictability and meaningfulness of mothers' beliefs.

REFERENCES

Barry, H., Bacon, M. K., & Child, I. L. (1957). A cross-cultural survey of some sex differences in socialization. *Journal of Abnormal and Social Psychology, 55*, 327–332.

Bar-tal, D., & Guttman, J. (1981). A comparison of teachers', pupils', and parents' attributions regarding pupils' academic achievements. *British Journal of Educational Psychology, 51*, 301–311.

Bronfenbrenner, U. (1958). Socialization and social class through time and space. In E. E. Maccoby, T. M. Newcomb, E. L. Hartley (Eds.), *Readings in social psychology* (pp. 406–425). New York: Holt, Rinehart, & Winston.

Chatterjee, S., & Price, B. (1977). *Regression analysis by example.* New York: Wiley.

Clarke-Stewart, K. A. (1978). Popular primers for parents. *American Psychologist, 33*, 359–369.

Covington, M. V., & Omelich, C. L. (1979). It's best to be able and virtuous too: Student and teacher evaluative responses to successful effort. *Journal of Educational Psychology, 71*, 688–700.

Dix, T. H., & Grusec, J. E. (1985). Parent attribution processes in the socialization of children. In I. E. Sigel (Ed.), *Parental belief systems* (pp. 201–233). Hillsdale, NJ: Lawrence Erlbaum Associates.

Dweck, C. S., Davidson, W., Nelson, S., & Enna, B. (1978). Sex differences in learned helplessness: II. The contingencies of evaluative feedback in the classroom and III. An experimental analysis. *Developmental Psychology, 14,* 268–276.

Entwisle, D. R., & Hayduk, L. A. (1978). *Too great expectations: The academic outlook of young children.* Baltimore: The Johns Hopkins University Press.

Estrada, P., & Arsenio, W., Hess, R. D., & Holloway, S. D. (1985). *Affective quality of the mother-child relationship: Longitudinal consequences for children's school relevant cognitive functioning.* Manuscript submitted for publication.

Feather, N. T., & Simon, J. G. (1975). Reactions to male and female success and failure in sexlinked occupations: Impressions of personality, causal attributions, and perceived likelihood of different consequences. *Journal of Personality and Social Psychology, 31,* 20–31.

Goodnow, J. J. (1984). Parents' ideas about parenting and development. In M. E. Lamb, A. L. Brown, & B. Rogoff (Eds.), *Advances in developmental psychology* (pp. 193–242). Hillsdale, NJ: Lawrence Erlbaum Associates.

Greenwald, A. G. (1980). The totalitarian ego: Fabrication and revision of personal history. *American Psychologist, 35,* 603–618.

Heise, D. R. (1969a). Separating reliability and stability in test-retest correlation. *American Sociological Review, 34,* 93–101.

Heise, D. R. (1969b). Problems in path analysis and causal inference. In E. F. Borgatta & G. W. Bohrnstedt (Eds.), *Sociological methodology* (pp. 38–73). San Francisco: Jossey-Bass.

Hieronymus, A. N., Lindquist, E. F., & Hoover, H. D. (1978). *The Iowa Tests of Basic Skills.* Boston: Houghton-Mifflin.

Hildreth, G. H., Griffiths, N. L., & McGauvran, M. E. (1964). *Metropolitan readiness tests.* New York: Harcourt, Brace & World.

Holloway, S. D., & Hess, R. D. (1982). Causal explanations for school performance: Contrasts between mothers and children. *Journal of Applied Developmental Psychology, 3,* 319–327.

Holloway, S. D., Hess, R. D., Azuma, H., & Kashiwagi, K. (in press). Causal attributions by Japanese and American mothers and children about performance in mathematics. *International Journal of Psychology.*

Jones, E. E., & Nisbett, R. E. (1971). *The actor and the observer: Divergent perceptions of the causes of behavior.* Morristown, NJ: General Learning Press.

Kelly, G. A. (1955). *The psychology of personal constructs.* New York: Norton.

Kelly, G. A. (1963). *A theory of personality.* New York: Norton.

Marjoribanks, K. (1980). *Ethnic families and children's achievements.* Sydney, Australia: George Allen & Unwin.

McGillicuddy-DeLisi, A. V. (1980). The role of parental beliefs in the family as a system of mutual influences. *Family Relations, 29,* 317–323.

McGillicuddy-DeLisi, A. V., Sigel, I. E., & Johnson, J. E. (1979). The family as a system of mutual influences: Parental beliefs, distancing behaviors, and children's representational thinking. In M. Lewis & L. A. Rosenblum (Eds.), *The child and its family* (pp. 91–106). New York: Plenum.

Nicholls, J. (1976). Effort is virtuous, but it's better to have ability: Evaluative responses to effort and ability. *Journal of Research in Personality, 10,* 306–315.

Overall, J. E., & Spiegel, D. K. (1969). Concerning least squares analysis of experimental data. *Psychological Bulletin, 72,* 311–322.

Parsons, J. E., Adler, T. F., & Kaczala, C. M. (1982). Socialization of achievement attitudes and beliefs: Parental influences. *Child Development, 53,* 310–321.

Regan, D. T., Straus, E., & Fazio, R. (1974). Liking and the attribution process. *Journal of Experimental Social Psychology, 10,* 385–397.

Rheingold, H. C., & Cook, K. V. (1975). The content of boys' and girls' rooms as an index of parents' behavior. *Child Development, 46,* 459–463.

Russell, A., & Russell, G. (1982). Mother, father and child beliefs about child development. *Journal of Psychology, 110,* 297–306.

Specht, D. A. (1975). On the evaluation of causal models. *Social Science Research, 4,* 113–133.

Stolz, L. M. (1967). *Influences on parent behavior.* Stanford, CA: Stanford University Press.

Weiner, B. (1980). *Human motivation.* New York: Holt, Rinehart, & Winston.

Weiner, B., Frieze, I., Kukla, A., Reed, L., Rest, S., & Rosenblaum, R. M. (1971). *Perceiving the causes of success and failure.* Morristown, NJ: General Learning Press.

Whiting, B. B. (1974). Folk wisdom and child rearing. *Merrill-Palmer Quarterly, 20,* 9–19.

5 Prenatal Expectations, Postnatal Experiences, and the Transition to Parenthood

Jay Belsky
Mary J. Ward,
Michael Rovine
The Pennsylvania State University

It is widely recognized that a couple's first pregnancy and the arrival of a first child represents a major life transition. It is a period of life involving stress and requiring significant alteration in customary life patterns (Holmes & Rahe, 1967; Hultsch & Plemons, 1979), including both role transition and status change (Antonovsky & Kats, 1967; Myers, Lindenthal, Pepper, & Ostrander, 1972). Consider here the fact that the life event defined by the transition to parenthood involves commitment to bear and raise a child, high levels of physical and psychological investment associated with pregnancy and delivery, and the real and symbolic changes that accompany the addition of a small, relatively help-less, and extremely demanding new member to the family unit. There are also the real changes that undoubtedly occur in day-to-day living and require adjust-ment. From everyone's perspective, then, be they mother, father, husband, wife, or infant, the process of adding a new member to the family represents an event of some magnitude.

It is family sociologists such as Russell (1974) who have paid the most attention to the transition to parenthood on the assumption that, "the family is an integrated social system of roles and structures and that adding or removing members will force a major reorganization of the system. Simmel's role theory suggests that with the shift from dyad to triad, there is a disruption of affection and intimacy" (p. 294).

Given this point of departure, it is of little surprise that sociologists who are interested in the transition to parenthood have concerned themselves primarily with the degree to which *crisis* is experienced by couples following the birth of the first child. Indeed, the overwhelming majority of investigations that focus on marital change across the transition to parenthood are designed to identify central

119

tendencies in the ways in which families function before and after the birth of a first child. Thus, it is the experience of the "average couple" that is the primary focus of attention in most of this work.

It is obviously the case, however, that all families do not experience the transition to parenthood, or any other developmental phenomenon, in exactly the same manner. Although declines in marital satisfaction may characterize the response of most couples to the arrival of a first child, there can be little doubt that the relationship that exists between some spouses does not change over time and that other relationships improve or deteriorate to varying degrees. It comes as some surprise to developmentalists, trained to distinguish between continuity and stability in developmental change, and thus to appreciate the difference between developmental function and individual differences, that little of the family sociology of the transition to parenthood even considers the reality of individual differences. As a result, the determinants of individual differences in response to the transition to parenthood have not been systematically investigated.

The research reported in this chapter stems from a three-cohort longitudinal study known as the Pennsylvania Infant and Family Development Project. One of the primary goals of this research program, which follows some 250 families from the last trimester of pregnancy through their infant's first year of life, is to chronicle change in the marital relationship across the transition to parenthood and to determine those factors and processes that account for variation in marital change. The present report addresses one potentially influential process, that involving the discrepancy between expectations and actual experiences regarding the effects of a first child on individual and family life. Before considering the way in which a discrepancy between expectations and experiences may actually influence marital functioning, and the determinants of individual differences in marital change more generally, we briefly summarize what is known about how marital relationships generally are affected by the birth of the first child.

Changes Associated with the Transition to Parenthood

As noted already, the stress associated with the transition to parenthood has been principally a focus of sociological inquiry. This work has highlighted four general classes of problems (Sollie & Miller, 1980). The first of these involves the physical demands associated with caring for a child. Specifically, new parents report routinely an experience of stress caused by loss of sleep and constant fatigue. Such fatigue results from the extra work required in caring for a highly dependent child, especially in caring for the baby through the night, during normal sleeping hours. Mothers, not surprisingly, seem to be most susceptible to problems involving physical demands, as they are most likely to experience the "role strain" associated with adding to the pre-parenthood roles of spouse, housemaker, and employee, that of primary caregiver.

A second negative theme that emerges from investigations of the transition to parenthood focuses attention on strains in the husband–wife relationship. Complaints of new parents highlight reductions in time spent together as a couple, changes in the sexual relationship, and the belief that the child's needs take priority over those of the spouse. Some of this stress, it should be evident, results from the physical demands of caregiving. As a case in point, consider how fatigue resulting from waking in the middle of the night to care for the infant might dampen one spouse's interest in sex.

A third negative theme that emerges from inquiries into the transition to parenthood centers around the emotional stresses experienced by parents. Having total responsibility for the care and well-being of the child is one such source of emotional strain, especially as parents come to realize, sometimes slowly, that the responsibilities of parenthood last a lifetime. Doubts regarding one's competence as a parent, which even the most skilled parents experience at one time or another, represent another source of emotional strain.

The final set of negative feelings experienced by parents adjusting to the addition of a child to the family involves opportunity costs and restrictions; that is, there are things they are no longer able to do. Parents frequently comment about limits placed on their social lives, particularly on their freedom to travel or to decide to do something on very short notice. Many new parents discover that doing things while they are responsible for young children is a far more complicated enterprise than they ever imagined. Think for a moment about wanting to go to a movie but not being able to find a babysitter, or about the process of wrapping and unwrapping a baby in warm clothes in order to go shopping in the winter. In addition to the social costs and restrictions associated with parenting, there are also financial costs. Most important here is the loss of income and career opportunities experienced when one parent remains home as primary caregiver. Also significant economically are the expenses of raising a young child.

It would be a mistake to conclude from this account of stresses associated with the transition to parenthood that there are no gratifications and rewards associated with parenthood. Miller and Sollie (1980) have identified several major positive themes that emerge from inquiry into the first parental experience. The first of these includes emotional benefits resulting from the love, joy, happiness, and fun that routinely accompany child care (e.g., play). Indeed, most parents regard these benefits as outweighing whatever costs are associated with the transition to parenthood. A second positive theme involves the self-enrichment and personal development that parents frequently report experiencing upon undertaking parental responsibilities and obligations. As noted earlier, parents often report feeling more like an adult, becoming less selfish, and thinking more about the future. In sum, parenting seems to have a maturing effect upon individual development in adulthood (Gutmann, 1975). A sense of family cohesiveness is the third positive theme to emerge from studies. In many households children are viewed as a link that ties husband and wife together, possibly even more strongly than marriage vows, thereby adding to the sense of being a family. Strengthened relationships with extended families are also reported routinely (Belsky & Rovine, in press).

It should be clear from the preceding analysis that the transition to parenthood poses problems as well as gratifications (Russell, 1974). The relationship between problems and gratifications will no doubt determine whether or not the birth and rearing of a first child will support or undermine marital functioning and satisfaction. What this suggests, of course, is that although there are some common stresses and pleasures associated with the transition to parenthood, there is also likely to be great variation in the ways in which couples respond to this change in individual and family life. Indeed, this may explain why some studies indicate that the arrival of the first child disrupts the marital relationship, resulting in stress often to the point of crisis (Dyer, 1963; Feldman, 1971; LeMasters, 1957; Wainright, 1966), whereas other data indicate that adjustment to parenthood is only mildly or moderately stressful (Beauchamp, 1968; Belsky, Spanier, & Rovine, 1983; Feldman & Rogoff, 1968; Hobbs & Cole, 1976; Meyerowitz & Feldman, 1966; Russell, 1974; Uhlenberg, 1970; Waldron & Routh, 1981). It is conceivable that these investigations are picking up a great deal of within- and between-sample variation that, when averaged, leads to few consistent results.

Determinants of Individual Differences in Marital Change

It is one thing to assert that individual differences characterize the adjustment of families to the addition of a first child, or to document such variation, and it is quite another to explain the variation. Why do some marital relationships improve, whereas others deteriorate? Why do some remain unchanged? It is virtually impossible to answer these questions on the basis of the empirical literature in this area. As noted already, little systematic attention has been paid to individual differences and even less to the determinants of these differences. For the most part, the data that are available are inconsistent.

One hypothesis that has been explored repeatedly is that initial levels of marital satisfaction mediate the subsequent influence of parenthood on couples' transition to parenthood. However, it is not clear whether high or low levels of initial satisfaction should predict subsequent crisis, and this theoretical confusion is mirrored in the available evidence. Whereas Feldman and Rogoff (1968) reported that declines in marital satisfaction associated with the birth of the firstborn are greater for husbands and wives whose marital satisfaction was initially high, Dyer (1963) and Russell (1974) observed that high levels of initial adjustment to marriage were predictive of limited crisis scores. Ryder (1973) and

LeMasters (1957), in contrast, failed to discern any relationship between assessments of the marital relationship prior to and following the birth of the baby. Inconsistencies are also evident among reports examining the mediating influence of individual differences such as planned versus unplanned pregnancy (Dyer, 1963; Hobbs & Wimbish, 1977; Russell, 1974; Touke, 1974); preparenthood employment status of mother (Dyer, 1963; LeMasters, 1957; Russell, 1974); and prior preparation for parenthood (Dyer, 1963; Russell, 1974; Touke, 1974; Uhlenberg, 1970) on the degree to which marital crisis accompanies the transition to parenthood. To a great extent, the inconsistency that is so evident in the transition-to-parenthood literature stems from the absence of conceptual frameworks for considering factors that might mediate the quality of adjustment to parenthood. That is, in study after study, little or no rationale is provided as to why some variables are selected for consideration and others are not in efforts to account for variation in crisis experienced by couples. However, when the many measures included in these studies as mediating variables are clustered conceptually, greater consistency is evident among reports than when variables are considered singularly. This is most evident when one considers available data pertaining to the timing of the first birth.

Elder and Rockwell's (1979) life-course perspective on human development, which "assumes that the consequences of events . . . vary according to their context and timing" (p. 3), directs attention to data bearing on the timing and sequencing of parenthood. According to this point of view, societies, through the people who populate them, have implicit and explicit plans for when certain events should occur and in what sequences. In our society, for example, marriage is supposed to occur after graduation from high school, if not college; pregnancy is to follow, not precede, marriage. Events that are "off-time," either because they are early (adolescent pregnancy) or out of sequence (pregnancy before marriage) are likely to generate stress because they violate normative standards. When we look at studies of the transition to parenthood, this prediction is generally confirmed; adjustment to parenthood is easier the more normatively placed parenthood is in the life course. Specifically, crisis tends to be less severe when parents are older (Hobbs & Wimbish, 1977; Russell, 1974; Tooke, 1974), have been married for longer periods of time before conception (Dyer, 1963; Russell, 1974), and conceive after marriage (Russell, 1974).

It would be inappropriate to conclude on the basis of these data that timing matters simply because "on-time" events, by not violating cultural standards, generate greater social acceptance than "off-time" events. Indeed, the apparent influence of timing would seem to implicate *preparation* for the adoption of a role. In fact, societal standards and expectations are based, at least in part, on notions of *readiness*. A women with a spouse is presumed to be more ready to enjoy the task of parenthood, and an older individual is presumed to be more psychologically mature and thus able to provide the nurturance required to rear children successfully. Obviously, notions of readiness vary across time and place. In traditional and tribal societies adolescent marriage, pregnancy and parenthood are accepted, if not encouraged. In these contexts, however, support systems and socialization experiences enhance the preparedness of the individual to adopt the role of parent at so "early" an age.

Preparation for a role, implicated as it is by evidence concerning the importance of timing, is a complex notion. The preceding discussion of adolescent parents in traditional and tribal societies draws attention to the role played by socialization experiences and support systems in preparing individuals for the role of parenthood. However, we need to take note of the fact that individuals also prepare themselves for the role of parent in a number of ways. Some of these involve skill development and knowledge generation. Parents-to-be read books about childrearing, talk with friends and relatives more experienced than they, and may even attend special classes specifically designed to prepare them for childbirth and parenthood. The expectations parents have for how a baby will affect their lives may well be influenced by such experience. Regardless of whether expectations are affected by such experiences, it is probable that parents-to-be will vary in their expectations. Needless to say, they are also quite likely to vary in their experience of how the baby affects their lives, and thus in the degree to which their prenatal expectations actually match their postnatal experiences. It is the issues of prenatal expectations, postnatal experiences, the match between them, and the consequences of any discrepancies that are the principal focus of this report. We focus upon this topic because, in the fact of limited data and theory regarding the determinants of individual differences in marital change across the transition to parenthood, our own naive psychology (Heider, 1958) alerts us to the potential deleterious consequences of violated expectations.

Prenatal Expectation, Postnatal Experiences, and the Consequences of Violated Expectations

Although the transition to parenthood is a developmental phenomenon, few investigations of this individual and family event are longitudinal in nature. As a result, little is known about what parents expect before a baby is born and how it relates to the actual experiences they have. Many writers comment on the fact that expectant parents frequently romanticize the ways in which becoming parents and having children will affect individual and family life (LeMasters, 1957). Parenthood is judged by some as a means of bringing the couple closer together, of creating a shared interest for spouses, and of enhancing relations with extended family. Often unrecognized is the degree of real, and frequently stressful adaptation that goes on when an individual as dependent as a new baby is added to the family.

In the face of this widely shared view that many parents-to-be are poor judges of how having a baby will affect family life, it is interesting to consider the results of the only published study to address this very issue. Kach and McGhee (1982) had expectant parents respond to 29 statements referring to common problems, gratifications, and feelings having to do with "life with baby" approximately one month before the baby was born and again 2 months after the child's arrival in order to gather information on parents' prenatal expectations and postnatal experiences. No significant differences emerged when parents' post-partum perceptions were compared with their earlier expectations. These data clearly are not consistent with the notion that, on the average, parents underestimate or overestimate changes that accompany the transition to parenthood. If they can be replicated, there will be grounds for concluding that parents-to-be generally do not have romanticized ideas about how the birth of the first child will influence their lives. The first objective of the investigation presented in this chapter, then, is to determine whether Kach and McGhee's (1982) findings are replicable in a comparable middle-class sample in a different geographic region (Texas vs. Pennsylvania).

If we succeed in replicating the finding that parents-to-be are, in general, accurate in appraising the nature of the transition to parenthood, this will not imply that expectant parents are equally accurate in forecasting postnatal experiences. Nor will such central tendencies imply that variation in expectational accuracy is not of functional significance to the adjustment process. In fact, there are both theoretical and empirical grounds for expecting that inaccurate or violated expectations may undermine the adjustment to parenthood.

A naive psychology (Heider, 1958) suggests that the underestimation of difficult or stressful experiences, and the overestimation of benefits associated with role change, will exacerbate any difficulty in adjusting to the role and decrease the pleasures and gratifications routinely associated with the role. Stresses that are not sufficiently anticipated will likely be experienced more adversely, because they will require greater adjustment, and positive experiences that are overanticipated will likely be experienced less positively than would otherwise be the case, because they will be regarded as not as much as was expected.

What remains more uncertain than the consequences of events that turn out less positive or more negative than anticipated is the effect of events that turn out more positive and less negative than anticipated. On the one hand there is reason to expect that such a situation should cause routinely stressful experiences to be experienced less stressfully and positive experiences to be experienced more positively, because the individual has the opportunity to benefit from a "pleasant surprise." Indeed, such *violated expectations* may actually have a more positive impact on adjustment to parenthood than perfectly accurate expectations.

On the other hand, situations that do not reflect what was anticipated invariably require more coping than ones that turn out as expected. From this point of view, even pleasant surprises may prove stressful. This is the position adopted by many investigators of life events, and most of those who develop life-event schedules, because they regard coping with change, regardless of its valence, as stressful to greater or lesser extents. Unfortunately, there is no available empirical work that even addresses, much less tests these competing, and equally logical, hypotheses with regard to the accuracy/inaccuracy of expectations. Two investigations do suggest, however, that expectations that are discrepant from actual experiences are associated with greater stress in adjusting to parenthood.

In one study of 34 primarily middle-class couples interviewed during late pregnancy and again when infants were 6 months of age, it was found that women who expressed (postnatally) unexpected or surprise reactions to their new role of parent were most often those whose marital satisfaction and self-esteem declined over time (Garrett, 1983). In a related study, Kach and McGhee (1982) reported that a discrepancy score representing the absolute difference between prenatal expectations and postnatal reports correlated highly ($r = .74, p < .01$) with a postnatal measure of problems encountered in adjusting to parenthood in the case of mothers (the correlation in the case of fathers was insignificant). Unfortunately, it is impossible to tell on the basis of their report whether positive or negative discrepancies or both were principally responsible for this relationship. The second major goal of the investigation reported here, then, is to address this issue and determine whether violated expectations, whatever their direction, undermine marital quality, or whether pleasant surprises actually exert a neutral or even positive effect.

The Context of Violated Expectations

Although it is hypothesized that individual differences in marital change across the transition to parenthood will be directly influenced by the relationship between prenatal expectations and postnatal experiences, it would be naive to assert that this will be the major or only determinant of marital adjustment. As we have already noted, the timing of first birth in terms of both the life course of the individual parent and the marital relationship is an important source of influence. Other factors and processes invariably play a role also: the division of labor of the couple, the emotional and instrumental support received from friends and relatives, general personality characteristics of the parents, temperamental characteristics of the child, and the demands and satisfactions that derive from one's job. It is necessary to recognize, then, that change in marital functioning across the transition to parenthood is, in all likelihood, multiply determined.

We would expect, for example, that wives whose husbands contribute little to home and baby care, whose friends think she should put her baby in day care and return to work, and who are personally dissatisfied with the job of full-time homemaker will experience greater stress in the transition to parenthood and will find their marital relations particularly undermined by this life-course event. Similarly, the man whose job is emotionally and physically draining, who is psychologically inflexible, and whose baby sleeps poorly and cries a great deal will find that his marriage suffers across the transition period.

The empirical study of many of these processes is a major goal of the Pennsylvania Infant and Family Development Project. Obviously they are beyond the scope of this one chapter. Nevertheless, in certain ways they inform our principal concern—the match between expectations and experiences and the consequences of violated expectations for marital change across the transition to parenthood. To state it more simply, accurate or inaccurate expectations do not occur in a vacuum, but in a family characterized by a great many other processes. The actual influence of violated expectations is likely to depend, then, on this broader context. We hypothesize that other family stresses will exacerbate the deleterious effect of experiencing life with baby more negatively or less positively than anticipated prenatally. By the same token, we predict that the existence of personal and contextual support should buffer the marriage from the otherwise adverse consequences of violated expectations. The third goal of the present chapter, then, is to empirically address each of these issues.

Toward this end, we present two analyses. One will test the particular hypothesis that personal psychological resources play a stress-buffering role. More specifically, it is predicted that individuals with healthy, adaptive, ego-resilient personalities will be less affected by violated expectations than persons with less flexible personal styles. Our assumption, of course, is that some individuals will be more able to recover from and overcome the effect of having one's expectations violated than will others because of the personal psychological resources they bring to their experience.

Because there is evidence that parents with babies who cry a great deal and whose biological rhythms (i.e., sleep, waking, feeding) are irregular experience more stress in the parenthood role (Russell, 1974), our second analysis will test the specific hypothesis that couples experiencing the dual stress of violated expectations and a "difficult" baby will display more negative change in their marriage than will couples that experience only one or the other stress. Our assumption here is that the coping processes required to overcome violated expectations will be burdened by the challenge of dealing with an irritable and irregular infant.

Before assessing the effect of violated expectations on marital functioning, and the potential buffering role of parent personality and the undermining effect of a difficult infant temperament, a descriptive analysis of prenatal expectations and self-reported postnatal experiences is provided. Specifically, we examine the general relationship between what husbands and wives anticipate and experience, and how postnatal experiences relate to prenatal expectations.

METHOD

Sample

The subjects of this investigation are 61 caucasian families participating voluntarily in the second cohort of the Pennsylvania Infant and Family Development Project. All couples are in intact marriages and are bearing their first children. In general, the sample can be described as middle-class. Annual family income reported during an interview conducted in the last trimester of pregnancy averaged $22,475. Couples had been married at the time of this interview an average of 4.2 years. The mean age of mothers and fathers, respectively, was 26.5 and 28.0 years, and the two parents averaged 14.4 and 15.8 years of education. For two of every three couples, the first birth was planned.

Families were recruited for the study with the assistance of the largest obstetrical practice in our community. This medical group, which handles about 80% of all births, provided us with the names and phone numbers of married women expecting their first children; these households were then called to determine if parents-to-be would be interested in receiving a letter outlining the Pennsylvania Infant and Family Development Project. If they indicated they would, their addresses were obtained, a letter was sent, and a second phone call was made after they received the letter. Questions about the project were answered and if parents were interested, a prenatal visit was scheduled. At this visit the project was again explained, informed consent was obtained, and data collection was initiated.

Our records revealed that 40% of the families eligible for project participation (i.e., expecting first child and remaining in area through baby's first year) became involved in the project. There were several inducements to participate. First, opportunity to participate in an interesting research program; second, a free newborn behavioral assessment; third, free 1-year developmental assessments of the child; and fourth, free counseling regarding what to look for in searching for quality infant day care if such counseling was desired.

Design

The families participating in the project provided information about themselves at several times across the year of the study. During the prenatal phase of the project, an interview with the couple and individual spousal questionnaires were administered. Within a few days of the infant's birth, a newborn behavioral assessment was administered in the local hospital. At 1, 3, and 9 months postpartum 1-hour, naturalistic, home observations of mother–infant and mother-father–infant interaction were conducted. Following the observation of all three family members at 3 and 9 months, the couple interview and the individual spousal questionnaires first administered prenatally were readministered. Finally, at 12 and 13 months infant–parent attachment and infant exploratory functioning were assessed at the university laboratory.

Two data collections (prenatal and 3-month phases), and two domains of measurement are of principal concern to us here. One domain of measurement had to do with prenatal expectations and actual reports of the effect of the transition to parenthood on one's life. The other domain concerned the marital relationship. Data bearing on infant temperament and parent personality are of secondary interest to this report and are discussed in brief as the chapter demands.

Expectations and Actual Effects

Identical questions with somewhat different phrasing were asked of parents individually in the questionnaires in the last trimester of pregnancy and again at 3 months postpartum. At the time of the prenatal assessments, these questions were posed in terms of how parents expected the baby to affect a number of aspects of their lives. At 3 months the questions requested that they evaluate how the birth of the baby and the transition to parenthood actually affected these same domains of their lives.

Parents were queried about six specific domains of individual and family life using separate 7-point scales consisting of 5 to 12 questions. The six specific domains were marital conflict and cooperation, overall marital relationship, personal opinion of self, relations with extended family, relations with friends and neighbors, and shared caregiving arrangements. The specific items that formed each domain were culled from content analyses of open-ended interviews carried out on the 72 families participating in the first cohort of the Infant and Family Development Project.

Marital Conflict and Cooperation.   Five items queried parents about conflict and cooperation on issues like spending money, household division of labor, and recreation activities. Appraisals were made of the extent to which the baby would cause (prenatal) or had caused (postnatal) increased conflict and decreased cooperation. The midpoint of this and all but the shared-caregiving scale indicated that the transition to parenthood would have or had had no effect. The internal consistency of this and each of the other scales, both prenatally and at 3 months, is presented in Table 5.1.

Overall Marital Relationship.   Twelve items queried parents about the extent to which having a baby would increase/decrease or had increased/decreased aspects of the marriage such as partner's sensitivity to feelings, partner's respect, having fun with partner, pleasure in sexual relations, and expression of love for partner.

TABLE 5.1
Internal Consistency (Coefficient Alpha) of Six Subscales
of Expectations/Actual Effects of Transition to Parenthood
and of the Measures of the Marital Relationship

| | Time of Measurement | | | |
| | Prenatal | | Three Month | |
Expectation/Effect Subscale	Husband	Wife	Husband	Wife
Marital Conflict and Cooperation	.76	.79	.72	.70
Overall Marital Relationship	.90	.93	.92	.90
Personal Opinion	.85	.91	.87	.90
Extended Family	.83	.83	.82	.81
Friends and Neighbors	.64	.59	.57	.62
Shared Caregiving	.91	.92	.78	.78
Marriage Subscale				
Positive Interaction	.75	.79	.81	.83
Negative Interaction	.54	.63	.75	.74
Love	.86	.87	.86	.83
Conflict	.61	.70	.69	.73
Ambivalence	.84	.61	.78	.77
Maintenance	.71	.71	.74	.72

Personal Opinion.   Eight items queried parents about the extent to which the transition to parenthood would or already had increased or decreased certain feelings about themselves. Specific items assessed feelings such as sense of self as an adult, physical attractiveness, respect for oneself, self-confidence in facing a challenging task, and sense of self as a caring person.

Relations With Extended Family.   Twelve items asked parents about effects of parenthood on dealings with extended family. Specific items dealt with frequency of contacts, receiving unwanted advice, receiving emotional support, and receiving gifts and services.

Relations With Friends and Neighbors.   Six items queried parents about how the transition to parenthood affected their relations with friends and neighbors. Specific items included the strengthening of old friendships, the creation of new friendships, and the receipt of emotional support and instrumental assistance.

Shared Caregiving.   Seven items asked parents to appraise who would be or was responsible for tasks like changing diapers, dressing the baby in the morning, and getting up at night to care for the baby. The seven possible responses ranged along a continuum from 100% husband and 0% wife to 100% wife and 0% husband, with 50% each as the midpoint.

The Marital Relationship

At both times of measurement each spouse completed three scales assessing several aspects of the marital relationships as part of the pre- and postnatal questionnaires. One 14-item scale, developed by Huston (1983, Huston & McHale, 1984) using questions from Birchler and Webb's (1977) areas of change questionnaire, assessed satisfaction/dissatisfaction with marital interactions and produces two scales measuring negative and positive interpersonal events in the marital relationship (see bottom of Table 5.1 for the internal consistency of all marriage scales for this sample). This instrument requires a respondent to evaluate the extent to which he or she would like certain relationship events to occur more or less often than they do using a 7-point scale, with the midpoint defined by the response "about the same as it does now" and extremes defined by the responses "a great deal more than it does now" and "a great deal less than it does now." Positive events include "my partner expressing approval of me or complimenting me on something I did," "sharing leisure interests with my partner," and "talking with my partner about things that have happened." Negative events include "my partner acting bored or uninterested while I am talking," "my partner being critical of me or complaining about something I did or didn't do," and "my partner doing things, knowing that they annoy me."

Braiker and Kelley's (1979) four-factor scale of intimate relations is comprised of 25 questions and taps spouses' attitudes and beliefs about parties in the relationship, specifically, feelings of love and ambivalence, and the interpersonal character of the relationship both in terms of the extent to which the partners experience conflict and the extent to which they engage in activities to enrich, improve, and thereby maintain the relationship. Questions such as, "To what extent do you have a sense of 'belonging' with your partner" (love), "How often do you and your partner argue?" (conflict), "How confused are your feelings toward you' partner?" (ambivalence), and "How much do you tell your partner what you want or need from the relationship?" (maintenance) are responded to on a nine-point scale that ranges from very little or not at all to very much or extremely.

The third instrument employed assesses overall marital opinion or marital satisfaction and was developed by Huston (Huston & Robins, 1982) and modeled after Campbell, Converse, and Rodgers (1976) approach to assessing life satisfaction. With a series of 14 bipolar items (e.g., boring–interesting, lonely–friendly, miserable–enjoyable, hopeful–discouraging), this single-score instrument is designed to assess subjective response to the marriage relationship in a way that makes no assumptions about the underlying behavioral patterns on which the evaluation is based (Huston & Robins, 1982).

RESULTS

Two sets of analyses are presented, the first descriptive and the second explanatory in nature. The descriptive analyses focus on stability and change in the prenatal and postnatal reports of expected and actual effects of having a baby. The second set of analyses examines the relationship between violated expectations and postnatal family functioning.

Descriptive Analyses: Stability and Change

Two sets of analyses were employed to look at changes over time in parental reports. First, a 2 (Parent) × 2 (Time of Measurement), repeated measures multivariate analysis of variance, followed by univariate analyses using the same statistical model, were conducted to assess mean change in parental reports and differences between husband and wife reports. Because no significant interactions between the two factors in the model proved significant, either at the multivariate or univariate level, and because our principal interest is in the relationship between expectations and actual effects, only the results bearing on the cross-time comparison are presented and discussed. In addition to these analyses of central tendencies, simple Pearson correlations were generated within each time of measurement to assess the relationship between husband and wife reports and between each time of measurement to assess the stability of mothers' and fathers' reports.

Data bearing on the relationship between expectant parents' prenatal expectations and their postnatal experiences are presented in Table 5.2. Three of six specific mean comparisons (summed across husband and wife respondents) revealed significant change over time, and these differences were most likely responsible for the significance of the omnibus F test. Inspection of specific pairs of means displayed in Table 5.2 reveals that expectations of the effect of having a baby on the marital relationship were somewhat more positive than reported postnatal experiences. In contrast, relations with friends and neighbors turned out to be somewhat more positive than anticipated prenatally, though even prenatal expectations were in the range of a small positive effect. And finally, parents-to-be expected husbands to be somewhat more involved in caregiving than they turned out to be. Both prenatally and postnatally, however, the mean scores fall between the 40% husband/60% wife and 20% husband/80% wife responses.

Consideration of all the scores in Table 5.2 indicates that at both the prenatal and postnatal times of measurement parents expected and experienced small positive effects of having a baby. When the means in Table 5.2 are divided by the number of items comprising each scale, scale points vary slightly around the responses indicating a little increase in good things and a little decrease in bad things. In other words, the *average* parent neither anticipated nor experienced

TABLE 5.2
Stability and Change in Parental Prenatal Expectations
and Postnatal Experiences

Expectation/Effect Subscales	$\bar{X}$ Scores		F (1,60)	Stability Coefficients	
	Prenatal	3 Months		Husband	Wife
Marital Conflict	21.58	21.52	0.01	.11	.09
Overall Marriage	56.39	52.52	10.00**	.39**	.17
Personal Opinion	40.47	39.75	1.55	.49***	.35*
Extended Family	58.18	58.56	0.22	.52***	.30**
Friends and Neighbors	35.67	36.24	4.61*	.44***	.43**
Shared Caregiving	37.45	40.70	30.72***	.37**	.61***
Multivariate F(6,56) = 9.83***					

$*p < .05$
$**p < .01$
$***p < .001$

great positive or negative consequences of having a baby. This is not to say, however, that there were no individuals whose expectations were grossly violated; as we see, individual differences in violated expectations had some of the very consequences that were predicted.

The results of the cross-time stability analysis, displayed on the right-hand side of Table 5.2, are generally consistent with the results of the means analysis. Although the majority of coefficients reveal that husbands and wives maintained their rank ordering over time, the magnitude of the statistically reliable correlations are modest (range from .30–.61). There is evidence, then, of both change and stability. Expectations are not completely accurate, but neither are they completely inaccurate.

Explanatory Analyses: Violated Expectations and Their Consequences

We pointed out in the beginning of this chapter that the conception of violated expectations is complex. One can think in terms of experiences simply being different from what was anticipated, as being more negative than what was anticipated, or as being more positive than what was anticipated. Which conception of violated expectations is most important when it comes to trying to explain variation in marital change across the transition to parenthood? In order to address this issue two types of composite difference scores were generated using the prenatal reports of expectations and the postnatal reports of actual experiences.

The first difference score was designed to reflect the absolute difference between prenatal expectations and postnatal experiences across subscales. This *absolute violated expectations score* did not distinguish between violations of expectations in which events turned out more positive than anticipated and more negative than anticipated. The very nature of the differences did not matter in the creation of this measure, only in the degree of absolute discrepancy between prenatal and postnatal measures. The larger the absolute violated expectations score, the more postnatal experiences deviated, across all subscales, from prenatal expectations. The score was created by summing the absolute difference between prenatal expectations and postnatal experiences across each of the six subscales.

We labeled the second measure the *directional violated expectations score.* Differences reflecting the fact that events turned out more positive than anticipated were given positive values, and differences reflecting the fact that events turned out more negative than anticipated were given negative values. The directional difference score for each subscale were summed to create the composite directional violated expectations score. The more positive a score on this measure, the more events turned out more positive or less negative than anticipated; the more negative a score on this measure, the more events turned out less positive or more negative than anticipated; the closer to zero a score on this measure, the more events turned out just as anticipated.

Each of these difference scores, reflecting very different conceptions of violated expectations, were correlated with the 3-month marriage measures after controlling for prenatal marriage scores. These partial correlations enabled us to assess the relationship between violated expectations and *change* in marital functioning. The results of these analyses, carried out separately for husbands and wives, are displayed in Table 5.3.

A quick inspection of the table reveals two important trends. First, the relationship between violated expectations and marital change, regardless of the measure of violated expectations, is more pronounced in the case of wives than husbands. While 9 of the total set of 14 correlations achieved statistical significance in the case of wives, the corresponding figures in the case of husbands is 1 of 14. Moreover, the magnitudes of the correlations for wives tend to be larger than those for husbands.

The second trend in the data underscores the fact that the directional score seems to be a better predictor than the absolute score. Indeed, comparisons of pairs of correlations, using z transformations, indicate that six of the seven correlations involving directional discrepancy scores are significantly larger than those involving absolute discrepancies in the case of wives, and that one of the seven correlations involving the directional relationships is reliably larger than its counterpart involving absolute discrepancies in the case of husbands. In not a single instance, then, is a correlation involving the absolute difference method significantly larger than one using the directional difference method.

What does all this mean at the substantive level? First, violated expectations, however conceptualized and measured, do not appear to exert much of an impact

TABLE 5.3
Intercorrelation of Two Kinds of Violated Expectation Scores
and Three-Month Measures of Marriage,
Controlling for Prenatal Marriage

	Respondent					
	Husband			Wife		
Three Month Marriage	Directional Discrepancy	Absolute Discrepancy	Z^a	Directional Discrepancy	Absolute Discrepancy	Z^a
Positive Interaction	.00	−.08	NS	.30*	−.24*	3.04***
Negative Interaction	−.05	.06	NS	.21	−.18	2.16*
Love	.11	−.03	NS	.46***	−.30*	4.42***
Conflict	−.02	−.06	NS	−.22	.11	NS
Ambivalence	−.13	.01	NS	−.48***	.39**	5.12***
Maintenance	.15	−.05	NS	.27*	−.11	2.11*
Satisfaction	.30*	−.01	1.75*	.50***	−.33**	4.88***

^{a}Test of the difference between correlation coefficients
NS Nonsignificant
*$p < .05$
***$p < .001$

on husbands' marital appraisals. At the very most, 10% of the variance is accounted for in change in husband's marital satisfaction. In the case of wives, up to 25% of the variance in change in marital satisfaction is accounted for. Clearly, violated expectations seem to exert a more pernicious impact on women than on men.

More significant than this, though, is the kind of violations of expectations that seem to be most influential. Whereas any violation undermines the marital quality for women across the transition to parenthood, it seems to be the case that when events turn out less positive or more negative than anticipated that the transition to parenthood has the most deleterious effect on marital change, and that when events turn out more positive or less negative than anticipated the transition to parenthood has the most positive effect on the marriage over this developmental transition. After all, the correlations between the directional discrepancy score and the measures of marital change were consistently and significantly larger than those between the absolute discrepancy scores and the measures of marital change.

The data presented in Table 5.3, and the discussion through this point, still do not exhaust the possible ways of looking at the effect of violated expectations. Indeed, it remains unclear, even in the face of evidence substantiating the greater predictive power of the directional discrepancy score, exactly what accounts for this predictive power. Are the relationships between the directional discrepancy score and the measures of marital change a function of the *benefits* of being positively surprised when things turn out more positive or less negative than anticipated, or are they a function of the *costs* associated with events turning out more negative or less positive than anticipated? Because the directional discrepancy score subsumed both kinds of violated expectations at different ends of its scaling continuum, it is impossible to distinguish between these two alternatives in the analyses presented so far.

In order to address this limit of the directional discrepancy measure, and to further advance our understanding of *how* violated expectations affect marital change, the distribution of directional discrepancy scores was examined. Our goal here was to identify men and women for whom events turned out better than anticipated (positive scores) and those for whom events turned out worse than anticipated (negative scores). The directional discrepancy scores of these distinct subgroups of individuals were then separately correlated with the measures of postnatal marriage, again controlling for prenatal marriages, in order to assess the extent to which different kinds of violated expectations predicted marital change across the transition to parenthood. The results of these analyses are presented in Table 5.4.

Once again we see little relationship between violated expectations of any kind and change in husbands' marital evaluations. In the case of wives, however,

TABLE 5.4
Intercorrelation Two Additional Kinds of Violated Expectation Scores
and Three-Month Measures of Marriage,
Controlling for Prenatal Marriage[†]

	Respondent					
	Husband			Wife		
Three Month Marriage	Worse Than Anticipated (n = 28)	Better Than Anticipated (n = 27)	Z^a	Worse Than Anticipated (n = 25)	Better Than Anticipated (n = 31)	Z^a
Positive Interaction	.04	.16	NS	.21	−.07	NS
Negative Interaction	−.01	−.12	NS	−.07	−.04	NS
Love	.04	−.03	NS	.14	−.15	1.94*
Conflict	.17	.10	NS	−.39*	.14	1.94*
Ambivalence	−.34	−.08	NS	−.39*	.14	NS
Maintenance	.16	.00	NS	−.08	−.16	NS
Satisfaction	.03	.29	NS	.53**	.28	NS

[†]Excluded from analyses are nine husbands and eight wives for whom there was no difference between prenatal expectations and postnatal experiences (i.e., directional discrepancy score equal to zero).
[a]Test of the difference between correlation coefficient
[NS]Nonsignificant
*$p < .05$

not only do more consistent relationships once again emerge, but all those that are statistically reliable involve those women for whom events turned out less positive or more negative than anticipated. Indeed, in the case of marital conflict and ambivalence, it happens to be that the effect of events turning out to be worse than anticipated is actually statistically different (and greater) from the effect of events turning out more positive than anticipated. To put these findings in substantive terms, it can be concluded, on the basis of this refinement of the analyses and presented in Table 5.3, that it is principally when postnatal experiences turn out to be more negative or less positive than anticipated that marital conflict and ambivalence is heightened, at least from the point of view of women, and that marital satisfaction declines across the transition to parenthood.

The Context of Violated Expectations.   Although violated expectations appear to have a pernicious effect on the marital relationship, particularly in the case of women, we hypothesized that this effect would be buffered or enhanced, depending on the circumstances under which such violations occurred. Specifically, we predicted that under conditions of additional stress, as when a baby's temperament is "difficult," the negative consequences of violated expectations would be even greater. To test this hypothesis, we endeavored to determine whether the scores on the difficulty factor of Bates, Freeland, and Lounsbury's (1979) Infant Behavior Questionnaire (completed by mothers at 3 months) would on their own, and in interaction with violated expectations (as assessed by the directional discrepancy score), increase the amount of variance that could be accounted for in 3-month marital satisfaction. Thus, a hierarchical multiple regression analysis was conducted; the interaction between temperament and violated expectations was regressed onto marital satisfaction after first regressing prenatal marital satisfaction, temperament, and violated expectations on the dependent variable. The results of this analysis are displayed in the top half of Table 5.5. In the case of neither husbands nor wives did the interaction prove significant, though in the case of wives temperament explained 7% of the variance in postnatal marital satisfaction.

Our second hypothesis regarding the conditions under which violated expectations would influence marriage concerned the stress-buffering potential of a healthy, adaptive personality. Specifically, we hypothesized that an ego-resilient, flexible adult could overcome the stressful experience of being surprised by the strains of parenthood. To test this hypothesis an analysis identical to that just described for temperament was conducted using a measure of personality comprised of the standardized sum of four positively intercorrelated personality scales, three from the Jackson (1976, 1980) Personality Inventory and Personality Research Form (nurturance, interpersonal affect, self-esteem), and the fourth from the ego strength scale in Cattell's (1960) Sixteen Personality Factor Questionnaire (16PF). The results of this analysis, displayed in the bottom half of Table 5.5, indicated that neither personality in isolation, nor in interaction

TABLE 5.5
Prediction of Postnatal Marital Satisfaction
Using Violated Expectations and Particular Family Circumstances:
Infant Temperament and Parent Personality

	Husband			Wife		
	R^2	ΔR^2	F	R^2	ΔR^2	F
Temperament						
Prenatal Marriage	.29		24.50***	.16		11.96***
Temperament	.32	.03	2.68	.23	.07	5.99*
Violated Expectations	.41	.09	8.56**	.43	.20	18.37***
Temp. × Viol. Exp.	.41	.00	0.02	.43	.00	0.34
Personality						
Prenatal Marriage	.29		24.50***	.16		11.96***
Personality	.29	.00	0.57	.16	.00	0.01
Violated Expectations	.39	.10	9.29**	.40	.24	23.80***
Pers. × Viol. Exp.	.39	.00	0.11	.40	.00	0.03

with violated expectations, significantly predicted or added to the prediction of 3-month marital satisfaction.

In sum, neither a stress-enhancing effect of a difficult infant temperament, nor a stress-buffering effect of a healthy, flexible personality could be discerned with respect to marital change, because none of the interaction terms in the regression equation proved significant or increased the variance accounted for in the regression equation over and beyond the single main effect of violated expectations.

DISCUSSION

Over the past 2 decades, interest in the transition to parenthood has increased dramatically. Initially the topic was studied principally by family sociologists concerned with how marital relations change following a major restructuring of the family system. More recently, lifespan developmentalists have become intrigued with this developmental transition, and there are several reasons for this. From one perspective, the transition to parenthood represents a normative life event and thus has the potential for restructuring the life course of individuals and families, thereby affecting adult development. From a related perspective, the transition to parenthood represents a meeting ground for two disciplines, developmental psychology and family sociology, because at this point in time individual development begins for some individuals in the family (i.e., infant), roles are created (i.e., mother, father), and families are changed (from dyad to triad).

Most of the work done to date on the transition to parenthood has been descriptive in nature, either chronicling change that takes place in the marital relationship, or documenting the extent to which crises are experienced in coping with this life event. A major purpose of the present investigation was to move beyond the mere description of change to an analysis of the causes of variation in change. Before discussing our results with respect to this principle focus of inquiry, let us review what we discerned at the descriptive level.

Changes Across the Transition to Parenthood

The major focus on change in the current study involved the comparison of prenatal expectations and postnatal experiences. It was anticipated, on the basis of opinions expressed in both the popular and scientific literature, that parents-to-be would romanticize the effect of the baby on individual and family life. That is, they would overestimate the positive impact and underestimate the negative impact of the transition to parenthood. In general, the results of our inquiry failed to substantiate this view of romanticized prenatal expectations. In terms of central tendencies, the average mother and father only anticipated very slight positive effects of the baby on individual and family life, and these expectations, again at the level of central tendencies, were generally consistent with experiences reported postnatally.

In fact, even though three of six domains of measurement did reveal significant change between expectations and experiences, these changes were not always in the direction of romanticizing the effect of the birth of a baby. The actual effect of having a baby on relations with friends and neighbors turned out to be more positive than anticipated, though the effect of this event on marriage turned out to be less positive than anticipated. Finally, wives tended to be more responsible for infant care postnatally than both husbands and wives expected. In general, then, our results are consistent with those reported by Kach and McGhee (1982) who actually discerned no reliable differences whatsoever between prenatal expectations and postnatal experiences.

From a developmental perspective it is important to recognize that change is a multidimensional phenomenon. The results discussed through this point deal only with mean scores, and thus changes in central tendencies. Another way to look at change is from the vantage of individual differences, and this kind of change was examined by correlating prenatal-expectation with postnatal-experience measures. In the case of both husbands and wives, stability coefficients were predominantly reliable, even if moderate in magnitude. From both the standpoint of central tendencies and individual differences, then, it is clear that there is a general correspondence between prenatal expectations and postnatal experiences.

In view of these results, we need to ask why there was not a greater discrepancy between the prenatal and postnatal data sets. After all, it is widely assumed, even by us before we carried out this investigation, that parents-to-be romanticize how having a baby will affect their lives. Several possible explanations come to mind. One emphasizes measurement considerations, and especially the possibility that the instruments used were relatively insensitive to the phenomenon being studied. Although this possibility cannot be fully discounted, it needs to be noted that the measures of expectations and experiences were highly internally consistent, and certainly seemed valid on the basis of the data to be discussed shortly concerning the consequences of variation in violated expectations.

A possibly more compelling explanation of the general similarity between expectations and experiences has to do with the population being studied. All families volunteered for the study, had intact marriages, were middle or working class, and thus could be assumed to be reasonably well functioning. Moreover, the high levels of education of both husbands and wives certainly makes it likely that parents-to-be took advantage of the massive popular literature on the topics of pregnancy and parenthood and were thus reasonably well prepared for having a baby. This argument would seem to be buttressed by the fact that for 66% of the sample the baby was planned, and for an even greater percentage of families attendance at childbirth preparation classes preceded the child's arrival. Thus, it remains possible that a large portion of the population does romanticize the transition-to-parenthood process as is widely claimed, but that the sample studied in this investigation was exceptional in the anticipatory socialization experiences that the parents-to-be had provided themselves.

Violated Expectations as Determinants of Variation in Marital Change

Although it may be the case that expectations and experiences were more congruent than incongruent across the sample, it would be inappropriate to conclude that all parents-to-be proved equally accurate in forecasting the actual effect of the infant on individual and family life. In actuality, our sample displayed a great deal of variation and, as we observed, this variation was of great functional consequence, especially for mothers.

We predicted at the outset of this investigation that violated expectations would adversely effect marital relations. This prediction was based on our own naive psychology: When events deviate from what is anticipated, stress results and coping is required. What was initially unclear to us was the most optimal way of conceptualizing violated expectations. Although Kach and McGhee (1982) found both positive and negative deviations from expectations to be strongly associated with stress, especially in the case of mothers, it seemed to us that not all violated expectations would necessarily exert the same impact. Indeed we assumed that it was principally when events turned out less positive or more negative than anticipated that stress would be greater and, consequently, that marital functioning would be undermined.

To address this issue we first compared the predictive power of two conceptually distinct measures of violated expectations. Recall that one represented the absolute difference between actual experiences and expectations, and thus did not distinguish between changes in which events turned out better and worse than anticipated; the directional discrepancy measure, in contrast, was scaled so that positive and negative violations were at opposite ends of a continuum. The data were clear in demonstrating that the latter conceptualization and measurement of violated expectations, in which positive violations would have an effect distinctly different than would negative violations, was predictively stronger than the absolute discrepancy measure. These results led to the preliminary conclusion, especially in the case of mothers, that when events turn out less positive or more negative than anticipated, marriages change for the worse, whereas the opposite is true when events turn out less negative and more positive than anticipated.

In actuality, the continuous scaling of the directional discrepancy scale could not provide full support for this conclusion, because the correlations generated did not by themselves indicate whether positive violations or negative violations of expectations, or both, were responsible for the significant patterns of covariation that we discerned. To further illuminate this issue, we split the sample into two groups—those individuals who experienced negative violations, and those whose experienced positive violations. We then examined how their respective violated expectation scores correlated with the multiple measures of marital change. Whereas the evidence was by no means totally compelling, the data did suggest that, principally in the case of women, it is when events turn out worse than anticipated that marital functioning is undermined.

The fact that the impact of violated expectations, however conceptualized and measured, was more evident in the case of women is consistent with the results reported by Kach and McGhee (1982). It may be explained by the fact that it is mothers who invariably bear the major burden of the transition to parenthood. Women are more likely to be physically exhausted by the birth process itself, as well as by night wakings. Further, they are more likely to be responsible for routine baby care, especially in the first 3 months and particularly when they are breast feeding and/or have not returned to work. Household division of labor tends to become more traditional following the transition to parenthood (Cowen, Cowen, Coie, & Coie, 1978; Lamb, 1979) and, in this regard, recall that it was observed in this study that mothers were more involved in baby care than fathers than either men or women anticipated prenatally. It seems to be the case, then, that because women experience the greatest life style change following the arrival of a first baby that failure to accurately anticipate the nature of the baby's influence, and especially the tendency to overestimate the positive effects of this event, are associated with negative change in the marital relationship as evaluated by women.

The Context of Violated Expectations. We initially presumed that for both men and women sources of influence on the marital relationships other than violated expectations would mediate the impact of violated expectations on marital change. In this investigation we tested this hypothesis by examining the stress-buffering effect of an adaptive healthy personality and the stress-compounding effect of an infant with a difficult temperament. Of particular significance to us is the fact that these hypothesized mediators of the effect of violated expectations could not, in fact, be shown to mediate the effect of violated expectations. Although having a difficult-tempered infant undermined marital satisfaction, neither this stressor nor the support of a healthy personality made a significant contribution to the prediction of marital satisfaction in interaction with violated expectations. This result was a surprise. Although we anticipated that violated expectations would negatively influence marriage, we anticipated that this effect would be most apparent in the case of parents encountering *additional, independent* stress (i.e., a difficult temperament), and least for parents who possessed the personal psychological resources to adjust to the fact that their expectations had been violated. Because neither of these predictions were confirmed, it seems that the violated expectations function across the board and are independent of other stressors or supports. Two qualifications of this conclusion are necessary. First, it is based on acceptance of the null hypothesis (i.e., our inability to discern interaction effects). Second, it is certainly possible that the kind of buffering and stress-promoting processes we were pursuing with parent personality and infant temperament, respectively, might be discerned if other stresses (e.g., low income) or supports (e.g., strong social network) were empirically considered.

Implications

What lessons can be drawn from the data presented in this chapter, particularly with respect to intervention efforts that could be undertaken to facilitate a smooth transition to parenthood? Because violated expectations seem to exert a pernicious effect on marriage, especially the experience of wives, there seems to be cause for instituting opportunities for anticipatory socialization to help parents-to-be develop more realistic expectations about how having a first child will affect their lives. Obviously the task is not to raise anxieties; rather, the goal should be to alter idealized visions by making parents-to-be sensitive to the very real stresses and strains they are likely to encounter.

Childbirth education classes would seem to be an ideal place for such anticipatory socialization to take place. In the United States today these community services, offered by nonprofit organizations, are engaged by large numbers of families on a totally volunteer basis. It is unfortunately the case that these classes, which meet on a weekly basis for about 5–10 weeks during pregnancy, all too frequently focus exclusively on the relatively emphemeral event of childbirth. Although the reduction of childbirth fear is a worthy goal, it seems unfortunate that in many classes the opportunity to consider life after baby arrives is not realized. What might be done?

Strategies undoubtedly exist in the best designed courses for anticipatory socialization about life with baby. Merely providing expectant couples with an opportunity to share expectations should alert many parents to possibilities they have not considered sufficiently. Also helpful might be the inclusion of new parents in these groups to report on their own postnatal experiences. One would want to insure that such well intended activities did not generate too much concern, and achieving a balance between the wonderful and the troublesome should not be too difficult. Whether or not such strategic intervention actually results in fewer violated expectations and thereby positively affects the marital relationship is, of course, an empirical question.

ACKNOWLEDGMENTS

The work reported in this chapter was supported by the National Institute of Child Health and Human Development (No. R01HD15496-01A1), the National Science Foundation (No. SES-8108886) and by the March of Dimes Birth Defects Foundation (Social and Behavioral Sciences Branch, No. 12-64), Jay Belsky, Principal Investigator.

REFERENCES

Antonovsky, A., & Kats, R. (1967). The life crisis history as a tool in epidemiological research. *Journal of Health and Social Behavior, 8,* 15–21.

Bates, J., Freeland, C., & Lounsbury, M. (1979). Measurement of infant difficultness. *Child Development, 50,* 794–802.

Beauchamp, D. (1968). *Parenthood as crisis: An additional study.* Unpublished manuscript, University of North Dakota.

Belsky, J., & Rovine, M. (in press). Social network contact, family support, and the transition to parenthood. *Journal of Marriage and the Family.*

Birchler, G., & Webb, L. (1977). Discriminating interaction behaviors in happy and unhappy marriages. *Journal of Consulting and Clinical Psychology, 45,* 494–495.

Braiker, H., & Kelley, H. (1979). Conflict in the development of close relationships. In R. Burgess & T. Huston (Eds.), *Social exchange and developing relationships* (pp. 111–143). New York: Academic Press.

Campbell, A., Converse, P., & Rodgers, W. (1976). *Quality of American life: Perception, evaluation, and satisfaction.* New York: Russell Sage.

Cattell, R. (1960). *16 Primary Factors.* Champaign, IL: Institute for Personality and Ability Testing.

Cowen, C., Cowen, P., Coie, L., & Coie, J. (1978). Becoming a family: The impact of a first child's birth on the couple's relationship. In L. Newman & W. Miller (Eds.), *The first child and family formation.* Chapel Hills, NC: Carolina Population Center.

Dyer, E. (1963). Parenthood as crisis: A restudy. *Marriage and Family Living, 25,* 488–496.

Elder, G. H., & Rockwell, R. C. (1979). Economic depression and postwar opportunity in men's lives: A study of life patterns and mental health. In R. G. Simmons (Ed.), *Research in community and mental health* (Vol. 1, pp. 17–37). Greenwich, CT: JAI Press.

Feldman, H. (1971). The effects of children on the family. In A. Michel (Ed.), *Family issues of employed women in Europe and America* (pp. 9–16). Lieden, The Netherlands: E. F. Brill.

Feldman, H., & Rogoff, M. (1968). *Correlates of changes in marital satisfaction with the birth of the first child.* Paper presented at the American Psychological Association Meeting, San Francisco.

Garrett, E. (1983). *Women's expectations of early parenthood: Expectations versus reality.* Paper presented at the American Psychological Association Meetings, Anaheim, CA.

Gutmann, D. (1975). Parenthood: A key to the comparative study of the life cycle. In N. Datan & L. H. Ginsberg (Eds.), *Life-span developmental psychology: Normative life crises* (pp. 231–254). New York: Academic Press.

Heider, F. (1958). *The psychology of interpersonal relations.* New York: Wiley.

Hobbs, D. (1968). Transition to parenthood: A replication and an extension. *Journal of Marriage and the Family, 30,* 413–417.

Hobbs, D., & Cole, S. (1976). Transition to parenthood: A decade replication. *Journal of Marriage and the Family, 38,* 723–731.

Hobbs, D., & Wimbish, J. (1977). Transition to parenthood by black couples. *Journal of Marriage and the Family, 39,* 677–689.

Holmes, T. H., & Rahe, R. H. (1967). The social readjustment rating. *Journal of Psychosomatic Research, 11,* 213–128.

Hultsch, D. K., & Plemons, J. K. (1979). Life events and life span development. In P. B. Baltes & O. G. Brim, Jr. (Eds.), *Life-span development and behavior* (Vol. 2, pp. 206–229). New York: Academic Press.

Huston, T. (1983). *The topography of marriage: A longitudinal study of change in husband-wife relationships over the first year.* Plenary address to the International Conference on Personal Relationships, Madison, WI.

Huston, T., & McHale, S. (in press.). Sex role strain in marriage: A longitudinal study of the impact of having a child on the topography of the husband–wife relationship. In S. Duck & R. Gilmour (Eds.), *Key issues in interpersonal relationships.* Hillsdale, NJ: Lawrence Erlbaum Associates.

Huston, T., & Robins, E. (1982). Conceptual and methodological issues in studying close relationships. *Journal of Marriage and the Family, 44* 901–925.

Jackson, D. (1976). *Jackson personality inventory.* Gaslen, NY: Research Psychologists Press.

Jackson, D. (1980). *Personality research form.* Post Huron, MI: Research Psychologists Press.

Kach, J., & McGhee, P. (1982). Adjustment to early parenthood: The role of accuracy of pre-parenthood expectations. *Journal of Family Issues, 3,* 361–374.

Lamb, M. (1979). Influence of the child on marital quality and family interaction during the prenatal, perinatal, and infancy periods. In R. Lerner & G. Spanier (Eds.), *Child influences on marital and family interaction: A life-span perspective* (pp. 179–196). New York: Academic Press.

LeMasters, E. E. (1957). Parenthood as crisis. *Marriage and Family Living, 19,* 352–355.

Meyerowitz, J., & Feldman, H. (1966). Transition to parenthood. *Psychiatric Research Report, 20,* 78–84.

Myers, J. L., Lindenthal, J. J., Pepper, M. P., & Ostrander, D. K. (1972). Life events and mental status: A longitudinal study. *Journal of Health and Social Behavior, 13,* 398–406.

Miller, B., & Sollie, D. (1980). Normal stresses during the transition to parenthood. *Family Relations, 29,* 459–465.

Orden, S., & Bradburn, N. (1968). Dimensions of marital happiness. *American Journal of Sociology, 73,* 715–731.

Russell, C. (1974). Transition to parenthood: Problems and gratifications. *Journal of Marriage and the Family, 36,* 294–301.

Ryder, R. (1973). Longitudinal data relating marital satisfaction and having a child. *Journal of Marriage and the Family, 35,* 604–607.

Sollie, D., & Miller, B. (1980). The transition to parenthood as a critical time for building family strengths. In N. Stinnet & P. Knaub, (Eds.), *Family strengths: Positive models of family life* (pp. 19–36). Lincoln, NE: University of Nebraska Press.

Touke, S. (1974). *Adjustment to parenthood among a select group of disadvantaged parents.* Unpublished master's thesis, Montana State University.

Uhlenberg, B. (1970). *Crisis factors in transition of college students to parenthood.* Unpublished master's thesis, Otto State University.

Vincent, J. P., Cook-Messerly, N., & Linzy, M. (1980). A social learning analysis of couples during the second postnatal month. *American Journal of Family Therapy.*

Wainwright, W. (1966). Fatherhood as a precipitant of mental illness. *American Journal of Psychiatry, 123,* 40–44.

Waldron, H., & Routh, D. (1981). The effect of the first child on the marital relationship. *Journal of Marriage and the Family, 43,* 785–788.

6 Linking Parental Beliefs to Children's Social Competence: Toward a Cognitive-Behavioral Assessment Model

Maurice J. Elias
Michael Ubriaco
Rutgers University

Parents engage in innumerable behaviors toward their children and toward each other about childrearing issues. One important aspect of these behaviors is their contribution to socializing children for competent interpersonal functioning (Lippitt, 1968). Recent research suggests that parents' childrearing practices are an expression of a set of beliefs about how children become socially competent and how family environments should be structured for shaping their children's behavior (e.g., Laosa & Sigel, 1982). From this perspective, the concrete behaviors of a parent embody an entire configuration of influences that must be brought into focus when attempting to understand the competence of children. When there are two parents involved in guiding a young person's development, the complexities become far more intriguing and challenging to unravel.

Several researchers believe that parenting behaviors are strongly cognitively mediated, incorporating specific socialization influences on parents such as socioeconomic status, ethnic background, and their own parenting history (cf. Bacon & Ashmore, this volume). Emmerich (1969) argued that parents possess a set of goals or values concerning their children's behavior and a set of means–ends beliefs concerning ways to ensure their goals for their children are met. These goals and beliefs are the product of parents' own socializing experiences, and are more relevant as predictors of their behavior than indices of those background experiences would be. Emmerich's data were somewhat surprising. Beyond indicating the role of cognitive mediation in parental role functioning, he

147

found that parental goals were generally stable, often despite developmental changes in the child or feedback that the goals were inappropriate or difficult for the child to achieve. It seemed as if the cognitive mediation operated in a conservative manner, to the potential detriment of the needs of the growing child. Sigel (1983a, 1985) attempted to elaborate the process through which parental goals and beliefs operate by considering how knowledge is organized. He suggests that the array of inputs to parents concerning how they should socialize their children is filtered through a system of beliefs about children and childrearing. When Sigel analyzes parent–child interaction, he therefore places less emphasis on sequential exchange of observed behaviors; rather, he assumes that parents are using their belief systems as an unseen criterion for evaluating their child's responses and for selecting their next behavior. Some empirical support for this contention has been found, along with the suggestion that these beliefs will influence the child's social and emotional growth (McGillicuddy-DeLisi, 1982).

Although the hypothesized link of parental goals and beliefs to the social competence of children is intuitively clear, the data of Emmerich and Sigel and his colleagues (Laosa & Sigel, 1982) have yet to lend empirical support to the connection. Indeed, even the general findings must be tempered by noting that results seem to vary as a function of family configuration, age and sex of focal child, sex of parent, population subgroup, and content of experimental tasks. Harman and Brim (1981) and Lippitt (1968) emphasize the difficulties involved in sampling or controlling for the numerous mediating variables that have been identified as influencing childrearing beliefs and behaviors. Further, they point out that nomothetic research strategies will not be adequate to provide models of development that might apply for particular families. Models focused on within-family characteristics and their growth over time, with accompanying assessment procedures, would be invaluable tools for identifying needs prior to parent education or child or family intervention (Billings & Moos, 1982; Harman & Brim, 1981).

A growing number of researchers and theorists have been advocating a return to idiographic methods as a tool for theory building and articulating within-family models of how children's competence is socialized (Billings & Moos, 1982; Lippitt, 1968). This approach is a logical outgrowth of what Meehl (1954) labeled as the idiographic end point of nomothetic laws. At some point, individual or small group application of nomothetic principles contains intolerable error. The idiosyncratic nature of individual histories and the fact that the family context includes a blending of these histories requires access to the parameters of their uniqueness. Rather than articulate general developmental trends, work from an idiographic perspective would involve defining typologies of parental, familial, and child characteristics that seem to denote pathways toward, or away from, the acquisition of social competence by children.

This chapter uses the work of Emmerich (1969) and Sigel (Laosa & Sigel, 1982) as a basis for developing a cognitive-behavioral model for assessing the pathways between parental beliefs and children's social competence. By clarifying the nature and operation of these pathways and by specifying assessment procedures, it is hoped that a procedure for gathering information valuable for planning preventive and remediative family interventions can be developed. In the ensuing section, the primary constructs that define the pathways—parental beliefs, parental teaching strategies, family environment, and means–ends thinking—are defined and their interrelationship explored. Two criteria of children's social competence, social-cognitive problem solving abilities and behavioral adjustment in school, are also presented. Several pathways between parental beliefs and child outcomes are described, with an emphasis on illustrating the importance of assessing how mediating variables can influence the socialization process. The next major section describes assessment procedures used to operationalize the main constructs, and then results of data collected from four families are presented. Following a review of how the data refined the model, the chapter concludes with suggestions for future research.

Parental Beliefs, Parental Teaching Strategies, and Parental Actions Toward Children

There is mounting evidence in both the research and clinical literatures that the constructs of parental beliefs and parental teaching strategies are necessary components of any model seeking to predict or explain the socialization of competence in children (Sigel, 1985). Each of these constructs are defined here, and examples of studies showing a link to children's competence are provided.

Parental Beliefs. At the most general level, parental beliefs may be considered as a core set of values, with strong self-reference and self-evaluation implications, covering two areas: parents and children. Their form, basic nature, and interrelationship can be captured by viewing these beliefs as self-statements that are essential for informing parental action and interpreting interactions in childrearing contexts: "Children should _____ , therefore I must _____ ." Implicit in this statement is a set of values, or expectations, for parents' behaviors and children's behaviors. Kelly (1955) emphasized the stabilizing nature of cognitive constructs such as parental beliefs, in that they allow individuals to order and perceive realities, identify contrasts, and respond to the environment in a relatively consistent manner. Rotter (1982) expanded this formulation to more explicitly account for ways in which constructs influence behavior in specific situations. His view is that behavior in a given situation is a function of generalized and specific expectancies and the reinforcement value of goal attainment in that situation. These generalized expectancies may be thought of as higher-order beliefs about oneself and one's environment (e.g., locus of control, interpersonal trust, trustworthiness).

The importance of Rotter's theoretical perspective is (a) to identify parental beliefs with *goals,* and (b) to caution us about the multiplicity of goals and expectancies that may be involved in a specific situation. Undoubtedly, features of parental beliefs are shared among members of a given culture, socioeconomic status, ethnic or gender groups, and the like. However, it is likely that the interrelationship of socialization influences on parents lead their beliefs to be organized in an idiosyncratic manner (Sigel, 1985). The task of uncovering parameters relevant for a particular family requires one to examine *how* parents organize their beliefs (e.g., by physical location of situation; age and/or sex of child; sex of parent) or else to carefully define an aspect of childrearing about which parental beliefs are being elicited.

McArthur and Baron (1983) supplement the cognitive perspective by elaborating a mechanism through which belief systems operate. They use three major components in their explanation: events, attunement, and affordances. They posit that social interaction occurs, is perceived, and then is cognitively organized in terms of *events*. Events contain information that is of considerable adaptive significance for individuals. The information actually perceived is determined largely by a person's *attunement* (or expectancies) and by the *affordances* present in the situation. Affordances are properties of events containing important information that suggests particular actions (e.g., a room full of chairs suggests one should sit down). Information present in affordances is available to individuals and generally likely to be perceived. However, someone's attunement may interfere with picking up this critical information.

An example is useful here. A young child is at a large family gathering. She is talking to an older cousin, and repeatedly uses foul language. Father asks the child to stop several times. With each repetition, his face grows harsher, his voice louder and more threatening, his posture more rigid. However, the cousin keeps laughing and reinforces the younger child's use of unacceptable language. A particular sequence of self-statements by the father commences: children should not use foul language; children should obey their parents, especially in front of other family members; she is not obeying my words, therefore, I must hit her. Father proceeds to hit her, and stimulates a set of self-statements by the child: I must be a terrible child for him to do this to me in front of everyone, and without even giving me an extra chance to stop.

Let us assume the event is encoded as a "family visit." Father is attuned to appropriate behavior, obedience, and respect in front of family members. Daughter is attuned to cousin's reaction. Affordances were provided in the form of father's voice level, posture, facial cues and words, and daughter's reaction to the delight of her cousin. The information available was not picked up because the attunements were narrow and self-focused. Now, there is a likelihood that subsequent family visits may lead to heightened attunement by father for signs of unacceptable or disobedient behavior by his daughter, and heightened attunement by daughter for information suggesting she is not a worthwhile child. Of course, we oversimplify. Perhaps mother or a grandparent entered the situation after the hitting incident and mediated the example as described. Such an intervention, if timely and carried out by a person highly valued by the child, can shift the attunements and affordances of the child (and perhaps the father) and make a contribution to the child's subsequent adjustment.

There is some evidence supporting such formulations about parental beliefs and their link to children's social competence. Kelly (1955) strongly argued that adaptive functioning is best predicted by flexible, well-differentiated construct systems. Bacon and Ashmore (1982) found that parental beliefs have a strong evaluative emphasis and, in some cases, may be narrowed by poorly differentiated ideas about which behaviors should be encouraged or changed. Emmerich's (1969) research supported this idea, despite the populations studied and methods used being quite different. These studies suggest that a child whose parents' belief systems are organized too rigidly or without sufficient accommodation to environmental input could be at risk for poor social adjustment.

Another source of relevant information is the clinical literature. Newberger and Cook (1983) concluded a cognitive-developmental analysis of how parents view their role and the role of their children in relation to themselves. A parental awareness interview was developed in which parents were asked to respond to three vignettes, each addressing a problematic childrearing situation (e.g., conflicting demands on a working mother), and to a series of questions around eight basic tasks of parenthood (e.g., reasons and methods for discipline and for resolving conflict). Two samples were used in the study, one rural, the other urban. In each case, mothers of children identified by state protective service officers as suffering physical abuse or neglect were matched with mothers whose children had medical or developmental difficulties but no history of abuse or neglect. The aspect of parental beliefs studied was parental awareness of (a) influences on the development of the child, (b) reasons for childrearing rules, and (c) responsibilities in the parenting role. The authors found that control parents had available to them more comprehensive and differentiated beliefs to serve as points of reference when interacting with their children. The parents of maltreated children seemed to possess a belief system comprised mainly of their own views, deemphasizing social conventions and input from the behavior of the child. The resulting lack of flexibility seems to have had negative outcomes for both children and parents.

In the family therapy literature, there are many examples of ways in which parental expectations eventuate in children's developing maladaptive schema concerning their own social competence. Bradt's (1980) work with child-focused families is representative of these examples. In child-focused families, at least one parent views the role of parent as possessing *extremely* positive reinforcement value. Bradt (1980) notes that most such parents have experienced a significant loss of relationship with a parenting figure. They come to place an intense emphasis on indulging their own child as a means of recapturing the bonds they have lost. Because the maintenance of a strong parent–child bond is of superordinate importance, overt expression of negative affect, particularly conflict, tends to be avoided. Relationships with one's spouse and other family members are affected, as they are often viewed as competitive. The child in such systems develops a distorted sense of self and an impaired view of how interpersonal relationships should be conducted. The clinician's challenge is to establish the inappropriateness of the parental belief that the child can be the instrument of recapturing the lost relationship. Once this belief becomes explicit, the goal becomes a restoration of a balanced set of family relationships reflecting a *genuine* concern with the child's competence.

A final example is a cross-cultural study by Falicov and Karrer (1980). To illustrate how two cultures differentially socialize children's behavior, Falicov and Karrer (1980) explicate the parental beliefs of Mexican-American and Anglo-American couples. Mexican-American children are taught that they are part of a hierarchical system in which control, authority, and wisdom are associated with being elderly and male. In school, they tend to be, by Anglo-American standards, excessively deferential and subservient to male teachers and administrators. They also often seek out a high degree of warmth and nurturance from female teachers. When deferential and nurturance-seeking behaviors become problematic in class and are reported to parents at teacher conference time, the parents are often flattered—not the response consistent with most teachers' expectations or values. Failures to accommodate this culturally accepted pattern to prevailing norms have clear implications for the competence of the child.

Overall, parental beliefs reflect values about children's behavior and the parental role. There is evidence that it is a useful construct, and examples of how parental beliefs are associated with child outcomes were provided. However, children do not have direct access to their parents' beliefs. Rather, they develop expectancies about their parents and behavioral standards by becoming attuned to regularities and contrasts in patterns of parent behavior over time and across situations. Thus, a link must be made between parental beliefs and parental actions. The construct that provides much of this linkage is parental teaching strategies.

Parental Teaching Strategies.   Teaching strategies can be described as the approach used by a parent to influence the child's behavior in an interpersonal situation. Among the most salient of these situations are discipline encounters (Hoffman, 1979; Mancuso & Lehrer, this volume), child–peer or adult–child conflicts (Shure & Spivack, 1978), and educational or instructional experiences (Hess, Holloway, Price, & Dickson, 1982; Hess & McDevitt, this volume). Most research in this area involves either (a) observation of parent (usually mother)–child interaction around one or two tasks such as sorting, jigsaw puzzles, or story telling (e.g., Laosa, 1982; Sigel, 1982) or (b) presentation of hypothetical parent–child or child–child situations (e.g., Shure & Spivack, 1978; Zill & Peterson, 1982). Verbalizations or behavioral styles generally are seen as the independent variables, with the dependent variable usually some aspect of task performance by the child.

Researchers who focus on parent–child interaction vary in what they see as the critical relationship between teaching style and outcome. Hess and Shipman (1965) focused on the way in which a restricted or elaborated linguistic style affected cognitive growth of young children. Bee (1971), however, theorized that linguistic style is a less central characteristic than the way in which mothers focus children's attention on key aspects of the problem and make it "solvable" for them; her research supports her view. Sigel, McGillicuddy-DeLisi, Flaugher, & Rock (1983) believe that teaching strategies are valuable to the extent that they promote higher order mental operations in children, particularly representational thinking. Sigel argues that parents can accomplish this by using "distancing" strategies—verbalizations that lead a child to anticipate future actions or consequences, reconstruct past events, or employ divergent thinking skills (Sigel, McGillicuddy-DeLisi, & Johnson, 1980). This is contrasted with authoritarian strategies, which do not promote cognitive growth.

Sigel et al. (1983) examined strategies used by parents of communication-handicapped and nonhandicapped preschoolers when involved with a story telling and a paper folding task. The results were correlated with children's performances on a variety of cognitive measures, such as the WPPSI, an anticipatory imagery task, memory tasks, and a seriation task. In general, authoritarian strategies were associated with lower task performance; distancing was linked with higher performance (Sigel et al., 1983). However, several studies have found that affective feedback behaviors (e.g., verbal and nonverbal evaluative feedback) seemed more relevant to cognitive outcomes in children from $3\frac{1}{2}$ to $4\frac{1}{2}$ years old than were teaching strategies directed at stimulating the child's own thinking processes (Bee, 1971; Johnson & McGillicuddy-DeLisi, 1983). In McLaughlin's (1983) study, a less structured, free-play situation was used, rather than the highly specific tasks usually employed in this research area. His findings were in exact contrast to those of Bee, Johnson, and McGillicuddy-DeLisi. That is, he found verbal instructional strategies to be most salient for cognitive outcomes. However, his design did not address the array of family context variables implicated as mediators of the teaching strategies child outcome relationship by Sigel et al. (1983). The parent–child interaction research to date has perhaps been most successful in producing some suggestive findings about teaching strategies and cognitive competencies in children and in identifying many factors, such as age and sex of child, ordinal position, family constellation, and task demands, that influence the pattern of obtained results.

The alternative research strategy of presenting vignettes for parental reactions and correlating the strategies to various child outcomes suggests that a competence–performance distinction is being made by different researchers in their approaches to studying these constructs. Sigel (1985) notes that the social psychological literature has joined this issue around the prediction of attitude–behavior relationships. The construct of *intention* has been used to refer to the relationship between one's preference or strategy and the willingness one has to act in accordance with the strategy in a particular situation. Sigel (1985) provides examples of how a parent's anticipation of a child's negative response to a strategy may well lead to that preferred strategy being replaced by a less desirable, but more situationally appropriate, technique. Weick (1971) provides even more basic examples of how everyday events conspire to keep parents from functioning in accordance with their optimal strategies. Such events as a rush-hour commute or a long walk up the stairs into one's apartment at the end of a work day or shopping trip can make the use of commands or if-then statements quite appealing, even to parents who know that they "should" be engaging in a series of inquiry questions to help their child probe past events and future outcomes.

Nevertheless, there are instances in which the main effects of parental teaching strategies generated in response to hypotheical situations is sufficiently strong to be predictive of child outcomes. Newcomb, Huba, and Bentler (1983) investigated the kind of parental teaching strategies that might lead to substance use in middle school-aged children. They hypothesized that direct modeling would be a primary influence, but also considered that cognitive mediation (i.e., children's perceptions of parental substance use), might account for meaningful variance. Newcomb et al. (1983) found that the direct modeling hypothesis applied to marijuana use and the mediation hypothesis accounted for the most variance in children's pill and alcohol use. In addition to linking teaching strategies and children's competence, this study also suggests that children have an active, constructive role in inferring the message, or beliefs, behind parental strategies.

Another line of research with the vignette paradigm has moved in a complementary direction. Shure & Spivack (1978) have conceptually and empirically linked young children's interpersonal-cognitive problem solving skills with their behavioral adjustment. As children learn to think of alternative solutions, consequences, and detailed steps involved in solving problems, they are more likely to behave in socially acceptable ways (Spivack, Platt, & Shure, 1976). Mothers whose teaching strategies encouraged this kind of thinking in their preschoolers had daughers, but not sons, with higher levels of interpersonal problem solving skills. This replicated finding (Shure & Spivack, 1978) reinforces the idea that distancing and related teaching strategies can, under certain conditions, be associated with the development of children's social-cognitive or behavioral competencies. That this finding has emerged despite methodological variations and a host of intervening variables suggests that the parental teaching stretegies construct has considerable utility.

Interrelationship of Parental Beliefs and Parental Teaching Strategies. Aspects of the construct of intentionality, presented earlier, should temper expectations about finding a strong beliefs–strategies correspondence. In both of Sigel's major studies (Sigel et al., 1980; Sigel et al., 1983), the link between beliefs and strategies did not emerge as predicted. Some data suggested that narrowly stated beliefs, such as, "Children's learning occurs as a result of parental rewards and punishments," best predict type of strategy used. However, the error rate was sufficiently high so as to lend doubt to the generality of this result. Nevertheless, these findings both confirm previous observations about the numerous intervening variables operating on the childrearing system in any family, and provide support for the appropriateness of using idiographic methods in subsequent research. Indeed, the challenge of untangling the relationship of beliefs and strategies to each other and to children's competence is a formidable one. As noted earlier, it requires a selection of key variables, an explication of their interrelationship, and operationalization through assessment procedures. The next sections present a model incorporating these three components.

OUTLINE OF CONSTRUCTS WITHIN A COGNITIVE-BEHAVIORAL ASSESSMENT MODEL LINKING BELIEFS AND COMPETENCE

Before proceeding, it would be useful to provide a tangible context within which an application of an idiographic assessment of a family might occur. Two such contexts come immediately to mind. First, a family could enroll in a parenting education program. Prior to intervention, a needs assessment is required to determine strengths and weaknesses in the pattern of family beliefs and interactions. The second is more familiar: a clinical context. Perhaps the parents are unable to manage their child's behavior and/or cannot agree about parenting methods and philosophies. In any case, an assessment of the linkage between parental beliefs and the social competence exhibited by the child would provide essential information for use during treatment.

In both of these types of situations—normative or remediative—the nature of the assessment model to be presented is cognitive-behavioral. Variables such as parental beliefs are social-cognitive; strategies (which are both thought about and put into action) are cognitive and behavioral. A set of mediating variables is also hypothesized that explains the manner in which the family maintains a sense of stability and the specific way in which inputs from each patient fit together to provide socialization messages to children. The operation of factors that link the primary constructs (parental beliefs and teaching strategies) to the outcome (child's social competence) are discussed following definition of the primary constructs in the present study.

Definition and Interrelationship of Primary Constructs Used in the Present Study

Parental beliefs are conceptualized as superordinate constructs, composed of a network of specific beliefs, directed toward defining how a parent believes a child becomes socially competent in two critical socialization domains: with parents and with peers. Parents are asked to rate the extent to which a variety of factors, such as direct modeling, reinforcement, logical explanation, interpersonal experiences, or commands, influences the achievement of competence in a particular domain. From the profile of influences provided, inferences are made about the likelihood that a parent will consider or carry out a particular teaching strategy.

Perhaps the most explicit opportunity for parents to express their beliefs is in the context of interpersonal problem situations that arise in the family. Following a social learning analysis (Bandura, 1977), it was postulated that parents could react to children's problems with these primary teaching strategies: (a) modeling desired behaviors, (b) encouraging children to monitor what happens to them while they attempt to handle problems on their own, (c) provide appropriate reinforcements and sanctions, and (d) using verbal dialogues to help instruct the child on ways problem situations should be approached.

Our particular interest was in the latter teaching strategy. We view such a strategy along a continuum ranging from positive, cognitive growth-enhancing, to negative, dysfunction-promoting. In defining the continuum, we draw most heavily from Sigel et al. (1980, 1983) and Shure and Spivack (1978). Specifically, parents may *tell* children what to do (and potentially discourage a child's own initiative) or *suggest* alternative ideas (and encourage children to think) or *ask* children what they think about different aspects of the problem (and send a meta-communication of confidence in their abilities to think about and solve the problem). Of course, parents, in a particular situation, may use any combination of these three strategies. However, the weight of the evidence seems to indicate that parents tend to settle into relatively stable patterns of use of these strategies during interactions with their children (White, Kaban, & Attanucci, 1979), although these patterns may be situation and goal specific (Emmerich, 1969; Knight, Kagan, & Buriel, 1982). This is especially likely to the extent that teaching strategies, as expressed verbally and behaviorally, closely reflect parental beliefs about the proper course of development for children and the proper role of parents (cf. Newberger & Cook, 1983).

Although there are many indices of children's competence, two types have received strong empirical support and were of particular theoretical interest. Behavioral adjustment in school is most useful to demark particlularly poor or positive levels of interpersonal competence in a salient environment for children. For this purpose, school adjustment ratings contain a baseline comprised of other children in the school presently and other classes the teacher (rater) has observed in the past. Such ratings tend to be more robust than parent ratings as a general indicator of competence and have been associated with measures of peer status, particularly among elementary school-aged children (cf. Kendall & Hollon, 1981).

The second major aspect of competence involves the social-cognitive problem solving skills of children. There is growing evidence that skills such as interpersonal sensitivity, means–ends thinking, self-efficacy expectancies, qualitative strategy of problem resolution, and method of reacting to obstacles encountered when attempting to solve interpersonal problems are important for generalized, flexible social competence in children (Elias & Maher, 1983; Spivack et al., 1976; Urbain & Kendall, 1980). Especially in light of studies suggesting that children's cognitions affect the way they interpret expressions of parental beliefs and strategies, an assessment of social-cognitive skills seemed valuable.

Hypothesized Interrelationships.   Hypothesized interrelationships among the primary constructs in the assessment model are outlined in Table 6.1 Several points are especially noteworthy. The pathway from each belief to child outcomes is outlined separately and can be used to generate a series of hypotheses. For example, parents believing in the influence of adult reward and punishments may express that belief by using Telling as primary verbal teaching strategy and/or by frequently using positive and/or negative comment. The use of Telling and negative comments is predicted as facilitating poor problem solving thinking in the child. The use of positive comments is predicted to enhance both positive school behavior and well-developed problem solving thinking skills. The balance of Telling and positive and negative comments must be examined, however, before hypotheses about outcomes can be made.

Similarly, if parents also believe that their logical explanations are important influences, their use of a Suggesting strategy must be considered. Note that there

TABLE 6.1
Framework of a Cognitive-Behavioral Assessment Model:
Interrelationships Among Constructs Linking Parental Beliefs
to Children's Competence

Beliefs If a child primarily learns through:	*Teaching Strategies* *Then parents' behavior* *should primarily involve:*	*Child Outcome*[a] *And results for the* *child should be:*
1. Own Experiences	Asking	SPS+
	Suggesting	
2. Parents' Logical Explanations	Suggesting	Behavior+
	Telling	
3. Adult Rewards and Punishments	Telling	SPS−
	Frequent Use of	Behavior+
	Positive Comments	SPS+
	Frequent Use of	Behavior−
	Negative Comments	SPS−
4. Adult Modeling		

Note: No specific hypotheses are made concerning strategies and outcomes when parents believe most strongly in Adult Modeling.

[a]SPS+ refers to positive social-cognitive problem solving skills; Behavior+ refers to adequate social adjustment; SPS− and Behavior− refer to inadequate levels of these attributes

is an implicit assumption that the same strategy motivated by different beliefs may be conveyed differently by parents and therefore experienced differently by the child; this particularly applies to a Telling strategy. Overall, then, an assessment of the extent to which parents value or devalue certain sources of influence on their children leads to expectations that they will emphasize certain strategies and that these strategies will have the particular effects outlined in Table 6.1.

Table 6.1 also provides several hypotheses for an assessment that begins with information about a child's social-cognitive problem solving abilities and behavioral adjustment. By reversing the arrows, one can predict that poor problem solving thinking would be associated with a preference for Telling strategies, frequent use of negaitve comments, and an accompanying belief that children learn primarily through adult rewards and punishments. Within our model, poor adjustment is best predicted by the frequent use of negative comments in the context of a belief system emphasizing the role of rewards and punishments. In such a family, children's initiative, response to suggestions, or even attempts to comply with parental commands often would be met with disapproval. In the absence of guidance through positive reinforcement, such children would be likely to experience confusion with regard to appropriate standards for behavior and considerable frustration, anger, and diminished self-efficacy. This constellation of factors is likely to produce behavioral maladjustment (Rutter, 1975). Similarly, hypotheses can be generated about parental strategies and beliefs, based on an assessment of children's social problem solving skills and the parameters in Table 6.1.

Mediators of the Pathways Between Beliefs and Competence

Table 6.1 is incomplete in several important respects. First, no hypotheses were made about the sequelae of having a strong belief in the importance of adult modeling. Second, the model assumes that the belief systems of each parent in a family are concordant. Finally, it excludes the influence of several aspects of the family environment that mediate the extent to which some of the pathways in Table 6.1 have heuristic value. The following section briefly addresses each of these concerns.

The Role of Modeling. "Adult modeling" in Table 6.1 may be considered to denote a belief that children learn best through observing and imitating adults. To make specific hypotheses, however, something must be known about the content or processes being modeled. One relevant set of processes is the extent to which parents possess and model good means–ends thinking abilities. Shure and Spivack (1978), in their research with inner-city mothers, found that those who scored well on a paper-and-pencil measures of means–ends thinking also tended to report the use of Suggesting and Asking dialogue techniques when parenting.

Mothers lower in means–ends thinking tended to use commands and not supply explanations for their actions. Interestingly, it is also plausible that parents who are excellent means/ends thinkers may model an "adults solve the problems in this family" belief that may ultimately inhibit their children's problem solving thinking skills. Thus, parental modeling is conceptualized as a mediating influence that can enhance the socializing impact of other constructs in Table 6.1 depending on their relative presence or absence in a particular family.

Interparental Accord.   For the parental variables discussed in Table 6.1 and the mediating variables presented in this section, the additional consideration of the nature and extent of parental agreement is critical for predicting child outcomes. Rutter (1975) has forcefully articulated the role of parental discord in producing psychological disorders in childhood and adolescence. Bronfenbrenner (1979) has extended this argument to note that, whereas parental discord may not produce diagnosed psychopathology, children and youth from such environments have a greater likelihood of obtaining only a marginal level of social adjustment as adults. Lippitt (1968) provides a similar warning when discussing how children respond to discrepant socialization messages. Of particular concern are the procedures used by families to create some sense of resolution of these discrepancies (Gara, 1982; Stuart, 1980). The opportunity to observe family interaction is an essential assessment tool to determine the way in which each parent's beliefs, teaching strategies, means–ends thinking skills, and other behaviors impinge on the child and influence problem solving and behavioral adjustment.

Family Environment.   Moos (1974) has identified a set of factors that can be used to reliably describe family environments: opportunities for personal growth, nature of interpersonal relationships, and organizational structure. He has also begun to identify ways in which these environmental characteristics can be combined into typologies of adaptive family functioning (Billings & Moos, 1982). Of particular relevance to our model was the extent to which parents described the family environment as reflecting an emphasis on conflict-free, supportive relationships, independence among family members, and maintaining order and control. These factors can be important mediators of the relationships in Table 6.1 in that they provide a broad context around which behavioral strategies can be interpreted. Families characterized as having supportive relationships are generally environments in which children are well-adjusted; however, although an emphasis on order and control can also produce behavioral adjustment in the child, those characteristics are likely to inhibit problem solving thinking (cf. Billings & Moos, 1982). The way independence and supportive relationships in a family covary also reflect different types of family environments. A combination of supportive relationships with independence should facilitate problem solving thinking, particularly if parents' beliefs reflect the importance of children learning through their own experiences. If supportive relationships are lacking and independence is high, a resulting sense of detachment could imply poor problem solving or adjustment. Factors such as use of positive comments and Asking strategies could ameliorate some of the potential negative effect, however.

Conclusions

The cognitive-behavioral assessment model presented in Table 6.1 and elaborated in the discussion of mediating factors illustrates the complexity involved in linking parental beliefs to children's competence within a particular family. Yet, there is a challenge in attempting to understand the pathways and processes suggested by the model. Such assessment efforts, conducted from an idiographic perspective, can have both heuristic and practical significance. The following section describes how the primary constructs and mediating variables were operationalized. Four cases, two selected to allow the left-to-right directionality in Table 6.1 to be followed and two following the reverse directionality, are then described in detail.

PROCEDURES USED WITH FAMILIES

Families were recruited from elementary schools in a working-class community in central New Jersey through notices sent home with second-grade children. The four families selected for this report were part of a larger sample. Each was an intact family, three of which had two children and one had three. Two of the families were selected because the children displayed extreme levels of skills relating to social competence: one child had exemplary social problem solving skills and the other had very poor classroom behavior, as rated by the teacher. The other two families were characterized by spouses who disagree markedly in their beliefs about how children develop competence with peers and with parents.

A family assessment procedure was developed that involved a single home visit, lasting approximately two hours. The procedure consisted of two parts. First, a family interaction task in a game format was conducted for about 30 minutes, to help put the family at ease and measure the variables of interest without sensitizing the family to our specific foci. Then, a series of pencil-and-paper measures were administered separately to each parent. Assessments were conducted by two highly trained pairs of male and female undergraduate psychology majors. Specific instruments used to measure each of the primary constructs in the model are reported next.

Family Interaction Assessment

The Family Experience Game (FEG; Elias & Kelsey, 1981) provided stimulus situations for exploring individual and family problem solving. The FEG is a board game modeled on the work of Blechman & Olson (1976) and is designed to elicit responses to a wide range of problematic social situations and family issues. It incorporates assessment of individuals' social attitudes and skills with group planning and decision-making skills. During the play of the game, participants are presented with a variety of questions concerning common interpersonal situations and are asked about their typical thoughts, feelings and actions vis-a-vis those situations; occasionally, they are asked to role-play their responses. One part of the FEG, the family conference, affords an additional valuable opportunity for observing a family's group process. The family conference requires that all family members participate in discussion and decision making efforts and allows a relatively standardized focus on parental teaching strategies. Among the tasks given to families during the conferences were the following: planning a meal together for which everyone could help prepare something; deciding on events and timing for a family outing; and holding a discussion of how a family could reduce excessive viewing of the television. Although the entire procedure was audiotaped, only the family conference portions were coded for use in this study.

Coding of Family Interaction.   A coding system for parental responses is used to reliably classify verbal behavior into three major categories: (a) *Telling,* exemplified by parents statements telling a child what to do or telling the child what to do accompanied by a reason; (b) *Suggesting,* which included parents letting a child know about their feelings concerning the matter at hand, suggesting to the child possible consequences of an action, or suggesting an alternative approach to a problem for the child's consideration; and (c) *Asking,* which included parents asking the child to think about consequences without providing examples or asking the child to think about conceptions of the situation at hand and alternative solutions for it. The initiation of a statement denoted a new unit of analysis; these units could be coded using more than one category. In addition to reporting the modal strategy used across units, three other indices for which specific hypotheses existed were derived: percentage of units in which Telling, praise or reward, or negative statements were made.

Parental Beliefs Questionnaire

The Beliefs Questionnaire is based on Emmerich's (1969) work with the Parental Role Questionnaire, as well as the work of Sigel et al. (1980). The questionnaire is a paper-and-pencil device designated to assess parents' conception of the importance of an array of potential influences on the development of children's social competence. Short descriptions of a child acting in a positive, prosocial manner in two different situations, at home with the family and at play with peers, were used. Parents were asked to use a 5-point Likert scale (ranging from a very small influence to a very large influence) to report their beliefs about the importance of each of nine different learning pathways in creating the positive outcome. The nine choices include: the effects of the child's behavioral experiences; the parent's use of contingent rewards and punishments; modeling by parents, other adults or child peers; two types of verbal instruction by parents; one style of verbal instruction by teachers; and the child's affective experiences. Parents were also asked to specify and rate any additional influences that came to mind. The responses were reliably combined to form a profile of beliefs concerning four pathways of influence highlighted by social learning theorists: (a) competence experiences of the child, (b) modeling by adults, (c) verbal explanation by parents, and (d) parents' use of rewards and punishments (Bandura, 1977). For the current analysis, interpretation of the profile placed emphasis on patterns of influence most highly endorsed by parents, and contrasted these with influences perceived as relatively unimportant.

Family Environment Scale (FES)

The FES is a questionnaire developed by Moos (1974) and is designed to assess family members' perceptions of the social environment. Six of 10 scales from the short form of the FES were used. Three scales were combined to create Moos' Family Relationships Index (FRI): cohesion (supportiveness of family members), expressiveness (freedom of emotional expression), and conflict (the extent of open hostilities, scored in the reverse). Two scales were combined to create Moos' Systems Maintenance dimension: order and organization (planning and rule clarity) and control (rigidity of procedures). One additional scale, independence (encouragement of self-sufficiency), was also examined. The FES has excellent psychometric properties (internal consistency coefficients range from .64 to .89). In addition, its construct validity has been supported by over fifty studies (Holahan & Moos, 1982; Moos, 1974).

Parental Teaching Strategies Questionnaire

The Strategies Questionnaire presented six common child-oriented problem situations (e.g., exclusion from a group; hit by another child). In each situation, the child brings the problem to a parent. Seven alternatives are provided and the parent is asked to choose the alternative most consistent with what he or she would actually do if confronted with the situation. These seven choices map directly onto the three categories of the coding system used for FEG family conferences previously described, i.e., Asking, Suggesting, and Telling. The modal response across situations and the number of different categories selected were considered indicators of parents' preferred responses when their children are faced with difficulties.

Means–Ends Thinking

Parents' cognitive-social problem solving skills were assessed using a content-modified version of Platt and Spivack's (1975) Means–Ends Problem Solving (MEPS) procedure. Two stories, portraying interpersonal problem situations accompanied by positive final outcomes, were presented to each parent in written form.

One story concerned a quarrel between friends; the other involved becoming a neighborhood leader. Parents were requested to supply the middle of the story, i.e., the events that could have hypothetically taken place between the advent of the problem and its resolution. Answers were scored for total number of means and anticipated potential obstacles supplied. In our larger sample, interrater reliability across stories is in the high .90s. MEPS scores have been found to relate to various adjustment criteria within psychiatric populations, and they have been successfully used to discriminate between clinical and nonclinical populations (Platt & Spivack, 1975).

Social-Cognitive Problem Solving

At school, the Social Problem Situation Analysis Measure (SPSAM) was administered to each child. It consists of a series of cards depicting unfolding sequences of interaction during a problematic situation, such as coping with rejection by peers or wanting something another peer has. Scores are provided for interpersonal sensitivity, primary self-efficacy expectancies (consisting of the value of personal initiative and the valence of expected outcomes in the situations presented), means–ends cognitive problem solving (measuring alternative thinking and planning skills) and qualitative strategy for problem resolution (e.g., mutual compromise, aggression, nonconfrontation, wishful resolution). The latter three indices are also tapped as the child responds to examiner-provided obstacles to his or her responses. Both convergent and discriminate validity and satisfactory reliability have been reported in several studies (e.g., Elias, 1980).

Behavioral Adjustment in School

A revision of the Acting Out–Mood–Learning (AML) Scale was completed by classroom teachers. A series of recent studies has supported the utility of the AML as a moderately precise screening measure of adjustment (e.g., Durlak,

Stein, & Mannarino, 1980). For the present study, teachers rated children as outstanding, average, having difficulty in one or two areas (A, M, or L), or generally poor in adjustment.

ANALYSIS AND INTERPRETATION OF FAMILY ASSESSMENTS

Each set of variables in the theoretical model outlined earlier was assessed by a specific instrument, with the exception of parental teaching strategies. For the latter, both competence (self-report) and performance (FEG) indices were used. The resulting data provide rich and detailed information about each family. A summary of the most salient findings can be found in Table 6.2 The next section contains descriptions of each family, based on these data. Two families are presented from the perspective of beginning with the child outcome data, building a heuristic model by gradually adding the parent data. For the other families, the parental belief data are discussed first, followed by the remaining parent data and the indices of child outcome. Each description concludes with several hypotheses concerning implications of the interaction of different constructs and of the continuation of observed patterns over time for the development of social competence for the focal child.

The Warm Family

The Warm family has two children, both girls, aged 15 and 8 (Linda). Mr. Warm is a senior-level university professor with a doctorate, and Mrs. Warm is a secretary who completed 3 years of college. Linda showed excellent social problem solving skills (cf. Table 6.2). Her self-efficacy expectancies and means–ends thinking in peer-related situations were quite positive, and she maintained these levels when interpersonal obstacles were encountered. Most significant, however, was Linda's interpersonal sensitivity. Linda focused on feelings, was aware of various persons' perspectives in problem situations, and grasped situations quickly. Her modal style of problem resolution was to seek out mutual compromises. In school, her behavior was seen as satisfactory.

To obtain a better understanding of Linda, Mr. and Mrs. Warm's data were examined. Although MEPS data were not collected for the Warms, both behavioral and self-report data on parental teaching strategies were available. During the Family Experience Game, their preferred strategies were Suggesting and Asking, and they also used the highest level of praise and encouragement of any family assessed. In their responses to vignettes involving children, their modal strategy was Asking (e.g., "What are some ways you can join the group?"). The beliefs of both parents concerning factors influencing children's competence were generally concordant. Both parents rejected the ultimate value of direct

TABLE 6.2
Parameters for Analysis of Family Case Studies

Variable Sets	Family			
	Warm	*Agree*	*Firm*	*Apart*
Parental Beliefs[a]				
1. Child's Experience	+M	+M,F	−M,F	−F
2. Parents' Explaining	+M,F	−M,F	−F	+F
3. Adult Reward and Punish	−M		+M,F	+M
4. Adult Modeling		−F	+M,F	−M
Family Environment[b]				
1. Family Relationship Index	1	3	2	4
2. Independence	4	2	3	1
3. Maintenance	4	2	1	3
Parental Teaching Strategies[c]				
1. Self-Reported Modal Strategy	A	A	S	S
2. FEG Modal Strategy	S,A	S	S(F),A,S,(M)	A(F),A,S,(M)
3. FEB % Telling[d]	2.5,2.2	8.4,10.7	0,0	0,0
4. FEG % Rewards[d]	22.8,14.3	5.0,4.3	12.5,11.1	9.1,6.7
5. FEG % Negative[d]	0,0	0,0	0.3,7	9.1,0
Parents' Means Ends Thinking[b]				
1. MEPS Score	N/A	1	2	3

(continued)

TABLE 6.2 (Continued)

	Family			
Variable Sets	Warm	Agree	Firm	Apart
Child's Social Cognitive Problem Solving[e]				
1. Interpersonal Sensitivity	2	1	1	0
2. Primary Expectancies	2[g]	2	2	1[g]
3. Primary MECPS[f]	2	1	2	1
4. Obstacle Expectancies	2[g]	2	0	2[g]
5. Obstacle MECPS[f]	2	2	0	0
6. Primary Modal Strategy	mutual compromise	direct discussion	direct discussion	wishful resolution
7. Obstacle Modal Strategy	nonconfrontation	nonconfrontation	giving up	—
School Adjustment				
1. AML Scores	adequate	unsatisfactory	exemplary	adequate

[a] + denotes relatively strong influences; − denotes relatively weak influences; M denotes mother; F denotes father
[b] rank of scores in this sample; 1 denotes highest rank
[c] A = asking, S = suggesting, T = telling
[d] percentage of all responses for mothers, fathers in FEG
[e] 2 denotes presence of skill on both stories, 1 denotes presence on one story, 0 denotes absence of skill
[f] means-ends cognitive problem solving (alternatives, consequences, planning, anticipating obstacles)
[g] skill level slightly below the indicated score

authoritarian parenting strategies, and agreed on the importance of explaining the reasons for requests to children. Mrs. Warm particularly seemed to believe that parental punishment was not helpful, preferring her children to learn from their varied expreiences. Both parents perceived the family environment as highly relationship-oriented; they did not characterize the family as independent or as concerned with maintenance activities.

Interpretations and Hypotheses.   There are several factors that may account for Linda Warm's excellent problem solving skills. Her parents seem to encourage her problem solving efforts while attempting to be minimally controlling or negatively evaluative. Her interpersonal sensitivity may relate to the family's strong relationship orientation and corresponding tendency not to value independence. What may be most surprising is that, given Linda's problem solving capabilities, her school behavior is only satisfactory. By considering all of the parent data together, one can develop an explanatory hypothesis. The Warms have created a family context in which problem solving, warmth, and mutual support are accepted. They tend to be close-knit and not concerned with maintenance factors such as order and organization and rule clarity. Given the tendency of teachers to emphasize maintenance and given the likelihood that school has a lower reinforcement value for Linda than do her family relationships, it is possible that Linda would not feel it necessary to use her problem solving skills at their highest levels.

The point of this rather detailed analysis is to suggest that the generally positive results portrayed in the family assessment contain one caveat. There may eventually be some conflict between school and family values and it would be unfortunate for Linda if she were forced to make a choice between these two essential sources of socialization and support. Because such conflicts are not uncommon in families with children of elementary school age, it would seem beneficial for the Warms to attend a parent education program addressing this issue and its impact on children's competence (Harman & Brim, 1981).

The Agree Family

The Agree family has two children, both boys, age 10 and $7\frac{1}{2}$ (Rudy). Mrs. Agree is a homemaker and her husband is a salesman. Mr. Agree graduated from college and Mrs. Agree, high school. Rudy's teacher rated his behavior as highly unsatisfactory, especially in the areas of self-control and mood. Inerestingly, Rudy seems to possess more than adequate social-cognitive problem solving skills; in fact, in his responses to obstacles he showed highly positive self-efficacy expectancies and means–ends thinking.

Mr. and Mrs. Agree possess the highest level of means–ends thinking of any family assessed, indicating their ability to resolve difficulties with their peers. Their preferred teaching strategies are oriented toward facilitating children's decision making through Suggesting and Asking. In the Family Experience Game, Mr. and Mrs. Agree expressed a wide range of teaching strategies but the lowest proportion of feedback responses, either positive or negative, of any family assessed. The following excerpt from the FEG illustrates this point.

Task: *Plan a meal in which everyone will be involved. When will it be?*
Mrs. A.: First we have to decide what we're going to have.
Rudy: Fondue.
Brother: Go home!
Mrs. A.: Fondue?
Rudy: We haven't had it for a long time!
Brother: Let's get it and do it.
Mrs. A.: Well, everyone likes lasagna, right?
Brother: Yeah.
Mr. A.: It has to be a meal. How about breakfast?
Brother: Boring.
Mr. A.: How about breakfast? We can make pancakes.
Mrs. A.: Okay.
Brother: And strawberries.
Mrs. A.: Strawberries? Okay.
Rudy: You don't like pancakes.
Mr. A.: We can mix the flour and the milk. And the boys can help me with all the ingredients. And your mother can. . .
Brother: Get some strawberries. . .
Mr. A.: And cut the bananas and strawberries and things we might have with it.
Mrs. A.: That sounds good.
Brother: I'll make the coffee.
Mrs. A.: Okay?
Rudy: I'll help dad with the ingredients.
Dad: Who wants to break the eggs?
Mrs. A.: Wait. When's this gonna happen?
Brother: You!
Rudy: I want to break the eggs.
Mrs. A.: How about Sunday!
Brother: All right, Sunday morning.
Rudy: Well. . .
Mrs. A.: We don't even have to do it this weekend. We could do it next Saturday.
Brother: Just do it Sunday?
Mrs. A.: Sunday?
Brother: Yeah.
Mrs. A.: Okay.

Mr. and Mrs. Agree used Asking and Suggesting techniques almost exclusively. Their approach allowed the discussion to move from a dinner (fondue, lasagna) to a breakfast, and then for all family members to have input into the detailed plans. Through well-timed suggestions and statements of acceptance, the parents seemed to generate a *de facto* consensus into which no one seemed coerced. This pattern was replicated in other family conference questions as well. To summarize up this point, the picture is one of parents who are skilled at resolving problems with their peers, display a range of problem solving strategies for their children to observe, and also make suggestions to their children in problematic situations; also, they do not seem to emphasize the frequent use of praise or negative statements as a way of providing guidelines and boundaries for their children's responses.

The parental beliefs data provide some valuable added information. As Table 6.2 shows, Mr. and Mrs. Agree have remarkable concordance in their beliefs about how children become competent. They feel this occurs primarily through the child's experiences; parental authority, expressed as ordering, instructing, or modeling for children, was believed to have the least influence on children's competence. The parents differed, however, in their perception of the family environment. Mr. Agree sees the family relationships as in some disharmony; conflict is moderate, independence high, and maintenance was seen as absent. Mrs. Agree sees family relationships as moderately close; conflict is absent, independence moderate, and maintenance, particularly order and organization, was seen as high. Thus, although Rudy's parents agree that he will learn mainly from his experiences, they do not agree about the kind of environment the family is currently presenting.

Interpretation and Hypotheses.   Although the data do not provide an unambiguous picture of the reasons for Rudy's poor school adjustment, several hypotheses can be generated for further consideration. Rudy has been socialized to learn from his experiences; he has become a good problem solver and especially adept at overcoming obstacles, which he probably encounters at a rate higher than many of his peers. His household is not especially warm and people tend to go their own way. Perhaps most critically, he is given relatively few explicit external or self-control messages. Rather, Rudy is expected to extract rules of behavior inductively, from his experience. Mischel (1979) and Meichenbaum (1977) warn that lack of explicit, clear controls in young children is related to impulsive, acting-out behavior. It is also possible that Rudy is experiencing some tension resulting from Mr. and Mrs. Agree's different perceptions of the nature of the present family environment. One would predict that his negative behavior would be resistant to change unless his parents shifted their beliefs about the importance of specific, clear adult and parental guidelines in Rudy's becoming adequately adjusted to school.

The Firm Family

Mr. and Mrs. Firm have two children. Lisa is 8 years old and her brother is 6. Mrs. Firm is a medical assistant and Mr. Firm is a warehouse worker; both completed high school and 1 year of college. They have some interesting differences in the strength of certain beliefs about how children become competent. Mr. Firm believes that parents' use of rewards and punishments and parental modeling are the primary influences; he feels that children's learning by experience is less important. Mrs. Firm believes in these same influences but more strongly. In addition, she rejects the value of parental explanations as socializing tools; her preference is for direct adult, and especially parental, actions. The family environment is generally consistent with these beliefs. Maintenance was perceived as higher than for any other family assessed; independence was correspondingly low. These findings are mediated by the relatively high family relationship index. Apparently, the firmness of Mr. and Mrs. Firm is being carried out in a caring context. Both Rutter (1975) and Hoffman (1979) have indicated that the proper blend of parental warmth and control can produce prosocial behavior and positive adjustment in young children.

Mr. and Mrs. Firm's teaching strategies consistently expressed their beliefs. In the Family Experience Game, they exhibited relatively few different styles; their preference was to issue rather strong Suggestions and reinforce agreement with these. When there was disagreement, Mrs. Firm would express her disapproval. Neither parent made any explanatory statements.

Task: *Plan a meal in which everyone will be involved. When will it be?*
Mr. F.: Count me out.
Mrs. F.: Now, everyone's got to participate.
Sister: Oh my gosh.
Mrs. F.: Everyone can help cook. What can you make?
Sister: Well, all I can make is pan. . .
Lisa: I can make a cake.
Sister: I can make pancakes.
Mrs. F. Oh, you can make pancakes.
Sister: Yeah, and boiled eggs.
Lisa: Cake doesn't go with pancakes, though.
Mrs. F.: Well, what can you make that goes with pancakes?
Sister: Sunnyside eggs.
Lisa: And scrambled eggs.
Mrs. F.: Yeah, you're pretty good with omelettes, too.
Lisa: I could do sunnyside-up eggs.
Mrs. F.: Well, the pancakes are enough for one thing and one person.
Mr. F.: I can make the toast.
Lisa: That's right.

Mr. F.: I like that.

Mrs. F.: Okay. Sister makes pancakes, Lisa makes eggs, and you (Mr. F.) make the toast.

Lisa: What are you going to make?

Mrs. F.: I'll do sausages. Does that sound like a reasonable meal?

Lisa: I guess so.

Mr. F.: When are we going to do this?

Sister: Oh, gee.

Lisa: Sunday.

Mrs. F.: Sunday morning.

Mr. F.: Sunday morning.

What is most interesting is the complete sense of parental control in this family conference situation. Sister's reactions at two points: "Oh my gosh," and "Oh, gee," suggest that problem resolution is in the hands of the parents. Even though Mr. and Mrs. Firm encouraged discussion by Lisa and her sister, the parents stamped approval on decisions. Mr. and Mrs. Firm's suggestions—toast and sausages—were neither explained nor questioned, and Mrs. Firm's assignment of tasks was similarly accepted. Data from self-reported responses to vignettes showed Suggestions to be their modal strategy, although the behavioral responses have clarified the way in which these suggestions are used. In the context of all the other data, the parents' relatively good means–ends thinking skills may be thought of as modeling the value of problem solving for Lisa and/or reinforcing the notion that in this family, the parents are the problem solvers.

The impact of these parental factors on Lisa Firm is quite interesting. Lisa is seen as among the very best adjusted students in her class. Her self-control, emotional stability, and learning skills were all rated as exemplary by her teacher, much as Rutter (1975) and Hoffman (1979) might predict. Her social-cognitive problem solving skills, as shown in Table 6.2, were more than adequate in primary problem situations, i.e., when a problem such as rejection by peers is first encountered. However, when Lisa faced obstacles, her self-efficacy expectancies and means–ends thinking scores were quite low, and her predominant resolution strategy was to "give up." This finding is similar to that uncovered by Elias, Larcen, Zlotlow, and Chinsky (1978) and Elias and Gordon (1983): Positive adjustment can be based on a sense of support and respectful acquiescence to adult direction, and the latter may be incompatible with a strong divergent thinking and problem solving orientation.

Interpretations and Hypotheses.   Mr. and Mrs. Firm believe that parents and other significant adults shape their children's competence through their modeling, by providing rewards and punishments, and by making clear, directive suggestions. They also provide a family environment characterized by strong relationships and strong controls. Lisa Firm has emerged as an exemplary student, following school rules and procedures for behavior and learning. However, her social problem solving skill profile suggests an external locus of control and an inability to cope well with interpersonal obstacles. One might wonder how Lisa will function in a poorly structured environment, or when she makes the difficult transition from elementary school to middle school.

The Apart Family

The Apart Family has three children—two daughters, aged 20 and 6, and a son (Warren), aged 8. Mr. Apart works as a teacher and Mrs. Apart is a homemaker; she is a high school graduate and he has a bachelor's degree. The Aparts have widely discordant beliefs about how children become competent. Mrs. Apart believes that parent rewards and punishments are most important and that direct modeling is least valuable. Her husband believes that children respond to explanation; what children take from their independent experiences is of relatively little positive influence. The family environment is characterized by a high degree of independence and the lowest family relationship index of any family assessed; maintenance is also relatively low.

Data concerning the expression of parental beliefs adds to the image of a parenting system in disharmony. Mrs. Apart uses Suggestions, particularly those cast in an if–then framework. Mr. Apart's response to the self-report vignettes and the Family Experience Game were not consistent. Of note, however, was his preference for using a questioning approach in the FEG, while combining this with the highest proportion of negative comments of any parent assessed. Overall, the Aparts were the least facilitative of children's problem solving thinking of any parents assessed, and their own means–ends thinking tended to be low.

Warren was the focal child of our assessment. His school functioning was rated by his teacher as adequate. However, his problem solving scores were the lowest of any child assessed. Interpersonal sensitivity and primary self-efficacy expectancies were especially low, and his preferred primary problem resolution strategy was wishful or magical thinking. One might anticipate that Warren is able to adjust to his second-grade class but lacks the base of emotional support and problem solving skills to respond well to difficult or challenging environments. *The data as presented* represent a snapshot of a family system with a long history of shared experiences. If the discordant beliefs between the parents represent a continuing trend, however, one might consider Warren at risk for future difficulty, particularly in adolescence.

Interpretation and Hypotheses.   Mr. and Mrs. Apart exhibited beliefs and strategies associated with poor child outcomes. Their son Warren showed adequate school adjustment but deficits in social problem solving were apparent. The data suggest careful monitoring of Warren's functioning in school and with peers. The Aparts would also benefit from an intervention directed toward reducing the discrepancy in their parental beliefs and increasing positive family relationships. At some point, further development of Warren's problem solving competencies also seems advisable.

DISCUSSION

To develop hypotheses about family function—an explicit theory of each family system—we drew from the literature on parental beliefs, defined key constructs and their interrelationships, identified mediating variables, and operationalized these ideas within a cognitive-behavioral assessment model. Our assessment included a home visit of approximately 2 hours, a half-hour, in-school assessment of children's problem solving, and administering to teachers a brief rating scale. The information obtained is, of course, a small sample of a much larger, dynamic stream of interactive behavior within each family.

Nevertheless, the four families studied illustrate the complex and configural relationship between parental beliefs and teaching strategies and children's social competence. The pathways outlined in Table 6.1 were, for these families, valuable heuristics with which to organize information and generate hypotheses. However, the mediating variables identified—parents' means–ends thinking, perceptions of the family environment, and interparental accord—provided conceptual linkages that enhanced the internal consistency of interpretations made. Indeed, the case studies should confirm that there is generally no one-to-one correspondence between parental beliefs or teaching strategies and aspects of child outcomes.

The Firm family provides a clear example of the potential heuristic value of the cognitive-behavioral assessment model presented earlier. Parental beliefs, the family environment maintenance dimension, and parental teaching strategies indicate parental control, exercised through rewards, punishments and modeling, and what can be interpreted as firm Suggestions. Interestingly, most research on parental beliefs focuses extensively on parent characteristics, management strategies and verbal interactions (Laosa & Sigel, 1982; Sigel, 1983b). Data from the family relationship index, however, placed the previously noted findings in a new context and led to a more positive interpretation of the family structure for the focal child, Lisa. Further, when social problem solving under obstacle and non-obstacle conditions were compared, the significance of Lisa's exemplary school behavior was also refined. Perhaps her ability to cope with nonsupportive and/or poorly structured environments is lacking. This calls to mind an issue too involved to pursue here, but one that should be noted: socializing children for positive *adjustment* is not always identical to socializing them for generalized interpersonal and academic *competence* (cf. Elias & Gordon, 1983). If we were clinicians seeing Lisa, we would raise with Mr. and Mrs. Firm our concern about her ability to cope with interpersonal obstacles and we would inquire as to how they are preparing her to do that. As nomothetic researchers, we might be more inclined to focus on the main effect of parental influences leading to good problem solving overall and a high score on the teacher rating scale.

The absence of systematic correspondence of beliefs and behaviors poses a challenge to our assessment and hypothesis-generating model. Although Weick (1971) outlined practical reasons why beliefs might not always be followed, there is a deeper theoretical point to consider. The "intentionality" construct suggests that perhaps beliefs are not put into practice because they are prejudged as unlikely to be successful. This is consistent with the notion of bidirectionality of parent–child influence, at the levels of direct interaction and over a longer time span (cf. Sigel, 1983a). We view the evidence of White et al. (1979), Emmerich (1969) and others, particularly in the clinical literature, as indicating that parental beliefs tend to be stable; teaching strategies may be more changeable in the service of carrying out those beliefs, but many parents are loath to shift their strategies, even in the face of evidence that they are not well-received by the child.

It is our view that inconsistency of parental beliefs and teaching strategies is likely a function of the operation of belief systems other than those involving child-rearing, and the relative reinforcement values a parent holds for these systems. In cases of child maltreatment, a predominant belief that a parent should be the breadwinner and provider can lead to conflict with beliefs about being a patient and understanding parent, especially given conditions of economic impoverishment and personal humiliation. The belief system around being an economic provider may fuel frustration and lashing out, or withdrawal, that exceeds the reinforcement available for behaving in accordance with one's beliefs about how a competent parent should act. The attunements in such situations can shift dramatically, thereby increasing the likelihood of child maltreatment (cf. Belsky, 1981).

More direct evidence of the operation of conflicting belief systems can be found by examining our assessment procedures. An in-home assessment often mobilizes belief systems concerning the desirability of making a certain impression on others. We conjecture that this may account for the consistent finding in our sample that strategies displayed on the FEG were more facilitative of cognitive growth than were modal levels elicited in the more private, self-report vignettes. Both parenting and assessment situations cannot be interpreted outside of the matrix of beliefs and preferences that operate on all setting inhabitants. Such factors place some limits on the degree of comprehensiveness and inclusiveness that can be attained by the model in Table 6.1 and the mediating variables. However, they also suggest additional foci for more extended assessments.

The likelihood that multiple belief systems operate in unison (and competition) highlights an aspect of our assessment model in particular need of development: rules that can be used to combine information into typologies of family functioning. At present, there do not seem to be any criteria for defining, within the constructs identified in our model, necessary or sufficient conditions for promoting competent, marginal, or inadequate adjustment by children. Data from the Agree family raise the intriguing possibility that the *absence* of certain behaviors—negative comments—may be problematic for a child receiving few positive comments in an environment with relatively low support and cohesiveness. Also, interpretations of the overall pattern of the interplay of factors associated with the Agree child's poor school adjustment derives in part from the authors' own clinical and intuitive norms, norms that can be made more explicit as the model is used with greater frequency and breadth.

Another aspect of rules that needs to be explored involves ways to more systematically interpret data under conditions of low or moderate interparental accord. When should data from each parent be treated separately, and when should they be combined? When combining data, how should different scores be weighted? Children extract socialization messages from the intersection of a variety of aspects of parental belief systems. What predicts the salience of different messages? To what is the child most attuned? According to Rotter (1954), reinforcement value of each parent, both overall and in particular situations, must be considered. Shure and Spivack's (1978) work suggests that sex of parent may exert an important modeling influence on preschool-aged children; there is also the likelihood that the child's attunements change over the course of his or her development. Currently, we are preparing to analyze a sample of families with focal children in fifth grade and therein more closely examine the mediating roles of developmental level and gender, albeit in an exploratory manner. Indeed, previous work has already suggested the differential impact of various parental strategies within the preschool years (Bee, 1971; Johnson & McGillicuddy-DeLisi, 1983; Shure & Spivack, 1978). Much needs to be learned about patterns characteristic of the families of older children and adolescents and the continuities or discontinuities over time.

Directions for Future Inquiry

One premise of our study has been the value of an idiographic approach to assessment and data analysis as a tool for building our conceptual models of how children are socialized to become interpersonally competent. Sigel (1983b) has made a thorough analysis of models of parent–child research and, in so doing, provides criteria for examining how researchers make inferences about child outcomes. Our study reflects both the strengths and weaknesses of an idiographic approach. Specific areas of weakness include a small number of cases, failure to provide sequential analysis of family interaction patterns, failure to consider extrafamilial influences on parent and child functioning, and our exclusive focus on outcomes for one child in the family, with the implicit omission of sibling interaction patterns and indirect pathways of influence from parents to the focal child through the siblings. Although Table 6.1 presented pathways between the major variables in two directions (i.e., from beliefs to outcomes and vice versa), ours is not a true bidirectional interactive model (Sigel, 1983b). An additional weakness, noted earlier, is that the data are discussed mainly in terms of within-sample differences and without reference to some independently interpretable norms or criteria.

There are also several strengths of our approach, according to Sigel's (1983b) criteria. First, the array of factors covered and the attention to separate as well as joint parental influences begins to approximate the systemic nature of family socialization processes. Second, the case study approach seeks to integrate each piece of information about the family into a contextually rich explanation of its functioning. In more nomothetic approaches, information is compared with a central tendency and data that do not conform are treated as outliers, error variance that might cancel out across a large number of cases, or simply "unexplained variance." The goal of such studies is to establish some general laws of family functioning. However, Gara (1982) strongly argues that idiographic approaches must be further developed and refined. For the developmental researcher, program planner, or clinician interested in understanding the laws governing the dynamics of a specific family, particularly one in which the behavior of some member may be harmful to him or herself or others, there is little room for unexplained variance. A model that is of heuristic and predictive value and serves as a guide for effective intervention or developmental planning is essential. It is to accommodate research and theory building to this latter purpose that we have chosen to pursue our present program of inquiry.

The cognitive-behavioral assessment information can be used to generate an analysis and interpretation of the functioning of a particular family, as was presented for the four families in the present study. In the course of subsequent contacts with the family, the hypotheses generated could be put to a test, through naturalistic study, experimental manipulations, or through educative or remedial intervention. Has the assessment information served a heuristic purpose? Do interventions guided by one's model have the intended affects? What changes in the pathways among variables and in the influence of mediating factors do one's outcomes suggest? These and related questions, aggregated across numerous, well-documented examples, should indicate the extent to which the emphasis given to parental beliefs and teaching strategies as essential aspects of children's socialization for competence is warranted. Similarly, the utility of alternative assessment instruments and strategies can also be determined and procedures appropriately modified.

As more researchers consider using an idiographic methodology in conjunction with nomothetic methods, knowledge can advance at the level of general theory and also in the elaboration of middle-level constructs that are so essential for relatively specific predictions of behavior (Rotter, 1954; Wiggins, 1973).

Advances in single-case and replicated single-case study designs promise to give increasing rigor to idiographic methods (Barlow, Hayes, & Nelson, 1983). Such developments will eventually focus our attention away from seeking to establish the fact that parental beliefs, strategies, and behaviors influence child outcomes. Instead, we will be attuned to asking *how* this influence occurs in different family contexts and what factors serve to support or detract from the socialization of competence for our children.

ACKNOWLEDGMENTS

Preparation of this article was supported in part by a National Institute of Mental Health Grant to the first author and a William T. Grant Foundation Action-Research Grant to Maurice J. Elias and John F. Clabby. We gratefully acknowledge the assistance of John F. Clabby and the Middlesex, New Jersey, school system, especially Thomas Schuyler. We are also grateful to Richard Ashmore and David Brodzinsky for their helpful comments and suggestions on an earlier draft of this chapter.

REFERENCES

Bacon, M., & Ashmore, R. (1982). The role of categorization in the socialization process: How parents and older siblings cognitively organize child behavior. In L. Laosa & I. Sigel (Eds.), *Families as learning environments for children* (pp. 301–372). New York: Plenum.

Bandura, A. (1977). Self-efficacy: Toward a unifying theory of behavioral change. *Psychological Review, 84,* 191–215.

Barlow, D. H., Hayes, S. C., & Nelson, R. D. (1983). *The scientist practitioner: Research and accountability in clinical and educational settings.* New York: Pergamon.

Bee, H. (1971). Socialization for problem solving. In J. Aldous, T. Condon, R. Hill, M. Straus, & I. Tallman (Eds.), *Family problem solving* (pp. 186–225). Hinsdale, IL: Dryden.

Belsky, J. (1981). Early human experience: A family perspective. *Developmental Psychology, 17,* 3–23.

Billings, A. G., & Moos, R. H. (1982). Family environments and adaptation: A clinically applicable typology. *American Journal of Community Psychology, 10,* 26–38.

Blechman, L. A. & Olson, D. H. L. (1976). The family contract game: Description and effectiveness. In D. H. L. Olson (Ed.), *Treating relationships.* Lake Mills, IA: Graphic.

Bradt, J. O. (1980). The family with young children. In E. Carter & M. McGoldrick (Eds.), *The family life cycle: A framework for family therapy* (pp. 121–146). New York: Gardner Press.

Bronfenbrenner, U. (1979). *The ecology of human development: Experiments by nature and design.* Cambridge, MA: Harvard University Press.

Durlak, J. A., Stein, M. A., & Mannarino, A. P. (1980). Behavioral validity of a brief teacher rating scale (AML) in identifying high-risk acting-out children. *American Journal of Community Psychology, 8,* 101–115.

Elias, M. J. (1980). *Developing instructional strategies for television-based preventive mental health curricula in elementary school settings.* Unpublished doctoral dissertation, University of Connecticut.

Elias, M. J., & Gordon, S. B. (1983, December). *A hierarchy of social cognitive problem-solving skills underlying behavior performance.* Paper presented at the annual convention of the Association for the Advancement of Behavior Theory, Washington, DC.

Elias, M. J., & Kelsey, J. W. (1981). *The family experience: A new psychotherapeutic game for children and parents.* Paper presented at the annual meeting of the American Psychological Association, Los Angeles, CA.

Elias, M. J. Larcen, S. W., Zlotlow, S. F., & Chinsky, J. M. (1978, August). *An innovative measure of children's cognitions in problematic interpersonal situations.* Paper presented at the meeting of the American Psychological Association, Toronto, Canada.

Elias, M. J., & Maher, C. A. (1983). Social and affective development in children: A contemporary programmatic perspective. *Exceptional Children, 49,* 339–346.

Emmerich, W. (1969). The parental role: A functional-cognitive approach. *Monographs of the Society for Research in Child Development, 34,* (8).

Falicov, C., & Karrer, B. (1980). Cultural variations in the family life cycle: The Mexican-American family. In E. Carter & M. McGoldrick, *The family life cycle: A framework for family therapy* (pp. 383–425). New York: Gardner Press.

Gara, M. A. (1982). Back to basics in personality study in the individual person's own organization of experience: The individuality corollary. In J. Mancuso & J. Adams-Webber (Eds.), *The construing person.* New York: Praeger.

Harman, D., & Brim, O. (1981). *Learning to be parents: Principles, programs, and methods.* Beverly Hills, CA: Sage.

Hess, R. D., Holloway, S., Price, G., & Dickson, W. (1982). Family environments and the acquisition of reading skills: Toward a more precise analysis. In L. Laosa & I. Sigel (Eds.), *Families as learning environments for children* (pp. 87–114). New York: Plenum.

Hess, R. D., & Shipman, V. C. (1965). Early experience and the socialization of cognitive modes in children. *Child Development, 34,* 869–886.

Hoffman, M. L. (1979). Development of moral thought, feeling, and behavior. *American Psychologist, 34,* 958–966.

Holahan, C. J., & Moos, R. H. (1982). Social support and adjustment: Predictive benefits of social climate indices. *American Journal of Community Psychology, 10,* 403–443.

Johnson, J. E., & McGillicuddy-DeLisi, A. (1983). Family environment factors and childrens' knowledge of rules and conventions. *Child Development, 54,* 218–226.

Kelly, G. (1955). *The psychology of personal constructs.* New York: Norton.

Kendall, P., & Hollon, S. (1981). *Assessment strategies for cognitive-behavioral interventions.* New York: Academic Press.

Knight, G , Kagan, S., & Buriel, R. (1982). Perceived parental practices and prosocial development. *Journal of Genetic Psychology, 141,* 57–65.

Laosa, L. (1982). Families as facilitators of children's intellectual development at 3 years of age: A causal analysis. In L. Laosa & I. Sigel (Eds.), *Families as learning environments for children* (pp. 1–46). New York: Plenum.

Laosa, L., & Sigel, I. (1982). *Families as learning environments for children.* New York: Plenum.

Lippitt, R. (1968). Improving the socialization process. In J. Clausen (Ed.), *Socialization and society* (pp. 321–374). Boston: Little, Brown.

McArthur, L., & Baron, R. (1983). Toward an ecological theory of social perception. *Psychological Review, 90,* 215–238.

McGillicuddy-DeLisi, A. (1982). The relationship between parents' beliefs about development and family constellation, socioeconomic status, and parents' teaching strategies. In L. Laosa & I. Sigel (Eds.), *Families as learning environments for children* (pp. 261–300). New York: Plenum.

McLaughlin, B. (1983). Child compliance to parental control techniques. *Developmental Psychology, 19,* 667–673.

Meehl, P. (1954). *Clinical versus statistical prediction: A theoretical analysis and a review of the evidence.* Minneapolis, MN: University of Minnesota Press.

Meichenbaum, D. (1977). *Cognitive-behavior modification: An integrative approach.* New York: Plenum.

Mischel, W. (1979). On the interface of cognition and personality: Beyond the person-situation debate. *American Psychologist, 34,* 740–754.

Moos, R. H. (1974). *Family Environment Scale Manual.* Palo Alto, CA: Consulting Psychologists Press.

Newberger, C., & Cook, M. (1983). Parental awareness and child abuse: A cognitive-developmental analysis of urban and rural samples. *American Journal of Orthopsychiatry, 53,* 512–524.

Newcomb, M., Huba, G., & Bentler, P. (1983). Mothers' influence on the drug use of their children: Confirmatory tests of direct modeling and mediational theories. *Developmental Psychology, 19,* 714–726.

Platt, J. J., & Spivack, G. (1975). *Manual for the Means–Ends Problem Solving Procedures (MEPS).* Philadelphia: Hahnemann Community Mental Health/Mental Retardation Center.

Rotter, J. B. (1954). *Social learning and clinical psychology.* Englewood Cliffs, NJ: Prentice-Hall.

Rotter, J. B. (1982). *The development and application of social learning theory.* New York: Praeger.

Rutter, M. (1975). *Helping troubled children.* New York: Plenum.

Shure, M. B., & Spivack, G. (1978). *Problem solving techniques in childrearing.* San Francisco: Jossey-Bass.

Sigel, I. (1982). The relationship between parental distancing strategies and the child's cognitive behavior. In L. Laosa & I. Sigel (Eds.), *Families as learning environments for children* (pp. 47–86). New York: Plenum.

Sigel, I. (1983a, July). *The belief construct: A conceptual analysis.* Paper presented at the annual meeting of the International Society of Political Psychology, Oxford, England.

Sigel, I. (1983b, April). *Structural analysis of parent–child research models.* Paper presented at the meeting of the Society for Research in Child Development, Detroit, Michigan.

Sigel, I. (1985). A conceptual analysis of beliefs. In I. Sigel (Ed.), *Parental belief systems: The psychological consequences for children* (pp. 345–372). Hillsdale, NJ: Lawrence Erlbaum Associates.

Sigel, I., McGillicudy-DeLisi, A., Flaugher, J., & Rock, D. (1983). *Parents as teachers of their own learning disabled children.* Princeton, NJ: Educational Testing Service.

Sigel, I. E., McGillicuddy-DeLisi, A. V., & Johnson, J. E. (1980). *Parental distancing, beliefs and children's representational competence within the family context.* Princeton, NJ: Educational Testing Service.

Spivack, G., Platt, J., & Shure, M. B. (1976). *The problem-solving approach to adjustment.* San Francisco: Jossey-Bass.

Stuart, R. B. (1980). *Helping couples change: A social learning approach to marital therapy.* New York: Guilford.

Urbain, S., & Kendall, P. C. (1980). Review of social-cognitive problem-solving interventions with children. *Psychological Bulletin, 88,* 109–143.

Weick, K. (1971). Group processes, family processes, and problem solving. In J. Aldous, T. Condon, R. Hill, M. Straus, & I. Tallman (Eds.), *Family problem solving* (pp. 3–32). Hinsdale, IL: Dryden.

White, B. L., Kaban, B. T., & Attanucci, J. S. (1979). *The origins of human competence.* Lexington, MA: Lexington Books.

Wiggins, J. S. (1973). *Personality and prediction: Principles of personality assessment.* Reading, MA: Addison-Wesley.

Zill, N., & Peterson, J. (1982). Learing to do things without help. In L. Laosa & I. Sigel (Eds.), *Families as learning environments for children* (pp. 343–373). New York: Plenum.

VIEWS OF CHILDREN

7

Children's Concepts of the Family

David R. Pederson
Rhonda L. Gilby
University of Western Ontario

Although the nature of the family and its impact on the developing child has been extensively examined from the perspective of the anthropologist, psychologist and sociologist, there is relatively little known about the child's understanding of the family. This chapter considers the ways in which children think about the family and how their thinking changes with age.

Why is it important to consider the child's understanding of this concept? One answer to this question is that the study of children's comprehension of the family provides a significant addition to the growing literature on the development of children's social knowledge. Studies of children's understanding of death (White, Elson, & Prawat, 1978), reproduction and birth (Bernstein & Cowan, 1975), illness (Campbell, 1975), adoption (Brodzinsky, this volume; Brodzinsky, Singer, & Braff, 1984), friendship (Selman, 1980), justice (Damon, 1977), and various social institutions such as schools, stores, money, and payment (Furth, Baur, & Smith, 1976) exemplify this line of research. Because of the salience of the family in the life of the child, knowledge of that institution adds an important dimension to our understanding of his or her development. In addition, there is the practical consideration of helping children cope with the stress of parental separation and divorce. In order to help children comprehend the type of changes that are intrinsic to separation and divorce, it is important to have normative information regarding the way in which they think about the family at different ages.

Another reason for an interest in children's conception of the family is that this area has proven to be fruitful for the study of cognitive development. Piaget (1928) was among the first to recognize the usefulness of the study of kinship terms as a way of analyzing the child's understanding of reciprocal relationships.

More recently, Watson (1984) has reviewed the research literature on the development of children's comprehension of social roles. The evidence suggests that children's understanding of these roles follows a clear, orderly developmental sequence, beginning with simple role playing in the early preschool years and culminating in adolescence with an understanding of the formal properties of social roles within the family.

The study of children's concepts of the family is also relevant to research on concept formation. Rosch (1975, 1978) has proposed that natural concepts are learned on the basis of prototypic instances. Much of the developmental research stimulated by Rosch has focused on children's nonsocial concepts such as "dog" and "bird" (see Clark, 1983; Mandler, 1983). The study of children's concepts of the family extends this line of research into a social area with which children not only are quite familiar, but for which there exists considerable agreement among both children and adults as to the configuration of the prototypic instance of the concept.

Finally, the concept of the family provides an opportunity to test hypotheses about the influence of experiential factors on concept development. Young children appear to base their initial understanding of a concept on their experiences with exemplars of that concept (Anglin, 1979). All children are exposed to different exemplars of the "family"; thus there are wide individual differences in experience.

In his discussion of the acquisition of naturalistic concepts, Anglin (1977) emphasizes the distinction between a concept's intension, which is its defining properties, and extension, which is its typical or representative instances. We use this distinction as an organizing feature in our consideration of the development of the child's concept of the family. The analysis of the intensions of a concept revolve around the attributes and properties of the term. Children's ideas about the attributes of a family have not been extensively investigated, although there is some research on children's perceptions of parents and other family members, and their activities and functions. Presumably the defining properties of the term *family* would include an appeal to spousal and parental roles and kinship terms. Thus, the child's understanding of the concept of the family is directly built on his or her understanding of social and kin roles. These terms are much more clearly defined in North American culture than the term *family*. Even in cases where kinship terms are used informally, such as the use of the term *uncle* to refer to an adult male friend of the family, there appears to be no confusion in adults between this use and the formal definition (Ball, 1974; Schneider, 1980).

Schneider's (1980) monograph represents an analysis of the extension of the family concept. An extension of a term refers to those instances to which an informant is willing to apply that term. Schneider interviewed American adults and children and concluded that there is considerable agreement that the prototypic North American family consists of two parents and their children. However, unlike kinship terms, there is little agreement on an explicit set of rules for distinguishing instances from non-instances.

In the remainder of this chapter, we first review research relevant to the intension of the child's concept of the family. The acquisition of an understanding of kinship terms and social roles is discussed. The child's perceptions of family members and ideas concerning the activities and functions of a family are also examined. Following this, we present research on children's extension of the family concept, examining both the child's acceptance of various groupings as instances of a family, and the criteria that appear to be used by the child to distinguish instances from non-instances.

INTENSION OF THE FAMILY CONCEPT—WHAT IS A FAMILY?

Kinship Terms

Kinship terms are defined in terms of reciprocal relationships. *Brother* by definition implies the existence of another sibling, and *mother* implies a son or daughter. An understanding of these terms requires a comprehension of this reciprocity. Piaget (1928) interviewed children between 4 and 12 years of age about their knowledge of the terms *brother* and *sister* in order to examine the functions of egocentric thought and the development of children's understanding of reciprocity. Piaget discerned three stages of development. In stage one, *brother* is defined solely in terms of property features, in this case being a boy. Stage two involves the idea that there must be more than one child in a family for the terms *brother* or *sister* to be applicable, and thus marks the beginning of the understanding of the relational nature of the terms. By stage three, the child appreciates both the relational and reciprocal nature of the terms. Not until 11 years of age did more than 75% of the children fully comprehend the reciprocal nature of brother and sister. Danziger (1957), Elkind (1962) and Swartz and Hall (1972) have replicated Piaget's study and found virtually the same age progressions.

Haviland and Clark (1974) and Macaskill (1981) examined the acquisition of kinship terms using an analysis of relational components developed by Bierwisch (1970). Within this system, relational components, such as *parent of,* or its inverse *child of,* can be combined with property features, such as male or female, to produce a definition of kin terms. For example, the relationship of a person (X) who is mother of (Y) can be defined as (X parent of Y) (female X). In this example, there is one property feature (sex) and one relational feature (mother of). Grandfather of (Y) involves a recursive relational component—(X parent of A) (A parent of Y) (male X). Brother of (Y), involves the idea of reciprocal relationship, namely (X child of A) (A parent of Y) (male X). Finally, some terms involve recursive reciprocal relationships such as niece of Y: (X child of A) (A child of Z) (Z parent of Y) (female X). This system was utilized by Haviland and Clark (1974) to classify 15 common English kinship terms into four levels of semantic complexity based on an analysis of their relational components. Level I entries are the least complex, including a single relational component, such as son or daughter (X child of Y). Level II entries are somewhat more complex, including both the parent of and child of relational components. Thus, brother or sister (X child of A) (A parent of Y) are level II entries. Level III terms include a single relational component that is recursed, such as *grandmother* or *grandfather* (X parent of A) (A parent of Y). Level IV entries include both parent of and child of relational components plus recursion. Aunt or uncle (X child of A) (A parent of B) (B parent of Y) are examples. Haviland and Clark (1974) elicited definitions from 30 children ranging in age from $3\frac{1}{2}$ to $8\frac{1}{2}$ years. The level of semantic complexity proved to be a very important factor in determining the order in which these kinship terms are learned. The simpler the term semantically, the earlier its acquisition.

Macaskill (1981) used a sentence completion test to simplify the task requirements. She also distinguished between child-centered relationships defined by other people's relationship to the child (such as my mother, my grandfather) and other-centered relationships defined by the child's relationship to others (such as I am a daughter of, a grandson of). As would be expected from a cognitive developmental framework, child-centered kinship terms were generally acquired before other-centered terms. Macaskill reported that within these two categories, the sequence by which kinship terms were acquired was directly related to the semantic complexity of the relationship.

The acquisition of kinship terms appears to be largely dependent on the child's cognitive development and independent of his or her experience with relatives. Piaget (1928) noted that only children had no more difficulty in understanding the terms *brother* or *sister* than children who in fact had a brother or sister. Jordan (1980) similarly found that sex, family size, and birth order were not correlated with conservation of kinship roles. Haviland and Clark (1974) and Chambers and Tavuchis (1976) reported that the child's experience with relatives as indicated by parental questionnaire data did not correlate with the child's understanding of kin terms.

Social Roles Within the Family

The research on kin terms has focused almost exclusively on the conceptual problem of understanding reciprocal relationships. An understanding of the defining properties of the family implies more than the comprehension of kin terms. As Watson and Amgott-Kwan (1984) noted, knowledge of family roles requires at least two additional features. The first is an understanding of the content of social roles, e.g., knowledge of what a father does in his paternal role. The second is the realization that a given individual may occupy more than one family role relationship, for example a person may be father, a son, and a husband.

On the basis of Fischer's (1980) stage theory of cognitive development, Watson and Amgott-Kwan (1983) postulated three levels in the early development of parental role concepts, with two steps within each level. Level 1, single representations, involves the concept of a social role (Step 1), such as mother, and an idea of what behaviors are implied by that role (Step 2). Level 2, representational mapping, marks the acquisition of the concept of reciprocal social roles (Step 3), e.g., the understanding that to be a father implies having a child, and the idea that roles can be recursive (Step 4). For example, in Step 4 the child understands when a father becomes a grandfather and some of the characteristics of the grandfather role. Level 3, representational systems, reflects the idea that one individual can hold several family roles simultaneously. At Step 5 within this level the child understands that a person can hold two roles simultaneously, e.g., can be both a father and a grandfather. At Step 6 this notion is extended to three or more simultaneous roles, e.g., a person can be a son at the same time he is a father and a grandfather.

To test this model, Watson and Amgott-Kwan interviewed 3- to $7\frac{1}{2}$-year-old children about their understanding of parental roles. Generally, the 3- and 4-year-olds could describe parental roles, i.e., they had attained Level 1 knowledge; 5- and 6-year-olds knew about reciprocal social roles and by age 7, children understood the idea of simultaneous family roles. The six steps formed a hierarchial, Guttman scale and the highest step attained was strongly age-related.

Watson and Amgott-Kwan (1984) developed a similar analysis of the understanding of family roles appropriate for children between 5 and 13 years of age. They proposed an eight-step sequence, beginning at the representational systems level of the previous study and continuing through to an abstract definition of family in terms of the required presence of spousal and/or parental roles. As in the case of the understanding of parental roles, the proposed sequence formed an age-related, Guttman scale. Six-year-old children could explain family role intersections, i.e., they understood that someone could be in both a spousal and a parental role. At age 9, children understood that a traditional family consisted of parental and spousal roles and could apply those concepts across generations. For example, they understood that the mother in one family is the daughter in a previous family and eventually can become a grandmother. The idea that either a spousal role or a parental role can be used to define a family was understood by the 12-year-olds. At that age, children notice that a childless couple is like a traditional family because of the presence of spousal roles and different because of the absence of parental roles, and that a single-parent family has parental roles but lacks spousal roles. Only 6 of the 50 children interviewed attained step 8 (mean age 12 years). At this step, when asked for rules to define a family using a minimum number of people, children can explain that a parent and a child or a husband and a wife are the two conditions that meet that criteria.

Wynn and Brumberger (1982) studied the development of an understanding of family roles within the framework of a Piagetian identity problem. One hundred children, aged 3 to 12 years, were tested for their ability to maintain the constancy of identity of the role of mother, father, sister, or brother, in the face of irrelevant spatial transformation such as moving out of the family home. The children were presented with cutout figures representing a family grouping living in a house. A figure was then removed, for example the father because of divorce, and the children were asked, "Is he still a father?" and "Why?". Wynn and Brumberger developed a seven-stage classification system for responses following the levels described by Piaget (1968) for the acquisition of identity concepts. The stages progressed from a lack of identity of the family role, through an intuitive understanding, to identity based on concrete explanations, followed by explanations based on an understanding of birth and blood relationships, and finally to a clear differentiation of identity from role function.

The children in the study were also presented with a standard Piagetian conservation task in order to assess identity in the physical domain. Highly significant correlations were found between stage of responding for the "social identity" and "physical identity" tasks, indicating stage consistency across the two domains. In those cases in which consistency across domains was not apparent, the findings suggest that the children had learned to apply the concept of identity in the physical domain before the social domain.

The aforementioned literature would suggest that children's comprehension of kinship terms and their understanding of social roles appear to follow a predictable developmental sequence. Futhermore, at least in the case of kinship terms, these developmental sequences are apparently not strongly influenced by individual differences in children's experience with various relatives. Some incidental observations from Watson and Amgott-Kwan (1984) suggest that family social-role concepts may also be relatively impervious to the influence of direct experience. In their study, approximately half of the children in the two older age groups were attending an alternative school. The children in this school had completed a course on families in which family function, family roles and alternative family structures were extensively considered. This course culminated in a published book on children's views of divorce. In spite of this massive amount of specific experience directly relevant to the criteria for scaling the family social-role concepts, there were no significant differences in the highest step reached between these children and the rest of the sample.

Perceptions of Family Members

Another aspect of the intension of the concept of the family is the child's perceptions of the attributes of family members. All theories of social and emotional development place great emphasis on the child's experiences within the family. As a result, many investigators have examined the child's perceptions of his or her own family. Their interest appears to stem from a clinical perspective that assumes that the study of such perceptions will provide clues to the existence and causes of emotional maladjustment in the child. Some examples of the procedures used include the Bene Anthony Family Relations Test (Anthony & Bene, 1957; Bene & Anthony, 1957) in which the child drops cards denoting various feelings into boxes representing the members of his or her family, the Family Concept Q-Sort (Van der Veen & Novak, 1971), in which the child sorts items describing various aspects of family living into nine piles ranging from "most" to "least like my family", and the Family Drawing Test (Hulse, 1951, 1952) or the Kinetic Family Drawing Test (Burns & Kaufman, 1970) in which the child draws pictures of his or her own family. The procedures and findings have been used as personality assessment tools and therefore do not directly deal with the more general question of the development of the child's perceptions of the family.

A more relevant research approach has been an examination of the child's perceptions of his or her parents and other family members. A number of studies have shown that as early as the age of 3 years, the child has developed stereotypes concerning parental attributes. The father, in contrast with the mother, is perceived as being more punitive, fear-provoking, powerful, competent, dominating, and interfering (Emmerich, 1959, 1961; Harris & Howard, 1981; Kagan, 1956; Kagan, Hosken & Watson, 1961; Kagan & Lemkin, 1960). The mother is seen as more nurturant, facilitative, accepting, and nicer (Armentrout & Burger, 1972; Emmerich, 1959; Kagan, 1956; Kagan & Lemkin, 1960). These perceptions are present in varying age groups (Kagan & Lemkin, 1960), in father-present and father-absent families, in working- and non-working–mother families, and are often in contrast to parental reports of their own behavior (Aldous, 1972; Kohlberg, 1966).

Family members other than the parents have also been studied. Kahana & Kahana (1970) explored the changing meaning of the grandparent for children at three age levels. The children were questioned about their grandparents, asked to choose a favorite grandparent, and to give reasons for their preferences. A pattern of development markedly similar to that reported by Selman (1980) in his study of children's understanding of friendships was found. The youngest children (4–5 years) viewed the grandparent in egocentric and concrete terms, describing what their own grandparents gave to them and preferring indulgent grandparents who brought them gifts. Eight- and 9-year-olds focused more on the mutuality of the relationship with their grandparents, describing shared activities and preferring grandparents who joined them in their play. The oldest group (11–12 years) thought of their grandparents in more grandparent-oriented terms, such as intelligence or goodness, which was independent of the grandchild. Almost half of this older group was unwilling to state a preference for any particular grandparent. The authors suggested that the meaning of the role of the grandparent should be understood in the context of the changing needs of the developing grandchild.

Family-Related Activities

The defining or characteristic properties of a concept may also include information relating to duties and activities performed. Some research has provided information concerning children's ideas about the activities of individual family members. Connor, Greene, and Walters (1958) asked 10th-grade children and their parents to select from a list of activities what a good mother, a good father and a good child does. The list contained items that the authors had categorized as either traditionally oriented in that they were marked by rigidly conceived, role-stereotyped expectations (e.g., a good mother keeps the house in order, a good father earns a good income, and a good child obeys and respects adults), or developmentally oriented, emphasizing the growth and development of the individual (e.g., a good mother sees to her children's emotional well-being, a good father encourages his children to grow up in their own ways, and a good child enjoys growing up). In general, the children more frequently endorsed the traditionally oriented expectations of what a good mother, a good father, and a good child does, than either of their parents. Similarly, Weeks & Thornburg (1977) questioned 5-year-old children concerning the specific marriage-related roles they expected to play when they became married adults. Comparing the children's responses to responses given by their parents concerning expectations in their own marriage, the children were found to hold more traditional and less egalitarian views than their parents. Children generally supported the two specific role stereotypes of paternal power and maternal child care.

Powell and Thompson (1981) questioned preschoolers about their ideas concerning family-related activities ascribed to mother and father. They found that children, whether in two-parent or in single-parent families, maintained very traditional, sex-stereotyped views, describing "what mothers do" and "what fathers do" by referring to domestic activities. The authors concluded that preschool children seemed to perceive that mothers and fathers are "adults of a particular sex who live together with children and perform domestic functions" (p. 37). More generally, it has been found that children's perceptions of the functional roles of males and females in society tend to correspond to the functions ascribed to mothers and fathers (Dubin & Dubin, 1965; Hartley, 1960). For example, Hartley (1960) found that, for children aged 5 through 11 describing what women need to know or need to be able to do, 64% of the items mentioned were domestic activities.

Gilby (1979) studied children's ideas concerning the activities that must be performed within a family, and the family members who should perform these activities. Sixty children, aged 5 through 11, from two-parent families, were interviewed. In response to an open-ended question asking about the things that people in a family need to do, the most common responses were keeping the house clean, mentioned by 87% of the children, doing the cooking (63%) and making money (63%).

A more structured set of questions presented the children with three different family groupings (mother and father with two children, mother with two children, father with two children) and, for each grouping, the children chose the family member or members whom they thought should perform each of a series of family-related activities, including shopping, cooking, cleaning, repairing, and disciplining and nurturing children. Across the family groupings, few differences related to age were found, with the exception that older children more often than younger children considered that the children in a family would be able to perform these tasks.

In general, for the two-parent group, the traditional or sex-stereotyped response was the most common one for most of the activities presented (i.e., mother should do the cooking, keep the house clean; father should make the money, fix things that break). Also of note, however, is the finding that the second most common response was a more egalitarian one, with about one third of the children responding that both mother and father could perform the task. The parents of these children reported that the actual division of labor within their homes was divided more equitably than the stereotyped responses of the children might indicate.

When presented with a single-parent grouping (both mother-headed and father-headed), the children showed flexibility in their responses, re-assigning the task to another family member, generally the other parent, when the original performer of the task was no longer present. Thus, the absence of one parent within the family did not present a problem to these children in terms of the performance of family-related activities, and only a few children indicated that any task would not get done if one parent was not present.

Family Functions

Our final consideration with respect to the intension of the family concept relates to the child's ideas concerning the functions of a family. Cataldo and Geismar (1983), in their study of preschoolers' views about parenting and the family, questioned 4- to 5-year-old children about the ways in which parents help children to grow up, what children learn in families, and the things that families do together. For these children the most frequently mentioned parental function, expressed by 65% of the children, was the provision of food. Also mentioned were a number of specific activities relating to the daily tasks of child-rearing (35%), provision of surprises and special treats (20%), correcting and disciplining children (20%), and loving and helping children (20%). In thinking about what they learned in their families, most children (54%) mentioned being taught particular skills, such as riding a bike, singing a song, or learning to read. Thirty percent of the children mentioned being taught specific "dos and don'ts."

Gilby (1979) asked 5- to 11-year-old children and university students to respond to the following three questions: "Why do we need families?" Why is it nice to belong to a family?" and "What things do families do for children?" There was much overlap in the responses to these three questions, and responses were pooled and used to examine the more general issue of the functions of the family.

Responses given could be classified into the following six categories:

1. companionship—including people to be with, talk to, do things with;
2. raising and socializing children—including guidance, direction, discipline;
3. providing the necessities of life—including food, clothes, shelter, protection, health care;
4. doing things for each other and helping each other;
5. providing a positive emotional experience—including love, caring, support, happiness; and
6. making a contribution to society.

No age differences were found among the responses of the children, although certain differences were apparent between their responses and those of the university adults. A large majority of the respondents mentioned that families provide the necessities of life (88% of the children, 70% of the adults), and positive emotional experiences (65% of the children, 100% of the adults). The children were more likely to mention companionship (73% of the children, 5% of the adults), and doing things for each other (92% of the children, 25% of the adults) than the adults were. Conversely, children less often mentioned raising and socializing children (18% of the children, 70% of the adults), and virtually none of the children considered the societal contributions of a family, whereas one-fourth of the adults did. In agreement with Cataldo and Geismar's (1983) findings, the responses of the children tended to be very specific, concrete and individual-oriented. Children appeared to be very aware of their dependent state, and of the many things they would be unable to do on their own, if they did not have their families. The responses of the university adults were more general, abstract and society-oriented.

Research on children's perceptions of the functions of the family and the attributes of family members indicates that young children maintain very traditional views. This conclusion is congruent with the fact that young children tend to hold more rigid attitudes on sex roles than their parents (Maccoby, 1980) and are exceedingly pragmatic in reasoning about justice, authority, and friendship (Damon, 1977; Selman, 1980).

EXTENSION OF THE FAMILY CONCEPT—IS THIS A FAMILY?

We now turn to research on how a child distinguishes a configuration of people who are a family from those who are not—i.e., to the question of the criterial attributes that a child uses in responding to the question, "Is this a family?"

Previous Research

Piaget (1928) asked 7- to 13-year-old boys to define the word *family*. Piaget found three stages of development. In stage one (roughly ages 7 and 8), family included all people who lived with the child. By stage two (9 to 10 years of age), the idea of biological relationship was used, but the criteria of living together was still salient. Thus, nonrelatives living in with the child were not excluded as family members. At stage three (11 to 13 years), family was defined independently of time and place and was generalized to include all biological relatives. Thus, at this stage the idea of family included members of the extended family rather than only members of the nuclear family living with the child as in stage two.

Piaget's study of stages in the child's concept of the family did not herald a major interest in this issue. The next study was reported approximately 50 years later by Moore (1977) who noted the similarity between the stages that Piaget identified in the development of the family concept and the more familiar stages in the development of conservation. The purpose of her study was to explore the relation between the child's concept of the family and his or her stage of cognitive development as assessed by Piagetian conservation tasks. Taking advantage of Piaget's subsequent discoveries of the need for concrete materials in assessing young children's concepts, her procedures involved the use of drawings and various family configurations. Half of the children in her study were from mother-headed, single-parent families and half from two-parent families. Children at all stages considered a two-generation group (two parents and a child) and a three-generation group (grandparents, parents, and a child) to be a family. Most children (73%) also considered a childless couple to be a family, but only 53% considered a single-parent group to be a family. There was a tendency for children from single-parent homes to more readily accept such a grouping as a family, although the differences were significant only in the case of questions concerning a father-headed single-parent family. Compared with children in the preoperational and formal operational stages, concrete operational children were less willing to accept a single-parent group as an instance of a family. Powell and Thompson (1981) used a similar procedure in studying the family concept of preschool children. Almost all of the children accepted a two-generation grouping (two parents and their children) and a three-generation group (grandparents, parents and children) as a family. They reported that over 75% of the preschool children they interviewed accepted single-parent groupings as families, and that there were no significant differences between the responses of children in two-parent or single-parent families.

Developmental Differences

Gilby & Pederson (1982) examined age differences in children's concept of a family over a wide variety of stimulus configurations. To explore children's ideas about the extensions of the concept of a family, we developed the Family Concept Interview. The questions asked in this interview are presented in Table 7.1. In Part A, children were asked to list the members of their own family. Part B was designed to explore the child's image of a prototypical family. The children were shown 18 cardboard figures mounted with velcro on a posterboard. The figures depicted a baby, adults, and children of varying ages. The children were requested to pretend that they were going to visit a family that they did not know and to pick out the people who would be in that family. In Part C, we varied the dimensions of common residence, presence of children, single parenthood, genetic or legal relationship, and sex of adult partners. The child viewed paper dolls representing the specific configurations corresponding to each question.

There were 20 children from each of the following grades: kindergarten (mean age: 5 years, 11 months), Grade 2 (mean age: 8 years) and Grade 4 (mean age: 9 years, 11 months). Twenty unmarried university students (mean age 21 years, 3 months) were also given a questionnaire containing Parts B and C and were also asked to rate how each of the stimuli presented in Part C conformed to their image of a typical instance of the concept family. In a questionnaire directed to the parents of the children, we requested information about the composition of the child's own family and the frequency of the child's contact with grandparents, aunts, uncles, and cousins.

When asked to list family members, 85% of the kindergarten children, 75% of the grade 2 children, and all of the grade 4 children mentioned only members of their nuclear family. Except for one kindergarten girl omitting a sibling, there was perfect agreement between the children's and their parent's listings of family members. In Part B, 64% of the subjects constructed a family with two parents and their children and an additional 26% included grandparents. These results are congruent with Schneider's (1980) conclusion that for both children and adults, the prototypic family consists of parents and their children. The mean number of children in the constructed families was 3.2, with a range from 1 to 13. A baby was included in 78% of the children's constructions, in 60% of the female

TABLE 7.1
Questions Asked During the Family Concept Interview

Part A.	Who is in your family?
Part B.	The respondent is asked to construct a "typical" family from 18 figures presented, then asked to identify the people in the constructed family.
	(Figures corresponding to the people mentioned are presented)
Part C.	1. Here are Mr. and Mrs. Brown. They are married. They live together. They have no children. Are they a family?
	2. Here are Mr. and Mrs. Brown. This is their son Billy. They all live together. Are they a family?
	3. Here is Mrs. Brown and her son, Billy. They live together, just the two of them. Are they a family?
	4. Billy's father, Mr. Brown, lives in a different house. Is he in Billy's family?
	5. These are Billy's grandmother and grandfather. Are they in Billy's family?
	6. What if they live in a different city and he never sees them. Then, are they in his family?
	7. Here are Mr. and Mrs. Brown and Billy. They all live together. This is Billy's brother, Bob. He lives in a different city. Is Bob in Billy's family?
	8. Here are Mr. and Mrs. Brown and Billy. This is Billy's friend, Joe. They all live together. Is Joe in Billy's family?
	9. Here are Mr. and Mrs. Brown, with Joe. They are living together, just the three of them. Are they a family?
	10. Here are Mr. and Mrs. Brown and Billy. This is Miss Jones. She lives with them and helps take care of Billy. Is Miss Jones in Billy's family?
	11. Here is Mr. Brown and his son, Billy. They live together, just the two of them. Are they a family?
	12. Billy's mother, Mrs. Brown, lives in a different house. Is she in Billy's family?
	13. These are Billy's aunt, uncle and cousin. Are they in Billy's family?
	14. What if they lived in a different city? Then, are they in his family?
	15. Here is Billy, his brother, Bob, and their sister Sally. They live together, just the three of them. Are they a family?
	16. Here are Mr. and Mrs. Brown and Billy. They all live together, but they don't love each other. Are they a family?
	17. Here are two very good friends, Miss Black and Miss Smith. They live together. Are they a family?
	18. This is Mrs. Brown and Billy. This is her friend, Mrs. Green and her son, David. They all live together. Are they a family?

Note: Copyright (1982) Canadian Psychological Association. Reprinted by permission.

university students' constructions, but in none of the male university students' imaginary families.

Table 7.2 presents the percentage of subjects responding affirmatively to each question in Part C, the X^2 values, the significant pairwise comparisons, and the mean typicality rating of the university students. A married couple with their child (question 2) was considered to be a family by all of the subjects. There were no significant age differences in the judgments about a childless married couple (question 1), a married couple with a child who is not their own (question 9), in the inclusion of an aunt, uncle, and cousin as family members (question 13) or in the acceptance of a group without love (question 16). There were significant age differences for each of the remaining 13 questions.

Kindergarten children more readily accepted nonrelatives as family members than the other respondents (see questions 8, 10, 17 and 18). Also, kindergarten and grade 2 children were less likely to accept extended family and nuclear family members living in a different place to be part of the family (questions 4, 6, 7, 12 and 14). It appears that living together or having contact are the criteria that kindergarten children use to distinguish family from non-family groups. Thus, Piaget's (1928) early observations that 6-year-old children define family by common residence were replicated. However, contrary to Piaget's conclusions, young children are sensitive to factors other than living together. A further examination of Table 7.2 reveals that fewer than half of the kindergarten children accepted a childless couple, a single-parent family or a family that did not love each other as instances of a family. As Piaget reported, with increasing age, genetic or legal relationships become the defining attributes and the use of the criterion of living together becomes less important.

As in the case of kinship and family roles, experiential factors do not appear to have a strong influence on the young child's concept of the family. There was no obvious relation between the child's responses to questions about extended family members (i.e., questions 5, 6, 13 and 14) and the parental report of involvement with grandparents, aunts, uncles and cousins. Again returning to the data presented in Table 7.2, there is no simple relation between the university student's ratings of the typicality of a configuration as an instance of a family and the young child's acceptance of that grouping as a family. For example, two women living with their sons were considered very atypical, yet 85% of the kindergarten children said that they were a family. In contrast more typical instances such as aunt, uncle, and cousin or a childless couple were less acceptable as instances of the family for the kindergarten children. These results appear to be inconsistent with recent work on children's concept formation that suggests that young children's concepts tend to be restricted to highly prototypic instances (Clark, 1983; Mandler, 1983; Rosch, 1978). Young children have features in addition to typicality that they use when deciding if a group of people is a family.

Child and Parent Concepts

Although the prototypic families that children and adults constructed were very similar, kindergarten children's judgments about what was a family were based on very different criteria than those used by older children and adults. As in the case of research on kinship and on social role understanding, individual differences in the concept of the family were not related to the child's experiences

TABLE 7.2
Percentage of Subjects Responding Affirmatively
to Each Question Within Part C

Question	Group				$X^2(3)$[a]	Significant Pairwise Comparisons[b]*	Mean Typicality Rating[c]
	Kindergarten	Grade 2	Grade 4	University			
1. Mr. & Mrs. Brown	45	45	70	85	9.85		2.50
2. Mr. & Mrs. Brown, Billy	90	95	100	100	3.81		1.05
3. Mrs. Brown & Billy	55	40	80	95	16.64*	K-U, 2-4, 2-U	3.30
4. Is Mr. Brown in Billy's family	5	35	50	85	26.97*	K-4, K-U, 2-U, 4-U	—
5. Billy's grandparents	60	55	85	100	14.40*	K-U, 2-U	2.15
6. Billy's grandparents, live in a different city	0	35	85	85	41.38*	K-2, K-4, K-U, 2-4, 2-U	3.44
7. Brother Bob, lives in a different city	15	70	90	100	40.20*	K-2, K-4, K-U, 2-U	1.89
8. Mr. & Mrs. Brown, Billy & friend Joe	70	20	20	45	14.48*	K-2, K-4, K-U	4.72
9. Mr. & Mrs. Brown & Joe	80	60	40	70	7.47		3.95
10. Mr. & Mrs. Brown, Billy, Miss Jones	90	20	15	40	29.04*	K-2, K-4, K-U	4.47
11. Mr. Brown & Billy	45	45	75	95	15.82*	K-U, 2-U	3.00
12. Is Mrs. Brown in Billy's family	10	25	75	90	35.60*	K-4, K-U, 2-4, 2-U	—
13. Billy's aunt, uncle & cousin	45	55	80	85	10.01		2.68
14. Aunt, uncle & cousin, live in a different city	5	35	80	75	30.17*	K-4, K-U, 2-4, 2-U	3.72
15. Billy, brother Bob, sister Sally	70	40	70	100	17.14*	K-U, 2-U, 4-U	3.42
16. Mr. & Mrs. Brown, Billy, no love	15	55	55	70	13.36		4.32
17. Miss Black, Miss Smith	70	25	5	25	21.12*	K-2, K-4, K-U	5.58
18. Mrs. Brown & Billy, Mrs. Green & David	85	20	10	40	27.97*	K-2, K-4, K-U	5.58

[a]X^2 must exceed 14.10 using the Bonferroni X^2 statistic at $p < .05$.

*$p < .05$.

[b]K = kindergarten; 2 = Grade 2; 4 = Grade 4; U = University

[c]Lower ratings reflect a judgment of a closer match to the target of a typical family. Ratings ≥ 2.40 are significantly greater than the rating given to stimulus #2 at $p < .05$.

Note: Copyright (1982) Canadian Psychological Association. Reprinted by permission with relatives. Perhaps the child's ideas about families come from more direct tuition from parents. If that is the case, there should be a correspondence between a child's perception of family and the perceptions of his or her parents. To assess this issue, we conducted a study to compare the child's and parents' concepts of the family.

The subjects were 38 children (16 boys and 22 girls) enrolled at the University of Western Ontario Laboratory Preschools and 54 of their parents (27 mothers and 27 fathers). The average age of the children was 4 years, 4 months, with a range from 3 years, 9 months to 5 years, 2 months. They were, with one exception, living with both parents and had an average of 1.3 siblings (Mode = 1). For almost half of the children (44%), one of the siblings was less than 2 years of age, and thus might be considered by the children to be a baby.

The Family Concept Interview (see Table 7.1) used in the Gilby and Pederson (1982) study was modified with the attentional limitations of preschoolers in mind. Small Fisher-Price figures were used to help the child describe who was in his or her family, and Part C was shortened by omitting questions 9 to 14 and question 16. Two orders of questions were established so that half of the children were questioned about Billy and his family first, and the remaining children were given the more unusual groupings (such as the question about two women living together) first. Pilot testing revealed that many children tended to get into a "yes" saying response set, so a question about Mr. Smith who lived all by himself was added as a clear contrary instance to help break the set. The data from an additional five children were not used in the analyses because they either answered "yes" or "no" to all of the questions. The parents were requested to complete a questionnaire that contained the same questions asked in the children's interview, plus information about the amount of contact the child had with grandparents.

The most striking thing about conducting the interviews was that even the youngest children had definite ideas about the term *family*. Many of the children were surprisingly good informants in that they could articulate the criteria they were using in their judgments. The children listed with considerable accuracy the members of their own family, as reported by their parents. (The only obvious exception was the case of one girl who did not include her mother. Her mother reported the next day that her daughter realized her omission as she was describing the study at the dinner table that night.) As was the case in the previous study the vast majority of children included only members of the nuclear family, and only three children listed grandparents and one child mentioned a babysitter. All of the parents listed members of the nuclear family, although several commented that they considered other kin to be part of their extended family.

In Part B of the interview the child was shown 18 cardboard figures and asked to select figures to represent people who might be in an imaginary family. Although the task requirements are rather involved, we were surprised at how easily the preschool children understood our request. Only one child failed to produce some grouping that could be reasonably considered to be a family. (She produced a string of six mother–daughter pairs). The characteristics of these constructed families indicated a major degree of consensus about the stereotype of a family. A two-parent nuclear family accounted for 66% of the families. An additional 31% of the children added one or more grandparents. The mean number of children included was 2.9, with a range from 1 to 6. The modal family constructed by 36% of the children consisted of mother, father, son, daughter, and baby, with or without grandparents. A baby was included in 84% of the constructed families. Only three children constructed families that matched their own. The children apparently had clearly developed ideas of what constituted a family, and could use these to construct an imaginary family.

The parents were given a similar task in their questionnaire. As in the case of their children, most of the parents (87%) constructed a family that consisted of two parents and their children. Unlike their children, grandparents were included in only an additional 8% of the imaginary families. There was a baby in 56% of the fathers' and 75% of the mothers' constructed families. The modal imaginary family produced by 31% of the parents, consisted of mother, father, son, daughter and baby. Although the parents and children shared many of the same stereotypes of a typical family, there was no obvious relationship between the constructions of any one parent and his or her child. In only one case was there an identical construction.

In Part C the task was to make judgments about whether a given grouping of people was considered to be family. Chi-square analyses were conducted to test for differences between the judgments of the children and their parents. Initial analyses revealed no significant order, sex, or age (4 years or less vs. over 4 years) differences in the children's responses. There were no significant differences in the mothers' and the fathers' responses.

The percentage of subjects responding affirmatively to each question and the Yates-corrected X^2 values are presented in Table 7.3. The Bonferroni criteria were applied to control the experiment-wise error rate at the .05 level (Jensen, Beus, & Storm, 1968). Notice that the only question that the parents and children clearly agreed on was that Mr. Smith, living alone, was not a family. (Even here there was not unanimity, because several parents said he was a family on the logical grounds that everyone belonged to a family). The only other questions in which the parent and child responses were not reliably different using the conservative Bonferroni test were about the nuclear family (question 1), two women living together (question 10), and the childless couple (question 12). There were significant differences in all of the other questions. Furthermore, inspection of the pattern of differences suggests that preschool children have well-developed criteria that are different than the criteria applied by their parents. This pattern of responding certainly confirms our subjective impressions from the interviews.

As would be expected from previous research, many of the differences can be attributed to the salience of common residence as a primary criterion for the

TABLE 7.3
Percentage of Preschool Children and Parents
Responding Affirmatively to Each Question in Part C

Question	Group		Yates-Corrected $X^2(1)^a$
	Children	Parents	
1. Mr. & Mrs. Brown & Billy	84	100	6.72
2. Brother Bob, lives in a different city	29	98	47.23*
3. Billy's teacher, lives with Billy	40	11	8.64*
4. Billy's grandparents	55	94	17.89*
5. Billy's grandparents, live in a different city	16	83	38.50*
6. Mr. & Mrs. Brown, Billy, & friend Joe	76	32	15.60*
7. Mrs. Brown and Billy, just the two of them	42	96	31.22*
8. Is Billy's dad in Billy's family if he doesn't live with Billy and his mom?	24	83	30.32*
9. Billy, his brother Bob, and his sister Sally	47	85	13.32*
10. Mrs. Black & Mrs. Green, live together	24	6	4.80
11. Mrs. Black, son David & Mrs. Green, son Joe, they all live together	66	21	16.94*
12. Mr. & Mrs. Adams (childless couple)	45	69	4.27
13. Mr. Smith, lives by himself	6	11	0.22

^{a}X^2 must exceed 8.36 using the Bonferroni X^2 statistic at $p < .05$
*$p < .05$

children. Thus the questions about dad, brother Bob, and grandparents living in a different place produced the largest child–parent disagreements. The questions about teacher and friend Joe can also be explained on this principle. A second principle that preschool children employ more strongly than their parents is the image of the two-parent nuclear family. Thus, the departures from this norm (such as the single-parent mother and the siblings living together) resulted in lower proportions of children responding affirmatively. This sensitivity was also articulated by many of the children who justified their views by saying that Billy and his mother needed a father or that the three siblings needed a mother and father in order to be a family. Similar comments were made by those children who decided that Mrs. Green and Mrs. Black, with or without sons, were not a family. A third criterion used by many children involved the number of people in a group. By this criterion, families are relatively large groups. For example, the children who said that mother, father, and Billy (question 1) were not a family gave as the reason that there were not enough people. In fact, all but one of these children concluded that the addition of brother Bob would make the group large enough to be considered a family. The criteria of a spousal or genetic relationship, obviously used as the criteria by the parents, apparently was not employed by their children.

The results from these two studies are consistent with Piaget's (1928) earlier conclusions that for children less than 7 years old, the concept of the family is strongly rooted in the criterion of common residence. Although living together is a necessary condition for a cluster of people to be considered a family, it is not a sufficient condition. Even preschool children use additional criteria such as the presence of more than one generation and of at least three people. With increasing age, family comes to mean more and more the presence of spousal and genetic relationships. The finding that young children use perceptual criteria such as living together rather than the more abstract concepts of biological or legal relationships is, of course, expected. It would be a mistake to conclude, however, that such a perceptual focus is inappropriate or irrelevant. Indeed, those features which young children focus on are apt ones, in that typically they are found in the family, as defined by its more abstract relational terms.

As in the case of kinship terms and knowledge of family roles, children's extensions of their concepts of family are not related in any obvious manner either to their experiences with their own family and relatives or to their parents' concepts or what constitutes a family. It is clear from the two studies we conducted that children's prototype of a family more closely resembles the culturally accepted image of two parents, a son, a daughter, and a baby than it resembles their own family.

GENERAL CONCLUSIONS

What can we say about the family from the perspective of the child? The most obvious conclusion that applies to all of the research literature we surveyed is that young children have very different concepts of the family than older children and adults. The young child understands kinship, family roles, and the function and structure of the family in very material terms. In each case, the initial focus is on the salient physical features. In the use of kinship words, this physical feature is the sex of the individual; thus for a young child, *brother* means a young boy. Family roles are first understood in terms of stereotypical activities. The functions of the family are seen as providing food and shelter, and a family is defined as people who live together and have other physical features of a family such as children and two adults. This conclusion is consistent with the initial stages of development of children's understanding of friendship as outlined by Damon (1977) and Selman (1980). Young children also define friendship primarily in physical terms, e.g., a friend is someone who plays with me. Given what we know about the general cognitive strategy of young children to attend to a few features of any concept, the fact that a similar process applies to the understanding of the concepts of friend and family is not surprising.

With increasing age, children more easily comprehend the recursive and reciprocal nature of kinship terms; family roles are seen as intersections of spousal and parental roles, and families are identified by legal and genetic relationships. This general developmental progression from a focus on the material to a comprehension of more abstract concepts is a well-established principle in social cognitive development (Damon, 1977; Selman, 1980).

A second general conclusion is that the child's understanding of the family does not appear to be strongly influenced by the child's experiences with his or her family. Recall that Piaget (1928) reported that children who have siblings do not acquire an understanding of *brother* and *sister* more rapidly than only children. Piaget's observations have been replicated and extended to the child's experience with other relatives by Chambers and Tavuchis (1976), Haviland and Clark (1974), and Jordan (1980). In each case, the experiential factors examined were not related to rate of acquisition of the relevant kinship terms. Although the evidence about experience is most extensive in the literature on kinship, similar findings exist in the research on other aspects of the concept of the family. Our research showing that the families children construct are independent from their own family, from their contact with extended family members, and from the families their parents construct is consistent with this conclusion.

Perhaps less conclusive by themselves are comparisons of children in single-parent and two-parent families. Although Moore (1977) did report that children from single-parent families were more accepting of a single-parent group as an instance of a family, the differences were significant only for the more unusual example of a father-headed single-parent family. Using procedures similar to Moore's, Powell and Thompson (1981) found no significant differences between preschool children from intact and single-parent families in their acceptance of a single-parent group as a family. Finally, recall the incidental observations made by Watson and Amgott-Kwan (1984). They noted that children who received extensive tutoring in school on concepts of families and family roles were not markedly advanced in the acquisition of these concepts over children who did not have this intensive experience.

Although it is always difficult to provide convincing support for the null hypothesis, these results, at the very least, lead to the conclusion that there is no strongly established relation between children's family experiences and their concepts of the family. Unlike the first conclusion about orderly developmental progressions, we find this second conclusion to be rather surprising. It is generally agreed that young children's initial understanding is strongly influenced by their early encounters with instances of a concept (Anglin, 1977, 1979; Saltz, 1971). In the case of children's understanding of family and kinship terms, the specific experiential factors that would a priori seem to be relevant are not as important as would be predicted from the literature on concept formation. Although children and adults agree on the prototypic family, children appear to attend to different features than do adults when considering atypical instances. These different features, primarily common residence, number of people, and the presence of at least two generations, are apparently determined more by the child's cognitive status than by specific experiences within the family. Future research examining these features may provide important insights about the development of children's prototypes.

Research on children's concepts of family substantiates the conclusion that young children base their understanding of these concepts on one or two salient physical features. However, conclusions about the competence of young children are markedly influenced by the research methods employed (Gelman, 1979). Much of the research on kinship and family roles requires the child to produce definitions. It may be that this method seriously underestimates children's knowledge that would be revealed by methods focusing more on recognition procedures.

Although our own work has involved recognition tasks (see Part C in Table 7.1), up to now we have concentrated on presenting variations in the structure of the family. These variations would presumably focus the child's attention on physical features. Our procedure could be easily modified to examine emotional issues. As Holyoak and Gordon (1984) point out, the relation between affect and cognition is particularly murky. Although the quality of family life and the affective functioning of the family is presumably an important determinant of the impact of the family on the child's development, research on children's sensitivity to this dimension is notably lacking. There are at least two hints in the literature to indicate that young children may be sensitive to emotional factors. In our developmental study, we included one question about love (see question 16, Tables 7.1 and 7.2). Although there were no significant age differences, the kindergarten children seemed to doubt if a grouping they considered to be a family in question 2 would continue to be one if the individuals did not love one another. The second hint comes from some incidential observations reported by Wynn and Brumberger (1982). They were surprised at the number of children in their study who considered love to be an important element in their definition of a family, and who used love as a determinant of the constancy of family role relationships. For example, many children commented that the father could still be a father after he moved out of the house if he still loved the children. Love is probably an important defining attribute in our cultural vision of what constitutes a "real" family. In this sense the fictional television family, the Waltons, could be said to be a real family emotionally if not structurally. The responses to this question in our study and Wynn and Brumberger's observations suggest that young children may be particularly responsive to love and affection as an essential attribute of a family. Research on the acquisition of children's sensitivity to this affective aspect of the family may also provide an empirical base for the study of the child's perceptions of the functioning of his or her own family.

We conclude on a practical note. In spite of the aforementioned methodological caution, there is strong evidence that the young child's perspectives on the family are very different from the view that we as adults maintain. At a time when our cultural norms about family structures are quickly evolving, this gap may be confusing, especially for a child faced with a change in his or her family structure. As an example of the possible confusion, we offer the following recollection by the senior author of this chapter. I learned to read using "Dick and Jane" readers. Those of you who have missed that experience will need to know that the stories presented an extremely stereotyped family consisting of mother (wearing an apron), father (going off to work), Dick, Jane, and baby Sally. Note that this family corresponds exactly to the prototypic family produced by our preschoolers who presumably have never been exposed to Dick and Jane. I recall resonating so completely with the perspectives on family life presented in those readers that contrary to all of the evidence of real families that I knew, I assumed that everyone else but me lived in a huge white house with acres of green grass and their prototypic family. My early concepts do not seem much different from children's views depicted in more recent studies. Certainly we as adults need to recognize the strong tendency for children to maintain stereotyped views of the family. Children may need our help and support in broadening their perspectives, especially when they are confronted with realities that are markedly different from their ideal.

REFERENCES

Aldous, J. (1972). Children's perceptions of adult role assignment: Father-absence, class, race and sex differences. *Journal of Marriage and the Family, 34,* 55–65.

Anglin, J. M. (1977). *Word, object, and conceptual development.* New York: W. W. Norton.

Anglin, J. M. (1979). The child's first terms of reference. In N. R. Smith & M. B. Franklin (Eds.), *Symbolic functioning in childhood* (pp. 167–184). Hillsdale, NJ: Lawrence Erlbaum Associates.

Anthony, J., & Bene, E. (1957). A technique for the objective assessment of the child's family relationships. *Journal of Mental Science, 103,* 541–555.

Armentrout, J. A., & Burger, G. K. (1972). Children's reports of parental childrearing behavior at five grade levels. *Developmental Psychology, 7,* 44–48.

Ball, D. W. (1974). The "family" as a sociological problem: Conceptualization of the taken-for-granted as prologue to social problems analysis. In A. Skolnick & J. H. Skolnick (Eds.), *Intimacy, family and society* (pp. 25–40). Boston: Little, Brown.

Bene, E., & Anthony, J. (1957). *Manual for Family Relations Test.* London: National Foundation for Educational Research in England and Wales.

Bernstein, A. C., & Cowan, P. A. (1975). Children's concepts of how people get babies. *Child Development. 46,* 77–91.

Bierwisch, M. (1970). Semantics. In J. Lyons (Ed.), *New horizons in linguistics* (pp. 166–184). Baltimore: Penguin.

Brodzinsky, D. M., Singer, L. M., & Braff, A. M. (1984). Children's understanding of adoption. *Child Development, 55,* 869–878.

Burns, R. C., & Kaufman, S. H. (1970). *Kinetic family drawings (K-F-D): An introduction to understanding children through kinetic drawings.* New York: Brunner/Mazel.

Campbell, J. D. (1975). Illness is a point of view: The development of children's concepts of illness. *Child Development, 46,* 92–100.

Cataldo, C., & Geismar, L. (1983). Preschooler's views of parenting and the family. *Journal of Research and Development in Education, 16,* 8–14.

Chambers, J. C., & Tavuchis, N. (1976). Kids and kin: Children's understanding of American kin terms. *Journal of Child Language, 3,* 63–80.

Clark, E. V. (1983). Meaning and concepts. In J. H. Flavell & E. M. Markman (Eds.), P. H. Mussen (Series Ed.), *Manual of child psychology: Vol. 3. Cognitive development.* New York: Wiley.

Connor, R., Greene, H. F., & Walters, J. (1958). Agreement of family member conceptions of "good" parent and child roles. *Social Forces, 36,* 353–358.

Damon, W. (1977). *The social world of the child.* San Francisco: Jossey-Bass.

Danziger, K. (1957). The child's conceptions of kinship terms: A study of the development of relational concepts. *Journal of Genetic Psychology, 91,* 213–232.

Dubin, R., & Dubin, E. R. (1965). Children's social perceptions: A review of research. *Child Development, 35,* 809–838.

Elkind, D. (1962). Children's conceptions of brother and sister: Piaget replication study V. *Journal of Genetic Psychology, 100,* 129–136.

Emmerich, W. (1959). Young children's discriminations of parent and child roles. *Child Development, 30,* 404–420.

Emmerich, W. (1961). Family role concepts of children ages six to ten. *Child Development, 32,* 609–624.

Fischer, K. W. (1980). A theory of cognitive development: The control and construction of heirarchies of skills. *Psychological Review, 87,* 477–531.

Furth, H. G., Baur, M., & Smith, J. E. (1976). Children's conception of social institutions: A Piagetian framework. *Human Development, 19,* 351–374.

Gelman, R. (1979). Preschool thought. *American Psychologist, 34,* 900–905.

Gilby, R. L. (1979). *The development of the child's concept of the family.* Unpublished master's thesis. University of Western Ontario.

Gilby, R. L., & Pederson, D. R. (1982). The development of the child's concept of the family. *Canadian Journal of Behavioral Sciences, 14,* 111–121.

Harris, I. D., & Howard, K. I. (1981). Perceived parental authority: Reasonable and unreasonable. *Journal of Youth and Adolescence, 10,* 273–284.

Hartley, R. E. (1960). Children's concepts of male and female roles. *Merrill-Palmer Quarterly, 6,* 83–91.

Haviland, S. E., & Clark, E. V. (1974). 'This man's father is my father's son': A study of the acquisition of English kin terms. *Journal of Child Language, 1,* 23–47.

Holyoak, K. J., & Gordon, P. J. (1984). Information processing and cognition. In R. S. Wyer, Jr., & T. K. Srull (Eds.), *Handbook of social cognition: Vol. 1* (pp. 39–70). Hillsdale, NJ: Lawrence Erlbaum Associates.

Hulse, W. C. (1951). The emotionally disturbed child draws his family. *Quarterly Journal of Child Behavior, 3,* 152–174.

Hulse, W. C. (1952). Childhood conflict expressed through family drawings. *Journal of Projective Techniques, 16,* 66–79.

Jensen, D. R., Beus, G. B., & Storm, G. (1968). Simultaneous statistical tests on categorical data. *Journal of Experimental Education, 36,* 46–56.

Jordan, V. B. (1980). Conserving kinship concepts: A developmental study in social cognition. *Child Development, 51,* 146–155.

Kagan, J. (1956). The child's perception of the parent. *Journal of Abnormal and Social Psychology, 53,* 257–258.

Kagan, J., Hosken, B., & Watson, S. (1961). Child's symbolic conceptualization of parents. *Child Development, 32,* 625–636.

Kagan, J., & Lemkin, J. (1960). The child's differential perception of parental attributes. *Journal of Abnormal and Social Psychology, 61,* 440–447.

Kahana, B., & Kahana, E. (1970). Grandparenthood from the perspective of the developing grandchild. *Developmental Psychology, 3,* 98–105.

Kohlberg, L. (1966). A cognitive development analysis of children's sex-role concepts and attitudes. In E. E. Maccoby (Ed.), *The development of sex differences* (pp. 82–173). Stanford, CA: Stanford University Press.

Macaskill, A. (1981). Language acquisition and cognitive development: The acquisition of kinship terms. *British Journal of Educational Psychology, 51,* 283–290.

Maccoby, E. E. (1980). *Social development.* New York: Harcourt, Brace & Jovanovich.

Mandler, J. M. (1983). Representation. In J. H. Flavell & E. M. Markman (Eds.), P. H. Mussen (Series Ed.), *Manual of Child Psychology: Vol. 3. Cognitive Development* (pp. 420–494). New York: Wiley.

Moore, N. V. (1977). Cognitive level, intactness of family, and sex in relation to the child's development of the concept of family. *Dissertation Abstracts International, 37,* 4117B–4118B. (University Microfilms No. 77-3960).

Piaget, J. (1964). *Judgment and reasoning in the child.* Paterson, NJ: Littlefield, Adams. (Originally published, 1928).

Piaget, J. (1968). *On the development of memory and identity.* Barre, MA: Clark University Press with Barre Publishers.

Powell, J., & Thompson, D. (1981). The Australian child's concept of family. *Australian Journal of Early Childhood, 6,* 35–38.

Rosch, E. (1975). Cognitive representations of semantic categories. *Journal of Experimental Psychology: General, 104,* 192–223.

Rosch, E. (1978). Principles of categorization. In E. Rosch & B. B. Lloyd (Eds.), *Cognition and categorization* (pp. 27–48). Hillsdale, NJ: Lawrence Erlbaum Associates.

Saltz, E. (1971). *The cognitive basis of human learning.* Homewood, IL: Dorsey.

Schneider, D. M. (1980). *American kinship: A cultural account,* 2nd edition. Chicago: University of Chicago Press.

Selman, R. L. (1980). *The growth of interpersonal understanding.* New York: Academic Press.

Swartz, K., & Hall, A. E. (1972). Development of relational concepts and word definition in children five through eleven. *Child Development, 43,* 239–244.

Van der Veen, F., & Novak, A. L. (1971). Perceived parental attitudes and family concepts of disturbed adolescents, normal siblings and normal controls. *Family Process, 10,* 327–343.

Watson, M. W. (1984). Development of social role understanding. *Developmental Review, 4,* 192–213.

Watson, M. W., & Amgott-Kwan, T. (1983). Transitions in children's understanding of parental roles. *Developmental Psychology, 19,* 659–666.

Watson, M. W., & Amgott-Kwan, T. (1984). Development of family role concepts in school-age children. *Developmental Psychology, 20,* 953–959.

Weeks, M. O., & Thornburg, K. R. (1977). Marriage role expectations of five-year-old children and their parents. *Sex Roles, 3,* 189–191.

White, E., Elsom, B., & Prawat, R. (1978). Children's conceptions of death. *Child Development, 49,* 307–310.

Wynn, R. L., & Brumberger, L. S. (1982, June). *A cognitive developmental analysis of children's understanding of family membership and divorce.* Paper presented at the Twelfth Symposium of the Jean Piaget Society, Philadelphia.

8

Children's Knowledge of Adoption: Developmental Changes and Implications for Adjustment

David M. Brodzinsky
Dianne Schechter
Anne Braff Brodzinsky
Rutgers University

Each year tens of thousands of children in the United States are adopted. Many are the product of out-of-wedlock pregnancies. An increasing number are adopted when the court system intervenes and terminates the parental rights of biological parents because of abuse or neglect. Still others are the result of abandonment, voluntary relinquishment, or parental death. Finally, a sizable number of foreign-born children are being adopted each year (Feigelman & Silverman, 1983; Kadushin, 1974).

The exact number of children who are adopted each year is difficult to determine because national statistics on adoption are no longer compiled. The last report by the U.S. Department of Health, Education, and Welfare was for 1975, when 104,188 children were adopted (National Center for Social Statistics, 1976). Recent estimates suggest that there are approximately 1.5 million individuals in the United States under 18 years of age who are adopted—roughly 2% of the population of children (Kadushin, 1974). Of this total, slightly more than half were adopted by relatives. The remaining children—and the ones who have received the most attention by adoption researchers—were adopted by nonrelatives.

The focus on adoption by mental health professionals—aside from those individuals who are interested in behavioral genetics issues (cf. Horn, 1983; Plomin & DeFries, 1983; Scarr & Weinberg, 1983)—is based on the concern that the disruption of a relationship between the child and his or her initial caregivers (e.g., biological parents, foster parents, etc.) may place the child at greater risk for psychological and academic maladjustment than nonadopted peers. Furthermore, even when children are placed for adoption very early in their lives—thereby reducing separation effects (Yarrow, 1964)—there still is concern that other experiences and situations associated with adoption may render these children more vulnerable to adjustment problems. Some of the risk factors that investigators have speculated about include: (a) a more problematic prenatal and reproductive history (Bohman, 1970; Losbough, 1965); (b) a more complicated and anxiety-arousing transition to parenthood for adoptive parents (Kirk, 1964); (c) the existence of a social stigma surrounding adoption (Kirk, 1964); (d) the adoptee's confusion, uncertainty, and anxiety in dealing with his or her unknown origin (Sants, 1964; Sorosky, Baran, & Pannor, 1975; Stone, 1972); and (e) the stresses and strains surrounding the process of adoption revelation—i.e., the process through which the child is informed of his or her adoptive status and comes to understand its implications (Braff, 1977; Brodzinsky, 1984a; Brodzinsky, Singer, & Braff, 1984; Wieder, 1977).

Research generally has confirmed the increased vulnerability of the adopted child to psychological and academic problems. For example, although nonrelated adoptees constitute only 1% of the population of children, they represent approximately 4% to 5% of the children referred to child guidance clinics and other mental health facilities (Mech, 1973). Clinic-referred adopted children also are more likely than nonadopted clinic children to manifest aggressive and acting-out problems, as well as learning difficulties (Eiduson & Livermore, 1953; Kenny, Baldwin, & Mackie, 1967; Menlove, 1965; Offord, Aponte, & Cross, 1969; Reece & Levin, 1968; Schechter, Carlson, Simmons, & Work, 1964; Silver, 1970; Simon & Senturia, 1966; Taichert & Harvin, 1975). With respect to research on nonclinic children, the results, although less consistent, still point to increased psychological risk associated with adoption (cf. Brodzinsky, Schechter, Braff, & Singer, 1984). For example, Nemovicher (1960) reported greater amounts of hostility, dependency, tenseness, and fearfulness in adopted children than in nonadopted children. A higher incidence of emotional and academic problems also was reported by Bohman (1970), but only for adopted boys. A similar pattern of findings for emotional adjustment in adopted boys versus unadopted boys was observed by Seglow, Pringle, and Wedge (1972). Finally, in our own research (Brodzinsky et al., 1984), we found that both mothers and teachers rated adopted elementary-school-age children as significantly less well adjusted in psychological, interpersonal, and academic areas in comparison to a matched sample of nonadopted peers.

Assuming that adopted children are at greater risk for various developmental problems, the obvious question that needs to be addressed is the basis for their vulnerability. This chapter focuses on one factor that repeatedly has been mentioned by professionals in the adoption field as having a profound impact on the adjustment of the adoptive family—namely, the adoption revelation process. Specifically, we examine the *telling process,* as it is called, from the perspective of cognitive-developmental theory. In so doing, we provide an overview of data on developmental changes and individual differences in children's understanding of adoption, as well as data on the relationship between children's adoption knowledge and psychological adjustment in the family. Finally, it is argued that a cognitive-developmental approach provides the researcher and the clinician with a useful way of understanding many of the adjustment problems associated with adoption.

ADOPTION REVELATION: CURRENT PERSPECTIVES

In the past there was some belief that adoptive families might benefit from withholding adoption information from the child. Today, however, the consensus among adoption authorities is that children not only have a right to this information, but that failure to tell the child of his or her adoptive status places the child at increased risk for emotional problems should the child inadvertently become aware of the information at some later point in life—which happened all too often in earlier times (Lifton, 1979; Sorosky, Baran, & Pannor, 1979). The relevant question at present, therefore, is not whether to disclose adoption information, but *when, what,* and *how* to tell the child. Psychoanalytic theorists argue that telling should be withheld until the child has passed through the Oedipal stage (around 6–7 years), and therefore is less vulnerable to the confusion and anxiety of having two sets of parents, instead of one, with whom to identify (Peller, 1961; Wieder, 1977). The more common recommendation among social welfare professionals, however, is to begin the telling process early in the child's life—usually between 2 and 4 years—to be followed by periodic discussions and reinterpretation of the information throughout childhood (Mech, 1973).

Why is it that social workers and the majority of the mental health community have been so concerned about the need to begin the disclosure process in the first few years of the child's life? What benefits are assumed to accompany early telling? As we have noted elsewhere (Brodzinsky, 1984a; Brodzinsky et al., 1984), an early disclosure of adoption information is believed to provide a foundation for an honest and trusting relationship between parents and children. It is also assumed to relieve parents of the burden of deception—a burden that can weigh heavily on the parent–child relationship. In addition, early telling minimizes the chances that children will discover the truth about their family status from an outside, and potentially unfriendly, source. Furthermore, it gives parents time to adjust to their own status as adoptive parents, and to try out different ways of handling the disclosure process, prior to the time when children actively begin asking questions about their status. Finally, early telling is assumed to provide the child with a basic awareness of his or her unique family status, which in turn is assumed to be necessary for facilitating the child's adoption adjustment.

In their enthusiasm for promoting early telling, however, most of the professionals in the adoption community have overlooked a very important aspect of the adoption revelation process; namely, that this process involves two separate, but interrelated goals. The first goal, and the one most often emphasized, is *telling*. This is the parent's task—the goal that adoption authorities have promoted as being essential for the development of a healthy family relationship. The second goal, on the other hand, and the one most often ignored by adoption authorities and adoptive parents, is *understanding*. This is the child's task. Telling children about their adoptive status and the circumstances surrounding their relinquishment does not, in and of itself, guarantee that the child will understand the information provided (Brodzinsky, 1984a). In emphasizing the need for openness and honesty in parent–child discussions about adoption—the importance of which we certainly do not dispute—adoption professionals have neglected the cognitive components of the disclosure process. This neglect has resulted in increased confusion and uncertainty among adoptive parents—who look to the professionals for advice—regarding their children's reaction to adoption information.

Perhaps a brief anecdote will clarify what we believe is an all too common reaction among adoptive parents who begin to disclose adoption information during the preschool years, or earlier, without considering the ability of their children to assimilate the information. Several years ago, at a workshop for adoptive parents, a mother of a 7-year-old adopted boy expressed concern because her child was beginning to ask questions that suggested he was insecure about his adoptive family status. When the child was first informed about his adoption—at $3\frac{1}{2}$ years—he seemed to accept it quite well, she said. He began to label himself as adopted and, on request, would repeat the story about growing in another woman's body and then coming to live with his adoptive family. The parents were pleased that the child not only was able to understand these events, but had a very positive feeling about them. However, sometime between 6 and 7 years of age, according to the mother, the boy began to ask questions about the reasons for his relinguishment. Was he bad? Didn't his first mother like him? What if she changed her mind—could she come back and get him? And what about his adoptive parents—maybe they would give him up too if he wasn't good. These thoughts and questions were beginning to emerge more and more frequently in the child, the mother reported. What had gone wrong, she asked. Why had her child, who so readily accepted his adoptive status previously, suddenly developed such an insecure view of himself? Was it something she and her husband had done, or failed to do? Was it their fault?

As we suggested to the mother, it probably was not that she and her husband had done a poor job in disclosing adoption information to their child. The problem was in their expectations concerning what the early disclosure attempts had accomplished, and what was normal for children to understand about adoption at different ages. We asked her why she had assumed her child, as a preschooler, had understood the adoption information presented. She responded that the child was quite open and verbal about his adoption. Moreover, his description of the events underlying the adoption was very realistic—that is, they mirrored what he had been told. Because of this, she and her husband had simply assumed that their careful attempts to break down the adoption story into simple facts, and their gradual introduction of these facts into the life of the child, had been successful in fostering a basic understanding and acceptance of his adoptive status.

This anecdote is presented, not with the intention of suggesting that it represents the experience and expectations of all adoptive parents—for obviously it does not—but as an example of the kind of confusion, uncertainty, and anxiety that sometimes emerges when parents consciously or unconsciously accept, in toto, the assumptions underlying the policy of early telling.

We have argued elsewhere (Brodzinsky, Braff, & Singer, 1980) that early telling is based on a mechanistic conception of knowledge development. Parents are encouraged by adoption professionals and literature to begin disclosing adoption information in the early years of the child's life based, in part, on the assumption that the development of knowledge, including adoption knowledge, results from a slow, progressive, accumulation of facts, and that the child's understanding and acceptance of his or her adoptive status is linked to the gradual build-up of these facts. And yet this assumption, in our opinion, is at odds with the growing body of research on children's acquisition of social knowledge; specifically, those areas that are most closely associated with adoption—for example, knowledge of birth and reproduction, family roles and relationships, interpersonal motives, social rules and regulations, and moral/ethical principles (cf. Bernstein & Cowan, 1975; Damon, 1977; Furth, 1980; Kurdek, this volume; Pederson & Gilby, this volume; Rest, 1983; Selman, 1980; Shantz, 1983). Furthermore, it appears that the mechanistic assumptions underlying early telling have led parents to develop unrealistic expectations about their children's capacity to assimilate adoption information. For example, in our research (Brodzinsky, Braff, & Schechter, 1984), when parents were asked to predict their child's comprehension of adoption, they showed a strong inclination to attribute knowledge to the child where, in fact, little or none existed. This indicates that parents believe their children understand much more about adoption than they actually do. More often than not, parents are misled by the child's *working adoption vocabulary*. When parents hear their 3-, 4-, or 5-year-old children refer to themselves as adopted, and describe the way in which they came into the adoptive family, they simply assume that the children understand what it is they are talking about. We are arguing, however, that it is questionable, given what is known about the emergence of social knowledge, that these young children comprehend the meaning of adoption-related concepts—at least in the way parents expect and hope they will.

A Constructivist Approach to Adoption Revelation

An alternative way of looking at the adoption revelation process is from the perspective of a constructivist theory of knowledge development. The basic assumption underlying this conceptual approach is that children's knowledge of the world, including the personal and impersonal aspects of it, results not from a gradual accumulation of externally-derived facts, but from an active process of internal construction. This assumption is derived primarily from the cognitive-developmental theory of Piaget (1970) and the social-cognitive theory of Kelly (1955, 1963). Briefly, Piaget proposes that the individual is never just a passive recipient of information encountered in the course of transactions with the environment, but acts on and transforms the information in accordance with the organizational principles underlying his or her existing cognitive structures. Likewise, Kelly argues that we individually formulate our own personal system of constructs and consequently view the world through these constructs. Both of these theoretical systems emphasize the active nature of the human organism. The notion of an ontological real world is rejected, and in its place is found a world of self-construction—a world that has meaning, and hence can be known, only through an active assimilatory process.

Yet knowledge is more than the result of an individual's mental constructions. Individuals live in a social matrix, and hence are influenced by the mental constructions, belief systems, and actions of others. Thus, we agree with Youniss (1975, 1981) who has argued that knowledge is also tied to interpersonal interactions.

This very brief description of our epistemological position holds not only for the individual's general knowledge of the world, but more importantly for our purposes, for the child's knowledge of, beliefs about, and adjustment to, adoption. We suggest that children's comprehension of adoption undergoes the same kind of qualitative (as well as quantitative) change that characterize their knowledge of other aspects of the social and nonsocial world. Moreover, it is also assumed that at a given point in time, the capacity for assimilating adoption information presented by parents and significant others is limited by the nature of the child's existing cognitive structures. The task for parents is to recognize that children do not understand the world in the same way they do, and that any attempt at explaining adoption to children must take this fact into account. For parents to be successful in helping their children understand and cope with their adoptive status, they must monitor their children's adoption knowledge, and recognize that a working adoption vacabulary does not necessarily imply understanding and acceptance. Furthermore, disclosing age-appropriate adoption information, and developing age-appropriate expectations about children's adoption knowledge, also necessitates some general understanding of the nature of social-cognitive development and how it relates to adoption. From our perspective, existing adoption theory and research have not supplied the guidelines that would help parents achieve these goals.

UNDERSTANDING ADOPTION: A COGNITIVE-DEVELOPMENTAL PERSPECTIVE

When children are placed for adoption, it certainly can be assumed that there have been major socioeconomic and/or social-emotional impediments to their continued existence in the biological family. Understanding the nature of these impediments, conceptualizing the biological parent's decision to reliquish them, and tracing themselves through the adoption process, is the unique developmental task of adopted children. But what exactly is involved in understanding adoption? What is the conceptual basis for this family status? How does children's knowledge of adoption change with age? These are among the questions that have been the focus of the Rutgers Adoption Project (Brodzinsky, 1983).

Rutgers Adoption Project

The Rutgers Adoption Project was begun in 1979 as an attempt to understand the development and adjustment of adopted children and their families. The project originally focused on developmental changes in children's understanding of adoption and on factors predicting differential adjustment to adoptive family life during the school-age years. Recently it has been expanded to include issues related to the transition to adoptive parenthood (e.g., the nature of mother–infant attachment in adoptive families), as well as issues related to identity development among adolescent and young adult adoptees. In the work completed to date, we have compared adopted children with matched samples of nonadopted children. This strategy has allowed us to answer questions concerning the impact of adoption, as a unique form of family life, on children and parents. In addition, though, we also have been concerned with individual differences in the development and adjustment of adopted children and their parents. Consequently, we have examined the relationship between demographic, family structure, and family process variables and selected child and parent outcome measures. In this chapter, we restrict our discussion to the issue of children's understanding of adoption and its relationship to adoption adjustment.

Children's Knowledge of Adoption

Subjects and Procedure.   Our intitial sample of 200 children (102 girls and 98 boys) from 4 to 13 years of age, included 20 adopted and 20 nonadopted children in each of five age groups: 4–5 years, 6–7 years, 8–9 years, 10–11 years, and 12–13 years. Of the 200 children, 172 were Caucasian; the remaining were either black, Oriental, Latin American, or mixed race. The noncaucasian adopted children lived in Caucasian families. Adopted and nonadopted children were matched for age, sex, socioeconomic status, and family structure (only child vs. child with younger siblings vs. child with older siblings). All adopted children were placed for adoption prior to 2½ years of age.

Children's understanding of adoption was studied primarily by means of an open-ended interview. The interview focused on four aspects of adoption knowledge: (a) the nature of the adoptive family relationship; (b) the role of the agency as intermediary in the adoption process; (c) motives for adopting; and (d) motives for placing a child for adoption. A complete description of the interview procedure, including the list of questions used, can be found in Brodzinsky et al. (1984). Data on (a), (c), and (d) have been reported previously (Brodzinsky et al., 1984). For the purpose of this chapter, however, only an overview of (a)— children's understanding of the adoptive family relationship—is presented. Data on (b)—children's understanding of the adoption agency—is reported in detail in the next section.

Knowledge of the Adoptive Family Relationship.   Children's interview protocols were analyzed for their understanding of the adoptive family relationship. Specifically, we were interested in the ability of children to differentiate between adoption and birth as alternative ways of entering a family, as well as children's conception of the permanence of the adoptive parent-child relationship. Six levels of understanding were identified:

Level 0: Children show no awareness of the meaning of adoption; or responses are so idiosyncratic as to be unscorable.

Level 1: Children fail to differentiate between adoption and birth as alternative ways of becoming a member of a family. Instead, they either believe that all children are born to one set of parents, but then go to live with another set of parents, or they equate the birth process with being adopted.

(A. W.: 4 years, 7 months): Adoption is when you are born. (What do you mean?) You came out of a lady. (Tell me more about that.) Well, then you go to live with your parents. (Which parents?) Your adopted parents. You came out of one lady, but she's not your mommy. (Is that true for all children?) Sure, that's how it is. (Are all children adopted?) Of course they are. (You mean that all kids are born to one set of parents, but then are adopted by other parents?) That's what I said, didn't I?

Level 2: Children clearly differentiate between adoption and birth as alternative ways of entering a family, and they accept that the adoptive family relationship is permanent, but they do not understand why. Usually, they rely on a sense of faith ("My mommy told me.") or notions of possession ("The child *belongs* to the other parents now.") to justify the permanent nature of the parent–child relationship.

(S.T.: 6 years, 5 months): Adoption is when the first parents can't take care of you and so you are adopted by other people—your adoptive parents. They couldn't make a baby themselves. (Tell me more about being adopted.) Well, one thing I know is that my parents won't ever give me up. (Tell me how you know?) Cause my mommy and daddy said so. (When adults adopt a child, is that child theirs forever?) Yes, that's what I meant. (Can the first parents—the ones who made the baby—ever get the baby back after it is adopted?) No, never. (How come?) I don't know. I guess because it doesn't belong to them now.

Level 3: Children differentiate between adoption and birth, but now are unsure about the permanence of the adoptive parent–child relationship. Biological parents are seen as having the potential for reclaiming the child at some future, but unspecified time; or the adoptive family is seen as potentially undergoing some form of disruption that could lead to abandonment or relinquishment of the child.

(E.W.: 8 years, 1 month): (Once the parents adopt the baby is it theirs forever?) That's hard to say. I think about that sometimes. (Tell me about it.) Well, I think that if the birth parents wanted to, they could get the baby back. (How?) They could get the police or someone to find out where the baby lives and then go and ask for the baby back. (What would happen then?) I don't know. Maybe the police would make them give it back. (Why would the police do that?) I can't say. I'm not sure about all of this.

Level 4: Children's descriptions of the adoptive family relationship are characterized by a quasi-legal sense of permanence. Specifically, children invoke an authority figure such as a judge, lawyer, doctor, or social worker who in some vague way "makes" the parent–child relationship premanent.

(A.R.: 10 years, 7 months): When the parents adopt a child they go to the adoption agency and the people there help them to find a child like they want. (Tell me more.) They find a child whose parents don't want it and then they ask the people if they want their child adopted, and if they say yes, then they take the child and give it to the other parents. (Can the first parents change their mind?) No, not after they sign the papers. (What papers?) Some kind of papers the people at the agency have. (Once adults adopt a child is that child theirs forever?) Yes. Cause the people at the adoption agency make sure that the other people don't change their mind. (How?) I don't know really. But that's what they do.

Level 5: The adoptive family relationship is now characterized as permanent, involving the legal transfer of rights and/or responsibilities for the child from the biological parents to the adoptive parents.

(J.M.: 12 years, 5 months): (Suppose an important decision had to be made about the child after it was adopted. Who should make that decision—the adoptive parents or the birth parents?) The adoptive parents, of course. (Why?) Once you give up a child and he's adopted, then he doesn't belong to you anymore. You don't have the right to say he should do this or that. (Why is that?) It wouldn't be fair to the adoptive parents. The child is theirs and they have to take care of him. They're the ones who are responsible for how he should grow up. Besides, it would really mix up the adopted kid if the other parents suddenly came back into his life. (But what if the birth parents really wanted the child back?) No way.

When they signed the adoption papers, that's that. The law says it isn't their child anymore and they don't have to right to try and get him back and upset the whole family.

Knowledge of the adoptive family relationship was analyzed by assigning each child a numerical score corresponding to his or her level of understanding (e.g., level 0 = 0; level 1 = 1, etc.). A general linear model analysis of variance was then performed on the data—age, adoption status, and sex were treated as independent variables. Of the three main effects, only age was significant. Duncan's Multiple Range test indicated a significant difference between all adjacent age levels (see Brodzinsky et al., 1984 for additional details). See Table 8.1.

As one would expect, there was a marked increase in adoption knowledge with increasing age. The majority of 4–5-year-olds did not understand the meaning of adoption, even though all the children had known about their adoptive status for some time, and labeled themselves as adopted. The confusion of some of these young children was particularly evident in their fusing of the birth and adoption concepts. By 6 years of age, however, most children clearly differentiated between birth and adoption as alternative ways of becoming a family member. Furthermore, when asked about the nature of the adoptive parent–child relationship, 6–7- and 8–9-year-olds generally stated that the relationship was a permanent one, although they did not understand why. For the most part, these children appeared to be repeating, without understanding, the assurances offered by parents regarding the permanency of the family relationship. Other children, however, were not so confident about the permanent nature of the adoptive family relationship. For these children, the relationship was perceived as some-

TABLE 8.1
Frequency Distribution by Age and Adoption Status
of Children's Knowledge of the Adoption Relationship

Age and Adoption Status		*Level of Understanding*					
		0	*1*	*2*	*3*	*4*	*5*
4–5	Adopted	6	5	8	1	0	0
	Nonadopted	12	4	0	4	0	0
6–7	Adopted	1	2	12	3	2	0
	Nonadopted	4	1	7	7	1	0
8–9	Adopted	0	0	10	5	4	1
	Nonadopted	0	0	4	8	8	0
10–11	Adopted	0	0	2	1	14	3
	Nonadopted	0	0	0	4	9	7
12–13	Adopted	0	0	1	2	7	10
	Nonadopted	0	0	0	0	9	11
Mean Age	Adopted	5:4	5:6	7:2	8:8	10:4	12:5
	Nonadopted	5:6	5:9	7:3	7:10	10:10	12:5

what tenuous. Specifically, biological parents were seen as having the potential for reclaiming the adopted child at some future, but unspecified, time. In addition, some children were concerned about the stability of the adoptive family, believing that it could easily fall apart as the biological family had. By around 10 years of age, however, most children once again displayed confidence in the permanency of the adoptive parent–child relationship. The conceptual basis for the permanence at this level of understanding, although still somewhat vague, was more firmly rooted than earlier knowledge levels in societal rules and regulations, and specifically, in the authority granted to those figures who administer such rules—e.g., judges, lawyers, doctors, caseworkers, and the like. Still, it was not until 12–13 years that a majority of children recognized that adoption involves a legal transfer of rights, obligations, and responsibilities from biological parents to adoptive parents.

Knowledge of the Adoption Agency.   Children's interview protocols also were examined for their understanding of the functioning of the adoption agency. Specifically, we were interested in determining how children conceptualize the role of the adoption agency, and other third parties, that act as intermediaries in the adoption process. Five levels of understanding were identified:

Level 0: Children do not differentiate between adoption and birth, and hence have no knowledge of the adoption agency and its functions.

Level 1: Children differentiate between adoption and birth as alternative ways of entering a family, but still have no understanding of the adoption agency.

Level 2: Children recognize the existence of the agency or other third parties (e.g., orphanage, lawyer, etc.) that serve as an intermediary in the adoption process, but attribute no specific functions to the third party. The agency is seen as a *passive* intermediary, and often as a "collection center" or "holding center" for children in need of a home.

(D.F.: 6 years, 5 months): You have to go to some kind of place with lots of kids . . . you go there and see the kids, talk to them, and see if you like them. If you do, you take one home. (What else happens there? Tell me more about the place.) That's all I know. It's a place that has kids who don't have parents. People go there and get a kid . . . to make the kid their child.

Level 3: At this level, children recognize that the agency plays an *active* role as intermediary in the adoption process. Specifically, the agency is seen as a "processing center" for handling adoption requests. The emphasis, however, is on meeting the needs of prospective adoptive parents.

(I.T.: 9 years, 3 months): Well you go to the agency people and say that you want to adopt a child. They talk to you to find out about you and what kind of child you want . . . like a boy or girl, or maybe a little baby or an older child . . . they have you sign papers and they try to find a child for you . . . one that needs to be adopted. Sometimes it takes a long time . . . sometimes you have to go far away to get a child, like to a different country.

Level 4: The agency is now characterized not only as active, but also as an *evaluative* intermediary, one that assumes an advocacy role in protecting the rights and welfare of adopted children and the adults involved in the process. (W.H.: 13 years, 1 month): (Can anyone adopt a child?) That all depends. It depends on the person's background. If someone has been in jail for possession of narcotics, or they've been in jail for raping someone, or if they've been hospitalized for alcoholism, I don't think that they would let the person adopt a child because they might abuse it. (So how does the agency know all this?) Well, by investigating the person's life and like trying to find out as much as possible about their background . . . they have to see if the people are responsible . . . if they will really take good care of and love the child.

A general linear model analysis of variance was also performed on the adoption agency data. Once again, the main effect for age was significant, indicating a marked increase in knowledge of the adoption agency as intermediary with increasing age, $F(4, 180) = 122.49$, $p < .001$. Duncan's Multiple Range test indicated a difference between all adjacent age levels. No other main effects or interactions were significant.

As Table 8.2 indicates, most 4–5 year olds, in line with their difficulty in differentiating between adoption and birth, have little understanding of the adoption process. Between 6 and 9 years of age, however, a gradual recognition of the mechanics of the adoption process begins to unfold. At first, the adoption agency, and other third parties, are viewed as passive intermediaries; somewhat later, a more active role is attributed to them. In both cases, however, the primary focus of these intermediaries is on providing for the needs of prospective adoptive parents. An emphasis on the child's needs and welfare is minimal at this time, and only superficially dealt with by children. At most, children may pay lip service to the fact that the adoptee "needs a home" or "someone to care for and love him". It is not until 10–11 years that the majority of children recognize that the adoption agency, and other parties involved, play an evaluative role in the adoption process—a role that focuses on the child's rights and welfare as much, if not more, as the rights and welfare of prospective adoptive parents.

To determine the relationship between children's understanding of the adoptive family relationship and their understanding of the adoption agency, a Pearson Product Moment correlation coefficient was computed. As one might expect, a strong positive relationship was found ($r = .73$, $p < .001$).

Discussion.   The results of our research suggest that children's adoption knowledge undergoes clear, systematic changes with age. As in many areas of cognitive development, children's adoption knowledge initially is rather global and diffuse. With time, however, such knowledge becomes increasingly differ-

TABLE 8.2
Frequency Distribution by Age and Adoption Status
of Children's Knowledge of the Adoption Agency

Age and Adoption Status		Level of Understanding				
		0	1	2	3	4
4–5	Adopted	11	6	3	0	0
	Nonadopted	16	2	2	0	0
6–7	Adopted	3	5	9	3	0
	Nonadopted	5	7	6	0	2
8–9	Adopted	0	3	7	7	3
	Nonadopted	0	3	9	0	8
10–11	Adopted	0	0	3	5	12
	Nonadopted	0	0	4	4	12
12–13	Adopted	0	0	0	0	20
	Nonadopted	0	0	0	1	19
Mean Age	Adopted	5:5	6:7	8:1	8:11	11:11
	Nonadopted	5:9	6:10	8:2	11:1	11:6

entiated, as well as integrated into a more general matrix of social and nonsocial knowledge.

Developmental changes in children's comprehension of adoption are understood most easily when compared to changes in other areas of social cognition (Brodzinsky et al., 1980). Although space does not permit a thorough conceptual analysis of adoption and its relationship to other biosocial concepts, two specific domains of knowledge serve to explicate and support our position.

The initial task for the adopted child is to distinguish between adoption and birth as alternative ways of entering a family. In the absence of such a distinction, children cannot help but misunderstand or be confused about their family status. Bernstein and Cowan (1975) have clearly shown that preoperational children have a very distorted understanding of birth, based primarily on spatial causality and artificialism, and that it is not until the concrete operational period that a physicalistic (i.e., biological) notion of birth emerges.

If preschool-age children are unable to comprehend the biological basis of birth, how then are they to differentiate birth from adoption—the most basic goal of the adoption revelation process? The answer is that in most cases they cannot. Our results clearly point out that the majority of 4–5 year olds, and presumably younger children too, either have no idea of what adoption means, or interestingly, they produce distorted associations between the two processes—i.e., they either equate birth and adoption as one and the same process ("when you come out of the mommy's tummy that means being adopted"), or they suggest that all children are adopted ("well, first kids get to be born to one mommy, but then they go and live with their other mommy").

Related to the task of differentiating between birth and adoption is the child's task of integrating two sets of parents into his or her mental and emotional life. Even the most elementary presentation of adoption information usually involves the revelation of the existence of another woman (and sometimes a man) as central to the child's birth experience. Children are asked to understand and accept that they come from the body of one woman, their birth or biological mother, but not from the body of their own (i.e., adoptive) mother. It takes little imagination to recognize the potential confusion for young children. The woman who gave birth to them and who was once their mother, is no longer their mother; the woman from whose body they did not come from, but, in fact, who they are living with, is their mother. Is it truly possible for young children to make sense of this puzzle? Perhaps in a way it is, at least temporarily.

Piaget (1964), and more recently, Gilby and Pederson (1982) and Pederson and Gilby (this volume) have observed that young children generally define a family in terms of the people who live together. With increasing age, however, comprehension of the family changes, eventually leading elementary-school-age children to define family members of individuals who share a blood (i.e., biological) relationship. In this context, it is easy to see how for preschool and early school-age adopted children, parental assurances that they (the children) are part of the family usually are readily accepted. After all, the children do live with their (adoptive) parents and siblings—hence they are all part of the same family. However, it is quite conceivable that with increasing cognitive maturity children may become confused or upset about the issue of family membership. Having developed an understanding of biological relationships as the basis for family membership—a criterion that transcends time and space—children may begin to seriously question to whom they belong—the biological or adoptive family. Furthermore, increased knowledge about biological relationships may also stimulate concern regarding the whereabouts and status of the biological parents, as well as concern about the motives underlying the original relinquishment. Thus, an increase in social knowledge, particularly as it relates to family roles and relationships, may be a basis for the temporary feelings of uncertainty regarding the permanency of the adoptive family relationship that is sometimes seen in the elementary school years (Brodzinsky et al., in press).

Knowledge of birth and reproduction, and family relationships, are but two areas that children must master before they have a well consolidated and integrated sense of the adoption experience. Other areas that appear to be fundamental to children's comprehension of adoption are conceptions about the self and others, interpersonal motivation, social causality, interpersonal conflict, separation and loss, and the role and functioning of societal institutions. Thus, to understand the emergence of children's adoption knowledge one must recognize that it is embedded within the broader context of children's social-cognitive development. Although our current work has not yet empirically mapped out the developmental correspondences between adoption knowledge and other areas of social cognition, this approach would appear to be a fruitful avenue of research—as evidenced by recent investigations relating children's interpersonal reasoning and their understanding of marriage and divorce (Dana, 1982; Kurdek & Berg, 1983; Kurdek, Blisk, & Siesky, 1981).

Individual Differences in Adoption Knowledge

In this section, we examine the relationship between children's adoption knowledge and various demographic and family-related factors. Specifically, we are concerned with the question of how children's family structure, family background, preplacement history, and adoption revelation experiences influence their comprehension of adoption. These questions were examined for a sample of 156 adopted children between the ages of 6 and 11 years (76 females and 80 males). All adoptions involved intraracial placements. With the exception of three black, one Latin American, and two Oriental children, all subjects were Caucasian. The median adoption placement age for the children was 3.5 months (range = 3 days to 7.5 years).

Family Structure and Adoption Knowledge. It has been suggested that adopted children from different family structures show different patterns of psychological adjustment. For example, Kraus (1978) has reported that adopted children with younger siblings who are biologically related to the adoptive parents are at increased risk for psychological problems. Presumably, these children are more likely to fear rejection or abandonment now that parents "have achieved what they wanted all along"—biological children. Our own data, however, do not support a relationship between family structure and incidence of psychological and academic problems among adopted children (Brodzinsky, 1983). Yet, family structure could be related to children's adoption knowledge. Having siblings who are biologically related to the parents may accentuate the uniqueness of the adopted child's family status, thereby facilitating greater curiosity, questioning, and ultimately, greater understanding of adoption. Likewise, being the oldest of several adopted children may lead to greater adoption knowledge because the child has the opportunity of experiencing the adoption process again and again as each new child is brought into the family.

With these speculations in mind, we examined the development of children's adoption knowledge for five different family structures: only children ($N = 21$), children with younger adopted siblings only ($N = 35$), children with younger biological siblings only ($N = 32$), children with older adopted siblings only ($N = 32$), and children with older biological siblings only ($N = 18$). Children with other family structures ($N = 18$) were eliminated from these analyses. Preliminary analyses indicated no differences among the groups for children's age, family socioeconomic status (SES), mother's rating of children's health at the time of placement, number of foster placements, and timing of the initial disclosure of adoption information by parents. Children with older biological siblings only were placed for adoption significantly later than other children (mean = 6.7 vs 3.1 months).

Three measures of adoption knowledge were used: knowledge of the adoptive family relationship, knowledge of the adoption agency, and a combined adoption knowledge score. The latter was derived by summing the children's z-scores for the adoptive family and adoption agency concepts. Separate 5 (Family Structure) x 2 (Sex) general linear model analyses of variance were performed on the data. Results indicated no difference among the various family structures for any of the adoption knowledge variables; nor were there other significant effects. Thus, in support of our earlier findings (Brodzinsky, 1983), adoptive family structure plays little, if any, role in the development and adjustment of adopted children.

Family Background Factors and Adoption Knowledge. Researchers have suggested that certain demographic and preplacement history factors, as well as the timing of adoption revelation, may influence the adjustment of adopted children. For example, children who have been placed for adoption beyond the infancy years, who have been exposed to deprived, neglectful, or abusive conditions prior to placement, who have experienced multiple foster placements, and/or who have not been informed of their adoptive status until relatively late in the childhood or adolescent years have been found to have a higher incidence of adjustment problems than adopted children with less disruptive and problematic family histories (Bohman, 1970; Fanshel, 1972; Feigelman & Silverman, 1983; Kadushin, 1974; Kirk, 1964; Lifton, 1979; Mech, 1973; Yarrow, Goodwin, Manheimer, & Milowe, 1973; Yarrow and Klein, 1980). To date, however, no research has looked at the relationship between these type of family background factors and children's understanding of the adoption experience. It is quite conceivable, for example, that the more disruptive the preplacement history and the more deprived the current family environment, the less advanced the child's understanding of adoption—holding age constant, of course.

To examine this issue, Pearson Product Moment correlation coefficients were calculated between a host of family background variables and the three measures of adoption knowledge described earlier. The specific family background variables included child's age at placement (median = 3.5 months, mean = 6.5 months, sd = 15.6 months, range = 3 days to 7.5 years), number of foster placements (mean = .73, sd = .77, range = 0 to 4), maternal rating of child's health at time of placement (mean = 1.33, sd = .61, range = 1 [excellent] to 4 [poor]), adoptive family SES (mean = 2.3, sd = .92, range = 1 [highest] to 5 [lowest]), number of siblings in the adoptive family (mean = 1.28, sd = .93, range = 0 to 5), age when parents first began to refer to the child as adopted (mean = 1.96 years, sd = 1.51 years, range = 1 to 4 years), and age when parents first began to actively disclose adoption information to the child (mean = 3.42 years, sd = 1.40 years, range = 1 to 8 years). Correlations were calculated separately for three age groupings (6 and 7 years, 8 and 9 years, 10 and 11 years) in order to minimize the confounding of developmental changes in adoption knowledge with the relationship between family background and children's comprehension of adoption.

Inspection of Table 8.3 indicates virtually no relationship, at any of the ages studied, between children's understanding of adoption and the selected family background factors. The three correlations that were significant must be viewed skeptically, given the large number of correlations generated; at the .05 level, one would expect approximately three correlations to be significant by chance.

Discussion. Our results have been very consistent with regard to individual differences in children's adoption knowledge. Regardless of the child's preplacement history, family SES, family structure, or adoption revelation history, children's adoption knowledge followed essentially the same developmental path. Of particular interest is the finding that children's adoption status (i.e., adopted vs nonadopted) was unrelated to their comprehension of the adoptive family relationship or the adoption agency. Adoption status has also been shown to be unrelated (with a few exceptions) to children's awareness of the motives underlying adoption (Brodzinsky et al., 1984).

TABLE 8.3
Relationship Between Children's Adoption Knowledge
and Selected Family Background Factors by Age Level

Adoption Knowledge	Place	Fost	Health	SES	Sibs	First	Explain
			6–7 Year Olds				
Family Concept	.03	.07	−.10	.00	.17	−.03	.02
Agency Concept	−.05	.12	−.24	.02	.03	−.15	−.10
Combined Measures	−.02	.10	−.19	.01	.11	−.10	−.05
			8–9 Year Olds				
Family Concept	−.09	.03	−.12	−.09	.35**	.06	.02
Agency Concept	−.16	−.19	−.18	−.08	−.07	−.20	−.19
Combined Measure	−.14	−.11	−.16	−.11	.16	−.08	−.10
			10–11 Year Olds				
Family Concept	−.20	−.03	−.04	.19	−.03	−.33*	−.17
Agency Concept	.05	.11	.00	.26	.07	−.16	−.14
Combined Measure	−.09	.05	−.02	.27	.02	−.30*	−.19

*< .05
**< .01

Place = Child's age at placement; Fost = Number of foster placements; Health = Maternal rating of child's health at time of placement; SES = Adoptive family socioeconomic status; Sibs = Number of siblings in adoptive family; First = Child's age when parents first referred to him/her as adopted; Explain = Child's age when parents began to actively disclose adoption information.

On the surface, these results are surprising. It could easily be argued that the unique family experiences of adopted children should lead them to develop more advanced reasoning about adoption in comparison to nonadopted children. A similar argument could be made for children exposed to different types of family structure, different preplacement histories, and different adoption revelation histories. Consequently, one must ask whether our results are reliable, and whether there are data from other areas that could support their validity. These are reasonable and important questions, and they need to be addressed.

To begin with, interrater reliability in coding adoption knowledge was quite high (Brodzinsky et al., 1984). Furthermore, the fact that children's adoption knowledge was consistently independent of adoption status, family structure, family background, and family process variables, while at the same time being systematically related to age, is, in itself, quite impressive, and evidence in support of the validity of the data. In addition, results reported by a number of researchers in the area of children's understanding of the family are virtually identical to our own findings. For example, Piaget's (1964) early research on children's conception of the family indicated that only children had no more difficulty understanding the terms *brother* and *sister* than children who actually had siblings. Similarly, Jordan (1980) found that family size and birth order were unrelated to children's conservation of kinship terms. Other researchers have also documented that children's family structure and experience with relatives is unrelated to the development of family concepts (Chambers & Tavuches, 1976; Gilby & Pederson, 1982; Haviland & Clark, 1974; Pederson & Gilby, this volume).

Taken together, these findings support the position that children's development of knowledge, including concepts related to different forms of family life, is not the result of a gradual, progressive accumulation of facts or bits of information derived from specific experiences, as mechanistic theorists would suggest, but rather are due to a general process of internal construction. This constructivist perspective is in line with the theoretical orientation of Piaget (1970) and Kelly (1955, 1963) and with the recent theoretical and empirical work of social-cognitive researchers (cf., Chandler, 1977; Damon, 1977; Furth, 1980; Selman, 1980; Shantz, 1983).

Children's Psychological Adjustment and Adoption Knowledge

In previous sections, we alluded to the possibility that the emergence of children's knowledge of adoption might be related to their pattern of psychological adjustment. In this section, we address the issue directly. Specifically, the question of interest is whether children's adjustment to adoption, and/or their more general psychological and school-related adjustment, is associated with their level of awareness and understanding of the adoption experience. A corollary question is whether the relationship between these variables differs as a function of children's age.

The subject sample used to investigate these questions was the same one used for our previous analyses of individual differences in children's adoption knowledge. Specifically, the subjects were 156 adopted children (76 females and 80 males) divided into three age groups: fifty-three 6–7-year-olds, fifty-nine 8–9-year-olds, and forty-four 10–11-year-olds. All children, with the exception of four girls and two boys, were Caucasian. Children in the three age groups were comparable to one another with respect to family SES, number of siblings, number of foster placements, maternal ratings of child's health at the time of placement, child's age at placement, and child's age when parents began to disclose adoption information.

To examine the relationship between children's understanding of adoption and psychological adjustment, Pearson Product Moment correlation coefficients were computed, within each age group, between the three measures of adoption knowledge described previously (adoptive family concept, adoption agency concept, and combined adoption knowledge score) and three separate composite measures of psychological adjustment. The first composite measure reflected children's general level of psychological adjustment (CPA), and was composed of three scores: (a) an overall school adjustment score from the Hahnemann Elementary School Behavior Rating Scale (Spivak & Swift, 1975)[1]; (b) an overall social competence score from the Child Behavior Profile (Achenbach, 1978; Achenbach & Edelbrock, 1979, 1981); and (c) an overall behavior problem score, also from the Child Behavior Profile. The second composite measure reflected children's adjustment to adoption per se (CAA), and was also composed of three scores: (a) a factor score derived from questionnaire data representing mothers' rating of children's adjustment to adoption; (b) a second factor score derived from questionnaire data representing mothers' rating of children's separation anxiety; and (c) a score derived from children's responses to three questions dealing with their adjustment to adoption. The third composite measure reflected parents' adjustment to adoption (PAA), and once again, was composed of three scores: (a) a factor score derived from questionnaire data representing mother's rating of her own and her husband's adjustment to adoptive parenthood; (b) a second factor score derived from questionnaire data representing mother's rating of her own and her husband's degree of involvement with their child regarding adoption-related issues (e.g., disclosing adoption informa-

---

[1]The overall Hahnemann school adjustment score was derived by subtracting the child's z-scores of the negatively valued subscales (i.e., intellectual dependency, failure anxiety, unreflectiveness, irrelevant talk, social overinvolvement, negative feelings, and inattention) from the z-scores of the positively valued subscales (originality, independent learning, school involvement, productive with peers, and school achievement). Subscales on the Hahnemann measure that are used with open classrooms only were excluded from our analyses.

tion, answering adoption-related questions, etc.); and (c) a third factor score derived from questionnaire data representing mother's rating of her own confidence in handling adoption-related issues with her child. All three composite scores of psychological adjustment were computed by arithmetically combining subjects' z-scores for the individual measures.

Inspection of Table 8.4 reveals that children's understanding of adoption is indeed related to psychological adjustment, both in children and their parents. However, the pattern of the relationship is very different for the three age groups. For 6–7-year-olds, children's adoption knowledge, especially their knowledge of the adoption agency, is *positively* related to general psychological and school-related adjustment (CPA). By contrast, all three measures of adoption knowledge are *negatively* related to maternal ratings of children's adoption adjustment, and are unrelated to parental adoption adjustment. At 8–9 years of age, children's adoption knowledge is *positively* correlated with both composite measures of children's psychological adjustment, as well as with the measure of parental adjustment to adoption. Finally, for 10–11 year olds, no relationship was found between children's adoption knowledge and measures of children's and parents' psychological adjustment.

TABLE 8.4
Relationship Between Children's Adoption Knowledge
and Composite Measures of Psychological Adjustment
by Age Level

Adoption Knowledge	CPA	CAA	PAA
6–7 Year Olds			
Family Concept	.09	−.33**	−.07
Agency Concept	.42**	−.22	−.14
Combined Measure	.28*	−.30*	−.12
8–9 Year Olds			
Family Concept	.26*	.12	.30*
Agency Concept	.10	.27*	.26*
Combined Measure	.22	.24*	.33*
10–11 Year Olds			
Family Concept	.05	.20	.18
Agency Concept	−.08	−.13	.08
Combined Measure	−.02	.03	.16

*$< .05$
**$< .01$

CPA = Children's psychological adjustment; CAA = Children's Adoption adjustment; PAA = Parent's adoption adjustment

Discussion.   How are we to interpret this complex, and apparently contradictory, pattern of findings? Do the results, in fact, make sense? Although we had not expected the negative relationships obtained for 6–7-year-olds, in retrospect, they are indeed understandable.

As we noted previously, preschool children have little, if any, awareness of the meaning of adoption. In the absence of such knowledge, their attitudes about, and adjustment to, adoption are likely to be highly dependent on the general atmosphere in the family. To the extent that parents provide the child with warmth, love, and acceptance, and are reasonably confident and show low anxiety in disclosing adoption information, the young child is likely to develop a very positive view of him or herself, and of adoption. In turn, parents' perception of the child's adoption adjustment are also likely to be positive. As children enter the elementary school years, however, their understanding of the adoption experience, particularly some of the complications that it entails, increases dramatically (Brodzinsky et al., 1984). Adoption is no longer viewed by the child in the unrealistically positive way found among so many preschoolers. In fact, it is quite common for school-age children to display occasional sadness, and even anger, regarding their relinquishment. We believe these emotions are both normal and age-appropriate, and reflect the beginning of a natural process of grief and bereavement that inevitably accompanies the adoption experience (Brodzinsky, 1984b). Adoptive parents, however, are very often surprised by their children's reactions. Having observed a generally positive outlook on adoption in their children during the preschool years, parents are now prone to mistake the child's newly emerging knowledge, and the expressed concerns that it entails, as reflecting problems in adjustment to adoption. In turn, this is likely to lead to less positive ratings of their children's adoption adjustment—as was found for the 6–7-year-olds.

But what about more general areas of adjustment—areas that are less tied to adoption? It would appear that parents of young school-age children make a distinction between adjustment to adoption per se, and general psychological and academic adjustment. Although greater adoption knowledge was associated with lower ratings of adoption adjustment among our 6–7-year-olds, it was related to higher maternal ratings of adjustment in more general areas of behavior, social competence, and school-related activities in these same children. One likely explanation for the latter finding is that children with advanced adoption knowledge are also likely to be the children who are advanced in others areas of intellectual competence. Parents, and teachers, recognizing the precocity of these children are, therefore, likely to rate them higher in overall adjustment.

A similar explanation holds for the positive relationship found for 8–9-year-olds between adoption knowledge and general psychological adjustment. That is, greater adoption knowledge is probably seen as a reflection of greater overall competence by parents and teachers. In turn, this perception is translated into positive, significant correlations between these variables. However, this does not explain the relationship between children's adoption knowledge and their adjustment to adoption. Whereas for 6–7-year-olds there was a negative relationship between these variables, for 8–9-year-olds, a positive relationship was found. We suggest that the shift in the pattern of relationship between adoption knowledge and perceived adoption adjustment reflects the gradual acceptance, by parents and children alike, of the normality, and in fact, beneficiality, of intellectually exploring all aspects of the adoption experience—even those that give rise to occasional feelings of sadness and anger. This change in attitude is probably due to the increased exposure of parents and children to adoption issues, particularly those related to questions about one's origin and the basis for one's relinquishment. This interpretation is supported by unpublished data from our project (Brodzinsky, 1984c) indicating that 8–9-year-olds show greater curiosity regarding the adoption experience, and have parents who are more involved with them regarding adoption-related issues, than either 6–7- or 10–11-year olds. Thus, as school-age children become more knowledgeable about adoption and have the time and opportunity to explore the many implications that this family status entails, they are likely to become more conformable with themselves, and consequently, be rated by others as better adjusted.

One of the more interesting findings for the 8–9-year-old group was the positive relationship between children's adoption knowledge and parental adoption adjustment. No such relationship was noted for the other two age groups. One possible explanation for this finding is that it is based on the increased parent–child involvement regarding adoption-related issues observed during this age period (Brodzinsky, 1984c). The more involved parents are with their children, and the more children are willing to communicate with their parents about adoption, the more aware parents will be regarding their children's adoption-related thoughts and fantasies. In turn, it is quite likely that parents will use this knowledge to help their children deal with concerns and conflicts about adoption, either by offering support, comfort, or advice, or simply by correcting the child's misperceptions. We hypothesize that such parent–child interaction is likely to facilitate parental confidence by decreasing uncertainty and anxiety regarding their ability to handle the child's concerns and adjustment problems. Increased confidence, in turn, would then be reflected in elevated self-ratings of adjustment by parents.

Finally, our data indicate that children's adoption knowledge was unrelated to their own, or their parents', psychological adjustment at 10–11 years of age. Inspection of Tables 8.1 and 8.2 suggests that this is probably due to a restricted range of scores (i.e., a ceiling effect) for adoption knowledge among these older subjects. An alternative possibility, however, is that psychological adjustment is simply less affected by purely cognitive factors in the preadolescent and adolescent years. By this age, most children are fully aware of what it means to be adopted, although clearly, some of the more abstract and subtle nuances are still to be mastered. Psychological adjustment, therefore, may be less tied to the young adolescent's understanding of adoption per se, than to other, more emotionally based factors, such as the personal meaning that that understanding has for the individual. For example, just what does relinquishment mean to the young adolescent? In what way does it fit into the ever-changing dynamics of his or her personality and self-system? As children enter adolescence, they are much more prone to personalize knowledge—that is, to incorporate it into their developing conception of self. If this is the case, then the role of cognition in adoption adjustment is likely to be complicated in the early adolescent years by important psychodynamic considerations (cf., Sorosky et al., 1975; Stone, 1972).

IMPLICATIONS AND FUTURE DIRECTIONS

The focus of the Rutgers Adoption Project, to date, has been to delineate developmental changes underlying children's comprehension of adoption, and to examine various factors associated with psychological adjustment among adopted elementary-school-age children. In this chapter we have reviewed some of our findings, especially as they relate to children's adoption knowledge. Our results have been clear—children undergo systematic, age-related changes in their conception of adoption that remarkably parallel the type of changes reported by researchers in other areas of social-cognitive development. We have also shown that children's adoption knowledge is unrelated to specific family status, structure, or experience. Finally, our data indicate a significant relationship between children's adoption knowledge and their psychological adjustment in the family; the pattern of the relationship, however, varies as a function of children's age level.

What implications can be drawn from these findings? Specifically, what do they tell us about the development and adjustment of adopted children and their parents? Generally, it appears that young children are more limited in their understanding of adoption than most adoption authorities, mental health professionals, and adoptive parents had realized previously. This lack of awareness has led many adoptive parents, who typically seek advice from these authorities and professionals, to develop unrealistic expectations regarding the likely outcome of their early attempts at disclosing adoption information to children. Furthermore, from our clinical contact with adoptive families, it also appears that many school-age adopted children are actively struggling with issues of separation and loss, and that parents frequently mislabel and misunderstand what their children are experiencing. Rather than representing emotional disturbance, or poor adjustment to adoption, these attempts by school-age children to understand the basis for their relinquishment—which often include overt displays of sadness and anger—actually are normal, age-appropriate, and probably inevitable, components of the adoption experience. Like reactions to parental death and divorce, they represent children's grief and bereavement in response to parental loss. Unlike these other areas, however, most adopted children are struggling with the loss of parents whom they never knew, or for whom they have only vague, and probably distorted, memories. Furthermore, unlike children who have lost parents through death or divorce, adopted children typically have lost all ties to their biological family and heritage. Thus, their loss is even more pervasive, and potentially problematic as these individuals enter adolescence and begin to deal with issues of identity.

Our research and clinical experience with adoptive families has convinced us that many parents have little awareness of the type of developmental changes that children undergo in adjusting to adoption, nor do these parents appear to recognize the normality of their children's grief reactions. In their need to be like other parents, and to have their children be like other children, adoptive parents often ignore the many differences that exist between adoptive family life and nonadoptive family life. In essence, these parents adopt what Kirk (1964) has called a "rejection-of-difference" coping strategy. The problem with this strategy is that it all too often leads to a conspiracy of silence among family members regarding adoption. Such an atmosphere makes it difficult for children to deal constructively with their feelings of being different, out-of-place, and the like. Simply put, it prevents adopted children from coming to grips with what one 9-year-old boy called, "the master question of my life—why was I given up for adoption?".

For adoptive parents to foster positive psychological growth in their children, they must acknowledge the differences that exist between their family and nonadoptive families (Brodzinsky, 1984b; Kirk, 1964); and they must create an atmosphere that allows for open and honest exploration and communication about adoption among all family members. Creation of such an atmosphere is made easier when parents have a well delineated set of guidelines concerning adoption adjustment. Specifically, adoptive parents need to be better informed about the developmental changes underlying children's understanding of, beliefs about, and adjustment to, adoption. Such information will help parents develop more realistic expectations concerning adoption adjustment, and the appropriate level and sequence of information to share with their children. A concomitant effect should be reduction in parents' anxiety regarding their ability to handle children's adjustment problems.

The Rutgers Adoption Project has been underway for 6 years. In that time we have produced a number of potentially important findings regarding children's adjustment to adoption. The question now is where do we go from here?

To begin with, it must be recognized that children's adjustment to adoption is an area receiving insufficient attention in the research community. Although much has been written about adoption, both in professional and lay publications, the bulk of the material is based on casework or clinical observations, not empirical research. Furthermore, much of the empirical research that has been reported, to date, is seriously flawed by methdological shortcomings (cf., Brodzinsky et al., 1984); and it has tended to be atheoretical in nature. It is to state the obvious, therefore, to say that developmental and child clinical investigators must develop well controlled, systematic, and theoretically based programs of research in this area. We believe our efforts represent a constructive beginning in this direction. Furthermore, it is our opinion that a cognitive-developmental framework, such as the one we have adopted, provides researchers and mental health professionals with useful insights into the process of adoption adjustment.

As to our own plans, we believe that it is important to replicate our findings using a longitudinal design. Although age-related changes in children's adoption knowledge were found, it is impossible to determine, given our cross-sectional design, whether the observed patterns represent true intra-individual developmental changes, or simply inter-group age differences (cf. Baltes, Reese, & Nesselroade, 1977). We are particularly interested in delineating the ways in which children's grief reactions manifest themselves across the childhood and adolescent years and the kind of responses these reactions elicit in parents. We are also very interested in examining the belief systems of adoptive parents regarding issues in child development in general, and adoption in particular, and the way in which these beliefs impact on specific parenting behaviors, and ultimately, parent and child adjustment patterns. In conclusion, the issues with which we are presently concerned center on the fundamental question of the role of knowledge and beliefs as determinants of behavior and adjustment. In this regard, we see our work as highly compatible with our co-contributors in this volume.

ACKNOWLEDGMENTS

Research reported in this chapter was supported in part by a grant to the first author from the National Institute of Mental Health (MH 34549).

REFERENCES

Achenbach, T. M. (1978). Child behavior profile, I: Boys aged 6–11. *Journal of Consulting and Clinical Psychology, 46,* 478–488.

Achenbach, T. M., & Edelbrock, C. S. (1979). The child behavior profile: II. Boys aged 12–16 and girls aged 6–11 and 12–16. *Journal of Consulting and Clinical Psychology, 47,* 223–233.

Achenbach, T. M., & Edelbroch, C. S. (1981). Behavioral problems and competencies reported by parents of normal and disturbed children aged four through sixteen. *Monograph of the Society for Research in Child Development, 46,* (No. 1, Serial No. 188).

Baltes, P. B., Reese, H. W., & Nesselroade, J. R. (1977). *Life-span developmental psychology: An introduction to research methods.* Monterey, CA: Brooks/Cole.

Bernstein, A. C., & Cowan, P. A. (1975). Children's concept of how people get babies. *Child Development, 46,* 77–91.

Bohman, M. (1970). *Adopted children and their families: A follow-up study of adopted children, their background environment, and adjustment.* Stockholm, Sweden: Proprius.

Braff, A. M. (1977). Telling children about their adoption: New alternatives for parents. *American Journal of Maternal Child Nursing, 2,* 254–259.

Brodzinsky, D. M. (1983). *Adjustment factors in adoption.* (Rep. No. MH34549). Washington, DC: National Institute of Mental Health.

Brodzinsky, D. M. (1984a). New perspectives on adoption revelation. *Adoption and Fostering, 8,* 27–32.

Brodzinsky, D. M. (1984b) *Children's adjustment to adoption: A psychosocial perspective.* Unpublished manuscript.

Brodzinsky, D. M. (1984c). *Developmental changes in parent–child interaction in adoptive families.* Manuscript in preparation.

Brodzinsky, D. M., Braff, A. M., & Schechter, D. E. (1984) *Adoptive mothers' perception of their children's adoption knowledge and beliefs.* Manuscript in preparation.

Brodzinsky, D. M., Braff, A. M., & Singer, L. M. (1980 January). *Adoption revelation: A cognitive-developmental perspective.* Presented at the conference on Piagetian Theory and the Helping Professions. University of Southern California, Los Angeles.

Brodzinsky, D. M., Schechter, D. E., Braff, A. M., & Singer, L. M. (1984) Psychological and academic adjustment in adopted children. *Journal of Consulting and Clinical Psychology, 52,* 582–590.

Brodzinsky, D. M., Singer, L. M., & Braff. A. M. (1984). Children's understanding of adoption. *Child Development, 55,* 869–878.

Chambers, J. C., & Tavuchis, N. (1976). Kids and kins: Children's understanding of American kin terms. *Journal of Child Language, 3,* 63–80.

Chandler, M. J. (1977). Social cognition: A selective review of current research. In W. Overton & J. Gallagher (Eds.), *Knowledge and development* (Vol. 1, pp. 93–148). New York: Plenum Press.

Damon, W. (1977). *The social world of the child.* San Francisco: Jossey-Bass.

Dana, R. S. (1982). Psychological conceptions of marriage and divorce in children aged five to ten years. *Dissertation Abstracts Interactional, 43,* 272.

Eiduson, B., & Livermore, J. (1953). Complications in therapy with adopted children. *American Journal of Orthopsychiatry, 22,* 795–802.

Fanshel, D. (1972). *Far from the reservation.* Metuchen, NJ: Scarecrow Press.

Feigelman, W., & Silverman, A. R. (1983). *Chosen children: New patterns of adoptive relationships.* New York: Praeger.

Furth, H. G. (1980). *The world of grown-ups: Children's conceptions of society.* New York: Elsevier.

Gilby, R. L., & Pederson, D. R. (1982).The development of the child's concept of the family *Canadian Journal of Behavioral Sciences, 14,* 111–121.

Haviland, S. E., & Clark, E. (1974). 'This man's father is my father's son': A study of the acquisition of English kin terms. *Journal of Child Language, 1,* 23–47.

Horn, J. M. (1983). The Texas Adoption Project: Adopted children and their intellectual resemblance to biological and adoptive parents. *Child Development, 54,* 268–275.

Jordan, V. B. (1980). Conserving kinship concepts: A developmental study in social cognition. *Child Development, 51,* 146–155.

Kadushin, A. (1974). *Child welfare services.* New York: Macmillan.

Kelly, G. A. (1955). *The psychology of personal constructs. I and II.* New York: Norton.

Kelly, G. A. (1963). *A theory of personality.* New York: Norton.

Kenny, T., Baldwin, R., & Mackie, J. B. (1967). Incidence of minimal brain injury in adopted children. *Child Welfare, 46,* 24–29.

Kirk, H. D. (1964). *Shared fate.* New York: Free Press.

Kraus, J. (1978). Family structure as a factor in the adjustment of adopted children. *British Journal of Social Work, 8,* 327–337.

Kurdek, L. A., & Berg, B. (1983). Correlates of children's adjustment to their parents' divorces. In L. A. Kurdek (Ed.), *New directions for child development. Vol. 19: Children and divorce* (pp. 47–60). San Francisco: Jossey-Bass.

Kurdek, L. A., Blisk, D., & Siesky, A. E. (1981). Correlates of children's long term adjustment to their parents' divorce. *Developmental Psychology, 17,* 565–579.

Lifton, B. J. (1979). *Lost and found.* New York: Dial Press.

Losbough, B. (1965). Relationship of E.E.G. neurological and psychological findings in adopted children. *A Medical Journal of E.E.G. Technology, 5,* 1–4.

Mech, E. V. (1973). Adoption: A policy perspective. In B. Caldwell & H. Ricuitti (Eds.), *Review of child development research* (Vol. 3, pp. 467–508). Chicago: University of Chicago Press.

Menlove, F. L. (1965). Aggressive symptoms in emotionally disturbed adopted children. *Child Development, 36,* 519–532.

National Center for Social Statistics. (1976). Social and Rehabilitation Service. *Adoption in 1975 at 4-11.* Washington, DC: U.S. Department of Health, Education, and Welfare.

Nemovicher, J. A. (1960). A comparative study of adopted boys and nonadopted boys in respect to specific personality characteristics. *Dissertation Abstracts International, 20,* 4722.

Offord, D. R., Aponte, J. F., & Cross, L. A. (1969). Presenting symptomatology of adopted children. *Archives of General Psychiatry, 20,* 110–116.

Peller, L. (1961). Comments on adoption and child development. *Bulletin of the Philadelphia Association for Psychoanalysis, 11,* 145–154.

Piaget, J. (1964). *Judgment and reasoning in the child.* Paterson, NJ: Littlefield, Adams. (Originally published, 1928).

Piaget, J. (1970). Piaget's theory. In P. H. Mussen (Ed.), *Carmichael's manual of child psychology* (Vol. 1, pp. 703–732). New York: Wiley.

Plomin, R., & DeFries, J. C. (1983). The Colorado Adoption Project. *Child Development, 54,* 276–289.

Reece, S. A., & Levin B. (1968). Psychiatric disturbances in adopted children: A discriptive study. *Social Work, 1,* 101–111.

Rest, J. R. (1983). Morality. In J. H. Flavell & E. M. Markman (Eds.), *Handbook of child psychology. Vol III: Cognitive development* (pp. 556–629). New York: Wiley.

Sants, H. J. (1964). Genealogical bewilderment in children with substitute parents. *British Journal of Medical Psychology, 37,* 133–141.

Scarr, S., & Weinberg, R. A. (1983). The Minnesota adoption studies: Genetic differences and malleability. *Child Development, 54,* 260–267.

Schechter, M., Carlson, P. V., Simmons, J. Q., & Work, H. H. (1964). Emotional problems in the adoptee. *Archives of General Psychiatry, 10,* 37–46.

Seglow, J., Pringle, M. K., & Wedge, P. (1972). *Growing up adopted.* Windsor, England: National Foundation for Educational Research in England and Wales.

Selman, R. L. (1980). *The growth of interpersonal understanding.* New York: Academic Press.

Shantz, C. U. (1983). Social cognition. In J. H. Flavell & E. M. Markman (Eds.), *Handbook of child psychology. Vol III: Cognitive development* (pp. 495–555). New York: Wiley.

Silver, L. B. (1970). Frequency of adoption in children with the neurological learning disability syndrome. *Journal of Learning Disabilities, 3,* 11–14.

Simon, N. M., & Senturia, A. G. (1966). Adoption and psychiatric illness. *American Journal of Psychiatry, 122,* 858–867.

Sorosky, A. D., Baran, A., & Pannor, R. (1975). Identity conflicts in adoptees. *American Journal of Orthopsychiatry, 45,* 18–27.

Sorosky, A. D., Baran, A., & Pannor, R. (1979). *The adoption triangle: The effects of the sealed record on adoptees, birth parents, and adoptive parents.* Garden City, NY: Anchor Books.

Spivak, G., & Swift, M. (1975). *The Hahnemann Elementary School Behavior Rating Scale manual.* Philadelphia: Hahnemann Medical College and Hospital.

Stone, F. H. (1972). Adoption and identity. *Child Psychiatry and Human Development, 2,* 120–128.

Taichert, L. C., & Harvin, D. D. (1975). Adoption and children with learning and behavior problems. *The Western Journal of Medicine, 122,* 464–470.

Wieder, H. (1977). On being told of adoption. *Psychoanalytic Quarterly, 46,* 1–23.

Yarrow, L. J. (1964). Separation from parents during early childhood. In M. Hoffman & L. Hoffman (Eds.), *Review of child development research* (Vol. 1). New York: Russell Sage Foundation.

Yarrow, L. J., Goodwin, M. S., Manheimer, H., & Milowe, I. (1973). Infancy experiences and cognitive and personality development at ten years. In L. Stone, H. Smith, & L. Murphy (Eds.), *The competent infant* (pp. 1274–1281). New York: Basic Books.

Yarrow, L. J., & Klein, R. P. (1980). Environmental discontinuity associated with transition from foster to adoptive homes. *International Journal of Behavioral Development. 3,* 311–322.

Youniss, J. (1975). Another perspective on social cognition. In A. Pick (Ed.), *Minnesota symposium on child development* (Vol 9, pp. 173–193). Minneapolis: University of Minnesota Press.

Youniss, J. (1981). A revised interpretation of Piaget (1932). In I. Sigel, D. Brodzinsky, & R. Golinkoff (Eds.), *New directions in Piagetian theory and practice* (pp. 191–202). Hillsdale, NJ: Lawrence Erlbaum Associates.

9 Children's Reasoning About Parental Divorce

Lawrence A. Kurdek
Wright State University

In 1982, the number of divorces in the United State declined for the first time since 1962. An estimated 1,170,000 couples divorced in 1982, 3.5% fewer than in 1981 (National Center for Health Statistics, 1985). Although this trend suggests that the divorce rate is levelling off, there is still a sizeable number of children who experience the stress occasioned by family disruption and reorganization. In 1982, 8.2% of children of all races under 18 years of age (5.1 million children) were living with a divorced mother; 5.0% of these children (3.09 million) were living with a separated mother. The percentage (and number) of children living with a divorced or separated father was 1.1% (658,000 children) and 0.4% (255,000 children), respectively (U.S. Bureau of the Census, 1983). Rates for black children are higher than those for white children. Because these data exclude divorced parents who had remarried at the time of the survey, these percentages underestimate the number of children affected by parental divorce. Based on information obtained from a large-scale national probability sample of 11- to 16-year-old children in 1981, Furstenberg, Nord, Peterson, and Zill (1983) estimate that about 39% of all children of all races will experience the marital disruption of their parents by their 15th birthday.

Because family instability has been related to emotional and behavioral pathology (e.g., Furstenberg, Nord, Peterson, & Zill, 1983; Guidubaldi, Perry, Cleminshaw, & McLoughlin, 1983; Hetherington, Cox, & Cox, 1982; Kalter & Rembar, 1981; Links, 1983; Mannheim, 1983; O'Leary & Emery, in press; Rutter, 1979; Wallerstein, 1984), children of divorced parents have been considered to be at psychological risk (Anthony, 1974). However, as recent reviewers of the children and divorce literature point out (Atkeson, Forehand, & Reikard, 1982; Biller, 1981; Blechman, 1982, Clingempeel & Reppucci, 1982; Emery,

233

1982; Emery, Hetherington, & DiLalla, 1984; Furstenberg et al., 1983; Hetherington, Cox & Cox, 1979; Kanoy & Cunningham, 1984; King & Kleemeier, 1983; Kurdek, 1981; Leahey, 1984; Shinn, 1978; White & Mika, 1983), numerous interacting factors mediate positive or negative consequences of parental divorce for children. Although these reviewers comment on methodological and conceptual problems of existing studies, certain trends and patterns are emerging across studies that differ in sample characteristics, measures, and number of assessment points.

One of the purposes of this chapter is to highlight these trends. The conclusions of previous integrators of the children and divorce literature are summarized along with noted methodological and conceptual limitations. It emerges from this summary that children's own views of parental separation have not been widely assessed. A second purpose of this chapter is to argue for the usefulness of a cognitive-developmental approach to the study of the effects of divorce on children. In this context, data from several recent studies are presented in a preliminary attempt to provide normative developmental data on children's own perceptions of various aspects of their parents' divorce. In addition, specific areas of reasoning about divorce are linked to developmental changes in social cognition. Finally, the implications of a cognitive-developmental approach for both clinical assessment and clinical intervention are discussed.

THE EFFECTS OF DIVORCE ON CHILDREN: EMPIRICAL TRENDS AND CRITICISMS

Interest in the effects of divorce on children has evolved from a more general interest in the effects of father absence on children (e.g., Herzog & Sudia, 1973). Because divorce is qualitatively different from other reasons for father absence (e.g., death, employment, or military duty), it has emerged as an area of investigation in its own right. The flurry of research activity in this area is reflected in the appearance of both the *Journal of Divorce* and several critical reviews of studies examining the impact of divorce on children's cognitive, emotional, social, sex role, and personality development (Atkeson et al., 1982; Biller, 1981; Blechman, 1982; Clingempeel & Reppucci, 1982; Emery, 1982; Emery et al., 1984; Hetherington & Camara, 1984; Hetherington et al., 1979; Kanoy & Cunningham, 1984; King & Kleemeier, 1983; Kurdek, 1981; Lamb, 1977; Leahey, 1984; Magrab, 1978; Shinn, 1978; Thompson & Gongla, 1983; White & Mika, 1983). These reviewers agree that despite limitations of extant empirical studies, several themes appear to be reliable.

The methodological limitations of the children and divorce literature are readily apparent:

1. Samples have been small and nonrepresentative, including mainly white, middle-class parents and children who have participated voluntarily.

2. Subjects have not been systematically classified in terms of length of time since parental separation, a time when major psychological changes would be expected to occur.

3. Studies have been retrospective rather than prospective, making it likely that subjects may distort and selectively attend to past details.

4. Studies of children in clinic settings have not been balanced with studies of children in nonclinic settings.

5. Appropriate comparison groups are lacking; e.g., children whose parents are separated or divorced should be compared with children whose parents are together and experiencing either low or high degrees of marital discord.

6. Comparisons between intact and divorced families have not controlled for differences in social economic status, income source, and occupational prestige.

7. Children of differing ages have been aggregated into one group rather than placed in distinct developmental groups.

8. Because mothers have traditionally assumed the role of custodial parent, parent gender has been confounded with custodial status.

9. With a few major exceptions, studies have been cross-sectional rather than longitudinal or longitudinal-sequential, making it difficult to assess both cohort effects and intraindividual age changes.

10. Studies have often included more than one child per family, leading one to question the independence of observations.

11. Measures have been used without documenting their reliability and validity.

In addition to these methodological problems, several conceptual limitations have also been noted:

1. The theoretical grounding of studies has most frequently been crisis theory, with few linkages made to other relevant theoretical perspectives, e.g., cognitive-developmental, social learning, ego control, or psychoanalytic.

2. Parental divorce has not been viewed as a multilevel ecological process whose effect on children is influenced by cultural attitudes toward divorce, social support available to the single-parent family, interparent relations in the postseparation period, parental appraisals of the divorce, and the child's own competencies for dealing with stress.

3. Divorce has not been viewed as a long-term process that results not only in changes in parents' financial and social support resources but also in children's relations with parents, siblings, relatives, and peers.

4. Divorce has not been viewed from a developmental and life-cycle perspective in which adaptive and maladaptive responses are seen as age-dependent and linked to the life transitions of both parents and children.

5. The divorce adjustment process has not been viewed as a reciprocal process involving both parents and children.

Despite the above methodological and conceptual criticisms, several consistent themes have emerged across studies differing widely in methodology:

1. The initial impact of separation/divorce is stressful for both parents and children; however, for most parents and children this stress diminishes appreciably as the family system reorganizes and stabilizes.

2. Children's reactions to parent separation are developmentally related.

3. Children's adjustment to the separation is negatively related to parental discord, especially when children are openly exposed to conflict.

4. Relative to girls, boys in their mothers' custody are more negatively affected by parental separation, particularly in the acquisition of acting-out and aggressive behaviors and poor self-control skills.

5. Children's adjustment is related to the quality of parenting provided by both parents in the postseparation period. For the custodial parent, this involves the use of authoritative discipline and adequate financial resources; for the noncustodial parent, this involves a pattern of regular and reliable visitation.

6. For the majority of children, parental divorce results in a dramatic decrease in the amount of contact with the noncustodial parent.

7. Parental divorce is associated with positive consequences for children, notably the acquisition of developmentally appropriate levels of responsibility and self-sufficiency.

Children and Divorce: A Cognitive-Developmental Perspective

Traditionally, the study of stress in adults has relied on adults' listing significant life events occurring over a specified period of time (e.g., Holmes & Rahe, 1967). More recently, such listings have been improved to allow adults to appraise the positive or negative consequences of significant life events (e.g., Sarason, Johnson, & Siegel, 1978). This method of appraisal is also found in the divorce literature in which the source of almost all of our information about adults' experience of separation and its consequences is the adult him or herself (Bloom, Hodges, & Caldwell, 1983; Hetherington et al., 1982; Kurdek & Blisk, 1983; Wallerstein & Kelly, 1980; Weiss, 1975). When one turns to the child and divorce literature, however, the source of information is shifted from the child to that of a parent, teacher, clinician, or trained observer. The anomalous nature of this situation is highlighted by a frequently cited paper entitled, *Divorce: A Child's Perspective* (Hetherington, 1979) that does not reference studies in which the children themselves have appraised aspects of the divorce experience. From a cognitive-developmental perspective, children who experience parental divorce actively structure and interpret the complex events transpiring before, during, and after the separation within the confines of their stage of cognitive development. Consequently, children's views of divorce-related events need not be congruent with those provided by individuals outside of the child's phenomonological frame of reference (Kurdek, Blisk, & Siesky, 1981; Young, 1983).

Nonetheless, it is understandable why past researchers have not systematically collected information from children. First, children may be seen as innocent victims of parental discord who should be spared the stress, anxiety, and embarrassment that might result from talking about the divorce with a stranger. Secondly, parents may mistakenly assume that the children both are unaware of parental discord and know little about the events surrounding the divorce. Finally, one may question how accurately children can reflect on their own thoughts and feelings. The metacognitive, self-reflective skills of young children in particular may not be well developed (Brown, Bransford, Ferrara, & Campione, 1983).

The reticence of investigators to probe children's perceptions of parental divorce can be balanced by at least two reasons why such a method of study is important. First, from a basic science standpoint, children's reasoning about parental divorce extends social cognitive developmental research into an applied setting (Shantz, 1983). How children make sense of divorce-related experiences may involve a variety of social cognitive skills that include: (a) taking the perspective of both parents; (b) focusing on intention rather than negative consequences, (c) making causal attributions about outcomes that are predominantly negative; (d) empathizing with parents and siblings; and (e) reasoning about parent roles as well as marriage and divorce as social institutions. Given the importance of these types of skills, the study of children's reasoning about parental divorce fits nicely into Selman's (1980) cognitive-developmental model of interpersonal understanding, which describes children's understanding of themselves and social relationships as a series of age-related levels. Consequently, one would predict that children's reasoning about divorce would evidence qualitative, stage-like, developmental shifts. Indeed, Longfellow (1979) has established conceptual correspondences between developmental levels of perspective taking, interpersonal reasoning, and reactions to divorce. As is shown below, empirical studies have provided support for a relation between interpersonal understanding and reasoning about the divorce.

The second reason why children's reasoning about parental divorce is important is that children's appraisal of divorce-related events may affect their adjustment to the divorce. Lazarus and Folkman (1984) view stress as a continuous feedback process involving the person and the environment. Cognitive components are relevant at two points in this process: first in terms of expectations of efficacy that occur prior to the stress, and second in terms of appraisals that follow the stress. It is on this second point that clinicians have focused attention. For example, Wallerstein (1983) has conceptualized children's divorce adjustment process as a series of six coping tasks that are added to the customary tasks of childhood and adolescence. Four of these tasks are cognitively oriented: acknowledging the reality of the marital rupture, resolving anger and self-blame, accepting the permanence of the divorce, and achieving realistic hopes regarding one's own relationships. Other clinicians (Gardner, 1976; Mendell, 1983; Tessman, 1978) have futher observed that children often construct problematic perceptions about both the nature of parental divorce and their causal role in the divorce decision. These perceptions include: thoughts of abandonment by the custodial parent, expectations of peer ridicule and rejection, seeing oneself as having to hold the family together, believing that improved behavior will result in parental reconcilication, blaming one parent exclusively for the divorce, and blaming oneself for the divorce.

These problematic appraisals that children construct about the divorce are reminiscent of descriptions of faulty information processing in adult depressives. Beck, Rush, Shaw, and Emery (1979), for example, postulate that misperceptions of reality cause depression and anxiety (cf. Golin, Sweeney, & Shaeffer, 1981). The type of cognitive errors found in depressives are described in Table 9.1 along with analogous comments of children experiencing parental divorce. If

TABLE 9.1
Cognitive Errors Found in Depressed Adults
and Illustrative Divorce-Related Comments in Children

Cognitive Error	Description of Error	Divorce-Related Comment
Arbitrary Inference	Drawing a conclusion when evidence is lacking or when evidence is actually contrary to the conclusion drawn	"My parents will get back together and see that they have made a big mistake."
Selective Abstraction	Focusing on a detail taken out of context, ignoring more salient features of the situation, and viewing the whole experience on the basis of this fragment	"Mom and Dad always fought, and never should have gotten married in the first place."
Overgeneralization	Drawing a conclusion on the basis of one or more isolated instances	"My mom will leave me all alone just like she left Dad."
Magnification	Exaggerating the meaning or significance of an event	"My friends will never speak to me now that they know that Mom and Dad are getting divorced."
Personalization	Relating external events to oneself in the absence of evidence for making such a connection	"If it weren't for me, Mom and Dad would still be together. The divorce is my fault."
Dichotomous Thinking	Viewing an experience from one of two opposing perspectives	"My Mom rather than my Dad caused all of the trouble in the family."

cognition is causally linked to affective and behavioral disorders, then the study of children's reasoning about parental divorce would provide a foundation for intervention strategies designed to assist children in revising faulty perceptions regarding the divorce. The intervention strategy of most relevance is rational-emotive therapy, a cognitive therapy designed to teach, to modify, or to replace dysfunctional cognitive-emotive links. These goals are accomplished by differentiating between feelings and thoughts, differentiating between rational and irrational beliefs, and disputing irrational concepts and beliefs. Although this technique has been developed and refined with adults, it has recently been applied to children (Bernard & Joyce, 1984; Ellis & Bernard, 1983).

TOWARD A DEVELOPMENTAL, NORMATIVE DESCRIPTION OF CHILDREN'S REASONING ABOUT PARENTAL DIVORCE

Researchers have adopted several strategies for studying children's reasoning about parental divorce. Two of these strategies are nondevelopmental in focus, and two are developmental. In the nondevelopmental strategies, either children of similar ages are interviewed or children of widely varying ages are interviewed. In both instances, responses from all children are analyzed as a single group. The first developmental strategy is quantitatively oriented. Here, children of differing ages are assessed, quantitative adjustment scores are derived, and these scores are correlated with chronological age. The second developmental strategy is qualitatively oriented. Here, children of various ages are grouped into distinct developmental status groups. This approach emphasizes age-related structural changes in reasoning, and blends nicely with cognitive developmental approaches to the study of social cognition (Selman, 1980).

Further Design Considerations

As would be expected from the foregoing discussion of limitations of the general children and divorce literature, studies specifically focusing on children's reasoning about divorce also have methodological problems. Three major problems of concern here are the use of small, nonrepresentative samples; uncontrolled variation in the time since separation; and the use of measures lacking psychometric data.

The studies focusing on children's reasoning about their parents' divorce are described in Table 9.2 along the dimensions of sample characteristics, measure information, and findings. The studies are grouped in terms of the nondevelopmental or the developmental strategies followed. Studies in Group A use single samples of children who vary widely in age. Studies in Group B also use samples of children varying widely in age, but they correlate scores with age. Studies in

TABLE 9.2
Description of Studies Investigating Childrens' Perceptions of Parental Divorce

Author(s)	n	Type of Group	Ages	Gender	SES	Time Since Separation
			Sample			
					A. Studies Using Samples	
Parish (1981)	606	Intact Divorce/Remarried Divorce/Not Remarried	"Grade school"	NR	NR	NR
Rosen (1977)	92	Divorce	9–28 yrs.	45M 47F	white, middle class	6–10 years
Wallerstein & Kelly (1980)	131	Separated/Divorced	3–18 yrs.	63M 68F	white, middle class	at separation, follow up 18 months and 5 years later
					B. Studies Using Samples with Wide Age Variation	
Kurdek, Blisk, & Siesky (1981)	58	Divorce	8–17 yrs.	28M 30F	white, middle class	4 yr. average

	Measure		
Title/Type	*Description*	*Reliability*	*Findings*
with Wide Age Variation			
Personal Attributes Inventory for Children	Check which of 30 positive or negative adjectives describe self, mother, and father	NR	Relative to children of intact homes, children of divorced/remarried or divorced/nonremarried homes reported less congruence between ratings of self and ratings of father
open ended interview	Seven questions asked: (1) Should parents stay together for the sake of the children? (2) What type of access to noncustodial parent do you prefer? (3) How much were you adversely affected by the divorce? (4) Was the divorce satisfactorily explained to you? (5) Has the divorce affected your desire to marry? (6) Did your sibs help you adjust to the divorce? (7) What parent behaviors were most distressing to you?	NR	—79% did not want to stay with parents in conflict —61% desired free access to the noncustodial parent —43% did not feel negatively affected by the divorce; 24% felt they benefitted —45% were satisfied with the explanation of divorce; 38% were dissatisfied —77% felt parental divorce has no influence on own marriage plans —53% felt sibs were of help in adjusting to the divorce; 35% felt sibs made no difference
open ended interview	Questions covered 3 main areas: (1) Feelings about visitation, (2) Approval of divorce decision, and (3) Anger at parents	NR	VISITATION: at time of separation, 20% were content with pattern, 40% were excited about it, and 33% were disappointed; 11% were genuinely reluctant to visit APPROVAL: at time of separation, 25% approved; at 18 month followup, 20% fully approved; at 5 year followup, 28% strongly approved ANGER: at time of separation, 33% were angry at one or both parents; at 18 month followup, 25% were intensely angry at one or both parents
and Correlating Scores with Age			
Open-ended questionnaire	For Understanding the Divorce, 14 questions were asked: (1) What does it mean when 2 people get divorced? (2) Why don't your Mom and Dad live together any more? (3) Do you think your Mom and Dad will ever live together again? (4) Do you think anyone is to blame for your Mom and Dad not being together like they used to be? (5) What are some of the bad things about your Mom and Dad not living together? (6) What are some of the good things about your Mom and Dad not living together? (7) What is your (custodial parent) like? (8)	97% perfect inter-rater agreement; Cronbach's alpha for a quantitative adjustment score = .24	—Understanding the Divorce was significantly positively correlated with age, but Feelings About the Divorce was not —Gender differences on both measures were nonsignificant —Feelings about the divorce were more negative than was Understanding of the divorce —Almost all children did not blame themselves for the divorce —53% defined divorce in psychological terms —the most negative feelings about the divorce referred to news of the divorce, the least negative to the in-

(continued)

TABLE 9.2 (*Continued*)

Author(s)	n	Type of Group	Ages	Gender	SES	Time Since Separation
				Sample		
Kurdek & Berg (1983)	70	Divorce	6–18 yrs.	36M 34F	white, middle class	13.17 months average
						C. Studies Using Samples of One Age
Ambert & Saucier (1983)	4539	Parents Together Parents Separated Parent Widowed	12–19 yrs.	M, F (*n* NR)	NR	NR
Fine, Moreland, & Schwebel (1984)	241	Divorced (100) Intact (141)	Mean Age 19.6 yrs.	44M, 56F 56M, 85F	Middle Class	At Least 8 yrs.
Camara (1979)	NR	Intact Divorce	9–11 yrs.	"equal M and F"	white, middle class	2–3 years

Measure			
Title/Type	Description	Reliability	Findings
	What is your (noncustodial parent) like? (9) Have you told many friends that your Mom and Dad don't live together? (10) Do you think it matters to your friends that your Mom and Dad don't live together? (11) Are there any ways in which you think you're different from your friends? (12) What do you do when your (noncustodial parent) comes to visit? (13) What are some of the big differences between the way things are now between you and your (noncustodial parent) and the way they were when your Mom and Dad lived together? (14) Do you think you'll ever get married?		fluence of the divorce on peer relations —understanding the divorce and feelings about the divorce were not significantly correlated —in a 2 year followup, thoughts and feelings about the divorce showed significant stability; feelings became significantly more positive with regard to loss of noncustodial parent and peer relations
	For Feelings About the Divorce, a 34 item Likert format scale was used which focused on: News of the Divorce, Loss of Noncustodial Parent, Peer Relations, Family Relations, and Emotional Responses	Cronbach's alpha = .75	
Open-ended questionnaire and structured objective inventory	Understanding the Divorce questionnaire described above, and a 60 item structured inventory assessing Peer Ridicule and Avoidance; Paternal, Maternal, and Self Blame; Fear of Abandonment; Hope of Reconciliation	Cronbach's alpha for questionnaire and inventory = .50 and .78, respectively	—scores from two measures significantly positively correlated with age partialled out —age significantly positively correlated with inventory but not with questionnaire scores —significant gender difference on inventory scores with girls giving better adjusted answers than boys
or One Age Group			
Structured Rating	Parents were rated separately on seven bipolar objectives (e.g., warm-cold)	NR	—compared to fathers from intact families or fathers from widowed families, fathers from separated families were seen as least strong, honest, competent, and able to give good advice by girls; boys saw these fathers as least important
Parent-Child Relationship Survey	Assessed subjects' perceptions of the current relationship with either Mother or Father. Factor scores derived for Mother were: Positive Affect, Resentment/Role Confusion, Identification, and Communication. Factor scores derived for Father were: Positive Affect, Father Involvement, Communication, and Anger	Cronbach alphas for subscale scores ranged from .61 to .94	—compared to subjects from intact families, subjects from divorced families rated Mothers as low on Communication and Positive Affect and Fathers as low on Communication, Involvement, and Positive Affect
Open ended interview	Using role play and displays of different family groups, questions focused on concepts of family, par-	NR	—no differences between children from intact and divorced families on (a) What a family is, (b) What

(continued)

TABLE 9.2 (*Continued*)

| Author(s) | n | Type of Group | Sample | | | Time Since Separation |
			Ages	Gender	SES	
Freed (1979)	51	Divorce	"latency aged"	NR	white, middle class	at least 1 year
Ganong, Coleman, & Brown (1981)	321	Divorce (48) Reconstituted (48) Intact (225)	15–17 yrs.	NR	white, middle class	NR
Hammond (1979)	165	Divorce (82) Intact (83)	Grades 3–6	NR	NR	NR
Luepnitz (1979)	24	Divorce	median: 19 years	12M 12F	white	Divorce occurred before respondent was 16
Parish (in press)	1409	Intact Divorce/Remarried Divorce/Not Remarried Death/Remarried	NR	NR	NR	NR

Title/Type	Measure Description	Reliability	Findings
	ent roles, and experience of parental divorce		function a family serves, (c) What criteria are for a family, (d) attributing the status of family to a single parent and child, and (e) assigning conventional roles to parents —relative to children from intact families, children from divorced families (a) tended not to include a father in a family display and (b) were less likely to identify coresidence and nurturance as attributes of mothers and fathers —parent conflict or divorce did not influence children's own plans for marriage or children
Bene-Anthony Family Relations Test Porter Parent Acceptance Scale	Assessed positive, negative, and neutral feelings towards parents	NR	Children felt positively or ambivalently toward the custodial mother, positively toward the noncustodial father; negligible number of negative feelings
Marriage Attitude Scale Divorce Attitude Scale Marriage Role Expectations	Assessed positive or negative feelings about marriage and divorce as well as marriage roles	NR	—no differences among groups on attitudes toward marriage, marriage role expectations, or preferred family size —adolescents from reconstituted families were more positive than adolescents from intact or divorce families on attitudes toward divorce
Attitude Toward Family Questionnaire Hammond Children of Divorce Questionnaire	Assessed ratings of family happiness, time and attention received from parents, possible positive consequences of divorce, control children have over reuniting parents		—for boys only, family rated as less happy and less time and attention received from parents in divorce than intact family —compared to children from intact families, children from divorced families more frequently indicated (a) that divorce could have positive consequences and (b) that children have no control over reuniting parents —for children of divorced families, most negative consequence of divorce was not seeing the noncustodial parent; most positive consequence was cessation of parental conflict
Open-ended interview	Three questions asked: (1) Which aspect of the divorce was the major stressor? (2) How enduring were the effects of divorce? and (3) How did you cope with the distress of the divorce?	NR	50% of the sample reported initial parent conflict to be the major stressor of divorce; 16% saw no aspect of the divorce as being stressful
Personal Attribute Inventory	Check which of 30 positive or negative adjectives describe self, mother, and father	NR	compared to intact and two death groups, both divorce groups rated mothers and fathers as more negative

(continued)

TABLE 9.2 (*Continued*)

Author(s)	n	Type of Group	Ages	Gender	SES	Time Since Separation
				Sample		
Reinhard (1977)	46	Death/Not Remarried Divorce	12–18 yrs.	18M 28F	"white collar"	Less than 3 years
Schlesinger (1982)	40	Divorce	12–18 yrs.	17M–23F	white, middle class	average 5 yrs.
Warshak & Santrock (1983)	44	Divorce	6–11 yrs.	22M 22F	white, middle class	average 3.3 years

Measure			
Title/Type	Description	Reliability	Findings
99 item Likert scale objective measure	Questions of measure focused on the following content areas: News of Divorce, Loss of Noncustodial Parent, Acceptance of Parent, Changes in Family Relations, School Performance, Peer Relations, Behavior Reactions, Emotional Responses, General Reactions, and Post Divorce Conflict	Spearman-Brown = .83 for total scale; .13 to .54 for subscales	More than 50% of the subjects: —were not happy about the divorce decision, but denied anger about it —saw the divorce as a mature, sensible decision —denied unpleasant or rejecting feelings toward mother or father —saw themselves as having acquired self reliance and responsibility as a result of the divorce —did not conceal the divorce from friends —did not see peers as rejecting because of the divorce —denied sacrificing social life for the sake of the custodial parent —most negative feelings focused on News of the Divorce and Changes in Family Relations
Open-ended interview	Question: Did parents discuss the separation decision with you?	NR	55% indicated that parents had not discussed the divorce decision with them
Open-ended interview	Eight questions asked regarding: (1) Perception of family roles, (2) Attitude toward each parent, (3) Desire for contact with parents, (4) Feeling about separation from parent, (5) Understanding of concept of divorce and reason for parental divorce, (6) Prediction of own marital status, (7) Post divorce family change, and (8) Attitude toward parental remarriage	NR	UNDERSTANDING OF DIVORCE —25% had no recall of having been told about the divorce —55% saw parents divorcing because of incompatibility —0% blamed self for the divorce ATTITUDES TOWARD THE DIVORCE —30% saw no advantages from the divorce; of those who did, most mentioned reduction in parent conflict —30% saw no disadvantages to the divorce; of those who did, most mentioned reduced availability of noncustodial parent —84% wished parents would reconcile, but only 5% expected that they actually would POSTDIVORCE CHANGES —79% saw unavailability of noncustodial parent as a major changed occasioned by the divorce —more than 67% were dissatisfied with the frequency of visitation —about 50% saw both parents as being nicer to be with since the divorce —about 50% described the most recent visit with the noncustodial parent positively —21% felt that they have spent less

(continued)

TABLE 9.2 (*Continued*)

Author(s)	n	Type of Group	Sample Ages	Sample Gender	Sample SES	Time Since Separation
Zill (1978)	2161	Never Married (80) Separated (157) Divorced (180) Unhappily Married (48) Happily Married (475) Very Happily Married (1159) Widowed (62)	7–11 yrs.	M F	stratified probability sample	NR

D. Studies Using Samples

| Kurdek & Siesky (1980) and Kurdek & Berg (1983) | 182 | Divorce | 6–8 yrs. 9–12 yrs. 13–18 yrs. | 28M, 27F 31M, 29F 40M, 38F | white, middle class | average 30 mo. |

Measure			
Title/Type	Description	Reliability	Findings
Open ended interview	Questions focused on perceptions and feelings about parents and the type of treatment received at home. Specific focus on perceived neglect and humiliation	NR	time with the custodial parent since the divorce REMARRIAGE —31% disliked the custodial parent's dating —59% expected the custodial parent would remarry —64% expected the noncustodial parent would remarry —62% favored remarriage of custodial parent vs. 37% favoring remarriage of noncustodial parent —relative to children in intact families, children in divorced families reported more frequent boredom, loneliness —relative to children of happily married parents, children of separated/divorced parents felt rejected and belittled —relative to other groups, children of unhappily married parents felt most neglected and humiliated —no differences among groups on feelings about schoolwork —relative to other groups, children living with mother but without father had more negative perceptions of home environment

Divided into Distinct Developmental Groups

open ended interview	(See listing of 14 questions above for Kurdek, Blisk, & Siesky (1981))	97% perfect interrater reliability	YOUNG SCHOOL AGED (6–8 years) —most (35%) defined divorce as physical separation —35% saw their parents as not living together because their marriage had ended; another 35% attributed this to parents' incompatibility —81% did not think their parents would reconcile, but most (48%) could not give a reason —83% did not blame anyone for the divorce, but those who did blamed either the father (29%) or both parents (29%) —Most (40%) could not think of a bad consequence of the divorce; those who did most often mentioned loss of the noncustodial parent (31%) —27% saw one of the good consequence of the divorce as being the end of parent conflict —Most described both mother and fa-

(continued)

TABLE 9.2 (*Continued*)

| Author(s) | n | Type of Group | Sample | | | Time Since Separation |
			Ages	Gender	SES	

	Measure		
Title/Type	Description	Reliability	Findings
			ther in positive terms (62% and 71%, respectively)
			—Most (46%) did not tell their friends about the divorce even though 67% did not think the divorce mattered to their friends
			—Although most (67%) saw themselves as different from their friends, this was not due to the divorce
			—Most (65%) described visits with the noncustodial father as having a good time
			—The biggest contrast most children (31%) saw between the pre- and post-divorce periods was the change in contact with the noncustodial father
			—62% thought they would marry, although most (58%) did not know why
			—Gender differences were negligible
			OLDER SCHOOL AGED (9–12 years)
			—Most (49%) defined divorce in psychological terms and cited incompatibility as the reason their parents did not live together anymore
			—81% did not see the parents as reconciling; most saw this as due to parent incompatibility (45%)
			—60% did not blame anyone for the divorce, but those who did blamed the father (41%)
			—Most (57%) saw the loss of the noncustodial father as one of the bad things about the divorce
			—Most (43%) saw the end of parent fighting as one of the good things about the divorce
			—Most described both mother and father in primarily positive terms (74% and 53%, respectively)
			—Most (70%) told friends about the divorce and did not think the divorce mattered to their friends (68%)
			—Although most (57%) saw themselves as different from their friends, this was not due to the divorce
			—62% defined visits with the noncustodial father as having a good time
			—When asked to compare the pre- and post-divorce periods, most ei-

(continued)

TABLE 9.2 (*Continued*)

Author(s)	n	Type of Group	Ages	Gender	SES	Time Since Separation
			Sample			

Author(s)	n	Type of Group	Ages	Gender	SES	Time Since Separation
McCollum (1980)	66	Intact (33) Divorce (33)	Gr. 1, 4, 8	NR	NR	NR

| | Measure | | |
Title/Type	Description	Reliability	Findings
			ther commented on the decreased availability of the noncustodial father or couldn't think of any differences (each 26%) —64% thought they would marry, although most (47%) didn't know why —Gender differences were negligible ADOLESCENTS (13–18 years) —61% defined divorce in psychological terms —61% saw their parents as not living together because of incompatibility —91% did not think their parents would reconcile, primarily because of their incompatibility (56%) —61% did not blame anyone for the divorce; those who did blamed either the father (41%) or both parents (31%) —74% saw the loss of the noncustodial father as one of the bad things about the divorce —48% saw the end of the parent conflict as one of the good things about the divorce —While most (57%) described mother in positive terms, most described father in either positive (39%) or ambivalent (31%) terms —87% told friends about the divorce and most (83%) did not think the divorce mattered to their friends —While most (61%) saw themselves as different from their friends, this was not due to the divorce —68% described visits with the noncustodial father as having a good time —When asked to compare the pre- and post-divorce periods, most (35%) could not identify an area of difference; those who did, mentioned a personality change in parents, emotional distance from the noncustodial parent, or more contact with the noncustodial parent (each 16%) —75% thought they would marry, primarily because of love (34%)
Open ended interview	Assessed children's concepts of family and divorce	NR	—Gender differences were negligible —No differences in reasoning of children from intact or divorced families —Age differences more striking than family status differences:

(*continued*)

TABLE 9.2 (*Continued*)

Author(s)	n	Type of Group	Sample			Time Since Separation
			Ages	Gender	SES	
Neal (1983)	44	Divorce	3–6 yrs. 5–8 yrs. 9–12 yrs. 11–15 yrs.	NR	white, middle class	at least 18 mo.

Measure			
Title/Type	Description	Reliability	Findings
Open ended interview	Assessed understanding of aspects of divorce from a social cognitive perspective and a family systems perspective	83% mean interrater agreement	a) 4 and 8 graders, more than 1 graders, defined a family in reference to a nonobservable function b) 8 graders, more than 1 and 4 graders, attributed family status to a single parent and child c) 8 graders, more than 1 graders, said a family still existed after divorce d) 1 graders said a divorce could be caused by child misbehavior e) 8 graders were able to see the divorce from the perspective of both parents and could see the divorce as having positive consequences PRESCHOOLERS (3–6 years) —saw divorce as one parent's physically moving away —interpreted divorce in dyadic terms such that the child could cause the behavior of either parent EARLY SCHOOL AGED (5–8 years) —saw divorce in personal and egocentric terms —were aware of parent interpersonal conflict —interpreted the divorce in triadic sequential terms such that the child could cause a particular mother-father interaction —showed awareness of parents' thoughts and feelings —saw link between own behavior and parent subjective state such that child behavior could be linked to distress of parent OLDER SCHOOL AGED (9–12 years) —distinguished between parents' inner feelings and their outside behavior —divorce linked to parents' changing feelings about each other "on the inside"; feelings could change if parents tried hard enough —sensitive to parents' need for distance from each other —experienced conflict in loyalty to both parents PREADOLESCENT AND YOUNG ADOLESCENT (11–15 years) —aware of parents' stable personality characteristics —aware of the congruence of incongruence between parents' personal feelings and their interpersonal expressiveness

(continued)

TABLE 9.2 (*Continued*)

Author(s)	n	Type of Group	Sample Ages	Sample Gender	Sample SES	Time Since Separation
Wallerstein & Kelly (1980) and	131	Separated	3–5 yrs. 6–8 yrs. 9–12 yrs. 13–18 yrs.	19M, 15F 19M, 16F 18M, 26F 7M, 11F	mostly white, middle class	Children seen at time of parent separation
Springer & Wallerstein (1983)	14	Separated	12–14 yrs.	7M, 7F	white, middle class	Children seen at time of parent separation
Young (1983)	223	Separated	7–11 yrs. (112) 12–17 yrs. (111)	NR	NR	Children seen at time of parent separation

	Measure		
Title/Type	Description	Reliability	Findings
			—divorce attributed to parents' personality problems or irreconcilable differences
			—not aware that parents may be unaware of their own contradictions
Open-ended interview	Questions focused on: responses to and experience of parental separation and divorce; continuity and change in parent-child relations; and the network of support available to child outside of the home	NR	PRESCHOOL AND KINDERGARTEN (3–5 years)
			—were frightened, bewildered, and sad
Open-ended interview			—feared being left alone
			—constructed fantasy explanations to account for father's absence
			—blamed self for the separation
			YOUNG SCHOOL AGED (6–8 years)
			—were sad, yearned for father
			—feared being left without family, food, toys
			—felt anger at mother for driving father away
			—worried about having caused the separation
			—experienced divided loyalties
			OLDER SCHOOL AGED (9–12 years)
			—felt rejected, helpless, and lonely despite outer calmness
			—felt intense anger at parent blamed for the separation
			ADOLESCENTS (13–18 years)
			—felt hurried and pressed to grow up
			—worried about sex and marriage
			—felt anger and a sense of loss
			—experienced loyalty conflicts and a changing evaluation of parents; need to divide time between friends and parent
			—sensed an acquisition of maturity and realistic view of money
			—aware of details of divorce-related events; rarely surprised by divorce decision
			—saw sibs as source of conflict and security
Structured questions in objective rating format	Question focused on whom child blamed for the separation	NR	OLDER SCHOOL AGED (7–11 years)
			—82.7% blamed one or both parents:
			a) 37.8% blamed both parents
			b) 35.7% blamed father
			c) 9.2% blamed mother
			d) 17.3% blamed no one
			ADOLESCENTS (12–17 years)
			—77% blamed one or both parents:
			a) 50.7% blamed both parents
			b) 43.8% blamed father
			c) 5.5% blamed mother
			d) 0.0% blamed no one

Note. NR means Not Reported.

Group C use samples of children from one age level only, while those in Group D use samples of children that are divided into several distinct developmental subgroups. Although several studies have examined reasoning about divorce in samples of children whose parents are not divorced (e.g., Dana, 1982; Lowry, 1980; Wynn & Brumberger, 1982), only studies of children who have directly experienced parental divorce are considered here.

As can be seen from the description of samples in Table 9.2, most studies have involved small samples that vary widely in terms of the length of time passed since the parents' separation. That the majority of studies have included only white children and their parents is especially distressing when one considers that in 1982 the percentage of children under 18 years living only with their mother because of separation or divorce is larger for nonwhites than for whites (21% vs. 4% for separation, and 17% vs. 8% for divorce) (U.S. Bureau of the Census, 1983). The bias toward middle-class families is also problematic, because the negative consequences of divorce for children and parents have often been linked to a decrease in financial resources available to the single parent (Colletta, 1979; Weiss, 1984; Zill, 1978). Given these sample constraints, the generalizability of available findings is limited.

Measurement issues in this area revolve around how best to define and to assess children's divorce adjustment. The different methods used and the various sources of information tapped give testimony to the multidimensional nature of this construct (see Table 9.2). Despite this diversity, available measures can be categorized into those assessing children's general behavioral adjustment and those assessing children's divorce-specific adjustment.

Parents, teachers and trained observers, as well as children themselves, have provided information on children's general behavioral adjustment. In addition to open-ended interviews (e.g., Kurdek & Siesky, 1979), parents have completed standardized measures such as the Child Behavior Checklist (Stolberg & Cullen, 1983), the Personal Adjustment and Role Skills Scale (Pett, 1982), the Personality Inventory for Children (Kurdek et al., 1981), and the Louisville Behavior Checklist (Jacobson, 1978). Teachers have completed such scales as the Hahnemann Elementary School Behavior Rating Scale (Guidubaldi et al., 1983), The Health Resources Inventory (Kurdek & Berg, 1983), and the Kohn Social Competence Scale (Hetherington et al., 1982). Trained observers have observed parent–child interaction in a laboratory setting and child free play and social interaction in the school (Hetherington et al., 1982). Finally, children themselves have provided information by completing the Piers-Harris and Coopersmith self-esteem scales (Cooper, Holman, & Braithwaite, 1983; Kelly & Berg, 1978; Kurdek & Blisk, 1983; Lowenstein & Koopman, 1978; Mannheim, 1983).

The major advantage to the use of standardized measures such as those listed is that data are available on the measure's reliability and validity. Further, norms available from these measures allow one to assess how much a child experiencing parental divorce is deviating from peers of similar age and gender not experiencing parental divorce. The main drawback to these measures, however, is that their content does not address issues directly related to the divorce itself. Fortunately, such measures for parents and children are in the process of being developed and refined. As can be seen from the Measures section of Table 9.2, the most frequently used divorce-specific measure is the open-ended interview in which children respond to questions regarding various aspects of the divorce. Although these interviews often provide clinically rich information, they have little demonstrated reliability, do not control for biasing response sets or demand characteristics, and rely on well developed verbal skills. One recent improvement in the use of open-ended questionnaires has been the standardization of the questions asked (Kurdek et al., 1981; Warshak & Santrock, 1983) and the derivation of objective measures of adjustment from open-ended responses that lend themselves more readily to traditional assessments of reliability such as internal consistency and test–retest as well as correlations with other measures (Kurdek & Berg, 1983; Kurdek et al., 1981).

A second type of divorce-specific measure uses an objective response format to assess children's own thoughts and feelings about the divorce (Kurdek & Berg, 1983; Pedro-Carroll, 1983; Reinhard, 1977) or children's perceptions of parent marital conflict (Emery & O'Leary, 1982). The most extensively developed and validated of these measures is Berg's Children's Separation Inventory (Kelly & Berg, 1978; Kurdek & Berg, 1983). The current version of this 48-item, yes-no format scale controls for a yea-saying response bias and provides separate scores for the following scales: Peer Ridicule and Avoidance, Paternal Blame, Maternal Blame, Self Blame, Fear of Abandonment, and Hope of Reunification. Objective scales of children's specific divorce reactions and adjustment have also been developed for parents to complete: the Parent Separation Inventory (Kurdek & Berg, 1983), the Parent Inventory (Stolberg & Cullen, 1983), and sections of the Boulder Divorce Study Interview (Bloom, Hodges, & Caldwell, 1983; Hodges & Bloom, 1984).

As can be seen from Table 9.2, the reliability data available on objective measures of children's divorce adjustment are greater than those available for the open-ended interviews but still are not extensive. Few studies have examined the convergent validity of such measures, but the data available indicate some overlap among differing measures (Kurdek & Berg, 1983) as well as a moderately positive relation between children's divorce-specific adjustment and their more global personal adjustment (Kurdek & Berg, 1983; Kurdek et al., 1981). However, one drawback to these objective measures is the lack of normative developmental data. Consequently, although these measures make it easier to assess children's divorce-related thoughts and feelings, they provide no framework for judging a particular child's responses to be developmentally appropriate or clinically significant.

The final type of measure tapping children's divorce-related perceptions is projective in nature. For example, Warshak and Santrock's (1983) Projective

Story task involves questioning children about events in pictures of divorce-related scenarios. Responses are scored to obtain scores regarding attribution of blame, reconciliation beliefs and wishes, attitudes toward custody arrangements, and attitudes toward parental remarriage. Even though no reliability data are available for tasks such as this, their development is encouraging given findings that children are more likely to attribute socially undesirable or conflictual affect to ambiguous story characters that they ordinarily would censure with regard to themselves (Brody & Carter, 1982). Such measures would also be helpful in dealing with children who have difficulty directly talking about the divorce.

Given the problems with regard to sampling and measurement, it is difficult to draw firm conclusions about how children of differing developmental levels perceive aspects of parental divorce. The lack of systematically analyzed longitudinal data on children's reasoning about parental divorce further restricts our knowledge of how such reasoning changes over the course of the post separation period. Nonetheless, the data available do show some recurring themes and trends. What follows is a cautious attempt to piece together a picture of how children of differing ages reason about parental divorce. After this section, focus shifts to a consideration of what particular areas of reasoning show developmental differences and ties to social cognition. Because our most extensive knowledge of how children of various ages react to and reason about parental divorce comes from Wallerstein and Kelly (1980), their breakdown of children into four developmental groups preschool [(3–5 years), younger school-age (6–8 years), older school-age (9–12 years), and adolescents (13–19 years)] will be adopted. Age norms, of course, are approximate and not absolute. The results of studies using samples of either one age or one age group (Group C studies in Table 9.2), or several distinct developmental groups (Group D), are integrated with the Wallerstein and Kelly (1980) findings. Because children younger than preschool age do not have the cognitive and verbal skills required for self-report measures of interviews, the present "child's eye" view of divorce does not include studies directly assessing children of this developmental group. Nonetheless, several recent studies provide indirect information on how infants and toddlers might be affected by parental conflict and divorce.

Children's Views of Parental Divorce: Infants and Toddlers (3 months to 2 years). The results of a handful of recent studies indicate that even infants and toddlers react negatively to parental stress and interparent conflict. Three-month-olds have been found to respond negatively to simulated acts of maternal depression (Cohn & Tronick, 1983), while 1-to-2½-year-olds have reacted to naturally occurring and simulated instances of interparent conflict with distress and attempts at active intervention (Cummings, Zahn-Waxler, & Radke-Yarrow, 1981; Cummings, Iannotti, & Zahn-Waxler, 1985). The most frequently replicated finding in this area involves attachment. Infants younger than 2 years have been found to develop anxious-resistant and anxious-avoidant attachments to single mothers, especially when these mothers are stressed, report low marital quality, and/or have limited access to social support networks (Crnic, Greenberg, Ragozin, Robinson, & Basham, 1983; Egeland & Farber, 1984; Goldberg & Easterbrooks, 1984; Pastor, Vaughn, Dodds, & Egeland, 1981; Vaughn, Gove, & Egeland, 1980).

Children's Views of Parental Divorce: Preschoolers (3 to 5 years). The most relevant studies here are those by Neal (1983) and Wallerstein and Kelly (1980) (see Table 9.2). Taken together, these studies indicate that the cognitive and social-cognitive capabilities associated with preoperational thought color preschoolers' understanding of parental divorce. Under conditions that do not greatly simplify task requirements, preschoolers: (a) usually center on perceptually salient stimulus properties; (b) often fail to detect abstract, invariant relations among objects; (c) are unable to coordinate information about states and transformations; (d) confuse their own and others' subjectivity; (e) conceptualize relationships in terms of concrete, physical aspects; (f) focus on single subjective states; and (g) have difficulty differentiating between inner motives and outward actions or appearances (Gelman & Baillargeon, 1983; Selman, 1980; Shantz, 1983).

Given this type of information-filtering system, preschoolers' reasoning about parental divorce has several distinctive features. These children are more likely: (a) to focus on one parent's physically moving away rather than on interparent incompatibility; (b) to view themselves as having caused the divorce; (c) to have difficulty coordinating parents' positive and negative feelings about each other; (d) to be confused by the noncustodial parent's dovetailing assurances of love with concrete plans to leave the home; and (e) to see the parents' separation as temporary. Although this type of reasoning is logical from the child's standpoint, and even appropriate given his or her framework for interpreting reality, it is likely to leave the child frightened, bewildered, and sad. Unfortunately, a recent study suggests that preschoolers' home environments may not compensate for these thoughts and feelings and may even exacerbate them, especially if the custodial parent is working. MacKinnon, Brody, and Stoneman (1982) report that the home environments of 3-to-6-year-olds whose divorced mothers work are less cognitively and socially stimulating than those of similarly aged children whose married mothers do or do not work. On the other hand, Weinraub and Wolf (1983) indicate that positive mother–child interactions between single-parent mothers and preschoolers are facilitated if mothers receive parenting support and are satisfied with these supports.

Children's Views of Parental Divorce: Younger School-Age Children (6–8 years). In comparison to preschoolers, children of school-entering age have a basic logical competence that includes inferential reasoning, propositional reasoning, and some notion of possibility and necessity. On the other hand, these children have limited skills related to deductive reasoning and assessing statements against evidence (Braine & Rumain, 1983). Children in this age group also show impressive changes in their social reasoning. Unlike younger children, they acknowledge that different subjective feelings can exist simultaneously as long as they are not directed to the same object. Persons are viewed in terms of concrete, specific feelings and actions. Of special note here is that these children begin to recognize the psychological as well as the physical effects of conflict, although conflict and its resolution are seen as unilateral rather than reciprocal (Selman, 1980; Shantz, 1983).

Against this backdrop of changes in both logical and social reasoning, findings of Kurdek and Siesky (1980), McCollum (1981), Neal (1983), Wallerstein and Kelly (1980), and Warshak and Santrock (1983) provide a number of consistent themes (see Table 9.2). Although children in this age range still interpret divorce personally, egocentrically, and in terms of physical separation, they are beginning to be aware of parent conflict and parent incompatibility as reasons for the divorce. Although these children are unlikely to blame themselves for the divorce, they may worry that their behavior added to interparent distress. Shared blame does not seem to be well understood, as children are likely to blame one or the other parent. Although these children wish their parents would reconcile, they do not believe such a reconciliation will actually occur. These children see reduced conflict as a beneficial consequence of divorce, and regard the reduced availability of the noncustodial parent as a negative consequence. Visits with the noncustodial parent are described very positively, although they are not seen as occurring frequently enough. Many of these children do not willingly discuss the divorce with their friends.

Children's Views of Parental Divorce: Older School-Age Children (9–12 years). Relative to the other developmental groups, this age group's reasoning about parental divorce has been frequently studied (Camara, 1979; Freed, 1979; Hammond, 1979; Kurdek & Siesky, 1980; McCollum, 1981; Neal, 1983; Wallerstein & Kelly, 1980; Warshak & Santrock, 1983; Zill, 1978). The findings of these studies (see Table 9.2) indicate that children at this developmental level define divorce in psychological terms, and frequently cite parent incompatibility or changes "on the inside" as a reason for the divorce. They see the single parent and child as a legitimate family structure. They view the divorce from the perspective of each parent, and can recognize the parents' need to have distance from each other. Although they wish parents would reconcile, they do not see this as likely. They rarely blame themselves for the divorce, but may feel strongly ambivalent toward one or both parents. They may feel angry because of both loyalty conflicts and negative perceptions of the home environment. Similar to younger school-age children, these children view the cessation of interparent conflict as a positive consequence of the divorce, although they view the unavailability of the noncustodial parent as a negative consequence. Visits with the noncustodial parent are evaluated positively, but could occur more frequently. Unlike younger school-age children, these children usually tell friends about the divorce. Finally, these children do not see their parents' divorce as impacting on their own plans for marriage and even expect both parents to remarry eventually.

This type of reasoning meshes nicely with the logical and social reasoning skills of children at this developmental level. Compared to the logical reasoning of younger children, children's reasoning at this level is more organized, systematic, consistent, and self-regulated, although not yet organized in terms of hierarchically embedded systems of relations (Braine & Rumain, 1983; Brown et al., 1983). The qualitative advance in the nature of these children's social-cognitive skills is also of note. These children recognize that one can have conflicting feelings toward the same object, distinguish between inner motives and outer actions, view relationships as reciprocal rather than unilateral, recognize that one can "fake" feelings and put up a front, and understand that partners in a relationship share in both the generation and the resolution of conflict (Selman, 1980; Shantz, 1983).

Children's View of Parental Divorce: Adolescents (13–19 years). Adolescents capable of formal operational thought are able to reason hypothetico-deductively, can systematically derive all combinations of a set of elements, can vary one factor at a time in an attempt to isolate causal factors in a set of relations, and can monitor and regulate their own problem-solving processes (Braine & Rumain, 1983). This abstract, systematic character of adolescent thought is mirrored in the social cognitive skills of children at this developmental level. These skills include conceptualizing persons in terms of abstract traits, acknowledging the force of situational constraints and unconscious processes, engaging in self-reflective as well as recursive thought, attributing interpersonal conflict to personality clashes, and recognizing that conflict may strengthen a relationship (Selman, 1980; Shantz, 1983).

The complexity and sophistication of adolescent thought are clearly found in adolescents' reasoning about parental divorce and parent relationships (Ambert & Saucier, 1983; Fine, Moreland, & Schwebel, 1983; Ganong, Coleman, & Brown, 1981; Kurdek & Siesky, 1980; Luepnitz, 1979; Neal, 1983; Reinhard, 1977; Springer & Wallerstein, 1983; Wallerstein & Kelly, 1980) (see Table 9.2). Although adolescents do perceive parental divorce as stressful and recall hearing the divorce decision with dismay, they interpret divorce in terms of incompatability and regard the divorce decision as mature and sensible. They see irreconcilable differences between parents as precluding a reconciliation, and claim that the divorce has instigated positive personality changes in both parents. They know that parents often attempt to hide their "true" feelings. Self-blame for the divorce is extremely rare, and both parents are likely to be considered in an attempt to localize the blame for the divorce. Evaluations of the noncustodial father, in particular, may be negative. Anger is often expressed as a result of the decreased availability of the noncustodial parent, and the end of parent bickering is seen as a positive consequence of the divorce. Almost all adolescents told friends about the divorce, and some experienced conflict in deciding how to allot time between parents and friends. Visits with the noncustodial parent are generally evaluated positively. Adolescents regard the divorce as stimulating their own increased self-reliance and responsibility, although some do see themselves as being pressed to grow up. Generally, parental divorce has no impact on adolescents' own marital aspirations.

DEVELOPMENTAL DIFFERENCES IN AND SOCIAL-COGNITIVE CORRELATES OF CHILDREN'S REASONING ABOUT PARENTAL DIVORCE

Developmental Differences

In the previous section, descriptions have been provided of how children from differing developmental levels reason about aspects of parental divorce. In this type of normative approach, developmental level is of central concern. In this section, however, our focus shifts to particular areas of reasoning about parental divorce and how children of differing developmental levels reason about the same content area. In the next section, empirical evidence of a link between social cognition and reasoning about parental divorce is presented.

Two strategies have been followed in assessing developmental differences in children's reasoning about parental divorce. Neither has been used extensively. In the first strategy, children's responses to open-ended questions are content analyzed, and the resulting response categories are crosstabulated with categories of chronological age. The two studies providing the most systematic assessment of developmental differences by means of this strategy are Kurdek and Siesky (1980) and Kurdek and Berg (1983). The design of both studies was cross-sectional. Because children in each study were given the same open-ended questions, they are here combined into one sample in an attempt to provide a more reliable picture of differences in responses provided by children from three developmental groups considered before: younger school-age (6–8 years), older school-age (9–12 years), and adolescence (13–18 years). Age differences were assessed by constructing contingency tables whose two dimensions were developmental level (the three age groups listed previously) and response categories to a question. The open-ended questions, response categories, and illustrative responses are presented in Table 9.3. The trends summarized here are based on interpretations of significant ($p < .05$) X^2 values.

The content covered by each question and the percentage of children from each developmental group who provided specific responses to that question are summarized in Table 9.4. The most striking aspect of this table is the per-

TABLE 9.3
Items, Response Categories, and Illustrative Responses
for the Open-Ended Interview

1. What does it mean when two people get divorced?
   a) Marriage Dissolution ("They end their marriage.")
   b) Physical Separation ("They move away from each other.")
   c) Psychological Distance ("They grow apart from each other and lose their love.")
   d) Child-Oriented ("I get mad.")
2. Why don't your Mom and Dad live together anymore?
   a) Incompatibility ("They didn't get along.")
   b) Marriage Dissolution ("They aren't married anymore and got divorced.")
   c) Loss of Love ("They don't love each other anymore.")
   d) Affair ("Dad fell in love with another lady.")
3. Do you think your Mom and Dad will ever live together again? Why or why not?
   a) Incompatibility ("No, because they just don't get along.")
   b) Remarriage ("No, because Dad got married again.")
   c) Parent Report ("No, because Mom says so.")
   d) Child-Oriented ("Yes, because I want them to.")
4. Do you think anyone is to blame for your Mom and Dad not being together like they used to be?
   Who?
   a) Mom
   b) Dad
   c) Both Mom and Dad
   d) "Other Man/Woman"
   e) Child
5. What are some of the bad things about your Mom and Dad not living together?
   a) Loss of Contact with Noncustodial Father ("I don't get to see Dad too much.")
   b) None ("There are no bad things about it.")
   c) Adverse Child Feelings ("I get sad.")
   d) Friends' Reactions ("My friends feel sorry for me and pity me.")
6. What are some of the good things about your Mom and Dad not living together?
   a) No Parent Conflict ("Mom and Dad don't fight with each other anymore.")
   b) None ("There are no good things.")
   c) Improved Relations with Custodial Mother ("I'm much closer to Mom now.")
   d) Child-Related ("I get away with a lot more now.")
7. What is your Mom like? How would you describe her?
   a) Positive ("She's fun and nice and loves me.")
   b) Negative ("She's pretty mean and kicked Dad out of the house.")
   c) Positive and Negative ("Sometimes she's nice, but sometimes she's crabby.")
   d) Neutral ("She's tall and thin.")
8. What is your Dad like? How would you describe him?
   a) Positive ("He's nice and takes me to neat places.")
   b) Negative ("He's always too busy to have any time for me.")
   c) Positive and Negative ("Most of the time he's nice, but sometimes he can get real strict and
      demanding.")
   d) Neutral ("He's kinda old and has a mustache.")
9. Have you told many friends that your Mom and Dad don't live together?
   a) Yes

(*continued*)

TABLE 9.3 (Continued)

b) No

c) Some

10. Do you think it matters to your friends that your Mom and Dad no longer live together?

    a) Yes

    b) No

    c) Some

11. Are there any ways in which you think you're different from your friends?

    a) Divorce-Related ("Yes, because they live with their Mom and Dad and I live with just my Mom.")

    b) Not Divorce-Related ("Yes, we have different color of hair.")

12. What do you do when your Dad comes to visit?

    a) Affection ("I hug and kiss him a lot.")

    b) Talk ("We just sit around and talk about stuff.")

    c) Avoidance ("I make myself scarce.")

    d) Fun ("We go out and have a good time.")

13. What are some of the big differences between the way things are now between you and your Dad and the way they were when your Mom and Dad lived together?

    a) Infrequent Contact with Father ("Now I hardly get to see Dad.")

    b) More Contact with Dad ("I get to see Dad by myself more.")

    c) Personality Changes ("Dad's much nicer now and less strict.")

    d) Emotional Distance ("I feel less close to Dad now.")

    e) Living Arrangements ("Dad lives in a different house now.")

14. Do you think you'll ever get married?

    a) Attachment ("Yes, because I'll fall in love and want to be with someone.")

    b) Raise Family ("Yes, because I want to have lots of children.")

    c) Irrelevance of Parents' Divorce ("Yes, just because it didn't work for them doesn't mean it won't work for me.")

    d) Fear of Divorce ("No, it wouldn't work out and we'd get divorced.")

---

vasiveness of developmental differences. Seventeen responses were derived from the 14 questions (questions 3, 11, and 14 in Table 9.3 were coded for both yes/no answers and justification), and significant relations with developmental status were found for 13 of them.

As suggested by the discussion of normative responses at these developmental levels presented earlier, the obtained significant developmental trends are consonant with those reported in the social cognition literature (Selman, 1980; Shantz, 1983). Compared with younger children, older children reasoned about parental divorce in terms that were inferential, abstract, and psychological (e.g., incompatibility, emotional distance); were aware of interparent conflict and discord; provided differentiated descriptions of both parents; separated the divorced status of their parents from their own peer group status; and could provide both good and bad consequences of the divorce.

As impressive as these developmental differences are, the responses for which developmental status effects were nonsignificant are also of note. Children at all three developmental groups did not think parents would reconcile, blamed the noncustodial father more than either the custodial mother or both parents, de-

TABLE 9.4
Summary of Significant Developmental Effects
for Open-Ended Interview Items
for Combined Kurdek and Siesky (1980)
and Kurdek and Berg (1983) Samples

Questionnaire Item (from Table 3)	Developmental Pattern and Percentage of Children from Three Developmental Groups (6–8 years (n = 55), 9–12 years (n = 60), and 13–18 years (n = 78)) Giving a Particular Response
1. Definition of Divorce	—Decrease in Physical Separation (35%, 30%, 16%) —Increase in Psychological Distance (27%, 49%, 61%)
2. Why Parents Don't Live Together	—Increase in Incompatibility (34%, 49%, 61%)
3. Why Parents Won't Reconcile	—Increase in Incompatibility (26%, 45%, 55%)
4. Whether or Not Anyone Is to Blame for the Divorce	—Increase in "Yes" (13%, 32%, 38%)
5. Bad Things About the Divorce	—Increase in Loss of Contact with Father (31%, 57%, 74%)
6. Good Things About the Divorce	—Increase in No Parental Conflict (27%, 43%, 48%) —Decrease in Child-Related responses (25%, 17%, 5%)
7. Description of Custodial Mother	—Increase in Negative descriptions (0%, 2%, 12%) —Decrease in Neutral descriptions (21%, 2%, 0%) —Increase in Combined Positive and Negative descriptions (15%, 22%, 30%)
8. Description of Noncustodial Father	—Increase in Negative descriptions (4%, 19%, 22%) —Decrease in Neutral descriptions (15%, 2%, 4%) —Increase in Combined Positive and Negative descriptions (4%, 19%, 31%)
9. Whether or Not Friends Were Told of the Divorce	—Increase in "Yes" (37%, 70%, 87%)
10. Whether or Not Divorce Matters to Friends	—Increase in "No" (67%, 67%, 83%)
11. Why Self Is Seen as Different from Friends	—Increase in Divorce-Related Reasons (15%, 23%, 31%)
13. Differences Between Pre- and Post-Separation Periods	—Decrease in Infrequent Contact with Father (31%, 26%, 13%) —Increase in Emotional Distance (1%, 9%, 16%) —Decrease in Living Arrangements (25%, 5%, 5%)
14. Why Self Would Marry	—Increase in Attachment (19%, 15%, 34%) —Increase in Irrelevance of Parents' Divorce (0%, 2%, 12%)

scribed visits with the noncustodial father as having a good time, and thought they would eventually marry. There was no evidence that these children blamed themselves for the divorce, perceived themselves as being socially stigmatized, or feared marriage. Unfortunately, we saw these children about 4 years after the parental separation, making it possible that the nonproblematic nature of these responses could be the result of children's already having adapted to a re-organized family structure.

The second strategy for assessing developmental trends in children's reasoning about parental divorce is to correlate children's chronological age with quantitative scores derived from open-ended questions (e.g., Kurdek et al., 1981) or objective measures (e.g., Kurdek & Berg, 1983). When higher reasoning scores reflect the abstract, psychological, differentiated trends listed earlier, such reasoning is positively correlated with chronological age (Kurdek & Berg, 1983; Kurdek et al., 1981).

Social Cognitive Correlates

One theme of this chapter is that children's reasoning about parental divorce occurs in a larger context of social cognitive development. Specifically, such reasoning involves self-awareness, attributions of intentional behavior, conceptions of behavior in context, descriptions of others and oneself, inferences about others' psychological states and processes, inferences about causes of behavior, and the function and resolution of interpersonal conflict. Direct evidence of the relation between social cognition and divorce reasoning come from studies by Dana (1982), Kurdek and Berg (1983), and Kurdek et al. (1981).

Although the sample involved 45 5-to-10-year-old children whose parents were living together, Dana (1982) assessed children's reasoning about friendship along with their reasoning about marriage and divorce. He found a significant relation between age and reasoning about marriage and divorce ($r = .92$) and between reasoning about friendship and reasoning about marriage and divorce ($r = .93$). Kurdek et al. (1981) assessed the relation between a composite measure of interpersonal understanding (including reasoning about subjectivity, self-awareness and personality, and the beginning, maintenance and termination of friendship) and a composite measure of divorce understanding (including defining divorce in terms of psychological dimensions, attributing the parents' not living together to incompatibility, recognizing that the parents will not reconcile, not blaming oneself for the divorce, describing both parents in neutral or positive terms, telling friends about the divorce, and recognizing that the divorce does not matter to friends). For 58 children (mean age = 13.09 years) whose parents were divorced, scores from the two measures were significantly related ($r = .41$). Kurdek and Berg (1983), with 70 children whose mean age was 9.92, replicated this finding. The significant correlation between the interpersonal understanding and divorce understanding scores was .42. In addition, interpersonal understanding was significantly related ($r = .46$) to a second divorce-related measure that assessed the dimensions of peer ridicule and avoidance, fear of abandonment, hope of reunification, paternal, maternal and self-blame. For neither sample was the relationship changed much when age was partialled out. Thus, although data are not extensive, there is evidence of a moderate relation between how children reason about aspects of their social world and how they reason about parental divorce.

IMPLICATIONS AND APPLICATIONS

Our current knowledge about children's reasoning about parental divorce has implications for assessments of divorce adjustment and the nature of intervention strategies designed to offset the children's confusion and stress regarding parental divorce.

Assessments of Divorce Adjustment

Findings of a positive relation between chronological age and reasoning about parental divorce might lead one to conclude that older children are better adjusted to divorce than younger children. Based on this information alone, such a conclusion is unwarranted. Normal thoughts, feelings, and behavior—like abnormal thoughts, feelings, and behavior—must be anchored in a developmental context (Achenbach, 1982). It has been noted several times throughout this chapter that children's reasoning about parental divorce is linked to the development of logical and social reasoning. Thus, level of cognitive development influences the extent to which a child's reasoning about parental divorce is nonegocentric; focused on parents' thoughts, feelings and intentions; and grounded in an appreciation for the complex dynamics of interpersonal relations. A judgment of adjustment, then, must be made with the competencies and limitations of differing developmental levels in mind. Although reliable changes in reasoning about divorce do seem to occur with advancing age, evaluations of the normality of a particular child's reasoning need to be made within the context of that child's developmental level (Sroufe & Rutter, 1984).

This developmental focus points the way to much-needed research. Foremost is the development of measures that have norms available for differing developmental levels. Most work with a developmental focus has considered preschoolers, early school-age children, later school-age children, and adolescents as distinct developmental groups. Given the developmental differences that have been found, these divisions serve as a good starting point for further work in this area. Also needed are normed measures that vary in assessment method or source of information. There is persuasive evidence that single measurements are not as stable or representative as multiple measurements (Rushton, Brainerd, & Pressley, 1983). Thus, assessing children's reasoning about parental divorce should only be part of a more comprehensive assessment effort that utilizes parents, teachers, as well as the children themselves as sources of information. Such assessments will be most valuable when they are developmentally anchored.

The Design of Intervention Strategies

Interventions designed for children of divorced parents have had a wide range of focus. Most traditional dynamic therapies are extensions of family therapy (Gardner, 1976; Hajal & Rosenberg, 1978; Rosenthal, 1979) in which the therapist and custodial parent work together to help the child deal with confused thoughts as well as sad, angry, and scared feelings through talking and play. More recently developed are interventions designed for children alone. These programs are largely preventive in focus and reach children either at school (Cantor, 1977; Kalter, Pickar, & Lesowitz, 1984; Stolberg & Cullen, 1983; Stolberg & Garrison, 1985), at court (Benedek & Benedek, 1979), or in the community (Guerney & Jordon, 1979). Although these child-oriented programs differ in technique, they have as major goals helping children develop realistic appraisals of their own situation, helping children acquire knowledge and skills necessary for problem solving and dealing with anger, anxiety and sadness, and helping children feel good about themselves.

The data presented in this chapter may be helpful in meeting the goal of realistic appraisal (cf. Wallerstein, 1983). Children's reasoning about parental divorce has been significantly related to parent and teacher appraisals of general behavioral adjustment as well as to parent appraisals of divorce-specific adjustment (Kurdek & Berg, 1983; Kurdek, et al., 1981). These relations are important given that recently developed cognitive therapies for children attempt to modify maladaptive beliefs which maintain unwanted feelings and behavior (cf. Kurdek, in press). Through changing children's appraisal of upsetting events, changing children's inferences when distortions of reality precede negative appraisals, and instructing children in the use of verbal self-instruction techniques, therapists have guided children toward nonupsetting emotional responses and more adaptive behavior (Bernard & Joyce, 1984; DiGiuseppe & Bernard, 1983). Such cognitive approaches have also been blended with behavioral approaches. Although these cognitive-behavioral approaches do not seem to be more effective than either cognitive or behavioral strategies alone with adults (Miller & Berman, 1983), limited evidence suggests that cognitive components do potentiate the effects of behavioral approaches with children in the area of self-control (Kendall & Braswell, 1982).

Children's reasoning about their parents' divorce might be incorporated into cognitively-oriented divorce intervention strategies for children which have focused on the identification and cause of feelings, effective problem-solving and communication, and anger resolution skills (e.g., Stolberg & Cullen, 1983).

There is evidence in the moral reasoning literature that children exposed to peers' reasoning that is one or two stages above their own level of reasoning benefit from such exposure (Walker, 1983). Generalizing this approach, children of differing developmental levels could be brought together to discuss reasons for parental divorce, relations with both parents, parent reconciliation, and self blame. While adults would monitor the discussion process, keeping in mind the developmental trends highlighted earlier, children themselves would correct maladaptive beliefs regarding the divorce and catalyze a more accurate and adaptive interpretation of divorce-related events. Such interactions, of course, require cognitive and verbal abilities beyond that of preschool children (cf. DiGiuseppe & Bernard, 1983). The specific factors maximizing benefits from such an approach remain to be identified.

ACKNOWLEDGMENTS

I would like to extend my appreciation to Gene Siesky and Bert Berg for their help in applying my interest in social cognitive development to the problems of children experiencing divorce. I would also like to thank Pat Schmitt, Gene Siesky, Richard Ashmore, and David Brodzinsky for their critical reading of the paper, and Kay Paske and Cyndi Dawson for typing the manuscript.

REFERENCES

Achenbach, T. M. (1982). *Developmental psychopathology.* New York: Wiley.
Ambert, A., & Saucier, J. (1983). Adolescents' perception of their parents and parents' marital status. *Journal of Social Psychology, 120,* 101–110.
Anthony, E. J. (1974). Children at risk from divorce: A review. In E. J. Anthony & C. Koupernik (Eds.), *The child in his family* (pp. 461–477). New York: Wiley.
Atkeson, B. M., Forehand, R. L., & Rickard, K. M. (1982). The effects of divorce on children. In B. Lahey (Ed.), *Advances in clinical child psychology* (pp. 255–281). New York: Academic Press.
Beck, A. T. (1976). *Cognitive therapy and the emotional disorders.* New York: International Universities Press.
Beck, A. T., Rush, A. J., Shaw, B. F., & Emergy, G. (1979). *Cognitive therapy of depression.* New York: Guilford Press.
Benedek, R. S., & Benedek, E. P. (1979). Children of divorce: Can we meet their needs? *Journal of Social Issues, 35,* 155–169.
Bernard, M. E., & Joyce, M. R. (1984). *Rational-emotive therapy with children and adolescents.* New York: Wiley.
Biller, H. B. (1981), Father absence, divorce, and personality development. In M. E. Lamb (Ed.), *The role of the father in child development* (pp. 481–552). New York: Wiley.
Blechman, E. A. (1982). Are children with one parent at psychological risk? A methodological review. *Journal of Marriage and the Family, 44,* 179–195.
Bloom, B. L., Hodges, W. F., & Caldwell, R. A. (1983). Marital separation: The first eight

months. In E. J. Callahan & K. A. McCluskey (Eds.), *Lifespan developmental psychology: Nonnormative life events* (pp. 217–239). New York: Academic Press.

Braine, M. D. S., & Rumain, B. (1983). Logical reasoning. In J. H. Flavell & E. M. Markman (Eds.), *Handbook of child psychology, Vol. 3. Cognitive development* (pp. 263–340). New York: Wiley.

Brody, L. R., & Carter, A. S. (1982). Children's emotional attributions to self versus other: An exploration of an assumption underlying projective techniques. *Journal of Consulting and Clinical Psychology, 50,* 665–671.

Brown, A. L., Bransford, J. D., Ferrara, R. A., & Campione, J. C. (1983). Learning, remembering, and understanding. In J. H. Falvell & H. M. Markman (Eds.), *Handbook of child psychology, Vol. 3 Cognitive development* (pp. 77–166). New York: Wiley.

Camara, K. A. (1979). Children's construction of social knowledge: Concepts of family and the experience of parental divorce. *Dissertation Abstracts International, 40,* 3433-B. (University Microfilms No. 8001884)

Cantor, D. W. (1977). School-based groups for children of divorce. *Journal of Divorce, 1,* 183–188.

Clingempeel, W. G., & Reppucci, N. D. (1982). Joint custody after divorce: Major issues and goals for research. *Psychological Bulletin, 91,* 102–127.

Cohn, J. F., & Tronick, E. Z. (1983). Three-month-old infants' reaction to simulated maternal depression. *Child Development, 54,* 185–193.

Colletta, N. D. (1979). The impact of divorce: Father absence or poverty? *Journal of Divorce, 3,* 27–36.

Cooper, J. E., Holman, J., & Braithwaite, V. A. (1983). Self esteem and family cohesion: The child's perspective and adjustment. *Journal of Marriage and the Family, 45,* 153–159.

Crnic, K. A., Greenberg, M. T., Ragozin, A. S., Robinson, N. M., & Basham, R. B. (1983). Effects of stress and social support on mothers and premature and full-term infants. *Child Development, 54,* 209–217.

Cummings, E. M., Zahn-Waxler, C., & Radke-Yarrow, M. (1981). Young children's responses to expressions of anger and affection by others in the family. *Child Development, 52,* 1274–1282.

Cummings, E. M., Iannotti, R. J., & Zahn-Waxler, C. (1985). Influence of conflict between adults on the emotions and aggression of young children. *Developmental Psychology, 21,* 495–507.

Dana, R. S. (1982). Psychological conceptions of marriage and divorce in children aged five to ten years. *Dissertation Abstracts International, 43,* 272. (University Microfilm No. DG82-13448)

DiGiuseppe, R., & Bernard, M. E. (1983). Principles of assessment and methods of treatment with children. In A. Ellis & M. E. Bernard (Eds.), *Rational-emotive approaches to the problems of childhood* (pp. 45–88). New York: Plenum Press.

Egeland, B., & Farber, E. A. (1984). Infant-mother attachment: Factors related to its developments and change over time. *Child Development, 55,* 753–771.

Ellis, A., & Bernard, M. E. (Eds.). (1983). *Rational-emotive approaches to the problems of childhood.* New York: Plenum Press.

Emery, R. E. (1982). Interparent conflict and the children of discord and divorce. *Psychological Bulletin, 92,* 310–330.

Emery, R. E., Hetherington, E. M., & DiLalla, L. (1984). Divorce, children, and social policy. In H. W. Stevenson & A. E. Siegel (Eds.), *Child development research and social policy* (pp. 189–266). Chicago: University of Chicago Press.

Emery, R. E., & O'Leary, D. (1982). Children's perceptions of marital discord and behavior problems of boys and girls. *Journal of Abnormal Child Psychology, 10,* 11–24.

Fine, M. A., Moreland, J. R., & Schwebel, A. I. (1983). The long term effects of divorce on parent-child relationships. *Developmental Psychology, 19,* 703–713.

Furstenberg, F. F., Nord, C. W., Peterson, J. L., & Zill, N. (1983). The life course of children of divorce. *American Sociological Review, 48,* 656–668.

Freed, R. (1979). The emotional attitudes experienced by children of divorce in relation to their parents. *Dissertation Abstracts International, 39,* 7522-A. (University Microfilm No. DG0330594)

Ganong, L., Coleman, M., & Brown, G. (1981). Effect of family structure on marital attitudes of adolescents. *Adolescence, 16,* 281–288.

Gardner, R. A. (1976). *Psychotherapy with children of divorce.* New York: Jason Aronson.

Gelman, R., & Baillargeon, R. (1983). A review of some Piagetian concepts. In J. H. Flavell & E. M. Markman (Eds.), *Handbook of child psychology, Vol. 3. Cognitive development* (pp. 167–230). New York: Wiley.

Goldberg, W. A., & Easterbrooks, M. A. (1984). The role of marital quality in toddler development. *Developmental Psychology, 20,* 504–514.

Golin, S., Sweeney, P. D., & Schaeffer, D. E. (1981). The causality of causal attributions in depression. *Journal of Abnormal Psychology. 90,* 14–22.

Guerney, L., & Jordon L. (1979). Children of divorce—a community support group. *Journal of Divorce, 2,* 283–294.

Guidubaldi, J., Perry, J. D., Cleminshaw, H. K., & McLoughlin, C. S. (1983). The impact of parental divorce on children: Report of the nationwide NASP Study. *School Psychology Review, 12,* 300–323.

Hajal, F., & Rosenberg, E. B. (1978). Working with the one parent family in therapy. *Journal of Divorce, 1,* 259–270.

Hammond, J. M. (1979). Children of divorce. *Dissertation Abstracts International, 40,* 672-A. (University Microfilm No. 7916719)

Herzog, E., & Sudia, C. E. (1973). Children in fatherless families. In B. M. Caldwell & H. Ricciuti (Eds.), *Review of child development research* (pp. 141–232). Chicago: University of Chicago Press.

Hetherington, E. M. (1979). Divorce: A child's perspective. *American Psychologist, 34,* 851–858.

Hetherington, E. M., & Camara, K. A. (1984). Families in transition: The processes of dissolution and reconstitution. In R. D. Parke (Ed.), *Review of child development research* (Vol. 7, pp. 398–440). Chicago: University of Chicago Press.

Hetherington, E. M., Cox, M., & Cox, R. (1979). The development of children in mother-headed famiies. In D. Reiss & H. A. Hoffman (Eds.), *The American family: Dying or developing* (pp. 117–156). New York: Plenum.

Hetherington, E. M., Cox, M., & Cox, R. (1982). Effects of divorce on parents and children. In M. E. Lamb (Ed.), *Nontraditional families* (pp. 233–287). Hillsdale, NJ: Lawrence Erlbaum Associates.

Hodges, W. F., & Bloom, B. L. (1984). Parents' report of children's adjustment to marital separation. *Journal of Divorce, 8,* 33–50.

Holmes, T. H., & Rahe, R. H. (1967). The social readjustment rating scale. *Journal of Psychosomatic Research 11,* 213–218.

Jacobson, D. S. (1978). The impact of marital separation/divorce on children. *Journal of Divorce, 1,* 341–360.

Kalter, N., Pickar, J. & Lesowitz, M. (1984). School-based developmental facilitation groups for children of divorce. *American Journal of Orthopsychiatry, 54,* 613–623.

Kalter, N., & Rembar, J. (1981). The signitifance of a child's age at the time of parental divorce. *American Journal of Orthopsychiatry, 51,* 85–100.

Kanoy, K. W., & Cunningham, J. L. (1984). Consensus or confusion in research on children of divorce. *Journal of Divorce, 8,* 45–72.

Kelly, R. R., & Berg, B. (1978). Measuring children's reactions to divorce. *Journal of Clinical Psychology, 34,* 215–221.

Kendall, P. C., & Braswell, L. (1982). Cognitive-behavioral self-control therapy for children: A components analysis. *Journal of Consulting and Clinical Psychology, 50,* 672–689.

King, H. E., & Kleemeier, C. P. (1983). The effect of divorce on parents and children. In C. E. Walker & M. C. Roberts (Eds.), *Handbook of clinical child psychology* (pp. 1249–1272). New York: Wiley.

Kurdek, L. A. (1981). An integrative perspective on children's divorce adjustment. *American Psychologist, 36,* 856–866.

Kurdek, L. A. (in press). Cognitive mediators of children's adjustment to divorce. In S. A. Wolchik & P. Karoly (Eds.), *Children of divorce: perspective on adjustment.* New York: Gardner Press.

Kurdek, L. A., & Berg, B. (1983). Correlates of children's adjustment to their parents' divorces. In L. A. Kurdek (Ed.), *New directions for child development, Vol. 19. Children and divorce* (pp. 47–60). San Francisco: Jossey-Bass.

Kurdek, L. A., & Blisk, D. (1983). Dimensions and correlates of mothers' divorce experiences. *Journal of Divorce, 6,* 1–24.

Kurdek, L. A., Blisk, D., & Siesky, A. E. (1981). Correlates of children's long term adjustment to their parents' divorce. *Developmental Psychology, 17,* 565–579.

Kurdek, L. A., & Siesky, A. E. (1979). An interview study of parents' perceptions of their children's reactions and adjustment to divorce. *Journal of Divorce, 3,* 5–18.

Kurdek, L. A., & Siesky, A. E. (1980). Children's perceptions of their parents' divorce. *Journal of Divorce, 3,* 339–377.

Lamb, M. E. (1977). The effects of divorce on children's personality development. *Journal of Divorce, 1,* 163–174.

Lazarus, R. S., & Folkman, S. (1984). *Stress, appraisal, and coping.* New York: Springer.

Laheey, M. (1984). Findings from research on divorce. *American Journal of Orthopsychiatry, 54,* 298–317.

Links, P. (1983). Community surveys of the prevalence of childhood psychiatric disorders. *Child Development, 54,* 531–548.

Longfellow, C. (1979). Divorce in context. In G. Levinger & O. Moles (Eds.), *Divorce and separation* (pp. 287–306). New York: Basic Books.

Lowenstein, J. S., & Koopman, E. J. (1978). A comparison of the self esteem between boys living with single parent fathers. *Journal of Divorce, 2,* 195–208.

Lowry, C. B. (1980). A cognitive developmental analysis of children's understanding of social relationships. *Dissertation Abstracts International, 41,* 3579-B. (University Microfilms No. 8106406)

Luepnitz, D. A. (1979). Which aspects of divorce affect children? *Family Coordinator, 28,* 79–85.

MacKinnon, C. E., Brody, G. H., & Stoneman, Z. (1982). The effects of divorce and maternal employment on the home environments of preschool children. *Child Development, 53,* 1392–1399.

Magrab, P. R. (1978). For the sake of the children: A review of the psychological effects of divorce. *Journal of Divorce, 1,* 233–246.

Mannheim, C. (1983, April). *Post-divorce adjustment of school-aged children.* Paper presented at the meeting of the Society for Research in Child Development, Detroit, MI.

McCollum, M. G. (1981). Children's concepts of family and divorce. *Dissertation Abstracts International, 41,* 3209-B. (University Microfilms No. 8103417)

Mendell, A. E. (1983). Play therapy with children of divorced parents. In C. E. Schaeffer & K. J. O'Conner (Eds.), *Handbook of play therapy* (pp. 320–354). New York: Wiley.

Miller, R. C., & Berman, J. S. (1983). The efficacy of cognitive behavior therapies. *Psychological Bulletin, 94,* 39–53.

National Center for Health Statistics: Advance report of final divorce statistics, 1982. Deaths, United States, 1982. (1985). *Monthly Vital Statistics Report, 33,* No. 11. DHHS Pub. No. (PHS) 85-1120. Hyattsville, MD.: Public Health Service.

Neal, J. H. (1983). Children's understanding of their parents' divorces. In L. A. Kurdek (Ed.), *New directions for child development, Vol 19, Children and divorce* (pp. 3–14). San Francisco: Jossey-Bass.

O'Leary, K. D., & Emery, R. E. (in press). Marital discord and child behavior problems. In M. D. Levine & P. Satz (Eds.), *Developmental variation and dysfunction* New York: Academic Press.

Pastor, D., Vaughn, B., Dodds, M., & Egeland, B. (1981, April). *The effect of different family patterns on the quality of mother-infant attachment.* Paper presented at the meeting of the Society for Research in Child Development, Boston, MA.

Pett, M. G. (1982). Correlates of children's social adjustment following divorce. *Journal of Divorce, 5,* 25–39.

Reinhard, D. W. (1977). The reaction of adolescent boys and girls to the divorce of their parents. *Journal of Clinical Child Psychology, 6,* 21–23.

Rosen, R. (1977). Children of divorce. *Journal of Clinical Child Psychology, 6,* 24–27.

Rosenthal, P. A. (1979). Sudden disappearance of one parent with separation and divorce. *Journal of Divorce, 3,* 43–54.

Rushton, J. P., Brainerd, C. J., & Pressley, M. (1983). Behavioral development and construct validity: The principle of aggregation. *Psychological Bulletin, 94,* 18–38.

Rutter, M. (1979). Maternal deprivation, 1972–1978: New findings, new concepts, new approaches, *Child Development, 50,* 283–305.

Sarason, I. G., Johnson, J. H., & Siegel, J. M. (1978). Assessing the impact of life changes. *Journal of Consulting and Clinical Psychology, 46,* 932–946.

Selman, R. L. (1980). *The development of interpersonal understanding.* New York: Academic Press.

Shantz, C. U. (1983). Social cognition. In J. H. Flavell & E. M. Markman (Eds.), *Handbook of child psychology, Vol. 3. Cognitive development* (pp. 495–555). New York: Wiley.

Shinn, M. (1978). Father absence and children's cognitive development. *Psychological Bulletin, 85,* 295–324.

Springer, C., & Wallerstein, J. S. Young adolescents' responses to their parents' divorces. In L. A. Kurdek (Ed.), *Children and divorce* (pp. 15–28). San Francisco: Jossey-Bass.

Sroufe, L. A., & Rutter, M. (1984). The domain of developmental psychopathology. *Child Development, 55,* 17–29.

Stolberg, A. L., & Cullen, P. M. (1983). Preventive interventions for families of divorce: The Divorce Adjustment Project. In L. A. Kurdek (Ed.), *New directions in child development, Vol. 19, Children and divorce* (pp. 71–82). San Francisco: Jossey-Bass.

Stolberg, A. L., & Garrison, K. M. (1985). Evaluation of a primary prevention program for children of divorce. *American Journal of Community Psychology, 13,* 111–124.

Tessman, L. H. (1978). *Children of parting parents.* New York: Jason Aronson.

Thompson, E. H., & Gongla, P. A. (1983). Single parent families. In E. D. Macklin & R. H. Rubin (Eds.), *Contemporary families and alternative lifestyles* (pp. 97–124). Beverly Hills: Sage Publications.

United States Department of Commerce, Bureau of the Census. (1983). Marital status and living arrangements: March 1982. *Current Population Reports,* Series P-20, No. 380.

Vaughn, B. E., Gove, F. L., & Egeland, B. (1980). The relationship between out-of-home care and the quality of infant–mother attachment in an economically disadvantaged population. *Child Development, 51,* 1203–1214.

Walker, L. J. (1983). Sources of cognitive conflict for stage transition in moral development. *Developmental Psychology, 19,* 103–110.

Wallerstein, J. S. (1983). Children of divorce: The psychological tasks of the child. *American Journal of Orthopsychiatry, 53,* 230–243.

Wallerstein, J. S. (1984). Children of divorce. *American Journal of Orthopsychiatry, 54,* 444–458.

Wallerstein, J. S., & Kelly, J. B. (1980). *Suriviving the breakup.* New York: Basic Books.

Warshak, R. A., & Santrock, J. W. (1983). The impact of divorce in father-custody and mother-custody homes: The child's perspective. In L. A. Kuraek (Ed.), *Children and divorce.* (pp. 29–46). San Francisco: Jossey-Bass.

Weinraub, M., & Wolf, B. M. (1983). Effects of stress and social supports on mother–child interactions in single and two-parent families. *Child Development, 54,* 1297–1311.

Weiss, R. S. (1975). *Marital separation.* New York: Basic Books.

Weiss, R. S. (1984). The impact of marital dissolution on income and consumption in single parent households. *Journal of Marriage and the Family, 46,* 115–128.

White, S. W., & Mika, K. (1983). Family divorce and separation: Theory and research. *Marriage and Family Review, 6,* 175–192.

Wynn, R. L., & Brumberger, L. S. (1982, June). *A cognitive developmental analysis of children's understanding of family membership and divorce.* Paper presented at the meeting of the Jean Piaget Society, Philadelphia, PA.

Young, D. M. (1983). Two studies of children of divorce. In L. A. Kurdek (Ed.), *New directions in child development, Vol. 19, Children and divorce* (pp. 61–70). San Francisco: Jossey-Bass.

Zill, N. (1978, February). *Divorce, marital happiness and the mental health of children: Findings from the FCD National Survey of Children.* Paper presented at the meeting of the National Institute of Mental Health, Bethesda, MD.

10 Coping with Abuse: Children's Perspectives on their Abusive Treatment

Sharon D. Herzberger
Trinity College

Howard Tennen
University of Connecticut School of Medicine

The ways in which parents discipline their children have for centuries aroused the attention of philosophers and social historians. To the literature on the ethics and logic of discipline and its application in various eras (e.g., DeMause, 1974; Locke, 1913), psychologists have added investigations of the effectiveness of discipline (Parke, 1970; Walters & Grusec, 1977), the factors involved in parents' choice of discipline (Dix & Grusec, 1985; Zahn-Waxler & Chapman, 1982), and the consequences of various forms of discipline on the child (Becker, 1964). Much less is known about the child's experience of discipline and punishment. A few diaries (cf. DeMause, 1974) and clinical records (e.g., Kempe & Kempe, 1978) describe how individual children view parental discipline, but few empirical studies (Halperin, 1981; Herzberger, Potts, & Dillon, 1981) have investigated the issue. Most of our knowledge about children's perceptions of discipline is indirect, and is inferred from studies of parents' behavior, the home environment, and the effects of discipline upon the child's behavior.

A child's interpretation of his or her circumstances has been shown to affect, among other factors, academic achievement (Dweck, 1975), peer interaction (Goetz & Dweck, 1980), coping with illness (Tennen, Affleck, Allen, McGrade, & Ratzan, 1984), and the dynamics of schizophrenia (Rabkin, 1965). Therefore, one would expect that the child's perception of disciplinary interactions would also affect his or her behavior. It is not always possible, however, to infer how a given child interprets an event. The child's view of the world changes with age and increasing cognitive sophistication (Flavell, 1977; Piaget, 1930), and a child of any age may interpret cues from the social environment in ways that do not coincide with the perceptions of his or her parent or an external observer. As Kagan (1977) has remarked with reference to children's reactions to parental rejection, it "is not a specific set of actions by parents but a belief held by the child" (p. 46) that affects subsequent development. Understanding the child's interpretation of discipline should therefore add considerably to our knowledge of the dynamics of disciplinary interactions.

In this chapter we examine children's perspectives on severe discipline, concentrating on physically abusive family situations.[1] We attempt to outline the link between such perspectives and the behavioral and emotional development of the abused child. The effects of abuse on children varies widely (Kent, 1976; Martin & Beezley, 1977) and the variation is attributed to differences in the type of abuse, the age of the child, and the general home atmosphere (Kinard, 1979). Little attention has been given to the cognitive strategies that may help or hinder a child's attempts to cope with an abusive situation. This chapter reviews the literature on the abused child's perceptions of the family, information on the consequences of abuse, and the literature on coping with stressful and uncontrollable events in an attempt to understand the behavioral and emotional consequences of abusive discipline.

The term *abuse* is fraught with ambiguity. Most researchers and social service professionals consider only *intended* harm to be abusive. There is a good deal of disagreement, however, about how severe a child's injury must be for its infliction to be labelled abuse (Giovannoni & Becerra, 1979) and about the circumstances under which we attribute intent and blame (Herzberger & Tennen, 1985a, 1985b). Definitions of abuse naturally affect whether the abusive label will be applied (Parke & Collmer, 1975; Straus, 1978), as do other factors, such as the characteristics of the parent, child, and observer (Giovannoni & Becerra, 1979; Herzberger & Tennen, 1985a, 1985b). These factors complicate efforts to summarize and integrate the research evidence. Furthermore, physical maltreatment is sometimes accompanied by a negligent or emotionally abusive environment (Herzberger et al., 1981; Kempe & Kempe, 1978), and no study has satisfactorily controlled for the effects of family environment when examining the consequences of physical abuse. In the discussion to follow we consider the interaction between physical and emotional maltreatment.

The Abused Child's Environment: The Observer's Perspective

Before examining abused children's perceptions of their environment, we consider the environment from an outside observer's perspective in order to identify

---

[1]It is common to consider abuse as one end of the disciplinary continuum. Abuse generally takes place within the context of a disciplinary interaction, albeit one that has "gone too far". Furthermore, attempts to identify characteristics of parents, such as sadism or other psychopathological qualities, have failed (cf. Parke & Collmer, 1975). Thus, recent examinations of child abuse have concentrated on such factors as parent–child interactions and stress—factors common to an examination of other forms of discipline.

cues that may be available to the abused child. The child abuse literature points to a number of consistent differences between abusive and nonabusive home environments. Many abusive parents, for example, appear ill-informed about child development (e.g., Galdston, 1965; Steele & Pollock, 1968). As a consequence, they tend to hold unrealistic expectations about their child's capabilities, and often misunderstand the motivation behind a child's actions (Mancuso & Lehrer, this volume). They appear particularly prone to expect advanced behaviors and to presume motives beyond their child's developmental ability. Cunningham (1972) gives a graphic example of a mother's unrealistic interpretation of her 2-year-old's behavior: "Look at her give you the eye! That's how she picks up men—she's a regular sexpot!" (p. 14). When the child's abilities and interests at a given age are not understood, it is possible to attribute willful malevolence.

Another characteristic of abusive parents is an expectation that the child will be responsive to the parent's emotional and physical needs (Spinetta & Rigler, 1972). Some researchers (Fontana, 1968; Steele & Pollock, 1968) claim that abusive parents lack sufficient nurturance during their childhood and, consequently, expect their own children to supply the love and attention they crave. Although case studies report dramatic examples of precocious children fulfilling parent's desires (e.g., Davoren, 1968), by and large, the reversal of roles is incomplete and the parent sees the child as a disappointment (Martin, 1977).

Abusive parents also tend to apply discipline inconsistently (cf. Parke & Collmer, 1975). Rather than using a few discipline techniques in a consistent fashion (the strategy common to nonabusive parents), abusive parents use many forms of discipline and apply them haphazardly (Elmer, 1967). Furthermore, abusive parents do not provide their children with consistent standards for behavior. Young (1964) found that over 80% of abusive parents failed to state explicitly expectations about their child's behavior and responsibilities. The inconsistent application of discipline and the lack of consistent standards for behavior often lead to more intense and severe discipline as parents search for methods to control the child's continued misbehavior (Parke & Collmer, 1975).

Finally, there seems to be less verbal and physical interaction among members of families with abused children (Burgess & Conger, 1978). The interaction that does occur is often negatively toned, with abusive parents being unresponsive to their child's requests and showing less support and approval. The differences between abusive and nonabusive families are mainly due to the mothers' behavior. Less dramatic differences are observed among fathers in abusive and nonabusive households.[2] Children in abusive households, in turn, tend to mimic

---

[2]It should be noted that Burgess and Conger (1978) compared interaction styles among family members in households in which one or more children were abused versus those in which no children were abused. Their analysis did not consider which parent or child was involved in the abusive relationship. Thus, although we might assume that some of the fathers in abusive households were the abusers, the authors did not confirm this.

their mother's behavior, interacting less with other family members than do control children.

Inconsistency, coldness, lack of empathy, and high expectations are more likely to be found in abusive than nonabusive households. They are not, however, present in all abusive homes, nor can the environment of a given household continually be so characterized. As Martin, Beezley, Conway, and Kempe (1974) observed, the home atmosphere varies across abusive families from generally normal parenting with the exception of occasional abusive acts to severe and continual rejection and physical abuse of the child. Thus, abusive families show some diversity, and children from these families are likely to vary in their interpretation of the treatment they receive.

The Consequences of Abuse

Studies of the effects of abuse show the wide range of methodological sophistication found in the larger literature on abuse. Studies with methodological control tend to examine one or a few behaviors in abusive and nonabusive samples. Less controlled studies attempt to catalogue the behavioral and emotional problems of a group of abused children in the absence of an appropriate comparison group, which does not allow one to assess whether the characteristics of abused children are prevalent among children in all troubled households. Because no study has separated satisfactorily the effects of physical abuse from the effects of debilitating emotional treatment, it is often difficult to discern the exact causes for any given effect (Jayaratne, 1977). Finally, although it is common to attribute pathological characteristics of abused children to their mistreatment, problems of assuming cause and effect are evident. Some characteristics of these children may have existed prior to, and perhaps predispose the child to, harsh parental discipline (Friedrich & Boriskin, 1976). With these caveats in mind, we discuss qualities that purportedly distinguish abused children from their nonabused counterparts.

Perhaps the most commonly reported finding is that abused children are aggressive (cf. Kinard, 1979, 1980). Martin and Beezley (1977) found aggression and oppositional behavior in a substantial proportion of their abused sample. Kent (1976) reported similar findings in a study that controlled for the effects of socioeconomic status. George and Main (1979) found increased aggression already evident among abused toddlers, who more frequently assaulted peers and harassed day care workers by threatening and spitting. Similar "acting out" behaviors, such as delinquency and aggression, have been noted among other samples also exposed to inconsistent childrearing practices (Glueck & Glueck, 1950, 1968).

Another commonly reported finding is wariness on the part of the abused child. George and Main (1979) report that abused toddlers were less likely than nonabused toddlers to approach caregivers in response to positive overtures.

When they did approach, it was more likely to be from the side or rear. Hypervigilance has also been reported by Martin and Beezley (1977) and Kempe and Kempe (1978).

Studies by Dodge and his colleagues (Dodge, 1980; Dodge & Frame, 1982; Dodge & Newman, 1981) on aggressive (but not necessarily abused) children suggest that cognitive processes mediate aggression and wariness or hypervigilance. Dodge and Newman (1981) report that aggressive boys are more likely than nonaggressive boys to attribute unwarranted hostility to peers. These biased attributions in aggressive boys may be due, in part, to their quick response to stimuli and their relative inattention to available social cues. Because the attributional bias was not evident following positive acts by peers, Dodge and Frame (1982) hypothesized that these behavioral tendencies may be due to a "paranoid" perspective that predisposes aggressive boys to feel that they, but not others, are targets of peers' hostility. The anticipation of hostile interactions leads to vigilance for signs of impending hostility and to aggression against potential offenders. In fact, aggressive boys *were* more likely than nonaggressive boys to be targets of others' aggression (Dodge & Frame, 1982). Although Dodge and his colleagues did not select abused children for their studies, their results may be relevant to abused samples. Their work suggests that when children learn at home that the world is a hostile place and they watch for signs of potential hazards, they may be quick to initiate aggression and respond aggressively to events that others might find innocuous.

Another characteristic of many abused children is low self-esteem (Martin & Beezley, 1977). The abused child's feelings of unworthiness could derive from the experience of emotional mistreatment and excessive parental expectations. Their docility and acceptance (Kinard, 1979), withdrawal and apathy (Martin & Beezley, 1977) and belief that they deserve the treatment they receive from their parents (Kempe & Kempe, 1978) may reflect this sense of unworthiness.

As we have noted, some clinical studies report a precocity among abused children (Martin & Beezley, 1977). Davoren (1968) provides a poignant example of an 18-month-old girl who put down her bottle to cross the room and comfort her sobbing mother. When her mother was soothed, she returned to her bottle. We do not know how many abused children develop a sophisticated "role reversal" in response to abuse, nor the consistency of such behavior among affected children. Neither do we know the base rate of such behavior among the general child population.

Perceptions of Abuse

The previous discussion implies that children's interpretations of abusive incidents are important determinants of the sequelae of abuse. Interpretations of abusive acts appear to affect the tendency to behave aggressively, the emotional development of the child, and the child's subsequent interaction with his or her parent. A few studies have examined the interpretations of abused individuals. These studies are discussed next.

The abused child's view of his or her family is likely to be different in many ways from that of other children. Herzberger et al. (1981), for example, interviewed 8- to 14-year-old abused and nonabused boys. Abused boys described their parents in more negative terms and characterized their treatment more negatively than the nonabused sample. The following examples demonstrate these differences:

Fourteen-year-old: (Describing abusive mother) Mean . . . just out of whack . . . no responsibility whatsoever. . . She had problems with her family . . . She just took them all out on me. (Describing abusive father) The same as my mother . . . he'd drink a lot. He'll pick up my mother and throw her out the door, throw her against walls . . . he did the same thing to me.

Nine-year-old: (Describing abusive mother) Not very good . . . She would whoop us with an extension cord and she would put my brother outside the house with no shoes on. (Describing non-abusive stepfather) He was real nice to me like if I would take some of my grandfather's money he would sit down and talk to me about it.

Thirteen-year-old: (Describing non-abusive mother) . . . She was OK, cause she like stuck up for me and stuff. She tried to keep me out of trouble.

Abused children also felt more emotionally rejected and more fearful of their parents. For example, when asked whether their parents cared about them or liked having them around, children remarked:

Nine-year-old: (Describing abusive mother) She didn't like me very much . . . she would put me out of the house . . . I would get blamed for most of the things and she would believe my sisters, but she wouldn't believe me and my brother.

Fourteen-year-old: (Describing abusive mother) . . . Every time I wanted to talk to her or watch TV with her, she'd move away . . . If I go to where she is to, you know, keep company then she moves away. So I was by myself most of the time.

Eleven-year-old: (Describing non-abusive mother) Yes, cause when I would play, after the game our coach would take us out to pizza place, I would forget to tell her and she'd get worried . . . We cracked a lot of jokes. (Describing abusive father) Sometimes . . . he played with me sometimes . . . He hit me sometimes, but since I was a big boy then, I would take that stuff.

Contrary to some clinical evidence (Kempe & Kempe, 1978), abused children in this study realized that their family situation was different from that of other children. One 9-year-old remarked, "I don't think other families whoop their kids with extension cords." A 14-year-old, discussing grandparents with whom he had lived, stated: "They watched over me and just took good care of how a normal kid is supposed to be taken care of." In contrast, he described his own parents as different from other families because "they broke a lot of laws with the world."

The apparent ease with which these children discuss a parent's role in their abuse should not obscure the considerable ambivalence they experience about their parents and some children's denial of feeling emotionally rejected (Halperin, 1981). One 11-year-old said his abusive mother was "nice, likeable, sometimes playful. If one person do something and all the rest of them didn't, so that she don't know who did it, so she gave us all a couple of lickings." Another 11-year-old said that his abusive father "showed me he cared in a different way . . . he gave me a father's way of giving love. Like going fishing." Interestingly, Halperin (1981) found no differences in perceptions of parents between abused and nonabused siblings, suggesting that it is the overall home atmosphere and general parent–child interaction rather than the physical act of abuse that may prompt the different feelings and behaviors of abused children relative to controls.

Several other studies examined abused and nonabused adolescents' views of discipline. Amsterdam, Brill, Bell, and Edwards (1979) found that, among teenagers, those who received the most severe discipline, including abuse, were most likely to believe it was deserved. The distinction must be made, however, between deserving punishment and deserving abuse. Herzberger et al. (1981) report that the abused children in their sample admitted performing behaviors that would prompt disciplinary action, but rejected the intensity of the discipline their parents chose. One 14-year-old remarked, "I wasn't no angel neither. I did things wrong, you know . . . they had like 3/4 of the reasons to hit me, but not that hard" (p. 86). Thus, although some reports (Amsterdam et al., 1979; Kempe & Kempe, 1978) reveal that children view parental discipline as rightful, this response may not be common among abused children, nor is the interpretation of this finding straightforward.

Herzberger (1983) suggests that abusive treatment may be considered legitimate by the child to the extent that abuse is perceived as normative (a high proportion of children in one's neighborhood or peer group are treated similarly) or when the circumstances under which punishment occurs are generally considered proper. Proper circumstances may include extreme misbehavior on the part of the child and the use of physical punishment techniques that differ in severity, but not quality, from normal discipline. For example, hitting with a strength great enough to induce bruising may be seen as more appropriate than burning or forcing the child to drink a noxious substance. Hitting is more normative, even though the parent may have gone too far, and the resulting injury is not always foreseeable. Burning, however, produces a planned, intentional injury. These ideas are supported by the judgments of social service and legal professionals (Giovannoni & Becerra, 1979), but remain to be tested among victims of abuse.

A pilot study (Libbey & Bybee, 1979) examined whether abused adolescents would regard certain treatment as abusive. Discussion revealed that most of the adolescents believed that hitting one in the head could be termed abusive, whereas spanking and using a belt could not. Thus, some forms of punishment that authorities or researchers might perceive as abusive may not be so perceived by the victims. A study by Herzberger and Tennen (1985b) supports this finding. Young adults were asked to judge disciplinary interactions between a parent and child. Some of the discipline methods would be termed abusive by social service and legal professionals (hitting the child with a leather strap on bare skin; banging the child against the wall several times). After reading the cases and making judgments about the severity, appropriateness, and possible consequences of such treatment, participants were requested to note whether they had experienced similar discipline as a child. Those who had experienced similar discipline judged it to be less severe and more appropriate than those who had not experienced it. Furthermore, the former were less likely to label the discipline as abuse and were more likely to hold the child responsible for incurring such treatment. These findings demonstrate the importance of examining the meaning of abuse from the victim's perspective.

From the Victimization of Abuse to Its Sequelae: Mediational Processes

There seems to be a broad range of emotional and behavioral responses to abusive treatment in childhood. Some children are devastated by the abuse; they withdraw and become depressed, or perhaps become hypervigilant for imminent aggression. Other children appear to survive the trauma with a sense of esteem and dignity. Their emotional life is not impoverished and their response to others is empathic. These behavioral and emotional disparities are paralleled by differences in children's interpretations of their victimization. Some children acknowledge their parent's blameworthiness, whereas others interpret the abuse as a sign of caring or may blame themselves for the abuse.

The remainder of this chapter is devoted to an exploration of the processes through which abusive parental treatment may affect the child. Our discussion draws on the wealth of literature on social cognitive development and coping with uncontrollable life events. Although the discussion is supported where possible by research involving abused children, much of the material presented is drawn from other populations. Our aim is not to review only confirmed and well supported ideas, but, through informed speculation, to provide the impetus for further research into an important, yet underinvestigated, topic.

Variations in Abuse and the Home Environment. Few studies have examined the relationship between particular forms of abuse, qualities of the abusive environment, or demographic characteristics of the child and the symptoms exhibited by the child victim. Martin and Beezley (1977), who have extensively examined the home environment, note that abused children who are oppositional, who withdraw, or who show other behavioral problems are more likely to live in "sub-optimal" homes (moving from home to home, unstable home environment, parental emotional disturbance) than are children who exhibit compulsive or precocious patterns of behavior. Symptom frequency was positively associated with the number of home difficulties. The frequency of abuse may also affect the consequences. Children who have been subjected to repeated abuse are more likely to be aggressive than are children exposed to less frequent abuse (cf. Kinard, 1979). However, there is some suggestion that continued severe abuse is likely to leave a child with depressed affect and docile behavior (Kagan, 1977; Rohner, 1975).

Child's Gender. The child's gender may also influence the effects of abuse. Feshbach (1970) suggests that, due to cultural pressures, girls are less likely than boys to respond to severe punishment with aggression. Not only are girls more often penalized for aggressive behavior, but parental expectations may affect the likelihood of an aggressive response. If parents attribute misbehaviors differentially according to the gender of their child (as do teachers; see Dweck, Davidson, Nelson, & Enna, 1978), this may suggest a mechanism by which girls and boys would respond differently to abuse. Our own preliminary investigations suggest that parents may in fact think differently about the misbehaviors of sons than of daughters. Parents were interviewed about the types of punishment they use with their children and whether their choice of punishment varies according to the characteristics of the child. Some parents readily admitted using different punishments with male and female children and attributed their behavior to differences they perceived between sons and daughters. One parent stated that boys "require more active discipline" since they are "more active, energetic and aggressive." Another parent stated that she would not need to use harsh punishment to correct a daughter's misbehavior because "girls have more of a desire to please." To the extent that these characterizations are generalizable and are conveyed to the child, they may induce more compliant, less aggressive behaviors among girls.

Parent's Gender. The abuser's sex may also affect the consequences to the child in several ways. First, children are more likely to model the behaviors of the parent with whom they most identify, commonly the same-sex parent (Bandura, 1969). If the identificand is abusive, the child may be more likely to adopt an aggressive behavioral style. Second, abuse by the parent to whom the child is more attached may be especially debilitating (cf. Yarrow, 1963). As one parent in our pilot study said, "The child spends more time with the mother and develops a stronger bond with her. . . . Children are amazed and alarmed when their mother spanks them or yells at them. Their feelings are hurt."

There is also some indirect evidence that abuse by the father may not have the same consequences as abuse by the mother. Herzberger et al. (1981) found that abused children offer uniformly positive descriptions of nonabusive mothers and more variable and negative descriptions of nonabusive fathers. For example, children were asked if their parent cared about them, gave them a lot of love, and liked having them around. While children reported significantly more positive feelings about nonabusive mothers than abusive mothers, abusive and non-abusive fathers did not differ on these dimensions. In fact, children reported that nonabusive fathers cared about them as much as abusive mothers. Children also thought that their mothers felt "bad" about hitting them much more often then did their fathers. These results are consistent with stereotyped perceptions of fathers and mothers (cf. Dubin & Dubin, 1965). If fathers are expected to be cold and aggressive, confirmation of these characteristics may be less harmful to the child than similar characteristics displayed by mothers. Mothers, who are stereo-typed by children as nuturant, sympathetic, and less powerful than fathers (cf. Dubin & Dubin, 1965), will seem particularly rejecting if their behavior contra-dicts these beliefs. We would then expect more dire emotional consequences of maternal than paternal abuse.

Two studies suggest that stereotypes of gender differences in parenting may indeed operate in this fashion. Potts and Herzberger (1981) found that fathers may engage in emotionally rejecting and cold behaviors with relative impunity. College students who responded to a questionnaire about their upbringing some-times perceived their father's lack of interest and involvement in family life in a benign way (e.g., reporting that father showed interest and love by earning money to contribute to the family). Mothers who showed the same lack of involvement were termed emotionally abusive. Herzberger and Tennen (1985a) obtained similar responses from young adults who read hypothetical case studies of abusive incidents. Parents were described as engaging in behavior that might be termed abusive, such as hitting the child with a leather strap or banging the child against the wall repeatedly. When the behavior was ascribed to a father, it was rated as more severe and more abusive than when the behavior was ascribed to a mother. The abusive behavior was seen, nonetheless, as particularly inap-propriate when performed by the mother and was less likely to be described as the child's responsibility.

Child's Age. One of the most important factors affecting the emotional and behavioral outcomes of abuse—but one that has received scant attention—is the age of the child at the time of abuse. Although evidence is scarce, some investi-gators (e.g., Kinard, 1979) suggest that abuse during infancy is particularly harmful, because the infant needs a consistent, reliable, trusting relationship. The child's response to severe discipline may also vary with age. Kinard (1979) reviews reports indicating that aggressive acting out by a child is more frequently associated with abuse at a younger age. This finding is generally attributed to the learned inhibition of aggression among older children (Sears, Maccoby, & Levin, 1957).[3]

Differences in cognitive sophistication may also explain why age is an important mediator of the effects of abuse. The young child has difficulty understanding emotions and thoughts that are not apparent and, therefore, depends upon surface information to understand others (Shantz, 1975). Before school age, children also do not generally reflect upon themselves and they possess no spontaneous self-concept (Secord & Peevers, 1974; Selman & Byrne, 1974). Consequently, they are not readily aware of their own characteristic styles of behavior or thought and may be more prone to accept the image of themselves provided by others.

Younger children also have a qualitatively different style of thinking about moral issues and cause-and-effect (Piaget 1930; 1932). Young children tend to maintain an external locus-of-control orientation (Mischel, Zeiss, & Zeiss, 1974), feeling that they are relatively powerless to influence their physical and social world. Complementing this trend is a belief in "immanent justice," the belief that misbehaviors will inevitably be punished, and a belief in the "God-like" authority and correctness of parents (Piaget, 1932). These characteristics may predispose the young child to accept parental rules and behavior. Their more rudimentary analysis of causation makes young children less likely to understand the many reasons why people behave the way they do, and they are less likely than older children to analyze others' intentions and motivation (cf. Flavell, 1977).

At first glance, this analysis may appear to contradict findings that aggressive acting out decreases with age (Kinard, 1979). Increasing cognitive skills should permit older children to recognize the inappropriateness of parental abuse, leading to rebellion and acting out. Although some adolescents behave aggressively and provocatively toward parents (Libbey & Bybee, 1979), it is the young child who, despite a cognitive style that encourages unquestioning obedience, is more likely to respond to aggression with aggression. One answer to the apparent contradiction may reside in the coping strategies adopted by children of varying ages, a topic to be discussed later. The target of the child's aggression may provide another clue to the contradiction. Kinard (1980) suggests that the aggression of young children is displaced. Children are likely to model parental aggression, but perform this activity outside of the home with peers. Thus, the young child may accept the parents' judgment in the use of physical discipline and imitate parental aggressive behaviors, but may be wise enough not to reciprocate directly.

---

[3]Examination of the effect of age of onset of abuse is complicated by a failure to control for the longevity of abusive treatment and the nature and frequency of abuse at each age.

Learned Helplessness as a Response to Abuse.   If there is one characteristic common to many abusive situations, it is that the child is exposed to unpredictable circumstances beyond his or her control. As noted previously, a number of studies (cf. Parke & Collmer, 1975) point to the inconsistent nature of discipline in abusive families. A parent may respond dramatically to a particular behavior or incident on one occasion, then respond with restraint on another occasion. From the child's perspective, it may appear as if parental responses are independent of his or her own behavior. The learned helplessness model (Seligman, 1975) makes some specific predictions regarding people's responses to uncontrollable outcomes. When children (or adults) begin to believe that important outcomes are independent of their own responses, the belief generalizes to new situations where control is actually attainable. Behavioral or emotional manifestations of learned helplessness include withdrawal, lowered self-esteem, anxiety and depression.

A child exposed to inconsistent childrearing techniques and adverse treatment such as abuse may be a prime candidate for developing the helplessness syndrome. It is difficult for a child to ascertain which of his or her behaviors should be eliminated if the response to them is inconsistent, thereby enhancing a sense of uncontrollability. Furthermore, certain behaviors are likely to be functionally equivalent to the parent, but not to the child. For example, if some of a young boy's mannerisms remind his mother of the most undesirable features of herself or her despised spouse (Martin, 1977), it is unlikely that the child will be able to ascertain the nuances that provoke abusive responses. Finally, even if the child could make such complicated discriminations, it may be impossible for him to change the behaviors or characteristics in question. The 2-year-old who cannot tie her shoes or fix her own dinner is not wilfully disobeying the parent, and the boy whose facial features remind the father of his hated uncle is unable to alter these circumstances.

Abramson, Seligman, and Teasdale (1978) suggest that a child's response to uncontrollable events will be mediated by the perceived causes of uncontrollability, and evidence suggests that adverse situations do activate causal questions in the minds of children (Tennen et al., 1984), as well as adults (Bulman & Wortman, 1977). The child may attribute the adversity to something about him or herself (*internal* attribution), to something outside him or herself (*external* attribution), or to some combination of attributions. The child's attribution may be to *stable* causes (causes that remain unchanged over time) or to *unstable* causes. Finally, the cause may be *global,* appearing in many other situations, or it may be *specific* to a unique set of circumstances. Attributions to internal, stable, and global factors are most devastating because they lead to the most widespread behavioral deficits as well as to feelings of low self-esteem.

This typology of attributions may be pertinent to child abuse. We know that many abused children believe that they deserve to be punished for their wrongdoings and some accept the severity of parental treatment (Amsterdam et al., 1979;

Herzberger et al., 1981; Kempe & Kempe, 1978). However, feelings of deservedness and self-blame need not lead to serious emotional disturbance. Self-blame can take two forms: blaming the trouble on one's behavior (one's actions or a failure to act) or on one's character or personality. Behavioral self-blame (Janoff-Bulman, 1979) may forestall helplessness and low self-esteem because children who blame their behavior for the abuse may seek ways to conform to parental wishes. These children may develop precocious or compliant behavior styles that, to the extent that these tactics are successful, can lead to renewed belief in control over life circumstances and enhance self-esteem. Children who attribute parental treatment to aspects of their character, however, do not have recourse to quick behavior changes, and may withdraw and develop a generalized chronic sense of unworthiness and helplessness.

Blaming oneself does not preclude other causal attributions. Over one-third of the abused boys in the Herzberger et al. (1981) study, for example, shared blame with their parents, indicating that their parents hit them partly because of the parent's "mean" character. Children who blame the parent in addition to or instead of themselves—particularly some intransient aspect of the parent's personality—*may* be able to maintain a better self-image, but predictions would be complex. Blaming the parent may create guilt feelings in the child that lead to more self-blame (Kernberg, 1975). Blaming the parent may also decrease the child's perception of control over abuse, further inciting feelings of helplessness, depression, and low self-esteem. In addition, some home circumstances do not encourage the child to attribute responsibility for abuse solely to the parent. For example, when an abused child's siblings are untouched, the child may be prompted to look inward for at least part of the cause.

The child who can point to ephemeral and external causes for parental treatment would be expected to suffer the least harm to self-esteem (see Witenberg, Blanchard, Suls, Tennen, McCoy & McGoldrick, 1983, for findings among hemodialysis patients). Cases abound of parents who engage in abuse after being laid off from work or being exposed to other stresses (Garbarino, 1977; cf., Gil, 1970). If children are capable of discerning the acute nature of the parent's distress and its correlation with parental behavior, they may make external attributions. External attributions may also result from noting that severe discipline is common among neighboring families and acceptable within society. These attributions may protect the child's self-esteem and his or her image of the parent, but as noted previously, they are unlikely to produce feelings of control. Thus, they may also contribute to the helplessness syndrome.

Inward Versus Outward Behavior. While the learned-helplessness model predicts many of the "inward" behaviors (Rothbaum, Weisz & Snyder, 1982) of abused children, such as withdrawal and despair, and when lowered self-esteem will appear (Abramson et al., 1978), the model does not predict the "outward" symptoms, such as temper tantrums and aggression, observed among many abused children (Libbey & Bybee, 1979; Martin & Beezley, 1977). In an attempt to predict the occurrence of inward and outward behavior, Rothbaum (1980) developed an integrated model of helplessness and reactance theories (Wortman & Brehm, 1975; Roth & Bootzin, 1974). Whereas helplessness theory predicts that inward behavior will follow from the perception of uncontrollability, reactance theory (Brehm & Brehm, 1981) predicts outward behavior in the face of uncontrollability or threatened behavioral freedom.

In his model, Rothbaum (1980) distinguishes between *loss* and *lack of control*. Loss of control refers to the contrast established by an expectation of control and the subsequent perception that an event is uncontrollable. Loss leads to outward behaviors such as protest, anger, and attempts to regain control. Lack of control refers to a current perception that one does not possess control, and occurs when a child (or adult) abandons hope of regaining control or when the expectations of control were never high. Relinquishment of control expectations leads to "inward" behaviors such as decreased response initiation, motivational deficits, and emotional dysfunction.

Rothbaum (1980) suggests that a belief in external locus of control mediates the recurring perception of lack of control. "Externals" expect that outcomes occur independently of their own actions and consequently engage in inward behaviors (cf. Lefcourt, 1976; Rothbaum, Wolfer & Visintainer, 1979). "Internals" believe that outcomes are associated with ability or the expenditure of effort and persevere even in uncontrollable situations because they have a generalized expectancy that goal-directed behavior leads to desired outcomes. It is only after considerable exposure to uncontrollable outcomes that internals succumb and show the withdrawal associated with helplessness (Cohen, Rothbart, & Phillips, 1976).

How then does a child develop aggressive, outward behavior? One explanation may be that the transition to helplessness is gradual, passing through a reactance stage (Wortman & Brehm, 1975). The individual who experiences loss of control reacts with anger for a while until reconciled to the seemingly unalterable circumstances. The hypothesized sequence is consistent with research on locus of control cited previously. Although not well documented, it has also been reported to occur among abused children (Kagan, 1977; Rohner, 1975). This logic suggests that cross-sectional investigations will find some children who adopt outward behavior patterns and who persist in attempts to regain control. A longitudinal study of such children, however, may ultimately reveal inward behavior patterns and a feeling of lack of control in the face of repeated abuse. The hypothesized sequence is also consistent with findings that outward responses to abuse are more evident among younger than older children. Studies that control for the longevity of abusive treatment would permit a test of this hypothesis.

Another explanation for the development of outward behaviors recognizes the inability to conceptualize the difference between proper and improper aggression

(Feshbach, 1978). Feshbach notes that children learn how to aggress by observing aggression and that eventually they also learn rules for the proper expression of aggression. To a young child, however, distinguishing between proper and improper aggression would be difficult—particularly if his or her parent engages in physical forms of discipline. Furthermore, young children's inability to empathize and take another's role (Shantz, 1975) renders them less able to anticipate the consequences of aggression for themselves and others. Thus, it is not surprising that younger children are more likely than older children to react to abuse by developing an outward behavior style (cf. Kinard, 1979).

In summary, an inward response to abuse is likely among children who have experienced recurring perceptions of lack of control, perhaps associated with an external control orientation. An outward response to abuse is likely among those who perceive a loss of control but retain hope for future control and among those who are too young to understand cause-and-effect and to empathize. Outward and inward behavior patterns may co-occur. Simultaneous patterns may correspond to different areas or sources of control (e.g., a girl believes she has *lost* control over her mother's discipline and *lacks* control over her father's discipline) or to a temporary state of ambivalent expectations about control, shifting between anger over loss of control and anguish over the possibility of never regaining control.

We have described characteristic responses to abuse and some mechanisms which may mediate responses. In the next section we discuss coping with adverse events more directly and will address the question of how a child copes with the stress of abuse in the absence of direct control. A related question is whether specific coping strategies selected by a child are associated with more or less emotional and behavioral disturbance. Finally, citing evidence from the stress and coping literature, we suggest that certain illusions may help a child cope with the stress of abuse.

Coping with Abuse.   A growing literature is investigating how people cope with adverse, and sometimes tragic, life events. A person's behavioral and cognitive attempts to deal with a stressor are referred to as coping strategies or responses. Coping strategies can be grouped into problem-focused coping strategies, which are direct attempts to alter a stressful event, and emotion-focused coping strategies, which are a person's attempts to regulate his or her emotional response rather than change the situation (Folkman & Lazarus, 1980; Pearlin & Schooler, 1978). Problem-focused coping is similar to what Rothbaum et al. (1982) call *primary control.* When a child or adolescent is first confronted with abuse, he or she may begin to cope by employing primary control responses. Fighting back (Libbey & Bybee, 1979), running away (Amsterdam et al., 1979), telling someone about the abuse (Amsterdam et al., 1979), or trying to change his or her own behavior in the hope of producing a less severe parental response (Davoren, 1968) represent primary control strategies. However, what emotion-focused or "secondary" control strategies are available to the child who finds that direct attempts to change response–outcome contingencies are unsuccessful? A number of secondary control strategies are available to the child experiencing stress (cf. Averill, 1973; Rothbaum et al., 1982). One strategy, *interpretative control* (Rothbaum et al., 1982), is to manage stress by ascribing meaning or purpose to it (see also Taylor, 1983). In response to the question "Why me?," victims of severe uncontrollable stress may point to "God's will," deservedness, or fate. Witenberg et al. (1983) found that end-stage renal failure patients who had not found an answer to the question "Why me?" were rated by their physicians and nurses as coping less successfully with their illness than patients who had found *any* answer. Maintaining interpretive control through appeal to "God's will" or fate may be unique to disaster victims and people with serious illness or disability. In the case of child abuse, we suspect that issues of deservedness are salient in the interpretation process. Preliminary evidence is provided by Amsterdam et al. (1979), who found that a significant proportion of adolescents viewed themselves as deserving punishment. In fact, as punishment became more severe, these adolescents reported being more deserving. Similar relationships between deservedness or self-blame and outcome severity have been observed in mothers of high-risk infants (Affleck, Allen, McGrade, & McQueeney, 1982) and mothers of children with early-onset diabetes (Tennen et al., 1984).

Another mechanism of secondary control available to an abused child is *cognitive control* (Pearlin & Schooler, 1978; Silver & Wortman, 1980; Taylor, Wood, & Lichtman, in press), by which one selectively attends to positive aspects of an adverse situation. Taylor et al. note several ways in which someone can evaluate the situation selectively: (a) comparing oneself with less fortunate others, (b) focusing on attributes that make one seem advantaged, (c) "creating hypothetical worse worlds," (d) construing benefit, and (e) creating standards by which one's own adjustment appears exceptional. From the abused child, one might hear that some kids do not have parents (comparison with less fortunate others to appear advantaged), that he or she was not thrown out of the house or permanently injured (creating worse worlds), that the abuse is a sign of caring (cf. Amsterdam et al., 1979; construing benefit) and that other kids who are hit by their parents get into more trouble or are "weird" (exceptional adjustment). What is perhaps most significant about both interpretive and cognitive control strategies is that they often involve distortions of "reality" and violations of "rational" thinking. Nonetheless, they may help the child cope with an otherwise devastating circumstance.[4]

---

[4]The effectiveness of cognitive control is appreciated by many psychotherapists. Watzlawick (1978), for example, specifically directs patients to redefine events with a positive connotation. Cognitive control has also been linked to better adjustment in seriously ill patients (Weisman & Worden, 1976–1977).

Retrospective control, which is similar to some types of interpretive control, refers to a belief that one's own behavior caused an uncontrollable adverse outcome (Thompson, 1981). This belief allows the person to maintain confidence in his or her capacity to control future adverse outcomes. As noted previously, characterological self-blame among abused children would be likely to result in the withdrawn, apathetic syndrome and may produce low self-esteem and feelings of unworthiness. In contrast, behavioral self-blame may lead to changes in one's behavior or attitudes in an attempt to reduce the incidence of future abuse. We would hypothesize the latter attributional style among children who cope with abuse by adapting their behaviors to fit parental needs and wants (Davoren, 1968). In an attempt to be "good" children (and, in effect, to be a parent to their parent), they try to alter the behaviors that may have precipitated previous abuse.

While predicted relationships between behavioral self-blame and successful coping have been reported (Bulman & Wortman, 1977; Tennen et al., 1984), behavioral self-blame does not always lead to successful coping (Witenberg et al., 1983). Retrospective control, in the form of behavioral self-blame may be most effective following a single adverse event, rather than one that is recurrent. Furthermore, behavioral self-blame may be especially detrimental when there is no possibility of regaining control (Bulman & Wortman, 1977). There may be many situations, for example, in which abuse is independent of effort on the child's part to change his or her behavior. Even the literature that demonstrates precocious role-reversal activities of some abused children does not suggest that this activity precludes all future abuse (Davoren, 1968). The child's attempts to be better and better will still lead to experiences of uncontrollability and may eventually result in increased passivity and withdrawal.

Of course, behavioral self-blame may not indicate an attempt to gain control. We might conjecture that self-blame can serve to maintain a positive image of the abusing parent. By accepting causal responsibility for the abuse, the child can continue to feel good about a parent who was, after all, "showing that s/he cares" (cf. Amsterdam et al., 1979). As noted previously, such idealization may result from guilt over aggressive feelings toward that parent, or, at a more primitive level, it may represent a need for protection against what is perceived as a dangerous and chaotic world (Kernberg, 1975). Thus, behavioral self-blame can represent retrospective control "I'll be different from now on and avoid abuse") or cognitive control.

A final issue regarding a child's use of retrospective control to cope with abuse is the question of whether self-blame in children represents a motivated attempt to adapt or the cognitive limitations of the child. In response to this interesting alternative explanation, we note that Amsterdam et al. (1979) found that 52% of the adolescents they interviewed interpreted punishment as a sign of caring and 23% of the adolescents blamed themselves for the punishment they received, a result that is inconsistent with the notion that cognitive immaturity leads to self-blame.

A recent study by Tennen et al. (1984), although not investigating abuse, further suggests that children's self-blame for aversive events is not merely a reflection of cognitive immaturity. These investigators asked diabetic children ages 8 to 17 to describe their illness and its causes. The sophistication of a child's conception of his or her illness was coded on a hierarchical scale from preconceptual through formal operational thinking (Piaget & Inhelder, 1969). Children who took personal responsibility for their illness were rated by physicians and nurses as coping better than children who made external attributions. Furthermore, self-blaming children did *not* express more primitive illness concepts.

Another coping strategy, *vicarious control,* is the belief that the aversiveness of an uncontrollable event or circumstance can be obviated by believing in the efficacy of a powerful other or by sharing the other's control and power via identification (Bandura 1969; Rothbaum et al., 1982). The abused child can attain vicarious control by believing in the efficacy and potency of the nonabusing parent. By ascribing benevolent motives and control to the nonabusing parent, the child can, at least temporarily, reduce the stress of abuse. Of course, a nonabusing parent may be physically unavailable, may deny the abuse, or may collude with the abuser. Attempts to gain vicarious control in such circumstances would lead to disappointment and further despair.

The second route to vicarious control, sharing control through identification, is akin to identification with the aggressor (Freud, 1923). By identifying with the abusing parent, the child can share (in fantasy) his or her control over the abusive situation. Children who attempt to gain vicarious control in this way might be expected to show the "outward" behaviors of aggressiveness and delinquency.

A final control strategy, which we might term *symbolic control,* may be derived from Wangh's (1962; see also Langs, 1976) description of "evocation of a proxy." With this strategy, the abused child attempts to master the perception of uncontrollability and its associated affects by evoking the same perceptions and feelings in others. By recreating the dreaded perceptions and affects in someone else, the child can obviate his/her own distress through a process similar to projective identification. Freud (1920) presents the following example of this process:

> If a doctor examines a child's throat, or performs a small operation on him, the alarming experience will quite certainly be made the subject of the next game, but in this the pleasure gain from another source is not to be overlooked. In passing from the passivity of experience to the activity of play the child applies to his playfellow the unpleasant occurrence that befell himself and so avenges himself on the person of this proxy. (pp. 15–16)

Because symbolic control is a relatively primitive (though pervasive) mechanism, we would expect its use to be most prevalent among young children. The abused child may demonstrate attempts at symbolic control in his or her play by pretending to threaten, frighten, and hurt playmates, or without the playful quality, in which case the child is labelled by others as aggressive or a behavior problem. Symbolic control requires that the proxy be someone who will succumb to the evocation, which leads to the prediction that such evocations will not be arbitrary. For example, we would not expect the child to evoke frightening perceptions and affects in his or her parents. Indeed, the child abuse literature suggests that the outward, aggressive behaviors are most often seen in younger abused children and often occur outside the home (Kinard, 1979, 1980).

Vicarious and symbolic control are subtle strategies which often transpire outside awareness. This may be one reason why little empirical evidence exists regarding these attempts to attain secondary control.

CONCLUDING REMARKS

A review of the child abuse literature reveals some apparently contradictory characteristics of abused children. Some investigators report aggressive acting out, wariness, and hypervigilance. Others stress depressed, docile behavior and low self-esteem. In addition to these contradictory behavioral clusters, there is considerable evidence of denial-like processes and attributional biases. Abused children, for example, may interpret abuse as a sign of caring and take personal responsibility for having been abused, or they may blame their parents for the treatment and see their parents as different from other adults.

While considerable research has identified the behavioral and emotional consequences of abuse, few studies have examined the processes through which abuse affects the child. In this chapter we contend that the examination of such processes is important. To do a proper examination, however, researchers must investigate what the child thinks and feels about his or her parental treatment. We have identified various factors that are likely to affect the child's interpretations of abuse, and have outlined various ways in which interpretations may influence the behavioral and emotional manifestations of abusive treatment. We viewed the consequences of abuse as attempts to gain control over the threats imposed by an abusive environment. In the face of abuse, the child will attempt to gain control over the abuser's behavior and may react with anger, aggression, and hypervigilance. Ultimately, however, the child may perceive that the home circumstances are unalterable. Borrowing from the work of Rothbaum (1980), we then propose that feelings of helplessness, characterized by depression, withdrawal and low self-esteem, may develop. Longitudinal studies are required to test the hypothesized sequence from reactance to acceptance of uncontrollability in abused children. Empirical support for the sequential hypothesis would clarify the apparent contradiction presented by evidence of both inward and outward behavior in the abuse literature.

When abused children are unable to attain direct or primary control, they may turn to secondary control stretegies. Secondary control strategies include finding purpose in the abuse, selectively attending to positive aspects of the abuse, attributing the abuse to one's own behavior, submitting to or identifying with powerful others, and evoking frightening perceptions and emotions in others. The concept of secondary control strategies explains what appears to be distortions and biases on the part of the abused child, while remaining within the context of current models of psychological control.

Although we have suggested a relationship between coping strategies and adaptational outcomes, we do not know the extent to which or the manner in which coping strategies affect the psychological development of the abused child. However, the apparent effectiveness of denial-like processes, perceptual biases, and attributional errors in coping with stress and illness leads researchers (e.g., Lazarus, 1983) and clinicians (e.g., Watzlawick, 1978) to question perceptual veridicality and reality testing as benchmarks of coping adequacy. Research is needed to test whether the relationships between coping strategies and outcomes found in other populations are manifested among abused children. Furthermore, research is needed to verify whether the proposed outcomes are indeed manifestations of coping strategies. For example, can one differentiate the self-blame associated with retrospective control from the self-recriminations of depression? Can we differentiate aggressive behavior in the service of vicarious or symbolic control from what may simply be imitative behavior? These questions remain to be answered.

Finally, we are not suggesting that social-cognitive variables and coping strategies are the only important mediators between abusive treatment and its consequences. In fact, research on the dynamics of abusive situations is needed from a myriad of theoretical viewpoints. Such research would inform us about the effects of abuse, and would also increase our understanding of how children respond to other stressful situations.

ACKNOWLEDGMENTS

The authors would like to thank Glenn Affleck for his contributions to our conceptualization of control strategies in abused children and to Laurie Pearlman for her helpful editorial suggestions.

REFERENCES

Abramson, L., Seligman, M. & Teasdale, J. (1978). Learned helplessness in humans: Critique and reformulation. *Journal of Abnormal Psychology, 87,* 49–74.

Affleck, G., Allen, D., McGrade, B., & McQueeney, M. (1982). Maternal causal attributions at hospital discharge of a high-risk infant. *American Journal of Mental Deficiency, 86,* 575–580.

Amsterdam, B., Brill, M., Bell, N. W., & Edwards, D. (1979). Coping with abuse: Adolescent's views. *Victimology, 4,* 278–284.

Averill, J. R. (1973). Personal control over aversive stimuli and its relationship to stress. *Psychological Bulletin, 80,* 286–303.

Bandura, A. (1969). Social-learning theory of identificatory processes. In D. A. Goslin (Ed.) *Handbook of socialization theory and research* (pp. 213–262). Chicago: Rand McNally.

Becker, W. C. (1964). Consequences of different kinds of parental discipline. In M. L. Hoffman & L. W. Hoffman (Eds.), *Review of child development research* (Vol. I, pp. 169–208). New York: Russell Sage Foundation.

Brehm, S. S., & Brehm, J. W. (1981). *Psychological reactance: A theory of freedom and control.* New York: Academic Press.

Bulman, R., & Wortman, C. (1977). Attributions of blame and coping in the "real world": Severe accident victims react to their lot. *Journal of Personality and Social Psychology, 35,* 351–363.

Burgess, R. L., & Conger, R. D. (1978). Family interaction in abusive, neglectful, and normal families. *Child Development, 49,* 1163–1173.

Cohen, S., Rothbart, M., & Phillips, S. (1976). Locus of control and the generality of learned helplessness in humans. *Journal of Personality and Social Psychology, 34,* 1049–1056.

Cunningham, B. (Feb. 23, 1972). Beaten kids, sick parents. *New York Post,* p. 14.

Davoren, E. L. (1968). The role of the social worker. In R. E. Helfer & C. H. Kempe (Eds.), *The battered child* (pp. 153–171). Chicago: University of Chicago Press.

DeMause, L. (1974). *The history of childhood.* New York: The Psychohistory Press.

Dix, T. H., & Grusec, J. E. (1985). Parent attribution processes in child socialization. In I. Sigel (Ed.), *Parental belief systems: The psychological consequences for children* (pp. 201–233). Hillsdale, NJ: Lawrence Erlbaum Associates.

Dodge, K. A. (1980). Social cognition and children's aggressive behavior. *Child Development, 51,* 162–170.

Dodge, K. A., & Frame, C. L. (1982). Social cognitive biases and deficits in aggressive boys. *Child Development, 53,* 620–635.

Dodge, K. A., & Newman, J. P. (1981). Biased decision-making processes in aggressive boys. *Journal of Abnormal Psychology, 90,* 375–379.

Dubin, R., & Dubin, E. R. (1965). Children's social perceptions: A review of research. *Child Development, 36,* 809–838.

Dweck, C. S. (1975). The role of expectations and attributions in the alleviation of learned helplessness. *Journal of Personality and Social Psychology, 31,* 674–685.

Dweck, C. S., Davidson, W., Nelson, S., & Enna, B. (1978). Sex differences in learned helplessness: II. The contingencies of evaluative feedback in the classroom and III. An experimental analysis. *Developmental Psychology, 14,* 268–276.

Elmer, E. (1967). *Children in jeopardy: A study of abused minors and their families.* Pittsburgh: University of Pittsburgh Press.

Feshbach, S. (1970). Aggression. In P. H. Mussen (Ed.), *Carmichael's manual of child psychology* (Vol. 2, pp. 159–259). New York: Wiley.

Feshbach, S. (1978). The development and regulation of aggression: Some research gaps and a proposed cognitive approach. In W. W. Hartup & J. DeWit (Eds.), *Origins of aggression* (pp. 163–187) Paris: Moutin.

Flavell, J. H. (1977). *Cognitive development.* Englewood Cliffs, NJ: Prentice-Hall.

Folkman, S., & Lazarus, R. (1980). An analysis of coping in a middle-aged community sample. *Journal of Health and Social Behavior, 21,* 219–239.

Fontana, V. J. (1968). Further reflections on maltreatment of children. *New York State Journal of Medicine, 68,* 2214–2215.

Freud, S. (1920). *Beyond the pleasure principle.* London: Hogarth Press.

Freud, S. (1923). *The ego and id.* London: Hogarth.

Friedrich, W. N., & Boriskin, J. A. (1976). The role of the child in abuse: A review of the literature. *American Journal of Orthopsychiatry, 46,* 580–590.

Galdston, R. (1965). Observations on children who have been physically abused and their parents. *American Journal of Psychiatry, 122,* 440–443.

Garbarino, J. (1977). The human ecology of child maltreatment: A conceptual model for research. *Journal of Marriage and the Family. 39,* 721–735.

George, C., & Main, M. (1979). Social interactions of young abused children: Approach, avoidance, and aggression. *Child Development, 50,* 306–318.

Gil, D. C. (1970). *Violence against children: Physical child abuse in the United States.* Cambridge, MA: Harvard University Press.

Giovannoni, J. M., & Becerra, R. M. (1979). *Defining child abuse.* New York: Free Press.

Glueck, S., & Glueck, E. (1950). *Unraveling juvenile delinquency.* New York: Commonwealth Fund.

Glueck, S., & Glueck, E. (1968). *Delinquents and non-delinquents in perspective.* Cambridge: Harvard University Press.

Goetz, T. E., & Dweck, C. S. (1980). Learned helplessness in social situations. *Journal of Personality and Social Psychology, 39,* 246–255.

Halperin, S. L. (1981). Abused and non-abused children's perceptions of their mothers, fathers and siblings: Implications for a comprehensive family treatment plan. *Family Relations, 30,* 89–96.

Herzberger, S. D. (1983). Social cognition and the transmission of abuse. In D. Finkelhor, R. J. Gelles, G. T. Hotaling, & M. A. Straus (Eds.), *The dark side of families: Current family violence research* (pp. 317–329). Beverly Hills, CA: Sage.

Herzberger & Tennen (1985a). "Snips and snails and puppy dog tails": Gender of agent, recipient and observer as determinants of perception of discipline. *Sex Roles, 12,* 853–865.

Herzberger, S. D., & Tennen, H. (1985b). The effect of self-relevance on moderate and severe disciplinary encounters. *Journal of Marriage and the Family, 47,* 311–318.

Herzberger, S. D., Potts, D. A., & Dillon, M. (1981). Abusive and nonabusive parental treatment from the child's perspective. *Journal of Consulting and Clinical Psychology, 49,* 81–90.

Janoff-Bulman, R. (1979). Characterological versus behavioral self-blame: Inquiries into depression and rape. *Journal of Personality and Social Psychology, 37,* 1798–1809.

Jayaratne, S. (1977). Child abusers as parents and children: A review. *Social Work, 58,* 5–9.

Kagan, J. (1977). The child in the family. *Daedalus: Journal of the American Academy of Arts and Sciences, 106,* 2, 33–56.

Kempe, R. S., & Kempe, C. H. (1978). *Child abuse.* Cambridge, MA: Harvard University Press.

Kent, J. T. (1976). A follow-up study of abused children. *Journal of Pediatric Psychology,* 25–31.

Kernberg, O. (1975). *Borderline conditions and pathological narcissism.* New York: Jason Aronson.

Kinard, E. M. (1979). The psychological consequences of abuse for the child. *Journal of Social Issues, 35,* 82–100.

Kinard, E. M. (1980). Emotional development in physically abused children. *American Journal of Orthopsychiatry, 50,* 686–696.

Langs, R. (1976). *The therapeutic interaction* (Vol. 2). New York: Jason Aronson.

Lazarus, R. S. (1983). The costs and benefits of denial. In S. Breznitz (Ed.), *The denial of stress* (pp. 1–30). New York: International Universities Press.

Lefcourt, H. M. (1976). *Locus of control: Current trends in theory and research.* Hillsdale, NJ: Lawrence Erlbaum Associates.

Libbey, P., & Bybee, R. (1979). The physical abuse of adolescents. *Journal of Social Issues, 35,* 101–126.

Locke, J. (1913). *Some thoughts concerning education.* Cambridge: Cambridge University Press.

Martin, H. P. (1977, August). The abusive environment and the child's adaptation. Paper presented at the annual convention of the American Psychological Association, San Francisco.

Martin, H. P., & Beezley, P. (1977). Behavioral observations of abused children. *Developmental Medicine and Child Neurology, 19,* 373–387.

Martin, H. P., Beezley, P., Conway, E. F., & Kempe, C. H. (1974). The development of abused children. *Advances in Pediatrics, 21,* 25–73.

Mischel, W., Zeiss, R., & Zeiss, A. (1974). Internal-external control and persistence: Validation and implications of the Stanford Preschool Internal-External Scale. *Journal of Personality and Social Psychology, 29,* 265–278.

Parke, R. D. (1970). The role of punishment in the socialization process. In R. A. Hoppe, G. A. Milton, & E. C. Simmel (Eds.), *Early experiences and the processes of socialization* (pp. 81–108). New York: Academic Press.

Parke, R. D., & Collmer, C. W. (1975). *Child abuse: An interdisciplinary analysis.* Chicago: University of Chicago Press.

Pearlin, L., & Schooler, C. (1978). The structure of coping. *Journal of Health and Social Behavior, 19,* 2–21.

Piaget, J. (1930). *The child's conception of physical causality.* London: Routledge & Kegan Paul.

Piaget, J. (1932). *The moral judgment of the child.* New York: Harcourt-Brace.

Piaget, J., & Inhelder, B. (1969). *The psychology of the child.* New York: Basic Books.

Potts, D. A., & Herzberger, S. D. (1981, April). Perceptions of emotionally and physically abusive treatment. Paper presented at the Society for Research in Child Development meeting, Boston.

Rabkin, L. I. (1965). The patient's family: Research methods. *Family Process, 4,* 105–132.

Rohner, R. P. (1975). Parental acceptance-rejection and personality development: A universalist approach to behavioral science. In R. W. Brislin, S. Bochner, & W. J. Loner (Eds.), *Cross-cultural perspective on learning* (pp. 251–269). Beverly Hills: Sage.

Roth, S., & Bootzin, R. R. (1974). The effects of experimentally induced expectancies of external control: An investigation of learned helplessness. *Journal of Personality and Social Psychology, 29,* 253–264.

Rothbaum, F. (1980). Children's clinical syndromes and generalized expectations of control. In H. W. Reese & L. P. Lipsett (Eds.), *Advances in child development and behavior* (Vol. 15, pp. 207–246). New York: Academic Press.

Rothbaum, F., Weisz, J., & Snyder, S. (1982). Changing the world and changing the self: A two process model of perceived control. *Journal of Personality and Social Psychology, 42,* 5–37.

Rothbaum, F., Wolfer, J., & Visintainer, M. (1979). Coping behavior and locus of control in children. *Journal of Personality, 47,* 118–135.

Sears, R. R., Maccoby, E. E., & Levin, H. (1957). *Patterns of child rearing.* New York: Harper & Row.

Secord, P. F., & Peevers, B. H. (1974). The development and attribution of person concepts. In T. Mischel (Ed.), *Understanding other persons* (pp. 117–142). Totowa, NJ: Rowman & Littlefield.

Seligman, M. E. P. (1975). *Helplessness.* San Francisco: Freeman.

Selman, R. L., & Byrne, D. F. (1974). A structural-developmental analysis of levels of role taking in middle childhood. *Child Development, 45,* 803–806.

Shantz, C. U. (1975). *The development of social cognition.* Chicago: University of Chicago Press.

Silver, R., & Wortman, C. (1980). Coping with undesirable life events. In J. Garber & M. Seligman (Eds.), *Human helplessness* (pp. 279–375). New York: Academic Press.

Spinetta, J. J., & Rigler, D. (1972). The child-abusing parent: A psychological review. *Psychological Bulletin, 77,* 296–304.

Steele, B. F., & Pollock, C. B. (1968). A psychiatric study of parents who abuse infants and small children. In R. E. Helfer & C. H. Kempe (Eds.), *The battered child* (pp. 103–147). Chicago: University of Chicago Press.

Straus, M. A. (1978). *Family patterns and child abuse in a nationally representative American sample.* Paper presented at the Second International Congress on Child Abuse and Neglect, London.

Taylor, S. E. (1983). Adjustment to threatening events: A theory of cognitive adaptation. *American Psychologist, 38,* 1161–1173.

Taylor, S. E., Wood, J. V., & Lichtman, R. R. (in press). It could be worse: Selective evaluation as a response to victimization. *Journal of Social Issues.*

Tennen, H., Affleck, G., Allen, D., McGrade, B., & Ratzan, S. (1984). Causal attributions and coping in juvenile diabetes. *Basic and Applied Social Psychology, 5,* 131–142.

Thompson, S. C. (1981). Will it hurt less if I can control it? A complex answer to a simple question. *Psychological Bulletin, 90,* 89–101.

Walters, G. C., & Grusec, J. E. (1977). *Punishment.* San Francisco: W. H. Freeman.

Wangh, M. (1962). The "evocation of proxy:" A psychological maneuver, its use as a defense, its purposes and genesis. In R. S. Eissler, A. Freud, H. Hartmann and M. Kris (Eds.) *The psychoanalytic study of the child, XVII* (pp. 451–469). New York: International Universities Press.

Watzlawick, P. (1978). *The language of change: Elements of therapeutic communication.* New York: Basic Books.

Weisman, A. D., & Worden, J. W. (1976–1977). The existential plight in cancer: significance of the first 100 days. *International Journal of Psychiatry in Medicine, 7,* 1–15.

Witenberg, S., Blanchard, E., Suls, J., Tennen, H., McCoy, G. & McGoldrick, D. (1983). Perceptions of control and causality as predictors of compliance and coping in hemodialysis. *Basic and Applied Social Psychology, 4,* 319–336.

Wortman, C. B., & Brehm, J. W. (1975). Responses to uncontrollable outcomes: An integration of reactance theory and the learned helplessness model. In L. Berkowitz (Eds.), *Advances in experimental social psychology* (pp. 277–336). New York: Academic Press.

Yarrow, L. J. (1963). Research in dimensions of early maternal care. *Merrill-Palmer Quarterly, 9,* 101–114.

Young, L. (1964). *Wednesday's children: A study of child neglect and abuse.* New York: McGraw Hill.

Zahn-Waxler, C. & Chapman, M. (1982). Immediate antecedents of caretaker's methods of discipline. *Child Psychiatry and Human Development, 12,* 179–192.

Author Index

301

Subject Index